SEX DISCRIMINATION AND EQUAL OPPORTUNITY

Sex Discrimination and Equal Opportunity

The Labor Market and Employment Policy

Edited by
GÜNTHER SCHMID
and
RENATE WEITZEL

St. Martin's Press   New York

Library of Congress Cataloging in Publication Data

Main entry under title:

Sex discrimination and equal opportunity.

    Includes index.
    1. Sex discrimination in employment - addresses, essays, lectures.
2. Women - Employment - addresses, essays, lectures. I. Schmid,
Günther, 1942-   . II. Weitzel, Renate.
HD6060.S47 1984   331.4'133   84-11450

ISBN 0-312-71333-9

CONTENTS

ABOUT THE AUTHORS

Anders Björklund, Research Associate at the Industrial Institute for Economic and Social Research in Stockholm, Sweden. His doctoral dissertation was on "Studies in Dynamics of Unemployment", of which several articles have been published in Scandinavian Journal of Economics, American Economic Review and Scottish Journal of Political Economy. Presently interested in the econometrics of panel data and program evaluation.

Rachel Eisenberg Braun, Graduate Student, Dept. of Statistics, George Washington University, Washington, DC, USA. Publications on "Economic Aspects of an Aging Population and the Material Well-Being of Older Persons", "Life Course Analysis and Multistate Demography: An Application to Marriage, Divorce and Remarriage."

Glen C. Cain, Professor in labour economics, Department of Economics, University of Wisconsin, Madison, Wisconsin USA. Main publications: Married Women in the Labor Force, 1966; Income Maintenance and Labor Supply, 1973; "The Challenge of Segmented Labor Market Theories" in Journal of Economic Literature, Dec. 1976.

Ludwig Eitel, Diploma in business administration, student of law at the Free University of Berlin, lecturer at the 'Fachhochschule für Wirtschaft' in Berlin. Main activities: trade union education work for works councils and workers representatives in board of directors (since 1978), research on issues of female discrimination. Publications: Collaborator of WSI-Project-Group 'co-determination at company and enterprise level'; collaborator of Pfarr/Bertelsmann: 'Lohngleichheit' (1981).

Pauline Glucklich, Senior Lecturer, Dept. of Management Studies, Civil Service College, Sunningdale, United Kingdom. Research and teaching field: Training women managers in the Civil Service and research into women in organisations. Main publications: Equal Pay and Opportunities (together with Snell, Polvall), 1981; Women, Work and Wages (together with Snell), Low Pay Unit 1982.

Siv Gustafsson is a Ph.D of Economics and holds a research position at Arbetslivscentrum, Stockholm, Sweden. Her main research has been concerned with microeconometric analyses of determination and structure of wages and salaries, specifically male-female earnings differentials and labor force participation in Sweden. Main Publications: Structure and Determination of Salaries in the Government Sector of Sweden, 1976; Cost Benefit Analysis of Early Childhood Care and Education, OECD 1978; Lifetime Patterns of Labor Force Participation, 1979.

Christine Jackson, Head of Research and Policy at the Equal Opportunities Commission (EOC), Manchester, United Kingdom. Author or co-author of numerous EOC-publications; co-author of Bail or Custody, Cobden Trust 1971; The Women's Directory, Virago 1976; Civil Liberty, Penguin 1978.

Christina Jonung, M.A. in Economics at the University of California Los Angeles 1970, is a researcher at the Department of Economics at the University of Lund, Sweden, where she also teaches labor economics. Her publications in English include "Sexual Equality in the Swedish Labor market", Monthly Labor Review, No. 10, Vol. 101, 1978. Migrant Women in the Swedish Labor Market, EIFO Report No. 3, Stockholm 1982. She also prepared the Swedish national report on the status of women in the labor market to the OECD in 1980. She is presently doing research on the occupational segregation by sex in the Swedish labor market.

Emma MacLennan is Deputy Director of the Low Pay Unit, an independent research and campaigning organisation in London. Her research and teaching fields are low pay in general, women's employment minimum wages, national insurance, small firms, service sector employment and child labor. Main publications: Minimum Wages for Women, 1980; Working Children, 1980; Insuring Poverty at Work (with Chris Pond), 1981; Women in Small Firms, forthcoming.

June Avis O'Neill, Senior Research Associate and Director of the Program of Policy Research on Women and Families, The Urban Institute, Washington, DC, USA. Her current research areas include: economic issues related to the employment and income of women, higher education finance, determinants of child support, the tax treatment of the family. Main publications: Resource Use in Higher Education, Carnegie Commission 1971; Financing Social Security, Congressional Budget Office, 1977; "Social Security-Fundamental Economic Problems and Alternative Financing Methods", National Tax Journal 1980; "A Time Series Analysis of Women's Labor Force Participation", American Economic Review 1981.

Heide M. Pfarr, Professor in Civil Law and Labor Law, Dept. of Law II, University of Hamburg, Federal Republic of Germany. Various publications in this area, among others: Lohngleichheit - Zur Rechtsprechung bei geschlechtsspezifischer Entgeltdiskriminierung (together with Bertelsmann), 1981. "Gleichstellung der Frau im Arbeitsleben - Vorschläge zur Rechtsreform", 1981.

Günther Schmid, Research Fellow and Deputy Director at the International Institute of Management, Science Center Berlin, Federal Republic of Germany; Privatdozent for Political Economy at the Free University of Berlin. Research and teaching areas: Labour Market Analysis and Labour Market Policy, Political Economy, Program Evaluation, Social Policy. Main publications: Funktionsanalyse und Politische Theorie, 1974; Bürokratie und Politik (together with Treiber) 1975; Steuerungssysteme des Arbeitsmarkts, 1975; Strukturierte Arbeitslosigkeit und Arbeitsmarktpolitik, 1980. Numerous articles in labour market analysis and labour market policy.

Renate Weitzel, Research Fellow at the International Institute of Management, Science Center Berlin, Federal Republic of Germany; Research areas: Labour Market Policies Related to Women, Flexible Working Time Patterns, Further Training. Publications: Arbeitszeitpolitik und arbeitszeitpolitische Steuerungsinstrumente, 1980: Möglichkeiten und Grenzen der öffentlichen Förderung von Teilzeitarbeit, 1981; Labour Market Policies Related to Women and Employment in the Federal Republic of Germany, 1982; Berufliche Bildung nach dem Arbeitsförderungsgesetz, 1983.

ACKNOWLEDGEMENTS

This book is part of the outcome of a larger study on "Regulation theory of the labour market: A comparative analysis of employment policy for the disabled and for women." The project has been financially supported by the German Research Foundation (DFG), and it was carried out by Günther Schmid (project leader), Klaus Semlinger and Renate Weitzel.

I am much indebted to Brigitte Müller who typed and corrected each contribution in this book. Thanks go also to the International Institute of Management which supported the production of the book, and last but not least to the individual authors. Each contribution has been written originally for this book.

Berlin, December 1983   Günther Schmid

ACKNOWLEDGMENTS

1 WOMEN IN THE LABOUR MARKET AND EQUAL OPPORTUNITY POLICY IN SWEDEN, UNITED KINGDOM, UNITED STATES AND WEST GERMANY: INTRODUCTION

GÜNTHER SCHMID

We are undergoing a "subtle revolution" (1) in the traditional relationship of women to work and family. One indicator of this change is the massive increase in women's economic activity, especially among married women with children. This increasing involvement of women in paid employment was an integral feature of the era of rapid economic growth from the Second World War to the early 1970s (2). However, the rising participation was not only a response to excess demand for labour which pulled women into the labour market. The fact that women's participation has continued to rise during the period of slow growth since 1974 shows that this development has deeper roots. There are also factors which push women into the labour market, such as the decreasing size of family, the destruction of traditional neighborhood systems, and women's increasing participation in higher education.

Despite the important role women play in the labour market today, little success can be registered with respect to qualitative criteria such as equal pay, equal employment opportunity, and equal share of home-work between men and women. Apart from the tension between their roles as homemakers and employees, women are in most countries still subject to provisions of the income tax and the social security system which penalize their wage-earning. Although wage differentials between men and women narrowed, a considerable difference can still be observed even holding constant qualification and working time differences. Women also face occupational overcrowding in "women's jobs" - those that are clerical and deal with health care, education, domestic work, or food service. Once in the labour force, they frequently hold marginal jobs, and they suffer more unemployment than men. Moreover, for working wives, an average week includes not only the hours of paid work but a considerable number of hours doing housework as well.

1

However, beyond these general trends, remarkable differences can also be observed between countries of comparable industrial development, both in quantitative as well as in qualitative terms. To give only a couple of highlights: Whereas in the United States labour force participation of women increased during the seventies from 48.9 % (1970) to 59.7 % (1980), in the Federal Republic of Germany it rose only slightly from 48.1 % (1970) to 50.0 % (1980). In Sweden, the acceleration of this trend was even greater than in the United States, and the labour force participation rates of the Swedish women are now only eleven per cent away from those of men (table 8, appendix).

In all countries, the bulk of women's employment increase was in services and related sectors. However, this trend was more pronounced in United States, Great Britain and Sweden than in Germany: Whereas in Sweden, six out of ten employees in private and public services are women, the ratio in Germany is only five to ten. On the other hand, in Germany half of the employment in agriculture is still female, whereas women make up a quarter or less in this sector in Sweden, Great Britain and United States. The income tax policy as well as the social security system in Sweden penalize wage-earning of women to a lesser extent than in Germany. The representation of women in labour market policies is generally higher in Sweden than in Germany. For some elementary comparative statistical data see tables 1 to 9 in the appendix.

The relatively limited success of equal opportunity policy in general, and some obvious differences in employment as well as in equal opportunity strategies among countries were the reasons to launch a project on "Women in Labour Market and the Effectiveness of Equal Opportunity Policy" at the International Institute of Management in Berlin in 1980. The aim of the project was not so much a comparison of many countries, but rather a systematic overview and an assessment of direct or indirect policy instruments to influence the functioning of the labour market in favour of equal employment opportunity for women. What are the mechanisms of direct or indirect discrimination on the labour market, and what are the factors obviously so strongly resisting positive equal opportunity policies? Which policy instruments in particular and which policy mixture are most likely to have a positive impact on equal employment opportunity, and what kind of administrative infrastructure is necessary to secure effective implementation?

Apart from pragmatic reasons, the selection of countries was guided by the criterion of which countries maintain a rich "policy mix" with regard to equal opportunity policies. Thus, beside the reference country West-Germany, Sweden, the United States and the United Kingdom have been chosen, because the Anglo-Saxon and the Scandinavian countries have a longer tradition of equal employment policy than most central European countries.

The outcome of the study were four country reports on the employment situation of women and on the policy mix of these countries (3). These national studies, which are currently available for those interested, were discussed at an international workshop in Berlin in December 1981. Specific issues of this discussion have been followed up and worked out to be presented in this volume. In the following, I will shortly summarize the individual contributions.

Anders Björklund looks at the "Male-Female Unemployment Differentials" in the four countries. He undertakes the first broader comparative analysis known in the literature on "unemployment dynamics", which means that he includes flows of unemployment and different aspects of unemployment duration. Such

2

a differentation is necessary for a better understanding of both the causal mechanisms and the welfare effects of unemployment. His main findings are that the major cause of the unemployment differentials between sexes - in most countries unfavourable for women - is the higher mobility into and out of the labour force that characterizes the labour market behavior of women. The unemployment costs for women are also higher, especially when taking into account the discouraged workers into the welfare function. However, the study also shows some slight improvement in the unemployment differentials for women, and it clearly implies that the higher risk of unemployment for women should not mainly be seen in the way the labour market works, but also in their greater domestic responsibilities in relation to men.

The most striking difference between men and women on the labour market is the work they do. Men and women are distributed differently between industries and occupations, and within most occupations they are employed at different levels and in different tasks of work. The occupational segregation of men and women is interesting for several reasons: other differences between men and women - wages, working conditions, working time - are related to differences in occupational distribution; one way to discriminate is by restricting the access of women or men to certain occupations; further, if discrimination through wage differentiation is restricted by law or agreements, employers may resort to employment discrimination.

Christina Jonung provides a thourough analysis of this issue from several angles. First she describes different methods to measure occupational segregation in labour markets. These measures are used to describe the development of sex segregation in the Swedish labour market from 1960 to 1975 and to compare it with Germany, Great Britain and the US. The sources of changes in the level of segregation are then identified with regard to structural changes, age groups, particular trades and occupations. Finally, the causes of occupational segregation and future trends are discussed.

The labour market in each of the four countries is characterized by a significant degree of occupational segregation. The pattern of segregation is similar in the sense that women are overrepresented in service, clerical and social work and underrepresented in administrative and manufacturing work. Although comparisons are hard to make and must be accompanied by reservations, the degree of occupational segregation appears to be higher in Sweden than in the other countries and possibly lower in Germany. In the US and Sweden the degree of occupational segregation is falling, in Germany and Great Britain it seems to be constant or rising.

Other important findings are the dependence of labour market segregation on the size and composition of the female labour force. Increasing labour force participation by women most probably involves a higher share of part-time work due to responsibilities in the household; because part-time work is concentrated in specific occupations and industries, a more segregated labour market is to be expected. Countries with a relatively low labour force participation rate today can, therefore, probably look forward to stable or even growing occupational segregation. On the other hand the increasing stability of labour force attachment of women contributes to desegregation; the lower and more rapidly decreasing degree of segregation of the under 35 age groups may be interpreted in this way. Furthermore, if opportunities of wage discrimination are reduced either by law or - as it is especially in Sweden the case - by collective agreements, employment discrimination may be intensified unless

3

legally or otherwise controlled. One hypothesis is that countries characterized by small wage differentials between men and women display a larger degree of occupational segregation.

Whereas occupational segregation is of more recent concern, analysis of earnings differentials between men and women has a long tradition in economic and sociological literature. However, explanations of these earnings differentials seem to vary with the increasing amount of econometric efforts to clear up this issue. The contribution by June O'Neill tries to solve this puzzle through a systematic comparison and evaluation of the recent literature. She first discusses the underlying determinants of earnings and of male-female earnings differences. Empirical studies of the pay gap are then reviewed. Because occupation is also an outcome of human capital investments and may also be a mechanism through which discrimination operates, the determinants of occupation and the relation between occupation and earnings are also emphasized.

In 1980 the female-male ratio was roughly around 70 per cent, except in Sweden where it ranged from 72 per cent to 90 per cent, depending on the particular measure of earnings used. In Germany, Sweden and in the United Kingdom women's earnings appear to have risen relative to men's over the past two decades; but there has been - on the average - virtually no increase in the United States despite the fact, that the United States was one of the first countries to adopt equal pay and equal employment legislation.

Concerning the determinants of the earnings gap, three broad factors are discussed: human capital investments and productivity, non-wage job characteristics such as tastes, home responsibilities and job requirements, and discrimination or institutionalized labour market barriers. Economic theory of discrimination provides a reason why discrimination might persists for a while, but it also provides - according to the authors view - reasons for optimism about the eventual erosion of discrimination, once legalized and institutionalized discrimination is eliminated. Differences in human capital investments and non-wage job characteristics seem to be prominent candidates for explaining persistent earning differences.

Empirical studies investigating the extent to which differences in human capital investment and other characteristics can account for the earnings gap explain a range from about 15 to 65 per cent of this gap, depending on data basis and method used, and excluding a few studies which explain virtually nothing or even 100 per cent. In as far the unexplained difference of earnings gap should be interpreted as "open discrimination" or - as Jacob Mincer suggests - "as a measure of our ignorance" is still an unresolved question. This leaves also uncertainties with regard to the role of policy. According to the authors view, some signs of change in the past decade provide reason for moderate optimistic expectations: Women have been increasing their schooling at the college and university level and have been marrying later and working longer. In some countries, the wage gap has already perceptibly declined, and the same can be observed among persons under the age of 35 in the United States.

Since the 1960's, governments of highly industrialized countries were increasingly put under pressure to engage in positive actions and in statutory protection of equal employment opportunity for women. The United States was certainly the leading country to introduce equal pay acts, anti-discrimination laws and affirmative action rules. Great Britain and later, the Scandinavian countries followed with similar rules and institutions enforcing these rules, and the central European countries - to some extent coerced by the European Commission in Brussels - also developed activities in this direction especially during the late seventies. To what extent this policy only reflected the increasing economic strength of women since World War II, and conversely to what extent women's position on the labour market was positively influenced by equal opportunity policies, is still a matter of controversal discussion. The following contributions provide a survey and an assessment of what has been done in this respect in the countries selected in this volume.

Rachel Braun starts with a description of the history and the present formal legal structure supporting American women in their fight for economic equality. Recent changes introduced by the Reagan Administration and controversial issues surrounding equal opportunity legislation are then discussed.

Whereas the Equal Pay Act (1963) is considered effective in remedying inequalities within an establishment, it cannot be used to raise the wages of women who work in predominantly female occupations or in establishments which employ too few men for comparison. The reaction to this failure was the development of the "comparable work" concept which, however, has eluded any workable practical definition. The U.S. also provides plenty of information on the problems which arise when the concept of discrimination is shifted from the unlawful "intention to discriminate" to the concept of "adverse impact". The U.S. is also the country with the most experiences in "affirmative action". Although the legality of affirmative action has been upheld in court decisions, a clear positive case, that could provide orientation, has not yet been decided. The bitterly contested case of Bakke vs. Regents, however, clearly denied the use of inflexible quotas. Finally, the case of the U.S. is a good demonstration for how important enforcing implementation agencies are to secure the effectiveness of equal opportunity laws. The cutbacks in both the staffing and budgets of the equal employment agencies under the Reagan Administration were clearly a setback for American's equal opportunity policy.

Pauline Glucklich examines the situation in Britain. Here, the Equal Pay and Sex Discrimination Acts do appear to have had some impact, particularly regarding income. It is not clear, however, how much of women's improved earnings position is to be attributed to equal opportunity policy, how much to income policy, and how much to the growth in female representation in trade unions. There are good arguments that a strong income policy in favour of low wage earners and an extension of collective bargaining to cover more female jobs might be more effective than to rely on the more selective approach of equal opportunity measures. It is also suggested that an effective general national minimum wage would probably have resulted in more lasting improvement in female earnings than the selective approach of the wages council machinery.

Broad consideration is given to the reasons why the Equal Pay and the Sex Discrimination Acts clearly failed to achieve equal pay or opportunity in the wider sense. As in the United States, the Equal Pay Act was not intended to overcome occupational segregation, and thus it was only effective at the company level. At this level, however, a lot of strategies evading the law can be observed, e.g., changing job content to prevent equal pay comparisons, introducing new grading schemes so that women end up with lower, altering job evaluation factors favouring men and restricting certain jobs only to fulltime workers. To be more effective, substantial amendments to the Equal Pay and Sex Discrimination Acts and correspondingly a strengthening of the main enforcement agencies - the Equal Opportunities Commission and the wage councils - are necessary.

Sweden previously stressed social and labour market policy instruments rather than anti-discrimination rules to promote equal opportunity. It was not until 1980 that the Equality Act between men and women at work was passed. Siv Gustafsson, therefore, starts with a historical review of social policy measures toward equalization in Sweden. Among the significant recent innovations is the separate taxation of earnings of husband and wife which increases the payoff to more equal distributions of paid work between spouses. Paid parental leave for childcare, not only for mothers but also for fathers, has been introduced. State subsidized daycare centers have also been substantially extended, but they still do not meet the demand. Calculating the costs and benefits of day-care, however, shows that the benefits for society are considerably greater than the costs. Sweden is also the country with the strongest labour market policy which has also effectively been used to improve women's position on the labour market.

The Equality Act between men and women at work consists of three parts: a ban on wage and employment discrimination, a request to the employer to actively promote equality at work (affirmative action), and as enforcing in-stitutions, the Equality Ombud and the Equal Opportunities Commission. It is interesting to note that the Equality Act in Sweden was championed by the Liberal Party against the hesitance and even resistance of the Social Democrats and the trade unions who essentially see equalization as a matter of social policy and collective bargaining. Another Swedish pecularity is the strong role of the collective bargaining system in the implementation of the Equality Act: no affirmative action, for instance, can be taken before there is a collective agreement between employers and employees' organizations.

In Germany too, it was not until 1980 that the Act on Equal Treatment was passed, and an external impulse was needed for the Federal Government to take the initiative: In 1975 and 1976 the EEC Council of Ministers has issued binding directives concerning the application of the principles of equal pay and equal treatment in employment. This does not mean that nothing has been done in terms of equal opportunity prior to this Act. Beside the quite explicit rules of the Basic Law ("Men and women shall have equal rights", and "no one may be prejudiced or favoured on account of sex"), several particular steps were made to explicitly prohibit discrimination, e.g., in the Works Constitution Act, in the Labour Law with its subsequent court interpretations, and the Family Reform Law of 1976 which abandoned the model of the housewife.

Heide Pfarr and Ludwig Eitel provide a comprehensive description and a critical assessment of German equal opportunity issues since World War II. Among other things, they develop a series of arguments why the present Equal Treatment Act is insufficient and probably quite inefficient: although the act introduced the reversal of the burden of proof in favour of women, at the same time it introduced the term "objective reason" as an additional exception;

because of its vagueness, it might now be easier for an employer to find such reasons. In addition, the act does not explicitly permit measures to ensure positive unequal treatment, and neither is there any mention of the problem of "indirect discrimination". The authors main point of criticism is that the German law to date with respect to equal rights for men and women has merely been developed to the point of prohibiting discrimination, and even in this respect the law has not gone far enough. However, what is needed essentially, are positive and supportive measures, since prohibitive measures might be circumvented, provoke other types of illegal behavior, and they involve high administrative and individual costs when violations occur and complaints are made. Especially the labour market seems to be a suitable policy area for intervention, and the Labour Law is considered as more susceptible to external regulation as the Family Law for instance. Essential elements of such a reform would be: positive discrimination in favour of women, an obligation of employers to organize work in such a way that the tasks can be performed by men as well as by women, militant enforcement agencies, and strengthening of the plant-level interest representation.

Christine Jackson looks at equalization policies from a more general point of view. She distinguishes three models: anti-discrimination legislation, positive discrimination or affirmative action, and equal opportunity policies. Anti-discrimination policy is the legislation of specific laws which make it unlawful to treat men and women differently. An important distinction is made between positive or reverse discrimination on the one hand, and affirmative or positive action on the other hand. Positive discrimination means giving preference to women, affirmative action means giving special encouragement and providing special programmes to try to reduce imbalances between the sexes. Equal opportunity policies are defined as those which intend to raise the level of women's qualification from entry into the labour market and to improve the compatibility of paid employment with domestic responsibilities.

The development and impact of British anti-discrimination legislation is discussed and compared with Sweden and, above all, with United States. So far, British anti-discrimination policy has had more of an educative effect than real impact on the improvement of the labour market position of women. What is lacking are powerful enforcement strategies, especially the threat of real financial sanctions which do exist - to some extent - in the US. It is argued that the strategy of positive or reverse discrimination should not be followed, because it is or would be socially and politically unacceptable, and because it is incompatible with anti-discrimination legislation. More promising are positive actions among which strategies of persuasion, mobilization of public opinions and monitoring are emphasized, and social policy strategies aimed at breaking down inequality at home and creating working conditions suitable for both men and women.

Emma MacLennan and Renate Weitzel undertake the first comprehensive comparative analysis of labour market policy in the four countries. Their basic concern is the way in which women's position in the labour market affects their access to unemployment benefits and inclusion in labour market policies, especially training, job creation and job preservation. It is shown that the nature of unemployment insurance systems operating in the countries surveyed is an important factor in the propensity of women to register. Systems based on the contributory principle which tend to exclude low income groups, part-time workers, seasonal and casual labour thereby exclude substantial numbers of women from liability and benefit. If they are unlikely to be eligible for benefit, there is less incentive for the unemployed, particularly discouraged workers, to register. Among the few non-contributory systems examined, the KAS system in Sweden seems to provide a suitable model in dealing with the specific disadvantages of women: eligibility for benefit under KAS is not dependent upon contributory tests but on registration for work, including part-time work.

In the same way that unemployment insurance systems based on contributory tests tend to exclude women and marginal workers, labour market policies which concentrate on the insured unemployed fail to meet the needs of these groups. This was particularly apparent when the West German provisions for adult training and retraining were considered. Furthermore, counter-cyclical policies which have the objective of reducing the number of registered unemployed can lose sight of those who fail to register or whose employment is tenuous. This is especially illustrated by the experience of public sector job creation in the United States. Finally, in all countries considered, job preservation policies are overwhelmingly concentrated on primary workers in traditional male manufacturing industries. To a considerable extent, labour market policy merely reflects the segmented labour market. The authors, therefore, stress the urgent requirement that women are defined as a priority group and policies are designed with sex inequalities instead of "sex neutrality", as long as women are disadvantaged on the labour market.

Up to this point, the contributions in this volume provide scattered descriptions and analytical evidence on the discrimination of women on the labour market, on different policy measures aimed at equalization, and on their real or potential impact to contribute to this goal. The following contribution by Glen Cain raises methodological questions of measuring discrimination and the impact of government programs. Cain first starts with the problem of adequately measuring labour supply and earnings. Because labour force participation rates are measured differently from country to country, and because they do not account for different working hours during the life cycle, he proposes an alternative measure - the lifetime labour supply measured in "hours worked per lifetime" as a fraction of total hours available for the 56-year span (age 14 to 70). His findings for the United States show the increase in women's market work to be less dramatic than that illustrated by labour force participation rates, but it is still substantial: Around 1900, the average woman could expect to spend about 8 per cent of her adult life in market work; by 1970 this fraction had increased to 13 per cent. The average man in 1900 could expect to spend about 43 per cent of his adult life in market work, and by 1970 this per cent had decreased to 25. Cain also provides convincing arguments why the earning differentials between men and women have to be interpreted with great caution, especially because of the changing composition of the labour force. He also raises doubts as to whether the usual econometric procedures are able to answer the question, if and to what extent labour market discrimination exists.

He therefore proposes a shift from the focus on market wage rates to income received during one's adult life, and, as a corollary, to shift from the individual market worker as a separate unit of analysis to the individual as a member of a household that shares total household income. A corresponding model is developed and illustrated. This model has not yet been empirically implemented, however, reasonable speculations suggest that the variance in expected lifetime income has increased, especially among women. Finally, conventional models for policy analysis are critized from a methodological point of view, and it is concluded that much effort is still required to develop adequate methods for the evaluation of government programs.

In the last contribution, I try to tie up the loose ends through a theoretical and comparative analysis of sex discrimination and equalization policies. In the first part of that chapter, different theories of discrimination are collected and evaluated according to the type of actors, their motivation and the mode of discrimination. Not all theories are equally relevant to sex discrimination in the labour market. The most influential theory of discrimination in economics, the theory of "taste for discrimination" developed by Gary Becker, does little to explain sex discrimination. More important but controversial in their empirical relevance are theories of monopsony based upon the assumption of lower supply elasticity of women in relation to men. The most promising approaches, however, are theories based on the motivating force of social customs and on pecuniary benefits with respect both to employers and employees, and theories based on the behavioral assumptions of traditional role orientation and on reducing uncertainties due to insufficient information.

In the second part, four principal forms of policy interventions to reduce labour market discrimination are identified and prominent examples from the four countries are evaluated: First, government itself can play a compensatory role through public finance or public employment; second, the state may try do directly influence the behavior of market actors through bans on discrimination, affirmative action or supportive policies; third, the state can provide incentives in order to influence individual behavior or attitudes indirectly, and fourth, the state can change the institutional framework of decision-making with respect to hiring, pay, promotion or job protection. Each of these forms of intervention has its specific strength and weakness.

Nevertheless, in practice, combinations of these different policy options are necessary. My approach, however, tends to argue that emphasis should be given to institutional changes, such as the reform of the tax and social security system to reduce disincentives of paid work for women, the extension of leave for childcare to fathers and the financing of such leave out of a common pool, and the establishment of independent and powerful equal opportunity agencies. Of equally great importance are the mobilization of public opinion and the heightening of consciousness on discrimination issues by the diffusion of information and by the institutionalization of monitoring systems both at the company level and various government levels. To a great extent, we look at reality as we think it should be.

NOTES

(1) Ralph E. Smith (ed.), The Subtle Revolution. Women at Work, Washington, D.C. 1979: The Urban Institute.

(2) OECD (Organisation for Economic Co-Operation and Development), Women and Employment, Paris 1980.

(3) Renate Weitzel, Labour Market Policies Related to Women and Employment in the Federal Republic of Germany, Manuscript, Berlin: International Institute of Management *), May 1982.

Lillemore Gladh and Siv Gustafsson, Labor Market Policy Related to Women and Employment in Sweden, Manuscript, Berlin: International Institute of Management*), December 1981.

Robert Elliot, Pauline Glucklich, Emma MacLennan, Chris Pond, Women in the Labour Market. A Study of the Impact of Legislation and Policy Toward Women in the UK Labour Market During the Nineteen Seventies, Manuscript, Berlin: International Institute of Management*), 1981.

June O'Neill and Rachel Braun, Women and the Labour Market: A Survey of Issues and Policies in the United States, Manuscript, Berlin: International Institute of Management*), November 1981.

*) International Institute of Management, Platz der Luftbrücke 2, D-1000 Berlin 42

APPENDIX

Table 1

Civilian Employment — Total (Thousands)

Year	USA	FRG	GB	SWE
1960	65 778	25 254	24 257	—
1965	71 088	26 699	25 327	3 692
1970	78 627	26 169	24 373	3 854
1975	84 783	24 798	24 593	4 062
1976	87 485	24 556	24 429	4 088
1977	90 546	24 511	24 505	4 099
1978	94 373	24 700	24 643	4 115
1979	96 945	25 041	24 806	4 180
1980	97 270	25 265	24 397	4 232

Changes (1970 = 100)

Year	USA	FRG	GB	SWE
1960	83.7	96.5	99.5	—
1965	90.4	102.0	103.9	95.8
1970	100.0	100.0	100.0	100.0
1975	107.8	94.8	100.9	105.4
1976	111.3	93.8	100.2	106.1
1977	115.2	93.7	100.5	106.4
1978	120.0	94.4	101.1	106.8
1979	123.3	95.7	101.8	108.5
1980	123.8	96.5	100.1	109.8

— not available.

Source: OECD Labour Force Statistics, Paris, own calculations.

11

Table 2

Civillian Employment, Males — Females

	USA		FRG		GB		SWE	
	Males	Females	Males	Females	Males	Females	Males	Females
1960	43 904	21 874	16 149	9 805	15 918	9 339	—	—
1965	46 340	24 748	16 848	9 851	16 361	8 966	2 357	1 335
1970	48 960	29 667	16 587	9 582	15 531	8 843	2 335	1 519
1975	51 230	33 553	15 432	9 366	15 046	9 546	2 342	1 720
1976	52 391	35 095	15 280	9 276	14 905	9 524	2 338	1 751
1977	53 861	36 685	15 217	9 294	14 878	9 627	2 314	1 785
1978	55 491	38 882	15 323	9 377	14 899	9 744	2 297	1 818
1979	56 499	40 446	15 459	9 582	14 894	9 912	2 315	1 865
1980	55 988	41 283	15 586	9 679	14 624	9 773	2 327	1 905

Changes (1970 = 100)

	USA		FRG		GB		SWE	
1960	89.7	73.7	97.4	102.3	102.5	105.6	—	—
1965	94.6	83.4	101.6	102.8	105.3	101.4	100.9	87.9
1970	100.0	100.0	100.0	100.0	100.0	100.0	100.0	100.0
1975	104.6	113.1	93.0	97.7	96.9	107.9	100.3	113.2
1976	107.0	118.3	92.1	96.8	96.0	107.7	100.1	115.3
1977	110.0	123.7	91.7	97.0	95.8	108.9	99.1	117.5
1978	113.3	131.1	92.4	97.9	95.9	110.2	98.4	119.7
1979	115.4	136.3	93.2	100.0	95.9	112.1	99.1	122.8
1980	114.6	139.1	93.9	101.0	94.2	110.5	99.7	125.4

— not available.

Source: OECD Labour Force Statistics, Paris, own calculations.

12

Table 3: Civilian Employment – Total, Breakdown by Sector (Thousands)

Year	USA Agri-culture[1]	USA Industry[2]	USA Others[3]	FRG Agri-culture	FRG Industry	FRG Others	GB Agri-culture	GB Industry	GB Others	SWE Agri-culture	SWE Industry	SWE Others
1960	5 458	22 087	38 233	3 623	12 661	9 670	1 005*	11 845	11 407	–	1 587	1 684
1965	4 361	23 742	42 985	2 966	13 379	10 354	846*	12 174	12 307	421*	1 480	2 060
1970	3 566	27 014	48 047	2 262	12 902	11 005	784	10 913	12 678	314	1 481	2 320
1975	3 476	25 996	55 311	1 823	11 408	11 567	668	10 013	13 912	261	1 448	2 384
1976	3 417	27 005	57 063	1 743	11 190	11 623	660	9 764	14 005	254	1 407	2 442
1977	3 383	27 996	59 167	1 655	11 103	11 753	656	9 767	14 082	248	1 360	2 504
1978	3 501	29 427	61 445	1 608	11 112	11 980	649	9 721	14 273	251	1 360	2 578
1979	3 455	30 402	63 088	1 558	11 233	12 250	634	9 666	14 506	242	1 360	2 631
1980	3 470	29 754	64 047	1 518	11 327	12 420	637	9 270	14 491	237	1 363	

Changes (1970 = 100)

Year	USA Agri-culture	USA Industry	USA Others	FRG Agri-culture	FRG Industry	FRG Others	GB Agri-culture	GB Industry	GB Others	SWE Agri-culture	SWE Industry	SWE Others
1960	153.1	81.8	79.6	160.2	98.1	87.9	128.2	108.5	90.0	–	–	–
1965	122.3	87.9	89.5	131.1	103.7	94.1	107.9	111.6	97.1	134.1	107.2	81.7
1970	100.0	100.0	100.0	100.0	100.0	100.0	100.0	100.0	100.0	100.0	100.0	100.0
1975	97.5	96.2	115.1	80.6	88.4	105.1	87.8	91.8	109.7	83.1	100.1	112.6
1976	95.8	100.0	118.8	77.1	86.7	105.6	84.2	89.5	110.5	80.9	97.8	115.7
1977	94.9	103.6	123.1	73.2	86.1	106.8	83.7	89.5	110.7	79.0	95.1	118.5
1978	98.2	108.9	127.9	71.1	86.1	108.9	82.8	89.1	112.6	80.0	91.9	121.5
1979	96.9	112.5	131.3	68.9	87.1	111.3	80.9	88.6	114.4	77.1	91.8	125.1
1980	97.3	110.1	133.3	67.1	87.8	112.9	81.3	84.9	114.3	75.5	92.1	127.7

* Secretariat estimates
– not available

1 Includes hunting, forestry, fishing.
2 i.e.: Mining and quarrying, manufacturing, electricity, gas and water, construction
3 Mainly wholesale and retail trade, transport, storage and communication, financing, insurance real estate and business service, community, social and personal services.

Source: OECD Labour Force Statistics, Paris, own calucaltions.

13

Table 4: Civilian Employment — Breakdown by Sector — Males (Thousands)

Year	USA Agri-culture¹	USA Industry²	USA Others³	FRG Agri-culture	FRG Industry	FRG Others	GB Agri-culture	GB Industry	GB Others	SWE Agri-culture	SWE Industry	SWE Others
1960	–	–	–	1 662	9 356	5 131	884*	8 741	6 293	–	–	–
1965	–	–	–	1 364	9 989	5 495	734*	9 055	6 572	–	–	–
1970	2 956	20 866	25 138	1 073	9 578	5 936	638	8 205	6 689	242	1 183	910
1975	2 882	19 949	28 399	854	8 548	6 030	534	7 586	6 927	193	1 155	994
1976	2 818	20 543	29 030	828	8 310	6 142	528	7 441	6 936	190	1 131	1 014
1977	2 758	21 253	29 850	787	8 240	6 190	531	7 410	6 937	183	1 104	1 026
1978	2 815	22 184	30 492	773	8 235	6 315	525	7 373	7 000	187	1 060	1 050
1979	2 771	22 818	30 911	744	8 324	6 391	512	7 331	7 051	181	1 052	1 082
1980	2 793	22 125	31 070	741	8 395	6 450	512	7 073	7 039	178	1 055	1 094

Changes (1970 = 100)

Year	USA Agri-culture¹	USA Industry²	USA Others³	FRG Agri-culture	FRG Industry	FRG Others	GB Agri-culture	GB Industry	GB Others	SWE Agri-culture	SWE Industry	SWE Others
1960	–	–	–	154.9	97.7	86.4	138.6	106.5	94.1	–	–	–
1965	–	–	–	127.1	104.3	92.6	115.0	110.4	98.3	–	–	–
1970	100.0	100.0	100.0	100.0	100.0	100.0	100.0	100.0	100.0	100.0	100.0	100.0
1975	97.5	95.6	113.0	79.6	89.2	101.6	83.7	92.5	103.6	79.8	97.6	109.2
1976	95.3	98.5	115.5	77.2	86.7	103.5	82.8	90.7	103.7	78.5	95.6	111.4
1977	93.3	101.9	118.7	73.3	86.0	104.3	83.2	90.3	103.7	75.6	93.3	112.7
1978	95.2	106.3	121.3	72.0	85.9	106.4	82.3	89.9	104.6	77.3	89.6	115.5
1979	93.8	109.4	123.0	69.3	86.9	107.7	80.3	89.3	105.4	74.8	88.9	118.9
1980	94.5	106.0	123.6	69.1	87.6	108.7	80.3	86.2	105.2	73.6	89.2	120.2

¹ Includes hunting, forestry, fishing.
² i.e.: Mining and quarrying, manufacturing, electricity, gas and water, construction real estate and business service, community, social and personal services.
³ Mainly wholesale and retail trade, transport, storage and communication, financing, insurance, real estate and business service, community, social and personal services.

* Secretariat estimates
– not available

14

Table 5: Civilian Employment — Breakdown by Sector — Females (Thousands)

Year	USA			FRG			GB			SWE		
	Agri-culture[1]	Industry[2]	Others[3]	Agri-culture	Industry	Others	Agri-culture	Industry	Others	Agri-culture	Industry	Others
1960	–	–	–	1 961	3 305	4 539	121*	3 104	5 114	–	–	–
1965	–	–	–	1 602	3 390	4 859	112*	3 119	5 735	–	–	–
1970	610	6 148	22 909	1 189	3 324	5 069	146	2 708	5 989	72	297	1 150
1975	593	6 047	26 913	969	2 860	5 537	134	2 428	6 985	68	326	1 326
1976	599	6 462	28 034	915	2 880	5 481	132	2 323	7 069	64	317	1 370
1977	625	6 743	29 317	868	2 863	5 563	125	2 357	7 145	65	303	1 416
1978	686	7 243	30 953	835	2 877	5 665	124	2 348	7 272	64	300	1 455
1979	684	7 585	32 178	814	2 909	5 859	122	2 335	7 455	61	308	1 496
1980	677	7 629	32 977	777	2 932	5 970	125	2 197	7 452	59	309	1 537
Changes (1970 = 100)												
1960	–	–	–	164.9	99.4	89.5	82.5	114.6	85.4	–	–	–
1965	–	–	–	134.7	102.0	95.9	76.7	115.2	95.8	–	–	–
1970	100.0	100.0	100.0	100.0	100.0	100.0	100.0	100.0	100.0	100.0	100.0	100.0
1975	97.2	98.4	117.5	81.5	86.0	109.2	91.8	89.7	116.6	94.4	109.8	115.3
1976	98.2	105.1	122.4	77.0	86.6	108.1	90.4	85.8	118.0	88.9	144.7	119.1
1977	102.5	110.0	128.0	73.0	86.1	109.7	85.6	87.0	119.3	90.3	102.0	123.1
1978	112.5	117.8	135.1	70.2	86.6	111.8	84.9	86.7	121.4	88.9	101.0	126.5
1979	112.1	123.4	140.5	68.5	87.5	115.6	83.6	86.2	124.5	84.7	103.7	130.1
1980	111.0	124.1	143.9	65.3	88.2	117.8	85.6	81.1	124.4	81.9	104.0	133.7

1 Includes hunting, forestry, fishing.
2 i.e.: Mining and quarrying, manufacturing, electricity, gas and water, construction.
3 Mainly wholesale and retail trade, transport, storage and communication, financing, insurance, real estate and business service, community, social and personal services.

— not available
* Secretariat estimates

15

Table 6: Civilian Employment by Sectors: Proportion of Women in per cent

Year	USA Agri-culture	USA Industry	USA Others	FRG Agri-culture	FRG Industry	FRG Others	UK Agri-culture	UK Industry	UK Others	SWE Agri-culture	SWE Industry	SWE Others
1960	n. a.	n. a.	n. a.	54.1	26.5	46.9	12.0	26.2	44.8	n. a.	n. a.	n. a.
1965	n. a.	n. a.	n. a.	n. a.	n. a.	n. a.	n. a.	n. a.	n. a.	n. a.	n. a.	n. a.
1970	17.1	22.8	46.2	52.6	25.8	46.1	18.6	24.8	47.2	22.9	20.1	55.8
1975	n. a.	n. a.	n. a.	53.2	25.1	47.9	20.1	24.2	50.2	26.1	22.1	57.1
1976	n. a.	n. a.	n. a.	52.5	25.7	47.2	19.9	23.8	50.5	25.2	21.9	57.4
1977	18.5	24.1	49.5	52.4	25.8	47.3	19.1	24.1	50.7	26.2	21.5	58.0
1978	19.6	24.6	50.4	51.9	25.9	47.3	19.1	24.2	50.9	25.5	22.1	58.1
1979	19.8	24.9	51.0	52.2	25.9	47.8	19.1	24.1	51.5	25.2	22.7	58.0
1980	19.5	25.6	51.5	51.2	25.9	48.1	19.6	23.7	51.4	24.9	22.7	58.4

n. a. = not available

Source: OECD Labour Force Statistics, Paris, own calculations.

Table 7: Civilian Labour Force, Total – Males – Females

Year	USA Total	USA Males	USA Females	FRG Total	FRG Males	FRG Females	GB Total	GB Males	GB Females	SWE* Total	SWE* Males	SWE* Females
1960	69 628	46 388	23 240	26 225	16 327	9 898	24 583	16 154	8 429	–	–	–
1965	74 455	48 255	26 200	26 846	16 953	9 893	25 626	16 589	9 037	3 738	2 360	1 378
1970	82 715	51 195	31 520	26 318	16 680	9 638	24 928	16 005	8 923	3 913	2 367	1 546
1975	92 613	55 615	36 998	25 872	16 055	9 818	25 459	15 753	9 705	4 129	2 373	1 756
1976	94 773	56 359	38 414	25 616	15 846	9 770	25 761	15 915	9 846	4 155	2 368	1 787
1977	97 401	57 449	39 952	25 541	15 735	9 806	25 955	15 929	10 026	4 174	2 350	1 824
1978	100 420	58 542	41 878	25 693	15 812	9 881	26 084	15 922	10 167	4 209	2 346	1 863
1979	102 908	59 517	43 391	25 917	15 876	10 041	26 150	15 824	10 326	4 268	2 359	1 909
1980	104 719	60 145	44 574	26 154	16 012	10 142	26 057	15 756	10 300	4 318	2 367	1 951

Changes (1970 = 100)

Year	USA Total	USA Males	USA Females	FRG Total	FRG Males	FRG Females	GB Total	GB Males	GB Females	SWE* Total	SWE* Males	SWE* Females
1960	84.2	90.6	73.7	99.5	97.9	102.7	98.6	100.9	74.5	–	–	–
1965	90.0	94.3	83.1	102.0	101.6	102.6	102.8	103.6	101.3	95.5	99.7	89.1
1970	100.0	100.0	100.0	100.0	100.0	100.0	100.0	100.0	100.0	100.0	100.0	100.0
1975	112.0	108.6	117.4	98.3	96.3	101.9	102.1	98.4	108.8	105.5	100.3	113.6
1976	114.6	110.1	121.9	97.3	95.0	101.4	103.3	99.4	110.3	106.2	100.0	115.6
1977	117.8	112.2	126.8	97.0	94.3	101.7	104.1	99.5	112.4	106.7	99.3	118.0
1978	121.4	114.4	132.9	97.6	94.8	102.5	104.6	99.5	113.9	107.6	99.1	120.5
1979	124.4	116.3	137.7	98.5	95.2	104.2	104.9	98.9	115.7	109.1	99.7	123.5
1980	126.6	117.5	141.4	99.4	96.0	105.2	104.5	98.4	115.4	110.4	100.0	126.2

* Sweden: Total Labour Force, 1960 not available.

Source: OECD Labour Force Statistics, Paris, own calculations.

17

Table 8: Total Labour Force Participation Rate*

Year	USA			FRG			GB			SWE		
	Total	Males	Females	Total	Males	Females	Total	Males	Females	Total	Males	Females
1960	66.8	97.1	42.6	70.3	94.4	49.2	71.7	98.1	46.1	74.3	98.5	50.1
1970	67.7	87.1	48.9	69.5	92.5	48.1	72.4	94.3	50.8	74.3	88.8	59.4
1975	69.1	85.4	53.2	67.9	87.0	49.6	73.8	92.2	55.3	78.5	89.2	67.6
1976	69.5	85.1	54.4	67.3	85.9	49.5	74.1	92.4	55.8	78.9	88.9	68.7
1977	69.9	85.4	55.1	66.9	85.2	49.3	74.2	91.8	56.5	79.2	88.1	70.0
1978	71.4	85.6	57.7	66.8	84.9	49.4	74.2	91.4	57.1	79.6	87.7	71.3
1979	72.1	85.7	58.9	66.8	84.5	49.6	74.5	90.7	58.2	80.5	87.9	72.8
1980	72.4	85.4	59.7	66.6	83.4	50.0	74.5	90.4	58.5	81.0	87.8	74.1
1981	72.7	85.1	60.7	66.1	82.3	50.1	73.8	90.0	57.5	81.0	86.5	75.3

* Total Labour Force x 100
  Population from 15 to 64 years

Source: OECD Historical Statistics, Paris 1983, Tables 2.6, 2.7, 2.8, vv. 34/5.

13

Table 9: Unemployment Total — Males — Females

Year	USA Total	USA Males	USA Females	FRG Total	FRG Males	FRG Females	GB* Total	GB* Males	GB* Females	SWE Total	SWE Males	SWE Females
1960	3 852	2 486	1 366	271	178	93	326	236	90	–	–	–
1965	3 366	1 914	1 452	147	105	42	299	228	71	44	20	24
1970	4 088	2 235	1 853	149	93	56	555	475	80	59	32	27
1975	7 830	4 385	3 445	1 074	623	452	866	707	159	67	32	36
1976	7 288	3 969	3 320	1 060	567	494	1 332	1 010	322	66	30	36
1977	6 855	3 588	3 267	1 030	518	512	1 450	1 051	399	75	35	40
1978	6 047	3 051	2 996	993	489	504	1 446	1 023	423	94	49	45
1979	5 963	3 018	2 945	876	417	459	1 344	930	414	88	44	44
1980	7 448	4 157	3 291	889	426	462	1 660	1 132	527	86	40	45

Unemployment Rates[1]

Year	USA Total	USA Males	USA Females	FRG Total	FRG Males	FRG Females	GB* Total	GB* Males	GB* Females	SWE Total	SWE Males	SWE Females
1960	5.5	5.4	5.9	1.0	1.1	0.9	1.3	1.5	1.1	–	–	–
1965	4.5	4.0	5.5	0.5	0.6	0.4	1.2	1.4	0.8	1.2	0.8	1.7
1970	4.9	4.4	5.9	0.5	0.6	0.6	2.2	3.0	0.9	1.5	1.4	1.7
1975	8.5	7.9	9.3	4.2	3.9	4.6	3.4	4.5	1.6	1.6	1.3	2.1
1976	7.7	7.0	8.6	4.1	3.6	5.1	5.2	6.3	3.3	1.6	1.3	2.0
1977	7.0	6.2	8.2	4.0	3.3	5.2	5.6	6.6	4.0	1.8	1.5	2.2
1978	5.9	5.0	7.1	3.8	3.0	5.1	5.5	6.3	4.2	2.2	2.1	2.4
1979	5.7	4.9	6.8	3.3	2.5	4.6	5.1	5.8	4.0	2.1	1.9	2.3
1980	7.0	6.7	7.4	3.3	2.6	4.5	6.3	7.0	5.1	2.0	1.7	2.3

1 All unemployment rates are calculated with respect to the total labour force.
– Not available.
* Registered wholly unemployed only.

Source: OECD Labour Force Statistics, Paris.

19

2 A LOOK AT THE MALE FEMALE UNEMPLOYMENT DIFFERENTIALS IN THE FEDERAL REPUBLIC OF GERMANY, SWEDEN, UNITED KINGDOM, AND THE UNITED STATES OF AMERICA

ANDERS BJÖRKLUND

1.   INTRODUCTION

Women can be discriminated or have an unfavourable position in the labour market in several ways. They can have lower wages than others, less attractive jobs in other respects than wages and they can suffer more from unemployment.

In this paper we will take a closer look at the unemployment differentials between sexes in the four countries studied in this volume, i.e. Great Britain, Sweden, the U.S. and West Germany. The main emphasis will be on various aspects of what has become known as "unemployment dynamics". This means that we extend the analysis to include not only unemployed but also the flows into and out of unemployment that form this group. In doing so we also emphasize different aspects of unemployment duration.

The main motivation for this look at the unemployment differentials is to contribute to a better understanding of both the causal mechanisms, and the welfare consequences of unemployment. The paper is also structured in this way. It starts with a short section (2) on the measurement of unemployment in the different countries and on the patterns and trends of the sex differentials. Then we try to shed some light on the causes of the sex differentials in the four countries treated here (section 3). This section presents the familiar "inflow times duration" decomposition of unemployment and data on the reason for having become unemployed.

Next we turn to a discussion of the welfare aspects of the sex-differentials in section 4. This section starts with a digression on different measures of unemployment duration and attempts to explain how they are related to each other. It is argued that duration measures, which highlight the situation for those currently unemployed, are probably more relevant to welfare analysis than measures which highlights the prospects for those who become unemployed at a certain point in time. Given some rather plausible assumptions about the costs of unemployment for the individual the total unemployment costs for men and women, and hence the cost differential, can be estimated.

In section 5 the main findings are summarized and some possible implications for policy issues and for further research are discussed.

2. THE MALE-FEMALE UNEMPLOYMENT DIFFERENTIALS

2.1 The Measurement of Unemployment in the Different Countries

All international comparisons of labor markets are complicated by different measurement methods and definitions of central labor market variables. This is particularly true of unemployment which is an imprecise concept that can be measured in several ways.

Our main concern in this paper is not to compare the aggregate levels of unemployment. The problems which arise when such comparisons are to be made have been analyzed in great detail in a study by the Bureau of Labor Statistics (International Comparisons of Unemployment (1979)). Instead, our main concern is to compare the sex differentials of unemployment in four countries. Consequently, the problems of measurement and definitions will concern us only when they are likely to affect the unemployment rates for men and women by different magnitudes.

The most "problematic" country as far as male-female comparisons are concerned is probably Great Britain. The reason for this is that the major source of unemployment statistics is the number of persons registered as unemployed at the Department of Employment's local employment offices. To be counted, persons must be out of work, searching for, capable of, and available for full-time employment (1). For several reasons this measure is likely to underestimate the female unemployment rate. Therefore we also present some data that are available from other sources of unemployment statistics. These are the General Household Survey (GHS) and the Census of the Population where a broader concept of unemployment is used. Both GHS and the Census count as unemployed those who in the reference week were not working and were looking for work, or would have looked for work if they had not been temporarily sick, or were waiting to assume a job they had already obtained.

Similar problems pertain to the West German unemployment data. The most important source for these are the administrative records of the Federal Employment Agency (see Freiburghaus (1979)). Job hunters at employment offices are registered as unemployed if they are between 15 and 65 years old, capable of work, employed presently for less than 20 hours a week, immediately available to take up employment and not just seeking very temporary (7 days or less) or part-time employment (less than 20 hours per week). This definition is very broad in the sense that workers on an involuntary part-time basis are included. On the other hand it is restrictive since those who are only looking for part-time jobs (less than 20 hours per week) are excluded. The latter requirement is likely to exclude many women from the statistics.

However, there is an additional data source in West Germany too. This is the annual microcensus which uses a definition of unemployment that is similar to the international conventions. Consequently, job hunting by other methods than via the Employment Offices is sufficient for being counted as unemployed. Furthermore, those who only are looking for part-time jobs are included. Involuntary part-time workers are excluded.

The least problematic cases for our purposes are Sweden and the U.S.. Very well developed monthly labor force sample surveys which strongly resemble one another are available in both countries. The main advantage of these surveys is that different types of unemployment or "idle capacity" are covered by the questions. This is crucial when male-female comparisons are to be made.

The most frequently used unemployment definition in both countries ("open unemployment") is based on a general seeking criterion (2). All part-time workers are counted as employed. The differences between the two countries are minor. In the U.S., job seeking students can be included among the unemployed whereas this category is excluded in Sweden. The reference period for job-hunting is four weeks (in the U.S.), but 60 days in Sweden.

2.2   Patterns and Trends of the Male-Female Unemployment Differentials

The aggregate time series of male and female unemployment rates and the differentials are presented in Tables 1a-d. These tables display many interesting features both between and within countries as far as unemployment differentials are concerned. First it can be seen that Great Britain differs from the other countries in one important respect; females have lower unemployment rates than males according to all measures. Registered unemployment data display much lower rates for women (the ratio between female and male unemployment rates never exceeds 0.65), but the differential is favourable for women when a more general search criterion is used too. This specific British pattern clearly requires an explanation.

In West Germany female unemployment has exceeded the male rate ever since 1970. However, during the late sixties the reverse pattern can be found. Consequently there has been a worsening trend for women.

Sweden and the U.S. are very interesting countries because of the detailed unemployment statistics that are available there. We can look at both open unemployment (i.e. unemployment according to a general search criterion), involuntary part-time and discouraged workers. It is important to note that all types of unemployment are higher for women than for men. Consequently, the common practice in both countries to present only figures on open unemployment underestimates the problems of women. This is not to say that the three types of unemployment should have equal weight in a measure of "total" unemployment. Actually it is likely that the individual welfare losses from involuntary part-time employment is lower than from open unemployment. In particular the social isolation that might be a consequence of open unemployment should not be as serious for part-time workers even if part-time work is involuntary.

Table 1a
Sex differentials of unemployment rates in Great Britain according to different measures

	1971 Census[a] all ages			Household survey[b] all ages			Department of Employment[c]			Department of Employment under 20		
	F	M	F/M	F	M	F/M	F	M	F/M	F	M	F/M
1970										1.4	3.4	0.41
1971	3.7	4.2	0.88	4.0	4.0	1.00				2.4	5.4	0.44
1972				3.6	4.8	0.75				3.1	6.8	0.46
1973				2.7	3.5	0.77				2.0	3.3	0.61
1974				2.8	2.8	1.00				2.0	3.6	0.56
1975				3.5	4.0	0.88	2.1	5.4	0.39	5.3	7.4	0.72
1976				4.8	5.4	0.89	3.4	7.0	0.49	8.0	9.1	0.88
1977				4.9	4.9	1.00	4.2	7.3	0.58	9.4	9.6	0.98
1978							4.3	7.1	0.61			
1979							4.2	6.6	0.64			
1980							5.5	8.5	0.65			
1981							8.0	13.5	0.59			

a Source: 1971 Census, Economic Activity, table 3.
b Source: Elliot, Glucklich, MacLennan, Pond 1981, Table 4:5.
c Source: Department of Employment Gazette.
d Source: See Layard (1982). The data relate to July and exclude "unemployed school-leavers".

Table 1b
Sex differentials of unemployment rates in West-Germany according to different measures

	Registered unemployment[a] 15–65 years			Census unemployment[b] 15 years and over			Registered unemployment[a] 15–19 years		
	F	M	F/M	F	M	F/M	F	M	F/M
1964									
1965									
1966	0.5	0.8	0.63	0.3	0.2	1,50	0.3	0.2	1.50
1967	1.7	2.4	0.71	1.3	1.4	0.93	0.7	0.9	0.78
1968	1.2	1.7	0.71	2.6	1.6	1.63	0.4	0.3	1.33
1969	0.8	0.9	0.89	1.3	0.8	1.63	0.4	0.2	2.00
1970	0.8	0.7	1.14	1.1	0.6	1.83	0.5	0.2	2.50
1971	1.1	0.7	1.57	1.4	0.7	2.00	0.7	0.4	1.75
1972	1.4	1.0	1.40	1.2	0.8	1.50	1.0	0.6	1.67
1973	1.5	1.0	1.50	1.1	0.7	1.57	1.4	0.7	2.00
1974	3.1	2.2	1.41	2.0	1.5	1.33	4.1	3.1	1.32
1975	5.4	4.3	1.26	4.5	3.9	1.15	6.5	5.3	1.23
1976	5.8	3.9	1.49	5.3	3.7	1.43	5.8	3.7	1.57
1977	6.0	3.7	1.62	5.7	3.5	1.63	6.6	3.9	1.69
1978	5.8	3.4	1.71	5.6	3.2	1.75	5.8	3.2	1.81
1979	5.2	2.9	1.79	5.3	2.7	1.96	4.3	2.0	2.15
1980	5.2	3.0	1.73				5.0	2.8	1.79
1981	6.9	4.5	1.53						

a Unemployment figures are yearly averages. Source: ANBA-Jahreszahlen 1981. Labor force definition is *Dependent Labor Force* (not including soldiers, civil servants).
Source: Schmid 1980 and own calculations based on unpublished material of the Federal Statistical Office: Micro-census.
b Unemployment figures according to Micro-Census.

Table 1 c
Sex differentials of unemployment rates in the U.S. according to different measures

	Open unemployment 16 years and older			Open unemployment 16–19 years			Involuntary part-time 16 years and over			Discouraged workers[a] 16 years and over		
	F	M	F/M	F	M	F/M	F	M	F/M	F	M	F/M
1964				12.6	15.8	0.80	–			–	–	
1965				13.9	14.1	0.99	–			–	–	
1966	4.8	3.2	1.50	14.5	11.7	1.24	–			–	–	
1967	5.2	3.1	1.68	13.5	12.3	1.10	3.5	2.2	1.59	–	–	
1968	4.8	2.9	1.65	14.0	11.6	1.21	3.2	1.9	1.68	–	–	
1969	4.7	2.8	1.68	13.3	11.4	1.17	3.2	2.0	1.60	1.3	0.4	3.25
1970	5.9	4.4	1.34	15.6	15.0	1.04	3.6	2.4	1.50	1.3	0.4	3.25
1971	6.9	5.3	1.30	17.2	16.6	1.04	4.0	2.5	1.60	1.3	0.3	4.33
1972	6.6	4.9	1.35	16.7	15.9	1.05	3.9	2.4	1.63	1.6	0.4	4.00
1973	6.0	4.1	1.46	15.2	13.9	1.09	3.6	2.2	1.64	1.3	0.4	3.25
1974	6.7	4.8	1.40	16.5	15.5	1.06	4.0	2.6	1.54	1.3	0.4	3.25
1975	9.3	7.9	1.18	19.7	20.1	0.98	4.9	3.4	1.44	1.9	0.6	3.17
1976	8.6	7.0	1.23	18.7	19.2	0.97	4.6	3.1	1.48	1.5	0.5	3.00
1977	8.2	6.2	1.32	18.3	17.3	1.06	4.6	2.9	1.59	1.7	0.5	3.40
1978	7.2	5.2	1.38	17.0	15.7	1.08	4.4	2.6	1.69	1.3	0.5	2.60
1979	6.8	5.1	1.33	16.4	15.8	1.04	4.3	2.6	1.65	1.1	0.5	2.20
1980	7.4	6.9	1.07	17.2	18.2	0.95	4.8	3.3	1.45	1.3	0.6	2.17
1981	7.9	7.4	1.07	19.0	20.1	0.95	5.3	3.5	1.51	1.5	0.6	2.50

Source: Employment and Earnings, various issues.
a   Includes those who do not belong to the labor force, desire a job, but are not seeking one because they do not think they can find employment.

Table 1 d
Sex differentials of unemployment rates in Sweden according to different measures

	Open unemployment 16–74 years			Open unemployment 16–19 years			Involuntary part-time work[a] 16–74 years			Discouraged workers[b] 16–74 years		
	F	M	F/M	F	M	F/M	F	M	F/M	F	M	F/M
1964	1.8	1.4	1.29	5.1	3.7	1.38	–	–	–	8.0	0.8	10.00
1965	1.8	0.8	2.25	4.2	1.9	2.21	3.9	0.9	4.33	7.6	0.7	10.88
1966	2.0	1.3	1.54	4.8	2.7	1.78	3.5	1.0	3.50	8.0	0.5	16.00
1967	2.3	2.0	1.15	5.8	4.7	1.23	3.8	1.2	3.17	7.8	0.6	13.00
1968	2.2	2.3	0.96	6.5	5.0	1.30	3.6	1.4	2.57	8.6	0.9	9.53
1969	2.0	1.8	1.11	5.4	3.8	1.42	3.7	1.2	3.08	7.6	0.8	9.54
1970	1.8	1.3	1.38	5.1	3.4	1.50	3.6	1.0	3.60	6.7	0.7	9.54
1971	2.8	2.4	1.17	8.4	7.1	1.18	4.0	1.1	3.64	6.1	0.8	7.62
1972	3.0	2.5	1.20	8.7	7.8	1.12	4.0	1.1	3.64	5.0	0.7	7.14
1973	2.8	2.2	1.27	8.0	5.8	1.38	3.8	1.1	3.45	4.7	0.6	7.83
1974	2.4	1.7	1.41	8.1	5.2	1.56	3.4	0.8	4.25	4.1	0.6	6.83
1975	2.0	1.3	1.54	7.1	4.2	1.69	3.1	0.8	3.88	3.5	0.7	5.00
1976	2.0	1.3	1.54	7.0	4.1	1.71	2.9	0.8	3.63	2.1	0.5	4.14
1977	2.2	1.5	1.47	8.1	5.4	1.50	3.0	0.9	3.33	1.9	0.6	3.20
1978	2.4	2.1	1.14	8.7	7.1	1.22	3.1	1.0	3.10	1.9	0.7	2.68
1979	2.3	1.9	1.21	7.9	7.0	1.13	3.1	0.8	3.88	1.5	0.7	2.10
1980	2.3	1.7	1.35	8.8	6.5	1.35	3.2	0.8	4.00	1.3	0.6	2.22
1981	2.6	2.4	1.08	10.5	8.2	1.28	3.9	1.2	3.25	1.5	0.8	1.82

Source: Labor force surveys, yearly averages.
a   Part-time workers who report ability and wish to work more.
b   Until 1975 discouraged workers were defined by the question "Would you have been searching for a job last week if you had thought that you could have found one in the are?" From 1976 on this question has been replaced by: "Would you have liked to have had work last week?" and "Could you have taken on work last week?"

Some other common patterns are also noteworthy. In both countries the open unemployment rate for males seems to be more sensitive to the business cycle than the one for females; the differentials are much lower during prosperity years. Furthermore an improvement for women can be found in both countries. In Sweden the improvement can only be found for discouraged workers but on the other hand this improvement is a very significant one. In the U.S. a positive trend for women in relation to men can be found both in the series for open unemployment and in the series for discouraged workers.

3.   AN APPROACH TO THE CAUSES OF THE UNEMPLOYMENT DIFFERENTIALS

3.1   "Inflow Times Duration" Decomposition

A natural point of departure for examining the causes of the male-female un-employment differentials is to apply the popular decomposition of unemployment into an inflow (or "turnover") component and a duration component:

(1) $U = F \times D$

where U denotes the number of unemployed, F is the inflow of new unemployment spells per period and D represents the average duration of unemployment spells. In terms of rates, (1) can also be written:

(2) $\dfrac{U}{L} = \dfrac{F}{L} \times D = u = f \times D$

where L denotes the labor force, u denotes the rate of unemployment and f is interpreted as the probability of an average labor force participant becoming unemployed during the period concerned. Because D, the average duration of unemployment spells, equals the inverse of the "escape-probability" of an unemployment spell, (2) provides a decomposition into inflow and escape prob-abilities. Obviously these components represent different mechanisms and hence causes of unemployment.

Before examining our empirical data some qualifications are necessary. The equations (1) and (2) only hold in a "stationary" or "stable" labor market with constant inflow and outflow. However, in practice the errors made when (1) and (2) are applied are small, at least when yearly data are used.

It is also important to realize what measure of unemployment is used; Swedish and American data are based on open unemployment whereas both British and German data reflect registered unemployment at the employment offices. Of course, the availability of relevant data is a restriction for applying the de-composition to another or more extended measure of unemployment. Suppose we were interested in the components for a measure of unemployment that in-cludes, say, both open and hidden unemployment. How would the components be affected? Without any formal exercise it seems intuitively clear that the more often spells of open unemployment precede or are preceded by spells of hidden unemployment, the more the duration component will be increased. The reason is, of course, that two (or more) separate spells will be "added to each other" and become one longer spell. On the other hand, the more often spells of open and hidden unemployment are separated by spells of employment and spells of voluntary labor force withdrawals, the more the   inflow   component

25

Table 2
Inflow and duration components of unemployment rates

Year	GB[a] F u	GB F f	GB F D	GB M u	GB M f	GB M D	SWEDEN[b] F u	SW F f	SW F D	SW M u	SW M f	SW M D	U.S.[c] F u	US F f	US F D	US M u	US M f	US M D	W-GER[d] F u	WG F f	WG F D	WG M u	WG M f	WG M D
1965							1.8	0.32	5.6	0.8	0.15	5.2												
1966							2.0	0.44	4.5	1.3	0.20	6.4							0.5	0.13	5.0	0.8	0.16	5.4
1967							2.3	0.35	6.5	2.0	0.21	9.7							1.7	0.20	4.7	2.4	0.25	5.0
1968							2.2	0.40	5.5	2.3	0.16	14.4							1.2	0.15	8.6	1.7	0.17	9.3
1969							2.0	0.35	5.7	1.8	0.21	8.6							0.8	0.12	8.1	0.9	0.12	9.3
1970							1.8	0.30	6.0	1.3	0.16	8.0							0.8	0.12	6.1	0.7	0.11	6.7
1971							2.8	0.29	9.5	2.4	0.17	13.9							1.1	0.14	7.6	0.7	0.13	5.6
1972							3.0	0.21	14.6	2.5	0.17	15.1							1.4	0.14	8.6	1.0	0.14	5.2
1973							2.8	0.22	12.8	2.2	0.12	18.3							1.5	0.16	9.1	1.0	0.15	6.7
1974							2.4	0.27	8.9	1.7	0.16	10.6	5.5	0.67	8.2	3.8	0.37	10.4	3.1	0.25	12.8	2.2	0.23	6.5
1975							2.0	0.20	10.0	1.3	0.13	10.4							5.4	0.31	16.8	4.3	0.29	9.5
1976	3.4	0.30	11.4	7.0	0.40	17.3	2.0	0.17	12.0	1.3	0.10	12.5							5.8	0.32	19.4	3.9	0.27	15.4
1977	4.2	0.34	12.5	7.3	0.40	18.2	2.2	0.19	11.7	1.5	0.11	14.2							6.0	0.32	19.2	3.7	0.26	13.8
1978	4.3	0.34	12.6	7.1	0.39	18.4	2.4	0.22	11.1	2.1	0.17	12.6							5.8	0.31	20.0	3.4	0.24	14.4
1979	4.2	0.35	12.0	6.6	0.38	17.3	2.3	0.21	11.2	1.9	0.14	13.5							5.2	0.28	18.6	2.9	0.22	12.6
1980							2.3	0.21	11.0	1.7	0.13	13.3							5.2	0.29	18.2	3.0	0.24	12.4
1981							2.6	0.17	15.0	2.4	0.15	15.7							6.9	0.31	22.6	4.5	0.28	16.0

a Inflow and unemployment data have been obtained from Department of Employment Gazette. Duration estimated as a residual from equation (2).

b Inflow and unemployment data from the Labor Force Surveys have been used (see Björklund (1981) for a presentation). Duration estimated as a residual from equation (2).

c Duration data have been obtained from Clark/Summers (1979) who used information about escape-probabilities. The inflow component was estimated as a residual.

d Unemployment and inflow data have been obtained from ANBA (see Table 1 d). Duration data until 1979 have been obtained from Freiburghaus (1979). He uses a method that to some extent takes the non-stationarity into account; therefore the products of the two components is not exactly equal to the unemployment rate. For 1980 and 1981 duration has been estimated as a residual.

will be increased. In both Sweden and the U.S. there are indications (3) of some mobility between the two unemployment statuses. Consequently it is likely that the duration component, at least to some extent, would be increased if an extended unemployment measure would be used.

The empirical data are presented in Table 2. In one respect West Germany differs from the other countries because the duration component has been higher for women than for men ever since 1970. It is hard to find any readily available explanation for this phenomenon. However, hypothetically, it is due to the different definition of unemployment used in West Germany. Involuntary part-time workers are included among the unemployed. It might be that many totally jobless spells precede or are preceded by spells of involuntary part-time work. And if involuntary part-time work is more common among women than among men, as it is in Sweden and the U.S., it might affect the duration component for women more than for men.

In both Sweden and the U.S., the higher unemployment rate for women is attributable to higher inflow-probabilities. The duration component is lower for women in both countries. It is also notable that the higher unemployment rate in the U.S. compared to Sweden completely can be explained by higher turnover in the U.S.

In Great Britain, finally, both components are higher for men than for women.

3.2   Reasons for Becoming Unemployed

Although useful for a first look at unemployment differentials, the decomposition in the preceding section is a very crude one even for causal analysis. The main reason for this is that the unemployed constitute a very heterogeneous group. In particular, the unemployed might have become unemployed in quite different ways. Some are entrants or reentrants to the labor force, some have left their previous jobs voluntarily and some have been permanently or temporarily laid off. Therefore the inflow-probabilities presented above do not represent any single cause or mechanism but a mixture of different ones.

The natural extension would be to disaggregate the stock of unemployed by reasons for having become unemployed and then apply the "inflow times duration" decomposition to each separate group. Unfortunately all that can not be done here. Unemployment data by reason are available only for Sweden, the U.S. and to a minor extent for West Germany. Furthermore the data needed for the decomposition are not available (4).

The available information is presented in Table 3. Two common features of the U.S. and Sweden can be found. Firstly, it appears that most of the unemployment differential between men and women in both countries is attributable to higher unemployment rates for entrants and reentrants. Actually the reentrants predominate in this group in both countries. Consequently we have been able to identify the mechanisms generating the unemployment differential quite well; it seems to be the mechanisms that are generating unemployment at the reentrance to the labor market. However, such unemployment can either be attributable to high mobility into and out of the labor force or to a difficult entry process. The "inflow times duration" decomposition   is   needed   to

Table 3
Causes of unemployment

SWEDEN [a]

	Total unemployment		Entrants/ Reentrants		Layoffs		Job undertaken completed		Others (incl. job leavers)	
	F	M	F	M	F	M	F	M	F	M
1975	2.20	1.33	0.88	0.38	0.32	0.27	0.39	0.33	0.43	0.35
1976	2.03	1.27	0.85	0.33	0.31	0.25	0.41	0.34	0.46	0.35
1977	2.17	1.50	0.84	0.40	0.30	0.34	0.54	0.41	0.49	0.35
1978	2.42	2.06	0.87	0.47	0.39	0.59	0.63	0.58	0.53	0.42
1979	2.34	1.86	0.82	0.45	0.37	0.43	0.69	0.58	0.46	0.40
1980	2.32	1.72	0.81	0.41	0.27	0.37	0.73	0.51	0.51	0.43
1981	2.63	2.35	0.87	0.52	0.40	0.66	0.89	0.74	0.47	0.43

THE U.S. [b]

	Total unemployment		Entrants/ Reentrants		Job losers		Job leavers	
	F	M	F	M	F	M	F	M
1973	6.0	4.1	3.3	1.5	1.7	2.0	1.0	0.6
1974	6.7	4.8	3.5	1.6	2.1	2.6	1.1	0.6
1975	9.3	7.9	4.1	2.1	4.0	5.2	1.2	0.7
1976	8.6	7.0	4.1	2.1	3.2	4.2	1.3	0.7
1977	8.2	6.2	4.2	2.1	2.8	3.4	1.2	0.7
1978	7.2	5.2	3.9	1.8	2.3	2.7	1.1	0.7
1979	6.8	5.1	3.6	1.7	2.2	2.7	1.0	0.7
1980	7.4	6.9	3.6	1.9	2.9	4.3	1.0	0.7
1981	7.9	7.4	3.8	2.1	3.1	4.6	1.0	0.7

WEST-GERMANY [c]

	Total unemployment		Without former employment		With former employment		Short-work [d]	
	F	M	F	M	F	M	F	M
1976	5.6	3.5	0.2	0.1	5.4	3.4	0.9	1.7
1977	5.9	3.3	0.3	0.1	5.6	3.3	0.6	1.5
1978	5.7	3.1	0.3	0.2	5.4	2.9	0.5	1.2
1979	5.1	2.4	0.3	0.1	4.8	2.3	0.5	0.4
1980	4.8	2.4	0.3	0.1	4.5	2.3	0.8	0.5

a   Source: Labor Force Surveys, yearly averages.
b   Source: Employment and Earnings, various issues.
c   Source: Unemployment figures (May) from ANBA. Labor Force figures: see Table 1 d.
d   Source: Schmid (1982).

distinguish between these two hypotheses. The available evidence from Sweden, which consists of rather imprecise inflow information, indicates that the differential can be attributed to the inflow component. The available evidence from the U.S., which consists of duration data that might differ from the data needed for these purposes (5), indicates the same. Therefore it seems as though the male-female unemployment differential in both countries for which these data are available is attributable to higher inflow rates to unemployment for reentrants to the labor force. This in turn can probably be explained by higher mobility into and out of the labor force for women compared to men. Actually this hypothesis is also supported by "outflow-data". The probability that an employed women leaves the labor market was about twice as high as that of men during seventies in Sweden (Heikensten (1982)). Marston (1976) presents similar evidence for the U.S..

A second common feature is that unemployment attributable to layoffs (or job losers) is higher for men than for women. Again, the rather inaccurate evidence available indicates that this is attributable to higher probabilities of being laid off for men. This finding is surprising because seniority rules are generally applied for layoffs (at least permanent layoffs) and women generally have lower tenure than men. The most reasonable explanation is that women are working in industries where layoffs are less frequent.

However, it is important to realize that this layoff pattern does not rule out discrimination against women as far as layoffs are concerned. It might be that women, with same tenure as men and working in the same industry, have higher layoff rates. A strict test of this hypothesis is beyond the scope of this paper.

The available information for West Germany is less comprehensive on this point. There is information on the unemployed with and without former employment prior to unemployment (i.e. entrants and reentrants to the labor force). Entrance and reentrance unemployment is higher for women than for men but only a negligible amount of the total differential between men and women is attributable to such unemployment.

It is also important to note that short-time work (Kurzarbeitergeld) is an important cyclical measure in West Germany (see Schmid 1982, p. 30). Since short-time work is a substitute for layoffs (in particular temporary ones) the cyclical fluctuation of unemployment is likely to have a different structure. Some figures on short-time work for men and women are presented in Table 3 too.

4.   WELFARE ASPECTS OF THE UNEMPLOYMENT DIFFERENTIALS

4.1   A Digression on Various Duration Concepts

The duration measure presented above is only one of several possibilities. It was used above because it shows the decomposition into "inflow"- and "escape"-probabilities which is useful for positive analysis of unemployment.

In order to explain the relationship between the duration measure presented above and some other ones which have been proposed it can be useful to make an analogy with a population of individuals.

The measure presented above is the expected or average duration of the spells that "flow in" during a certain period, i.e. week. If we make an analogy with a population, it is the expected life-time of a newly born individual.

A second measure is the counterpart to the average age of the population. Consequently it is a measure of the average time that those currently unemployed (the _stock_ of unemployed) have been unemployed at a certain point of time. This statistic is very common since it can found in the unemployment statistics presented in most countries; of course it measures the average duration of unemployment until the time of the survey for those counted as unemployed in the survey. Hence it is an interrupted spell length for the currently unemployed.

A third measure has been proposed by Akerlof/Main (1981) and is implicit in the influential paper by Clark/Summers (1979). It measures the expected total duration of unemployment for those who are unemployed at a certain point of time. In terms of a population it is a measure of the expected life-time for the current population.

These three measures and the relationship between them are illustrated in Figure 1.

The figure displays two hypothetical patterns of unemployment. Both cases are static ones, i.e. the inflow and duration of spells are constant over a period of time.

The stock of unemployed and its inflow- and duration-components are the same in both cases. However, both the interrupted and the total spell durations of the unemployed differ in the two cases. It appears that these statistics are higher in Case 2 where there is dispersion in the duration of the spells. Actually it can formally be shown that the deviation between the average duration of unemployment spells (D) and the average total spell-duration for the currently unemployed (2 * T) is an increasing function of the variance of unemployment spells (see Salant (1977)). In most real labor markets there is a considerable deviation among spells of unemployment. Consequently the total spell-duration for the currently unemployed is much higher than the duration of all spells of unemployment.

Case 2 in Figure 1 can also be used to illustrate that different definitions of "the long-term unemployment rate" exist, i.e. an unemployment rate that excludes short-term unemployed defined in some way. Suppose that we can consider one week as "short" and five weeks as "long". From Case 2 in Figure 1 it appears that only 50 per cent of all spells are long. On the other hand it also appears that four out of six of the currently unemployed have been unemployed more than one week at the time of the survey. Actually this concept of the long-term unemployment rate is often used and published (6) in the U.S.. However, it can also be seen that even more of the currently unemployed (five out of six) experience long spells. As a consequence most unemployment spells can be short but still most unemployment can be observed among persons experiencing long spells.

Another relationship between two of the three summary measures of unemployment duration is also apparent from the figure (and from our notation). It appears that the total spell-length for the currently unemployed is two times

Figure 1.   Illustration of different statistics of unemployment duration

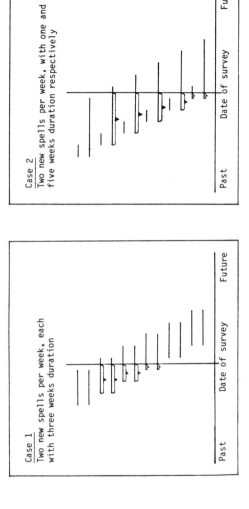

Case 1
Two new spells per week, each with three weeks duration

Case 2
Two new spells per week, with one and five weeks duration respectively

Stock of unemployed   : U = 6

Weekly inflow of spells   : F = 2

Average duration of spell   : D = 3

Average interrupted spell-
length for the unemployed   : T = 1/6 (2.5 + 2.5 + 1.5 + 1.5 + o.5 + o.5) = 1.5

Average total spell-length
for the unemployed   :2T = 1/6 (3 + 3 + 3 + 3 + 3 + 3) = 3

U = 6

F = 2

D = 3

T = 1/6 (4.5 + 3.5 + 2.5 + 1.5 + 0.5 + 0.5) = 2 1/6

2T = 1/6 (5 + 5 + 5 + 1 + 5) = 4 2/6

the interrupted spell-length in these static cases. This has a quite simple, intuitive explanation; the survey is equally likely to hit upon a specific spell at any time during its "life" so the average uncompleted length of a spell is likely to be half of its total length.

Of course all the summary measures of unemployment duration are needed if we want to provide a complete empirical picture of the unemployment phenomenon. Actually this is not enough, since it might also be interesting to describe the complete distributions of unemployment spells.

Before we turn to the more fundamental issue, how these measures should be used in view of different purposes, we take a brief descriptive look at the total spell-length for the currently unemployed. These are presented in Table 4.

Table 4
Average total unemployment-duration for the currently unemployed. In weeks

	Great-Britain[a]	Sweden[b]		The U.S.[c]		West-Germany[d]	
	M	F	M	F	M	F	M
1964	–	17.2	20.8	–	–	–	–
1965	59	20.6	11.8	–	–	–	–
1966	55	18.8	15.0	–	–	21.5	39.0
1967	55	20.4	20.6	–	–	33.5	42.8
1968	57	19.2	23.0	–	–	35.4	79.8
1969	60	23.0	26.0	–	–	28.9	76.3
1970	61	22.0	25.8	15.8	19.0	25.6	58.9
1971	61	29.8	24.8	20.2	24.6	29.6	44.2
1972	71	35.0	30.2	21.2	26.8	31.7	45.3
1973	77	36.6	30.4	17.6	22.4	34.7	51.0
1974	72	33.4	29.6	16.8	21.8	37.6	41.4
1975	62	32.4	29.8	25.2	30.6	48.0	50.8
1976	70	30.6	30.4	28.0	34.6	59.1	69.8
1977	78	32.8	28.2	25.0	31.8	63.9	73.8
1978	81	32.8	32.2	21.0	26.8	72.8	80.2
1979	–	33.4	33.8	19.2	24.0		
1980	–	29.2	33.0	20.6	26.4		
1981	–	32.4	33.6	23.4	31.0		

a   Main (1981).

b   The Labor Force Surveys.

c   Employment and earnings.

d   From Egle 1979, p. 54.

General note: All data have been estimated as two times the interrupted spell length, a procedure that presupposes a static condition.

Compared with the measure presented in Table 2, several interesting differences emerge. The most important difference is that the total unemployment duration for the currently unemployed is much longer than the duration of unemployment spells. In all countries the former measure is at least three times as high as the latter one. Consequently deviation in the duration of spells must be considerable.

This fundamental difference between the two different ways to look at the dynamics of unemployment was emphasized very efficiently by Clark/Summers (1979) in an article titled "Labor Market Dynamics and Unemployment: A Reconsideration." Even though they did not present the summary measure presented in Table 4 (7), they showed that most unemployment can be considered as rather long spells of unemployment. This was a reassessment of the commonly held view during the seventies, that most unemployment was "frictional" and very short-term. The latter only holds for unemployment spells.

A second interesting finding is that the male-female duration differential in West Germany now becomes favourable for women; whereas the duration of unemployment spells was longer for women than for men, the total unemployment duration for the currently unemployed is shorter. This indicates that the deviation in the duration of unemployment spells is lower for women than for men.

The sex-differentials in Sweden and the U.S. conform with the ones found in Table 2. In Sweden there are no systematic differentials and in the U.S. the duration for men is significantly higher.

In addition to these sex-differentials some very striking national differentials can be found in the table. Unemployment duration in West Germany and Great Britain is more than twice as long as in Sweden and the U.S. according to this measure. This is quite puzzling and definitely requires an explanation. One explanation could of course be that Sweden and the U.S. rely on survey information whereas West Germany and Great Britain have registration data. However, a look at some data on registered unemployment from Sweden did not support this hypothesis (8).

4.2   The Costs of Unemployment

Obviously all the measures discussed in the preceding section are necessary for a complete empirical picture of unemployment. It must be an important task for labour economists to provide the public and politicians with such a picture.

However, a more fundamental task is to point out how the different measures should be used and interpreted in view of different purposes. Suppose we want to estimate and compare the welfare consequences from unemployment for different groups, what measure should be used? Actually there is no consensus on this. This in turn is not surprising since very detailed information about the costs of unemployment for the individual is needed for such estimates. However, one interesting approach has been suggested by Layard (1981, 1982) perhaps stimulated by Hurd (1980). This approach shows that, at least as a first approximation, the unemployment costs for a certain group is proportional to the number of unemployed times the interrupted spell-length for the currently unemployed (9).

33

As a general approach to the problem it can be constructive to think of a cost function for unemployment. Let us denote the cost of one week of unemployment for one individual $\underline{i}$ with c_i and the total costs for all unemployment in the economy by C.

Then we have for a total level of unemployment denoted by U:

$$(3) \quad C = \sum_{i=1}^{U} c_i$$

If all unemployed were completely homogeneous in regard to the welfare consequences of unemployment, i.e. $c_i = c$ for all unemployed, then of course the structure of unemployment would not matter. If that were the case, only the level of unemployment would be important.

However, it is likely that the unemployed constitute a very heterogeneous group in regard to welfare consequences. The "costs" are likely to be a rather complicated function of the specific, individual situation. The duration of unemployment is of course one potential candidate here, and the level of unemployment compensation is another, with household composition being perhaps a third one.

It is obvious that some kind of simplification is needed in order to get an idea of the scale of the problem. If we regard the duration of unemployment as the single most important determinant of unemployment costs, a simple and tractable but still quite plausible specification is to make the costs for individual $\underline{i}$ (c_i) during his t'th unemployment week a linear function of unemployment duration:

$$(4) \quad c_i = a \cdot t_i$$

This specification implies that each additional unemployment week costs more than the preceding one, perhaps due to the decreasing marginal utility of leisure, social isolation or loss of on-the-job training possibilities.

The total unemployment costs for all unemployed during a certain week can easily be computed:

$$(5) \quad C = \sum_{i=1}^{U} a \cdot t_i = U \cdot \sum_{i=1}^{U} a \cdot \frac{t_i}{U} = U \cdot a \cdot T$$

i.e. the total costs are proportional to the number of unemployed times the average interrupted spell-duration. Consequently, this duration measure, at least as a first approximation, seems to be preferable to the one presented in section 3 for welfare analysis. Intuitively, this is reasonable since this measure includes the dispersion of the duration of unemployment spells and for welfare purposes this seems to be relevant.

Layard (1981, 1982) has motivated this cost function by using a compensated supply curve for labor i.e. the supply curve that emerges when the individual receives income compensation for the welfare losses from declining wages (and vice versa for increasing wages). Even though the calculation with such a supply curve is of little advantage to us, it raises another important question that must be answered when measuring unemployment costs for men an women.

Consider a compensated labor supply curve in wages and annual weeks (10). Furthermore, suppose that the supply schedule is approximately linear as in Figure 2 below. If there were no rationing in the labor market we assume that the individual wants to work 52 weeks at the market wage w*.

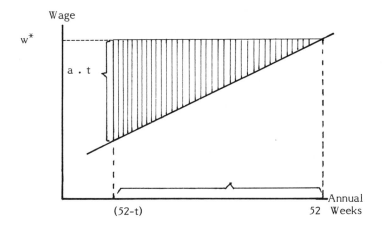

Figure 2: A linear compensated labor supply schedule

However, rationing is assumed to make the person unemployed for, say, t weeks. The virtue of the compensated supply curve is that the area above it - the shaded area in the Figure - measures the value of this loss. If, for the sake of simplicity, we assume that the schedule consists of discrete rectangles (11), the first, the second and the t'th week respectively will cost a, 2 . a, t . a. Consequently we have the same cost function as above.

Next we have to determine the "cost parameter" - or the slope of the supply schedule $\underline{a}$ for men and women. Actually it is likely to be <u>lower</u> for women because most labor supply studies have shown that the supply for women is more elastic. This in turn can be explained by higher productivity in home production for women. As a consequence it is less costly for women to be unemployed.

However, in my view it would be negligent to be less concerned about female unemployment for this reason. It is important to realize that unemployment costs are lower for women due to the existing institutional situation in the

35

labor market. This situation in turn is likely to reflect discrimination against women. It is probably this discrimination in the labor market that has made women invest more in skills for home production. In a sense then, discrimination against women reduces the absolute unemployment costs for women; the absolute unemployment costs for women are lower because women have less to lose by being unemployed. It is hardly appealing to use a cost measure with such properties. A simple way to avoid this problem is to estimate the unemployment costs as a fraction of the total "surplus" that can be achieved in the labor market if there were no constraints, i.e. no unemployment. Obviously this surplus is the total area over the supply schedule for all labor force participants. In terms of our notations it becomes (12):

$$(6) \quad L \cdot \sum_{t=1}^{52} a \cdot t = \frac{L \cdot 52 \cdot 53 \cdot a}{2}$$

whereby L denotes all labor. By dividing (5) by (6) (and multiplying by 52 to arrive at annual costs) we get:

$$(7) \quad \frac{u \cdot t \cdot 2}{53}$$

This measure only clarifies the extent to which a certain group is unable to realize its potential surplus from labor force participation because of rationing constraints. It is not affected by the total value of the surplus which in turn is likely to reflect discrimination.

The measure is applied in Table 5 where the cost differentials between men and women are presented. We must restrict ourselves to the sex differentials in the different countries; the international differentials of unemployment costs are likely to be affected by institutional differences that are not interesting for our purposes.

Table 5
Sex differentials of unemployment costs (u x T)

	SWEDEN			THE U.S.			WEST-GERMANY		
	F	M	F/M	F	M	F/M	F	M	F/M
1970	0.198	0.168	1.18	0.466	0.418	1.11	0.10	0.21	0.48
1971	0.417	0.298	1.40	0.697	0.652	1.07	0.16	0.15	1.07
1972	0.525	0.376	1.40	0.700	0.657	1.07	0.22	0.23	0.96
1973	0.512	0.334	1.53	0.528	0.459	1.15	0.26	0.26	1.00
1974	0.401	0.252	1.59	0.563	0.523	1.08	0.58	0.46	1.26
1975	0.324	0.194	1.67	1.172	1.209	0.97	1.30	1.09	1.19
1976	0.306	0.198	1.55	1.204	1.211	0.99	1.71	1.36	1.26
1977	0.361	0.212	1.71	1.023	0.986	1.04	1.92	1.37	1.40
1978	0.394	0.338	1.17	0.756	0.697	1.08	2.11	1.36	1.55
1979	0.384	0.321	1.20	0.653	0.612	1.07			
1980	0.336	0.281	1.20	0.762	0.911	0.84			
1981	0.421	0.403	1.04	0.924	1.147	0.82			

The pertinent countries here are the U.S. and West Germany. In the tables above we have seen that the unemployment rate is higher for women than for men. But we have also seen that unemployment duration for the currently unemployed is lower for women. What will the net effect on unemployment cost be?

For the U.S. it turns out that the costs for women are slightly higher than for men during years of prosperity but lower during recessions. This cyclical pattern mainly reflects that the male unemployment rate is more cyclically sensitive than the female rate, which in turn probably reflects the higher layoff probabilities for men.

For West Germany the table displays higher costs for women during most years. In addition, there is a negative trend for men compared to women.

For Sweden the negative situation for women remains as could be expected from the data presented above.

No British data are presented since none on average unemployment duration are available for the sexes. However, since the information presented in Department of Employment Gazette September 1978 on the distribution of unemployment duration indicates that the relevant duration measure is lower for women and the registered unemployment rate is lower too, our approach would give lower costs for women. However, the use of registered unemployment is questionable for comparisons between sexes.

Of course, these cost estimates must be interpreted with caution. They rely on a very simple cost function that, however, does not deviate from the common notion of the welfare consequences of unemployed. Still, I want to argue that some "cost function" - explicit or implicit - is needed if we want to answer the basic question raised in this section. It is an important task for future labor market research to quantify the welfare losses for various groups of unemployed. With a more detailed cost function than the one used here the target groups for selective labor market policies can be chosen with more care and the efficiency of the policies can hopefully be improved.

It is also important to stress that the approach is based on the assumption that all unemployment is due to rationing and hence is "involuntary". It might be argued that some unemployment, especially short-term, should be regarded as "voluntary". This would of course change the estimates, but not much necessarily because the short-term unemployed receive a low weight when this approach is used (13).

Even if the basic approach to unemploymet costs is accepted as a reasonable approximation some other objections can be raised. First, we could only compute the costs for open unemployment. If some of the discouraged workers should be included in a welfare relevant measure of unemployment, the costs for women might be considerably underestimated because in that case not only the unemployment rate for women would be increased relative to men but probably also the duration measure.

A second objection is that account should also be taken to recurrent spells of unemployment. The relevant question is of course whether our conclusions regarding sex differentials would be changed. Again we only have some information from the U.S. and Sweden. However, the available evidence do not change our conclusions (14).

5.   SUMMARY AND CONCLUSIONS

Let us summarize our major findings and see what conclusions can be drawn. Our look at the aggregate male-female unemployment differentials showed that Great Britain was an exception; according to all available measures of unemployment, the female rate was lower than the male rate. Is this an indication of favourable labor market conditions for women as far as unemployment is concerned, and in that case, are these conditions due to any specific policy measures applied in Britain?

We saw that women's unemployment was lower than men's even when a general job seeking criterion is used to define unemployment. However, it would be premature to draw any far-reaching conclusions from this information. To do this we must be sure that a man and a woman with equal "willingness to work" are equally likely to fulfill a general job-seeking criterion. There are strong reasons to believe that this is not the case in Great Britain. The unemployment benefit rules are likely to create much higher incentives for men to register at an employment office and hence fulfill at least one such search criterion. In particular, the condition to accept jobs with at least 30 work hours a week reduces the registration incentives for women. For further details see MacLennan and Weitzel in this volume and Donaldson (1979).

Actually, there is a need for more detailed unemployment information, like the one provided by the Swedish and the American surveys, in a labor market with an institutional setting like the British. In the three other countries female unemployment was considerably higher than that of males. On the other hand, the trends were different. Whereas improvement for women could be seen both in Sweden and the U.S., the opposite pattern could be observed in West Germany.

Our cause-oriented approach in Section 3 was to decompose male and female unemployment rates into components that are likely to reflect different causes of unemployment. The most detailed decompositions could be made for Sweden and the U.S.. The labor force surveys in these countries provide valuable information about the reason for having become unemployed even though it is restricted to the openly unemployed.

It turned out that the male-female unemployment differential could be attributed to a very specific "unemployment component" in both countries, namely the unemployment caused by reentrants to the labor force, which is much higher for women. Furthermore, the evidence indicated that the reentrance probability rather than unemployment duration for reentrants is higher for women. Consequently we can conclude that the major cause of the unemployment differentials between sexes is higher mobility into and out of the labor force that characterize the labor market behavior of women.

However, such an explanation is hardly valid for the unemployment differentials between teenage girls and boys, since at this age girls have no reason to be more mobile into and out of the labor force than do boys. What about the unemployment differentials for teenagers in the four countries? As   could be seen in Table 1 the girls have higher unemployment than boys in Sweden and West Germany whereas the opposite patterns was found in Great Britain and the U.S.. The causes behind these differences are probably to be found in the way that the transition from school to work is organized. In West Germany it is sometimes argued that the apprenticeship system is more favorable for boys than for girls (Schmid 1982). In Sweden there seem to be some legal restrictions that make the transition from compulsory school (at the age of 16) to work difficult. In particular, several occupations within the service sector that attract girls have an entry age limit of 18.

Another important finding in this section was that unemployment caused by layoffs is lower for women than for men in both Sweden and the U.S.. The probability of being laid off seems to be particularly lower for women. The explanation for this phenomenon is probably that women are working in industries where layoffs are less frequent than elsewhere.

An important issue, with obvious policy implications, is whether the hiring and the layoff behavior by employers is discriminatory against women in the sense that a woman with the same productivity as a man faces a higher probability of being laid off and a lower one of being hired. The aggregate time-series used in this paper can not answer this question. Probably microdata sets with panel properties would have be used for this purpose.

An important task for future research is to determine to what extent women have lower wages, worse jobs and higher unemployment due to discrimination in the sense defined above. However, our findings that women have jobs with lower layoff probabilities has an important implication for the approach that this research should take. It is reasonable to conjecture that all workers are willing to pay a premium in terms of lower wages for a job with a lower layoff probability (or some other negative attribute) at least as long as unemployment compensation is incomplete. If these attributes are not equally distributed among men and women (and the layoff probabilities obviously are unequally distributed) a partial analysis of wage differentials is likely to give misleading results. Consequently it seems reasonable to recommend that future studies on discrimination should analyze different job attributes such as wages, job quality and unemployment risks simultaneously instead of individually as has been done in this paper.

Is the higher unemployment for women something to be concerned about from the welfare point of view or can it be attributed to rather harmless "frictional" unemployment? This is the issue addressed in Section 4. An answer to this question clearly requires information on the welfare consequences of unemployment. It seems reasonable to assume that the individual welfare consequences are an increasing function of unemployment duration.

The section started with a digression on different concepts of unemployment duration. We showed that the average duration for those who become unemployed during a certain period is rather short but those who are unemployed at a specific date will be unemployed for quite a long time before they find employment (or leave the labor force). The former flow-oriented measure was around 12-18 weeks in Great Britain, 10-16 weeks in Sweden during the seventies, 8-10 weeks in the U.S. and 10-20 weeks in West Germany. On the other hand the latter numerically-oriented measure was much higher, around 60-80 weeks in Great Britain, 25-33 weeks in Sweden, 15-30 weeks in the U.S. and 30-80 weeks in West Germany. The latter figures are clearly an indication that most unemployment is attributable to rather long spells and hence can not easily be regarded as harmless and frictional.

In order to estimate the cost differentials of unemployment between sexes we postulated a specific cost function for unemployment; the cost of a certain unemployment week was assumed to be a linear function of duration. When this cost function was used it turned out that the unemployment costs for a specific group are proportionate to the unemployment rate times the numerically-oriented duration measure.

The empirical application of this formula demonstrated that the unemployment costs for women was lower than for men in Great Britain. However, the same objections as above can be raised against this result. In both Sweden and West Germany the female costs were highest. In the U.S. a cyclical pattern was found; the costs for males were highest during recessions and the costs for females were highest during years of prosperity. However, if only a fraction of the discouraged workers should be included in a welfare relevant unemployment measure the costs for females would probably be higher during recessions too.

Summarizing then, there are strong reasons to be concerned about the unemployment differentials between men and women at least in Sweden, the U.S., and West Germany.

Finally, can any more concrete policy conclusions be drawn from the calculations performed in this paper? Perhaps the data presented can be useful for assessing the impact of some specific labor market policy measures that have been applied in any of the countries. However, we will not attempt such analyses here. Instead it is important to stress that our findings support the view that the reasons for the unfavourable position of women regarding unemployment should not mainly be seen in the way the labor market works. The reason for the higher reentrance rate of unemployment for women is of course that women take higher responsibility for household work than men. This in turn forces women to interrupt their labor market careers with high unemployment risks as a consequence.

Therefore, it seems as, if such measures that increase the incentives for men and women to share the home responsibilities more equally between men and women, are needed not only to increase the equality between sexes in general - more equal labor force participation and investment in various types of human capital -, but also to reduce the unemployment differential. This conclusion is also supported by the promising trend towards smaller unemployment differentials in both Sweden and the U.S.. In these countries women have rapidly become more permanent labor force participants during the last decades. An optimistic forecast based on the findings in this paper is that countries that go on in this direction will also experience a narrowing unemployment gap between men and women.

NOTES

1) See Donaldson (1979).

2) See Björklund (1979) and Bureau of Labor Statistics (1979).

3) For the U.S. see Clark/Summers (1979). In Sweden about 40 per cent of the discouraged workers report that they have been actively searching for jobs during the last two years.

4) Actually, the data for Sweden are available (see Björklund (1981) but the precision becomes very low if we disaggregate both by reason and by sex.

5) The data are interrupted spell-lengths for the currently unemployed (see O'Neill and Braun (1981), page 50). The relationship between these data and the duration data needed for the decomposition is explained below.

6) It can be found in Employment and Earnings, the main source of unemployment statistics (published by the Bureau of Labor Statistics).

7) These were proposed by Akerlof and Main (1981).

8) Since the late seventies, all registered unemployed at the employment offices are counted monthly. Even though no measure of the average duration of unemployment is available, some frequency tables of duration exist. However, this information did not show any difference between registered unemployment and the data from the surveys.

9) Since the interrupted spell-duration is proportional to the total spell-duration the choice between these two measures is arbitrary.

10) To eliminate notations, we will not present hours worked per week here. However, it would only affect the subsequent results in the way that $\underline{a}$ would have to be replaced $\underline{a . H}^2$ in the cost function that follows.

11) The choice between discrete and continuous time does not change the qualitative nature of the results.

12) The formula for the sum of a finite arithmetic series is used. Here it becomes $\dfrac{52 . (1 + 52) . a}{2}$

13) This is also demonstrated by Hurd (1980).

14) In Björklund (1983) I suggest an alternative duration measure that probably is superior for groups who suffer from recurrent spells (especially youth). Some experiments with this measure with data from the retrospective surveys is Sweden and the U.S. did not change the results concerning male-female differentials much.

REFERENCES

Akerlof, G., and Main, B., "An Experience-Weighted Measure of Employment and Unemployment Durations", American Economic Review, December 1981, No. 5, pp. 1003-1011.

Björklund, A., "The Measurement of Unemployment in Sweden", IIM-papers 79-1d, Berlin 1979.

Björklund, A., "Studies in the Dynamics of Unemployment", Stockholm School of Economics 1981.

Björklund, A., "Measuring the Duration of Unemployment: A Note", Scottish Journal of Political Economy, Vol. 30, No. 2, June 1983, pp. 175-180.

Clark, K., and Summers, L., "Labor Market Dynamics and Unemployment: A Reconsideration", Brookings Papers 1979, I., pp. 13-72.

Donaldson, A., "The Measurement of Unemployment in Britain", IIM-papers 79-1a, Berlin 1979.

Egle, F., Ansätze für eine systematische Beobachtung und Analyse der Arbeitslosigkeit, Nürnberg (BeitrAB 36) 1979.

Freiburghaus, D., "The Measurement of Unemployment in the Federal Republic of Germany", IIM-papers 79-1d, Berlin 1979.

Freiburghaus, D., "Distribution of the duration of unemployment in the Federal Republic of Germany 1977-1979" (in German), IIM-papers 80-2, Berlin 1980.

Heikensten, L., "How are regional labor markets affected by changing employment?", Stockholm School of Economics, mimeo, 1982.

Hurd, M., "A Compensation Measure of the Cost of Unemployment to the Unemployed", Quarterly Journal of Economics, September 1980, No. 2, pp. 225-243.

Layard, R., "Measuring the Duration of Unemployment: A Note", Scottish Journal of Political Economy, November 1981, No. 3, pp. 273-277.

Layard, R., "Youth Unemployment in Britain and the U.S. Compared", in Freeman, R., and Wise, D., eds., The Youth Labor Market Problem: Its Nature, Causes and Consequences, University of Chicago Press, 1982.

Main, B., "The lengths of employment and unemployment in Great Britain", The Scottish Journal of Political Economy, June 1981, No. 2, pp. 146-164.

Marston, S., "Employment Instability and High Unemployment Rates", Brookings Papers 1976, I, pp. 169-203.

O'Neill, June, and Rachel Braun, Women and the Labour Market: A Survey of Issues and Policies in the United States, Washingtion 1982: Urban Institute, Mimeo.

Salant, S., "Search Theory and Duration Data: A Theory of Sorts", Quarterly Journal of Economics, February 1977, No. 9, pp. 39-57.

Schmid, G., Strukturierte Arbeitslosigkeit und Arbeitsmarktpolitik, Königstein/Ts. 1980.

Schmid, G., "Employment Policy in the Federal Republic of Germany: Lessons to be Learned", in: International Journal of Manpower, Vol. 3, No. 1 (1982), 24-31.

U.S. Bureau of Labor Statistics, International Comparisons of Unemployment, 1979.

3 PATTERNS OF OCCUPATIONAL SEGREGATION BY SEX IN THE LABOR MARKET

CHRISTINA JONUNG

1.   INTRODUCTION

Women's participation in employment has increased substantially in most industrial nations during recent decades. In this sense women have become more economically equal to men. However, the labor market conditions of women still differ significantly from those of men, e.g. with respect to hours of paid work, hours of home work, level of earnings and the rate of unemployment. The most striking difference between men and women on the labor market is the work they do. Men and women are, to a great extent, found in different spheres of economic activity and occupations, and within most occupations they are employed at different levels and with different work tasks. This paper focuses on economic equality as described by the pattern of occupational distribution of men and women.

There are several reasons why the occupational concentration of men and women deserves special attention. First, the strength and persistence of this social phenomenon in itself is such that it warrants a search for explanations. Second, other differences between men and women on the labor market, concerning e.g. wages, working conditions, work absenteeism, are related to differences in occupational distribution. However, it is not established whether occupation alone contributes to these disparities or whether a common underlying process causes the inequality of working conditions. Third, the occupational distribution of men and women is of interest from the perspective of discrimination in the labor market. One way to discriminate is by restricting the access of women or men to certain occupations. Further, if discrimination through wage differentiation is restricted by law or agreements, employers may increasingly resort to employment discrimination.

Occupational segregation is said to exist when men and women are differently distributed across occupations to an extent greater than would occur at random. Thus the term segregation as used here simply means that women and men predominate in different areas of the labor market. It does not imply anything about the process by which the job allocation takes place. It may be the result of processes on the supply side by which women and men, due to distinct preferences or different human capital investments, choose different occupations. It may also, as pointed out above, be the result of demand-side developments, whereby employers discriminate by assigning men and women to different types of work.

A starting point for the study of occupational segregation should be to establish its existence, and to describe its extent and character. This is the aim of this paper which is based on the Swedish labor market experience. The paper is organized in the following way. The first section describes different methods to measure occupational segregation in labor markets. The next section uses these measures to describe the development of sex segregation in the Swedish labor market from 1960 to 1975. Comparisons are then made with the experiences of other countries in focus in this book: Germany, Great Britain and the US. The following section identifies the sources of change in the level of segregation with regard to structural changes, age groups, particular trades and occupations. The final section deals with the causes of occupational segregation and future trends.

2.   MEASURING OCCUPATIONAL SEGREGATION

Occupational segregation has several dimensions. Strictly speaking, a total absence of occupational segregation in society would require an equal absolute number of men and women within each occupation, on the market as well as in home work outside the market (disregarding random differences and differences in population size). This can only be achieved if men and women have the same labor force participation rates (and their populations are the same). The level of female labor force participation is thus one aspect of segregation. The recent increase in women's rate of labor force participation means that women are moving from a strictly segregated area, the home, to a less segregated one - the market for paid labor. This, although an important aspect, is usually disregarded in studies of occupational segregation. The analysis is concentrated on differences between men and women in the regular labor market.

Confining the analysis to the regular labor market means that one has to take account of the number of men and women on the labor market and study the difference between men's and women's relative distribution across occupations. An equivalent alternative is to compare the percentage of women in single occupations to their share of the total labor force. The degree of under- or over-representation can be studied for single occupations or the information can be summarized by the aid of various segregation indices. Perfect integration prevails if men and women appear in each occupation in the proportions in which they are found in the total labor force, and total segregation exists if men and women work in completely different occupations.

One way to describe male and female occupational distribution is to tabulate the number, percentage share and percentage distribution of men and women for every occupation. This may be illustrative enough if the number of occupations is small, but it becomes difficult to comprehend as this number increases. Studying a large number of occupations, measures that summarize information are needed.

There are several such measures-segregation indices (1). The one most commonly used to measure occupational segregation is the "dissimilarity index". See e.g. the Economic Report of the President (1973), Stevenson (1975), Blau and Hendricks (1979), Gross (1968), Fuchs (1975), Roos (1981). The popularity of this index stems from the fact that it is easy to compute and has a clear interpretation. It will be used also in this presentation.

According to the dissimilarity index, the deviations between men's and women's relative distribution across occupations determine the level of segregation.

With the following notation:

W_i = the number of women in occupation i

M_i = the number of men in occupation i

W = the total number of women in the labor force

M = the total number of men in the labor force

the index, D, can be expressed as

$$D = \frac{1}{2} \sum_{i}^{n} \left| \frac{W_i}{W} - \frac{M_i}{M} \right| \cdot 100 \qquad (1)$$

The index is thus calculated as the absolute sum of the differences between the proportion of the female labor force in a certain occupation and the proportion of the male labor force in that occupation. The sum is divided by two and multiplied by 100 (2). Theoretically, the index can take any value between 0 and 100. The score of 0 indicates no segregation. The distribution of women is then identical to that of men. A value of 100 indicates total segregation with men and women in completely different occupations.

It is no problem to identify situations with no segregation or complete segregation and assign a value to them. The problem in measuring segregation is to assign a value to the distributions inbetween, i.e. when men and women are unequally distributed, but to some extent found in the same occupations. This must be done to evaluate whether segregation is increasing or decreasing. How should, for instance, integration that takes place within extremely male- or female-dominated occupations be evaluated in relation to integration within areas that are only moderately segregated? Different segregation indices evaluate occupational distributions and such changes in different ways.

The dissimilarity index takes no account of whether changes take place at the extremes of the distribution or in occupations close to full integration. Each occupation adds to the level of segregation in proportion to its size and the deviation between the share of women in the occupation and the share of women in the labor force (or the deviation between the proportion of the male labor force and the proportion of the female labor force in the occupation). A change from 5 to 10 per cent in the female share of an occupation is given the same weight as one of 30 to 35 per cent. It can be shown that the dissimilarity index is not dependent on the entire distribution of the labor force across occupations. It will only depend upon the distribution of men and women between occupations with an overrepresentation of women and occupations with underrepresentation of women. It can thus be calculated as

$$
D = \frac{\sum_{i=1}^{o} W_i}{W} - \frac{\sum_{i=1}^{o} M_i}{M} \tag{2}
$$

where $i = 1 \ldots\ldots o$ are those occupations where women are overrepresented in relation to their share of the labor force.

The major advantage of the dissimilarity index is that it can be interpreted as the share of women in the labor force that has to change occupations in order to make the distribution of women across occupations identical to that of men. Since the measure is symmetrical, it can alternately be interpreted as the share of the men in the labor force that has to be moved to make their occupational distribution identical to that of women.

The use of the index with this interpretation has been criticized on the ground that the measure does not take the total occupational structure as given. Transferring women into men's occupations in a way that the occupational distribution of women becomes identical to that of men is not an operation one could think of in practice. It would totally change the occupational distribution of the total labor force and almost wipe out those occupations where women form a large majority. However, if the issue here is to compare women's and men's occupations, the index is clearly valid. On the other hand, if the question is how many and what percentage would actually have to move in order to integrate the labor market we need another index. Such an index, C, compares women's relative distribution to the relative distribution across occupations of the total labor force

$$
C = \frac{1}{2} \sum_{i=1}^{n} \left| \frac{W_i}{W} - \frac{T_i}{T} \right| \cdot 100 \tag{3}
$$

T_i = the number of persons in occupation i

T = the total number of persons in the labor force

This index can be interpreted as the proportion of women in the labor force that must move in order to make women's occupational distribution identical to that of the total labor force. If these women are exchanged with men the total occupational structure will be left unchanged and the distributions of men and women will become identical.

I denote this index a concentration index, since it measures the degree to which women are concentrated and segmented from the rest of the labor force rather than the degree of segregation of men and women to different occupations. It has the drawback that its maximum is dependent on the share of women in the labor force and is equal to 100 minus the percentage of women in the labor force. It is thus not symmetrical for men and women. Any com-

47

parison of the concentration of men and women in the labor market, requires a separate calculation for men and for women.

Summary indices do not provide enough information about the pattern of segregation. Other dimensions are the dispersion of women and men across occupations (do we find women and men in all possible occupations?) and the level of concentration of men and women in particular occupations (are occupations with a large number of women also heavily female dominated?). One can study the share of the number of occupations that are all female/male or the share of the population that work in all female/male occupations. Other relevant information is the share of the female/male labor force in occupations sorted according to sex ratios.

The following section describes the occupational segregation in the Swedish labor market with the aid of the measures described above. The measures should only be taken as descriptive and not be interpreted as normative. The measures themselves say nothing about how desirable a situation or a certain change is. The evaluation of the desirability of a certain development requires value judgements.

3.   THE SWEDISH EXPERIENCE 1960-75

During the last two decades an unprecedented increase in the labor force participation rates of Swedish women has occurred. According to the yearly labor force surveys, 600,000 women have been added to the labor force and female labor force participation rates have increased from 54.5 in 1963 to 75.1 in 1980 for women 16-64 years of age. (3) Which areas of the labor markets have received all these women, what occupations have they taken up? The labor force surveys are sample surveys and do not allow a detailed study by occupations. Instead I will use census data for the years 1960, 1970 and 1975 for persons aged 16 and above working 20 hours or more to describe the female labor market by occupation. (4) According to the censuses women's participation rates rose from 32.0 in 1960 to 38.0 in 1970 and 42.2 in 1975 and women's share in the labor force from 30 per cent in 1960 to 35 per cent in 1970 and 39 per cent in 1975. The number of women added to the labor force was 241,000 in the sixties and 166,000 between 1970 and 1975.

Before describing the development of occupational segregation, I will briefly indicate the structure of labor demand during this period. The large rise in the labor force participation rates of women have to a considerable extent been a response to a growing demand for female labor. The expansion of employment opportunities during this period has primarily taken place in areas that traditionally have been the domain of women, such as the service sector, clerical work and, in particular, the public sector. Within the public sector, education had a particular high growth rate during the sixties, while health care expanded during the sixties and seventies. During the latter half of the seventies, social services have shown the highest growth rate, e.g. care for pre-school children, for the elderly and social work. The share of women in each sector of the economy has remained remarkably stable. The only major expansion of women in a major field of activity took place within health, education and welfare.

One way to illustrate the sex-segregated labor market is to tabulate the distribution of men and women across occupations. Table 1 provides information on

Occupational area

Table 1
Employed Persons by Sex and Occupational Area, 1960, 1970 and 1975

Occupational area		1960				1970				1975			
		Total	Men	Women	Share of Women %	Total	Men	Women	Share of Women %	Total	Men	Women	Share of Women %
Work in technology, natural science social sciences, arts, letters and fine arts	No.	417,099	257,828	159,271	38.2	646,070	371,005	275,065	42.6	780,393	414,532	365,861	46.9
	%	12.9	11.3	16.5		19.0	16.9	22.8		22.0	19.1	26.7	
Administrative work	No.	69,120	63,832	5,288	7.7	79,058	67,255	11,803	14.9	90,291	70,989	19,302	21.4
	%	2.1	2.8	0.6		2.3	3.1	1.0		2.5	3.3	1.4	
Accounting and clerical work	No.	271,481	92,833	181,648	66.2	370,948	97,306	273,642	73.8	406,926	95,568	311,358	76.5
	%	8.5	4.1	18.8		10.9	4.4	22.7		11.5	4.4	22.7	
Commercial work	No.	308,502	159,730	148,772	48.2	305,530	159,812	145,718	47.7	305,262	166,349	138,913	45.5
	%	9.5	7.0	15.4		9.0	7.3	12.1		8.6	7.7	10.1	
Agriculture, forestry and fishing	No.	437,802	401,281	36,521	8.3	272,304	218,519	53,785	19.8	215,943	170,902	45,041	20.9
	%	13.5	17.6	3.8		8.0	9.9	4.5		6.1	7.9	3.3	
Mining, quarrying	No.	15,642	15,579	63	0.4	12,578	12,395	183	1.5	11,143	10,846	297	2.7
	%	0.5	0.7	0.0		0.4	0.6	0.0		0.3	0.5	0.0	
Transport, communications	No.	235,470	196,979	38,494	16.4	221,363	180,842	40,521	18.3	224,771	182,594	42,177	18.8
	%	7.3	8.7	4.0		6.5	8.2	3.4		6.3	8.4	3.1	
Manufacturing	No.	1,152,078	992,000	160,078	13.9	1,154,098	985,913	168,185	14.6	1,102,996	930,154	172,842	15.7
	%	35.5	43.6	16.6		33.9	44.8	14.0		31.2	42.9	12.6	
Service work	No.	312,958	78,029	234,929	75.1	327,898	92,069	235,829	71.9	379,845	105,509	274,336	72.2
	%	9.7	3.4	24.3		9.6	4.2	19.6		10.7	4.9	20.0	
Military work	No.	17,869	17,869	0	0.0	16,702	16,702	0	0.0	23,347	23,347	0	0.0
	%	0.6	0.8	0.0		0.5	0.8	0.0		0.7	1.1	0.0	
TOTAL	No	3,241,021	2,275,957	965,064	29.8	3,406,549	2,201,818	1,204,731	35.4	3,540,917	2,170,790	1,370,127	38.7

Source: The Population and Housing Censuses of 1960, 1970 and 1975.

49

the number of men and women, their relative distribution and the proportion of women per occupation for a division of occupations at the one digit level. (5) Already at this aggregated level, it is apparent that men and women are found in quite different areas of work. The most important female areas are the occupational area "work in technology etc.", which also includes health and educational work, and "clerical work" and "service work". Men on the other hand have manufacturing as their major area of work, a sector that has remained roughly stable for men, but has experienced a decrease in relative importance for women. On the whole men's relative distribution across occupations has changed very little over the period. The two major changes are the decrease of workers within the agricultural sector and the increase in the share of men at work within "technology etc.". This rather well mirrors the general structural development of the economy.

The relative distribution of women has varied more in time. The largest change in the female labor market during the sixties and seventies has been the rapid expansion of the occupational area "work in technology", which now is the largest area for female workers. Within this area health and sick care and, to somewhat lesser extent, educational work are responsible for the large increase. Clerical work is another area with substantial increases both in numbers and percentage, especially during the sixties. Areas that have diminished in relative importance (but not in terms of numbers) are commercial work, manufacturing and service work.

The most common occupations for women in general also contain a very large proportion of women, often over 90 per cent. Table 2 displays the labor force according to the sex ratio of the occupation and illustrates the extent to which men and women work in male, female or mixed occupations. The table shows that a very small percentage, 5-6 per cent of the labor force, work in occupations that have a relatively even composition of men and women. This pattern has remained stable.

The proportion of all women in occupations that can be regarded as female occupations, i.e. with more than 60 per cent women, have remained exactly the same, 76 per cent. Out of the net addition of female workers to the labor force between 1960 and 1975 about three quarters took up female dominated occupations and only one quarter male dominated ones. Within the female-dominated occupations there has been a shift from the category with 60-80 per cent women to occupations with 80 per cent women or more. Many women have entered occupations that initially comprised 60-80 per cent women causing them to shift category and the category with 80-90 per cent women has consequently experienced a large increase in the number of women employed. The largest increase in total numbers employed have taken place in the category with 10-20 per cent women. Men as well as women show a strong increase in the proportion working in such occupations.

Extremely male dominated occupations are less common than before and the share of women working in such occupations has increased somewhat. About 10 per cent of all women work in occupations with more than 80 per cent men, while only 3 per cent of the men work in occupations with more than 80 per cent women. Finally, since 1975, there are no longer any occupations (listed on the three digit level) that are 100 per cent female. Aside from military work employing 1 per cent of the male labor force, only a few very small male occupations altogether without women remained.

Table 2
The Distribution of Employed Persons according to Percentage Females of the Occupation

Sex ratio % women		1960 Men	Women	Total	Share of Women %	1970 Men	Women	Total	Share of Women %	1975 Men	Women	Total	Share of Women %
0 – 10	%	68.9	4.3	49.6	2.6	62.9	4.4	42.2	3.7	45.6	2.5	28.9	3.4
	No	1,567,130	41,036	1,608,166		1,385,813	52,811	1,438,624		989,358	34,713	1,024,071	
10 – 20	%	11.2	3.8	9.0	12.6	17.2	5.4	13.0	14.8	31.0	7.6	22.0	13.4
	No	254,594	36,633	291,227		377,722	65,502	443,224		673,894	104,644	778,538	
20 – 40	%	10.0	7.7	9.3	24.8	7.8	5.5	7.0	8.0	9.5	5.7	8.0	27.4
	No	225,872	74,454	300,326		171,831	66,799	238,630		206,051	77,683	283,734	
40 – 60	%	3.0	8.0	4.5	53.1	4.1	8.6	5.6	53.6	5.1	7.9	6.2	49.5
	No	68,041	77,013	145,054		89,064	103,021	192,085		111,066	108,686	219,752	
60 – 80	%	6.2	40.6	16.4	73.6	5.4	28.2	13.5	74.1	5.5	24.9	13.1	74.0
	No	140,627	391,623	532,250		118,882	339,902	458,784		120,205	341,777	461,982	
80 – 90	%	0.6	9.3	3.2	87.4	2.3	22.4	9.4	84.3	2.6	24.2	10.9	85.7
	No	13,004	89,775	102,779		50,300	270,046	320,346		55,359	331,519	386,878	
90 – 100	%	0.3	26.4	8.1	97.4	0.4	25.5	9.2	97.4	0.7	27.1	10.9	96.2
	No	6,689	254,530	261,219		8,206	306,650	314,856		14,857	371,105	385,962	
0 – 100	%	100.0	100.0	100.0	29.8	100.0	100.0	100.0	35.4	100.0	100.0	100.0	38.7
	No	2,275,957	965,064	3,241,021		2,201,818	1,204,731	3,406,549		2,170,790	1,370,127	3,540,917	

Source: The Population and Housing Censuses of 1960, 1970 and 1975.

51

Table 2 conveys a picture of a very segregated labor market, but it is difficult to draw any conclusions about the increase or decrease in segregation from such a table. Such an evaluation requires a comprehensive measure of occupational segregation. As mentioned in the previous section, I have chosen to rely on the dissimilarity index. Calculations with other measures of occupational segregation, such as the Gini-index or Theil's enthrophy measure, not reported here, show the same trends. The results of the calculations of the dissimilarity index are displayed in Table 3.

The dissimilarity index indicates that regardless of the occupational level studied, occupational segregation has fallen between 1960 and 1970 and 1975. As pointed out in section 2 the dissimilarity index can be interpreted as the proportion of women that have to change occupations in order for women to obtain the same occupational distribution as men (or vice versa). Thus the figures state that while in 1960 74.5 per cent of the women in the labor force would have had to change occupation, in 1975 this was the case for 70.3 per cent.

Table 3
Dissimilarity index at the one-, two- and three digit level, 1960, 1970 and 1975

Year	Occupational level		
	one-digit	two-digit	three-digit
1960	49.2	66.8	74.5
1970	44.5	63.1	72.6
1975	43.6	59.8	70.3
change 1960-70	− 4.7	− 3.7	− 1.9
change 1970-75	− 0.9	− 3.3	− 2.3
change 1960-75	− 5.6	− 7.0	− 4.2

Source: Calculated from the Population and Housing Census of 1960, 1970 and 1975.

Generally, the more detailed an occupational division is studied, the more apparent is occupational segregation. As a result the dissimilarity index is quite a bit higher at the three-digit level than at the two-digit level, and higher at the two-digit level than the one-digit level. See Table 3. The degree of change in time also differs according to the level of aggregation. The reduction in segregation across major occupational areas and across occupational groups for the whole period has been larger than the reduction in segregation as estimated at the finer division - the three-digit level. A reduction in segregation across occupational groups must partly have been outweighted by an increased segregation within these occupational groups. Considering that the second period studied is only half as long as the first one, the reduction in occupational segregation, particularly as measured at the three-digit level, appears to have been much more rapid during the seventies than during the sixties.

4.   INTERNATIONAL COMPARISONS

How does occupational segregation in Sweden compare to that of other countries covered in this study - Great Britain, the US and Germany? Inter-

52

national comparisons of occupational segregation are difficult to make for several reasons. First, very aggregated occupational data are generally used in international comparisons. This obscures a great deal of the segregation, since, as we have shown, segregation is higher the more detailed the occupational level studied.

Second, different countries exhibit different stages with respect to industrialisation and the development of the service sector. This affects the occupational segregation of the labor market. Comparing countries with very different occupational structures may give a distorted picture, e.g. if there is a large agriculture sector segregation is likely to be low. On the other hand, it is of interest to study how industrialization and an expansion of services reflect in occupational segregation of the labor market, e.g. will the development of public services draw women from the manufacturing industry?

Third, female labor force participation rates differ between countries. Measures of occupational segregation do not include persons working at home. How do we compare and evaluate occupational segregation in two countries; one where a large part of the female population is occupied with family care outside the labor market and another country where a larger share of the female population works on the labor market, but in typical female social and service work?

The report Women and Employment, published by OECD, describes the degree and the character of segregation in the OECD countries. The pattern of segregation is depicted with the aid of "coefficients of female representation" for each occupational area, calculated by dividing the female share of employment in the occupational area by the female share of the total labor force. The data presented are at the one-digit level of the occupational classification.

According to this OECD publication, the aggregate pattern of occupational segregation for Sweden, displayed in Table 1, is similar to that of the other three countries as well. Women are overrepresented, relative to the share of women in total employment, in service, clerical and sales work in all countries and underrepresented in administrative work and in manufacturing, transport etc.. The most representative share in all countries is found within "professional, technical and related workers" (corresponding to the first occupational area in Table 1.

The degree of over- and underrepresentation differs somewhat among the four countries. Underrepresentation in administrative work is less pronounced in the US and Germany than in Great Britain and Sweden. The overrepresentation in services is higher in Great Britain and Sweden, and in clerical work is highest in the US and Sweden, but lowest in Germany. Women are overrepresented in agriculture in Germany, but underrepresented in the other countries.

The OECD also presents a comprehensive measure of segregation. The index is calculated as the weighted sum of the absolute deviations from unity of the coefficients of female representation, the weights being the proportion of the total labor force in each occupational area. (6) The index corresponds to twice the index of concentration (2) presented earlier. It is calculated at the one-digit level.

The report provides an index for Germany, 45.7, for the US, 51.1, and for Sweden, 50.4, respectively. According to the OECD results, occupational concentration is lower in Germany than in Sweden and the US. This is remarkable, since, for statistical reasons, we would have expected a lower value of this type of index for those countries, where women form a larger share of the labor force. (The concentration index compares the female occupational distribution to the occupational distribution of the total labor force of which the female labor force is a part). The figures further show a slight rise in occupational segregation, 1.1, for Germany and a small fall for Sweden, 1.2, and the US, 0.3, respectively, during the first part of the seventies (7).

An investigation aimed at studying the youth employment (Reubens (1983)) also contains information regarding sex differentials. This comparative study includes the US, Great Britain and Sweden. The study, based on census data at the three-digit level for each country, covers 1970 for the US, 1971 for Great Britain and 1975 for Sweden.

This study verifies that women in the US and Great Britain, as is the case in Sweden, are concentrated in a smaller number of occupations than men. The share of employment accounted for by the most common occupation for each sex is far greater for females than for males. Figures are given for the concentration in the top five per cent of the total number of occupations. For the adult population (over 25) these accounted for 29.4 per cent of the males and 64.1 per cent of the females in Great Britain, for 42.6 per cent of the males and 60.1 per cent of the females in Sweden and 40.5 per cent of the males and 56.6 per cent of the females in the US. While the degree of concentration of females in a limited number of occupations is of a similar level in the three countries, the concentration of males in a few occupations is significantly lower in Great Britain than in other countries. Apparently men in Great Britain are distributed across occupations to a larger extent than men in other countries.

An inspection of the most common occupation in the different countries shows a greater overlap between men's and women's most popular occupations in Great Britain than in the other countries, e.g. clerical work is a top occupation in Britain for men as well as women. Likewise the top occupations for each sex are more likely to be dominated by the same sex in Sweden than is the case in Great Britain.

On the basis of the above information one would expect a relatively lower index of dissimilarity for Great Britain, not because women are spread across more occupations but because men are less concentrated. This is also the case when compared to Sweden. Indices of dissimilarity for the adult population were estimated to 66.1 for Great Britain (223 occupations), 70.7 for Sweden (282 occupations) and 65.1 for the US (441 occupations).

Chapter 5 of the same book also includes some data for Germany. These are difficult to compare to those of the other countries, since they are calculated on a significantly lower number of occupations (87). But on the other hand, indices are given for three different years. The figures, 54.2 for 1960, 56.6 for 1979 and 54.7 for 1980, indicate a stable level of segregation in Germany during the last two decades. The index is significantly lower than the measure at the two-digit level for Sweden (57 occupations) as indicated in Table 3.

An international comparative study, made by Roos (1981), is based on data from similar sample surveys in different countries. Indices of dissimilarity were calculated on the basis of a division of occupations into 14 groups. The figures were for Germany 42.6, Great Britain 31.1, the US 46.8 and Sweden 60.0.

Segregation in a single country is especially well documented for the United States, see e.g. the Economic Report of the President (1973), Fuchs (1971), Gross (1968), Oppenheimer (1970), Reubens and Reubens (1977). The period 1960-70 is most carefully described by Blau and Hendricks (1979). Using a classification based on about 280 occupations, they calculated an index of dissimilarity of 68.4 in 1960 and 65.8 in 1970. In order to remove the biases introduced by changes in the occupational classification schemes between the census years, they also calculated an index based on 183 occupations with comparable data. The index computed on this basis amounted to 73.8 in 1960 and 70.7 in 1970. O'Neill and Braun (1981) report an index of 63.5 calculated on the basis of 419 occupations in the 1980 census. Judging from these studies, the degree of occupational segregation in the US is less than in the Swedish labor market. The speed of change registered for the US in the sixties was somewhat greater than that in Sweden, but somewhat slower in the seventies.

Hakim (1979) describes the pattern of differentiation between men's and women's work in England and Wales during the period 1901-1971. According to her, the development of occupational segregation during the decade 1961-71 is unclear; some indicators point to an increase, others to a decrease of occupational segregation. According to one measure the degree of overrepresentation of women in "female" occupations, i.e. occupations with a higher share of of women than in the labor force, had fallen slightly, while the underrepresentation in "male" occupation had remained stable. On the other hand, the distribution of the labor force by sex ratios shows that the percentage of women working in occupations with more than 60 per cent women has increased strongly during the decade. The table by sex ratios also gives a picture of a stronger and more stable domination of men in male occupations than women in female occupations. The author concludes that male inroads into women's preserves have not been counterbalanced by women's entry into typically male spheres of work.

A comparison between English and Swedish data shows that the percent of all men working within extremely segregated male occupations (90 per cent or more men in the occupation) is substantially higher in England. On the other hand, the concentration of women in female occupations appears to be higher in Sweden than in England. While 70 per cent of all Swedish working women are in occupations with 70 per cent or more women, this was only the case for half of all employed women in England and Wales in 1970. Furthermore, the degree of overrepresentation of women in "female" occupations and underrepresentation in "male" occupations was higher in Sweden in 1960 and 1970 than in England 1961 and 1971. However, by 1975 the degree of over- and underrepresentation had fallen and was identical to that in England and Wales in 1971.

In summation (8): the labor market in each of the four countries is characterized by a significant degree of occupational segregation. The pattern of segregation is similar in the sense that women are overrepresented in service, clerical and social work and underrepresented in administrative and manufacturing work. Although comparisons are hard to make and must be accompanied by reservations, the degree of occupational segregation appears to be higher in Sweden than in the other countries and possibly lower in Germany. In the US and Sweden the degree of occupational segregation is falling, in Germany and Great Britain it seems to be constant or rising.

5.   SOURCES OF CHANGE IN OCCUPATIONAL SEGREGATION

5.1   Structural vs. Sex Composition Changes

The index of occupational segregation may change in time due to one or both of the following two reasons: (a) a change in the degree of segregation (i.e. the deviation between the proportion of women in the occupation and the proportion of women in the labor force) within single occupations, and (b) a differential rate of expansion in occupations with different degrees of segregation. Here, I will refer to the two types of changes as a change in the sex composition within occupations and as a change in occupational structure. An increased share of women in the labor force can take place either through an expansion of the female dominated occupations or through an increased share of women within the separate occupations. If the increase in labor force participation rates have occurred mainly through an expansion of female occupations, the index can show an increase even if women have increased their share within the male-dominated occupations. It is of interest to separate the two types of changes in order to find out whether a fall in occupational segregation is due to men and/or women penetrating new areas of work or only to changes in the occupational structure.

A standardizing procedure can separate the change in the index due to changes in the sex composition of the occupation and the change due to the development of the occupational structure of the economy. (Fuchs (1975), Blau and Hendricks (1979)). If we are studying the development during the period 1960-1970, we can use the following standardizing procedure.

$$D_c = \frac{1}{2} \sum_i \left| \frac{(W_{i70}/T_{i70}) \, T_{i60}}{\sum ((W_{i70}/T_{i70}) \, T_{i60})} - \frac{(M_{i70}/T_{i70}) \, T_{i60}}{\sum ((M_{i70}/T_{i70}) \, T_{i60})} \right| . 100 \quad (4)$$

For the meaning of the symbols see section 2. This standardized index shows the result if the occupational structure had remained unchanged and all occupations had retained their 1960 employment, but the proportion of women in each occupation had changed as in 1970, i.e. D_c is the value the dissimilarity index takes as a result of <u>compositional</u> change. Alternatively one can standardize for 1960 sex proportions and estimate the index that would result solely from the development of the occupational <u>structure.</u>

$$D_s = \frac{1}{2} \sum_i \left| \frac{(W_{i60}/T_{i60}) \, T_{i70}}{\sum ((W_{i60}/T_{i60}) \, T_{i70})} - \frac{(M_{i60}/T_{i60}) \, T_{i70}}{\sum ((M_{i60}/T_{i60}) \, T_{i70})} \right| . 100 \quad (5)$$

The result of the standardization procedure is displayed in Table 4. If each sex had kept their proportion within each occupation in 1960, but the total number employed in each occupation had developed the way it actually did until 1970, the segregation index would have increased by o.4 per cent. If occupations had retained their 1960 employment, but attained the 1970 shares of men and women, the result would have been a decline in the index of 2.1 percentage points. The reduction in the segregation index between 1960 and 1970 is thus mainly due to a changed sex composition of the individual occupations. (The changes in structural and sex composition do not exactly add up to the actual change due to interaction between sex composition and structural changes. An interaction term is therefore included in Table 4).

Table 4
Sources of Change in the Segregation Index — Structural or Sex Composition Effects

Period	Actual index[a] change	Structural[b] effect	Composition[c] effect	Interaction[d] effect
1960-70	- 1.9	+ 0.4	- 2.0	- 0.3
1970-75	- 2.3	+ 0.4	- 2.8	+ 0.1
1960-75	- 4.2	+ 0.9	- 5.5	+ 0.4

a   estimated as $D_{1970} - D_{1960}$ and respectivity for each period
b   estimated as $D_s - D_{1960}$ and respectivity for each period
c   estimated as $D_c - D_{1960}$ and respectivity for each period
d   the interaction effect is the result of the interaction between structural and compositional effects.
Source: Calculated from the Population and Housing Census of 1960, 1970 and 1975.

During the period 1970-75, structural developments slightly increased segregation. The actual decline in segregation during this period is entirely due to a change in the sex composition within occupations in the direction of decreased segregation.

The change in occupational structure has been such that decidely male occupations (0-10 per cent female) have decreased in relative importance since 1960. The growth in areas that were made up of 10-20 pro cent women in 1960 and the even larger expansion of female occupations of 90-100 per cent women countered this effect. The result of these structural effects was to produce a slight increase in segregation.

As may be seen in Table 2, sex composition changes have been such that the share of women in occupations with 10-20 per cent women increased slightly over the period. The proportion of females in occupations with more than 60 per cent women remained constant, but there was a movement towards occupations with a more extreme sex composition. On the other hand, the share of men in the extreme male category fell, and instead the proportion increased in the 10-20 per cent category. Men also increased their proportion slightly in typically female jobs. The net result of these movements was a decline in segregation as measured by the dissimilarity index.

Blau and Hendricks in a study of the US labor market also separate structural and sex composition effects. They show that the decline of the dissimilarity index in the US in the period 1960-1970 primarily is due to a changed sex composition within occupations. This is the result of men moving into typical female professions and women taking up typical male sales and clerical jobs.

5.2   Male/Female Entry

Is it possible to find out whether desegregation has taken place mainly as the result of men moving into female occupations or   women   moving   into   male occupations? Section 2 pointed out that the dissimilarity index can be reduced to the difference between the share of the female labor force in occupations with an overrepresentation of women and the share of the male labor force in such occupations. By dividing the index into its parts, we can thus state whether the change in the index is due to women moving out of occupations with an overrepresentation of women or men moving into such occupations. The results are presented in Table 5.

Table 5
Sources of Change in the Index: Male or Female Movements

Period	Actual change	Change due to increase of women in male occupation	Change due to increase of men in female occupation
Total change:			
1960-1970	- 1.9	- 0.5	- 1.4
1970-75	- 2.3	- 1.1	- 1.3
1960-75	- 4.2	- 1.6	- 2.7
Sex composition change:			
1960-70	- 2.0	- 0.9	- 1.2
1970-75	- 2.8	- 1.5	- 1.3
1960-75	- 5.5	- 2.2	- 3.3

Source: Calculated from the Population and Housing Census of 1960, 1970 and 1975.

The drop in the index between 1960 and 1970 was to three-fourths the consequence of men moving into female occupations. Men's movements still contribute more to the change of the index in the period 1970-1975, but the change is then more evenly shared between the sexes.

The increased proportion of men found in female occupations is the result of both structural changes in the size of occupations and a changed proportion of men within the single occupations. In the lower part of Table 5, the part of the index change due to changes in the sex composition of occupations is separated according to male influx in female occupations and female movements to male occupations. The results are now different. The change in the index is more evenly divided between men and women in the period 1960-70. In the period 1970-75 the inflow of women to male occupations is somewhat more responsible for the change in the index. Structural changes have thus been such as to favor an increased share of the male labor force in occupations dominated by women. The reduction in the index due to changes in the sex composition of the single occupations is equally due to men and women moving into non-traditional areas.

The Swedish experience thus differs from the English one according to Hakim's (1979) conclusion that desegregation in England primarily is due to men entering female jobs.

5.3   Occupations

What areas of the labor market have the strongest segregation?   What   areas have contributed most to desegregation? Table 6 displays dissimilarity indices for each occupational area. The most segregated area is "work in technology etc.", that contains many of the professions within education, health and social care, but also several technical professions. The great inflow of women into this occupational area has not resulted in any reduction of the degree of segregation. In the second occupational area, the degree of segregation has actually increased. Women have reduced their relative share within private business administration and have entered administrative work within the public sector. Clerical work also shows increased segregation. There is a large decrease in the level of segregation within manufacturing and also within transport and communications. The impression from Table 6 is that segregation has decreased in contracting sectors of the economy. In occupational areas that have increased in relative importance, occupational segregation has remained constant or even increased.

Table 6
Dissimilarity Index by Occupational Area

Year	Occupational area									
	0	1	2	3	4	5	6	7-8	9	10
1960	72.1	21.7	30.9	60.0	48.7	85.6	83.3	67.1	65.7	0
1970	71.9	21.9	33.9	61.7	68.0	69.3	75.5	53.7	66.1	0
1975	70.1	26.6	37.3	59.6	47.1	34.8	71.3	47.2	64.6	0

0   Work in technology, natural and social sciences, art, letters and fine art.
1   Administrative work.
2   Accounting and clerical work.
3   Commercial work.
4   Agriculture, forestry, fishery (the large variations for the agricultural sector are due to changes in the procedure for counting female family workers in agriculture).
5   Mining, quarrying.
6   Transport, communications.
7-8 Manufacturing.
9   Service work.
10   Military work.
Source: Calculated from the Population and Housing Census 1960, 1970 and 1975.

What are some of the individual non-traditional occupations where men and women have increased their relative shares? I will restrict the presentation here to the seventies. During this period men have increased from 1 to 4 per cent as pre-school teachers, from 1 to 3 per cent as nurses and from 3 to 5 per cent as nurse's aides. Men have also increased their shares in female-dominated occupations in household work, such as catering supervisors, cooks and kitchen assistants.

Women have increased their share by about 4-6 percentage points in a number of male-dominated occupations in manufacturing. In many cases, however, this is more a consequence of a reduced number of men than an increased number of women in these occupations. Women's share has increased within metal furnacemen, metal annealers and case-hardeners, metal casters and   molders, opticians, watch-, clock- and precision-instrument makers, metal platers and coaters, telephone installers, and crane and hoist operators.

What is the situation for women in some high-status occupations? Women have increased their share of physicians from 18 to 23 per cent, dentists from 27 to 30 per cent, prosecuting attorneys from 4 to 11 per cent, court lawyers and judges from 12 to 16 per cent, and school principals from 12 to 15 per cent. In the various fields of engineering, women's share has increased very little and range between 1 and 5 per cent. The share of women among university teachers remains the same, 20 per cent.

5.4   Age

There are several theoretical reasons to expect occupational segregation to be less in the younger age groups. In these age groups, differences between men and women in educational level, work experience and on-the-job training - all factors, that have been said to influence sex differences in occupations and earnings - are less than in older age groups. Also if new attitudes and changes in sex roles are developing, we may expect to see more of these in younger age groups were the dependence on earlier experience for occupational choice is less.

Table 7 displays dissimilarity indices by age groups. Differences in the index by age groups are quite small. All age groups display the same trend towards reduced segregation. The speed of change appears to be somewhat greater for the age groups under 35, especially the age group 25-29, than for the older age groups. I have also compared the occupational distribution of younger women to that of older women and similarly for men (not displayed here). Differences in occupational distribution according to age are less than differences according to sex. However, the labor market of young men differed quite markedly from that of adult men. Age, experience and education lead men into new areas. The labor market of young women and adult women differed less. Young women, thus to a larger extent than is the case for young men, compete in the same labor market as adults of the same sex.

Table 7
Dissimilarity Index by Age

Year	Age								
	16-19	20-24	25-29	30-34	35-44	45-54	55-64	65-	All
1960	75.4	77.5	76.0	74.4	73.7	74.1	73.6	67.5	74.5
1970	73.5	73.8	72.4	71.9	72.8	73.5	73.7	68.8	72.6
1975	70.8	70.2	69.1	70.7	71.0	71.7	72.4	65.4	70.3

Source: Calculated from the Population and Housing Census 1960, 1970 and 1975.

The study by Reubens (1983) also included dissimilarity indices by the age groups 15-19, 20-24 and 25 +. For the US and Britain, as in Sweden, dissimilarity indices by sex calculated for the three age groups were very close. However, the German figures provided in the same book, show a significantly lower figure for men and women above 25 years of age. Thus, in Germany the labor market of young people is more segregated than the labor market for adults. Mayby the low labor force participation rate of German women means that the women that do remain in the labor market in Germany, in relation to men, on the average have less child-care responsibilities, higher education, more labor market experience, and are more market oriented than is the case for women, in relation to men, in the labor force of other countries.

5.5   Summary

Desegregation during the sixties and the seventies is the result of a decline in segregation within occupations that has counteracted an influence towards increased segregation from the development of the occupational structure. The change in sex composition is due to women, as well as men, increasing their proportion in non-traditional areas. However, some evidence suggests that an increased share of women in non-traditional occupations is due more to men exiting than women entering these fields. Attention should be paid to the nature of the non-traditional occupations where men and women increase their shares. Are they expanding or contracting areas? Finally, no strong trend towards reduced segregation resulting from the entry of the younger generation into the labor market can so far be discerned.

6.   CAUSES OF OCCUPATIONAL SEGREGATION

There are two basic approaches to analyze the existence and persistence of occupational segregation (9). One approach starts at the labor supply-side of the market and focuses on the division of labor in the home. According to this approach, the specialization of labor between family members results in differences between men and women in their supply of labor to the market and in the investments they make in education and training. A woman, it is assumed, plans her future on the premise that she will become a member of a household. On the basis of today's division of labor, she expects that the main part of the household work will be her responsibility. Since women know that they will probably have to be absent from the labor force during some periods and others will be able to use only part of their time for market work or will have to demand flexible hours of work, their educational investment will be differently oriented compared to that of men. Women will choose an education and an occupation that make it possible to combine home work and market work. Women's education will be shorter than men's since it does not pay to spend many years on an education if the possibility to use it is uncertain. The subject of study will be such that it relates to the functions at home, since this knowledge can be used both inside and outside the market. According to this theory, women will thus enter other segments of the labor market than men - those that can be combined with home responsibilities, but not those that give a high pay-off in connection with full-time work.

The same holds true for investments in the labor market. Women's greater ressponsibilities at home make it hard for them to fulfill the requirements of work-life continuity, i.e., long hours, travel etc. in many higher positions and male occupations. Their shorter time in the work force makes on-the-job training less profitable.

The second approach ascribes the different labor market experiences of men and women to discrimination. Discrimination can take several forms. Women may be paid less than men although they perform the same job; a woman's employment or promotion possibilities may be less favourable than a man's; the qualifications demanded may be set higher for a woman. Most important, employers often controll access to internal education and training which lead to higher levels and higher pay. Employers may discriminate women by not giving them the chance to accumulate such knowledge and by recruiting women only for occupations than cannot offer possibilities of advancement. The reasons for discrimination may be prejudice, misinformation, "statistical discrimination" by assuming that each individual woman has the characteristics of the average woman, or simply tastes and tradition among employers, other employees or customers.

If discrimination exists, it places women in a viscious circle. It prevents them from investing in on-the-job training and results in a lower returns from their education. Investing in a male occupation is very risky for a woman, since she does not know whether she will be the subject of discrimination or not. Staying in female occupations seems safer. If discrimination is reduced, it will take a long time for this information to spread among women, since few will find it worthwhile to take the risk to find out. Discrimination will make it relatively less costly for women to drop out of the labor market or to accept the main responsibilities at home. Employers can then point to the labor market behaviour of women and continue to discriminate against them.

The theories are not mutually exclusive. Both mechanisms may work at the same time and will then reinforce each other in viscious circles. The theories offer a variety of hypotheses regarding the persistence of occupational segregation over a period of time and the differences in occupational segregation across countries. Both would emphasize the direction of labor demand as important for the persistence of occupational segregation. According to the theory of the division of labor in the home, women will enter the market when demand increases in the female areas - those that are compatible with responsibilities outside the market. Since, according to the discrimination theory, women are restricted to certain areas, their inflow in the market will be related to the development of openings in these areas or the removal of barriers of entry to formerly male areas. The increase in labor force participation rates started relatively late in Sweden. In many other countries, an increase in market employment was due to the war economy, when women replaced men in industry. In Sweden, the rapid increase in labor force participation rates occured with the expansion of the public sector.

According to the division of labor theory, the availability of part-time work is a characteristic that will entice women to seek work. Part-time work may be more convenient to establish in certain occupations. Discrimination theories on the other hand point to part-time as one of the mechanisms used by employers to segregate women to certain areas. On both accounts one would expect countries that allow more part-time work to have a more segregated labor market. A recent Swedish study (Petterson 1981) of the part-time labor force finds that the major part of the variations between occupational areas in the share working part-time is related to variations in the share of new recruitment. This could indicate that part-time employment is more of an adjustment of labor demand to new forms of labor supply than a means of segregation.

The theory of the division of labor in the home points to a changed composition of the labor force as an important factor contributing to the persistence of labor market segregation. The typical background of the female worker has changed significantly in Sweden. Until the 1950's, a majority of the women in the labor force were unmarried and their careers were unimpeded by family bonds and children. Today a majority is married, not seldom mothers of young children, who share their time between care of their families and work outside the home. Earlier generations of well-educated women could also find and afford household help - something that is almost out of reach for the career women of today - and thus compete on more equal terms with men. Thus, a higher labor force participation rate most probably means a higher share of double-working women in the labor force. An expected result is a more segregated labor market.

According to human capital theory, the stronger the attachment of women to the labor force, the less segregation one should observe. According to the four country studies the stability of labor force attachment of Swedish females is higher than that of women in other countries. This is partly due to the availability of relative generous leaves of absence for child care. Women, who in other countries would have to leave the labor force in connection with childbirth, can keep their employment in Sweden. The development of a continuous attachment to the labor force should make women and employers more willing to invest in on-the-job training for younger generations. In the long run, this should reduce occupational segregation. The lower and more rapidly decreasing degree of segregation of the under 35 age groups may be interpreted in this way.

Discrimination can take the form of unequal pay for the same job for men and women, or restrictions on the employment of women in certain jobs. The acceptance of lower wages may be one method for women to bypass barriers of entry to male occupations. If opportunities for wage discrimination are reduced either by law or by collective agreement, the use of employment discrimination may be intensified unless also legally or otherwise controlled. One hypothesis is that countries characterized by small wage differentials between men and women would display a larger degree of occupational segregation. According to the country studies differences in labor earnings between men and women are smaller in Sweden than elsewhere, which is consistent with this hypothesis.

7.   FUTURE TRENDS

How will occupational segregation develop in the near future? Forecasts till 1990 concerning the occupational structure of the Swedish labor market predict a continued growth of employment in education and health care. Social services are expected to expand even more rapidly than before. No significant growth is expected for technical, manufacturing and clerical work. The demand for labor will thus primarily exist in typically female areas. Structural changes cannot be expected to significantly contribute to decreased segregation. The extent to which they do, will be due to an increased share of men in the female sectors of the economy. Any major changes in segregation will rely upon the willingness and ability of men and women to select non-traditional occupations.

Countries that have a relatively low labor force participation rate today can probably look forward to stable or growing occupational segregation. This will be due to changes in the composition of the labor force as more women with responsibilities for children enter the labor force. The countries that already have reached a relatively high level of labor force participation can probably expect slightly decreasing levels of segregation. As women plan for a more continuous attachment to the labor force, and as employers gain experience from the new labor force behavior, investments in market oriented human capital will be more profitable. This should affect occupational choice and occupational mobility. However, as long we find large differences between men and women in the amount of non-market work and responsibilities, we should expect the degree of occupational segregation to remain significant.

What labor market mobility is required by a policy of occupational desegregation? To gain a perspective, suppose that we want to totally integrate the labor force. What amount of labor transfer is required? The dissimilarity index describes how "dissimilar" men's and women's occupational distributions are by measuring the share of the female (male) labor force that has to change jobs in order to obtain the same occupational distribution as men (women). This is, however, not the transfer of labor desired to desegregate the market, since it would more or less deplete either the female or the male occupations. We wish to calculate the number (or share) to be transferred, while keeping the occupational structures intact. The concentration index, C, described in section 2, measures the share of women that need to exchange jobs with men in order to integrate the labor market. Such an exchange does not disturb the occupational structure.

According to the concentration index in 1960, a total integration of the labor force would have required 52.3 per cent of the female labor force to exchange jobs with men. In 1970 46.9 per cent would have sufficed and 43.1 per cent in 1975. However, since the number of women in the labor force has increased over this period, the necessary transfer in terms of number of persons to be moved has in fact grown. The 1960 index corresponds to about 505,000 women, the 1970 figure to 565,000 and 1975 to 590,525. The total number of persons that would have to change jobs, men and women, related to the total labor force has also actually risen. In 1960 it was 31.1, 1970 33.2 and in 1975 33.4 per cent. A total desegregation of the labor force today would thus involve more persons and a larger share of the labor force than ever before. Although a complete desegregation probably is not desired, the calculations seem to indicate that the problems confronting a policy of occupational desegregation have increased rather than decreased over time.

Should the decrease in segregation that took place during the sixties and the seventies be considered significant? In order to evaluate the magnitude of change, it is necessary to have some norm of comparison. What degree of desegregation was possible to achieve over this period? One cannot expect the employed to change occupations to a significant degree. Opportunities for integration are created by flows in the labor force: between declining and expanding occupations and into and out of the labor force.

A dissimilarity index resulting from two "experimental" hiring methods have been calculated. The first method is termed maximum equalization. Considering that the net addition to the labor force consisted of women and that the number of men has decreased, assume that the following structural changes occurred; the net addition of women to the labor force all entered male dominated occupations and the net decrease of men disappeared from male-dominated occupations. How much would the index have dropped? As indicated by Table 8 an actual decreased of 4.2 over the entire period 1960-75 should be compared to a maximum one of 25.9.

The notion of maximum equalization takes no account of the course of demand as reflected in the employment of different occupations. Instead, taking the occupational structure as given and following the method suggested by Blau and Hendricks (1979), construct a hiring pool consisting of the net addition of women to the labor force, women released from occupations with a declining number of women and men released from occupations with a declining number of men. Assume that all new hiring is sex-neutral and that all net increases in occupations were filled in the same sex ratio as prevails in the hiring pool.

Table 8
Actual and Possible Changes in the Dissimilarity Index

| Period | Actual change | Possible change | |
		Maximum equalization	Hiring pool
1960-70	1.9	17.4	13.6
1970-75	2.3	10.5	7.9
1960-75	4.2	25.9	18.5

Source: Calculated from the Population and Housing Census 1960, 1970 and 1975.

The fall in the dissimilarity index resulting from this procedure would have been much larger than the actual change. According to Table 8 in the period 1960-70, the decrease would have been 13.6 and 7.9 in the period 1970-75. If the random hiring method is applied to the entire fifteen year period the reduction would have been 18.5. The 1970's are characterized by a faster desegregation both in terms of actual performance and "possible" performance as measured by the random hiring method. In the 1960's the reduction in segregation was about 1/7 of "possible" change, while in the 1970's the actual change corresponds to 1/4 of the change resulting from a random hiring from the hiring pool.

The hiring pool method underestimates possible integration since it ignores opportunities for integration through replacement needs in the labor force. On the other hand, it overestimates the possibilities for integration since it ignores the background characteristics of the persons in the hiring pool in terms of preferences, schooling and occupational experience. Nevertheless, the impression is that the integration of the labor force has fallen far short of what would be possible to achieve, although showing a stronger progression in the early 1970's than in the 1960's. Thus, there is ample room for policies aiming at influencing occupational choice and employer recruitment procedures.

NOTES

*) Financial support for this research from the Swedish Council for Research in the Humanities and Social Sciences is graciously acknowledged. I wish to thank Siv Gustafsson, Marianne Sundström and Eskil Wadensjö for helpful comments, Ingemar Dahlstrand for conducting the computer and programing work and Yael Tågerud for typing the manuscript.

(1) For an overview see Duncan and Duncan (1955).

(2) The same index can be derived from a different starting point that relates the level of segregation to the deviation of women's representation in the single occupations from their average representation in the labor force, weighted by the size of each occupation. This is because an identical representation of men and women across occupations requires a female representation in each occupational identical to their total share in the labor force.

(3) In the labor force surveys, available since 1962, everyone who has worked at least one hour during the survey week or has been looking for work sometime during the 60 past days is included in the labor force.

(4) Comparable census data for the three years is only available for persons at work 20 hours or more. Occupational categories are made as comparable as possible over time, by sometimes adding two or more categories.

(5) The occupational categories are based on ISCO (International Standard Classification of Occupations), see OECD 1980 p. 76 ff. I have used the official Swedish translation of the categories.

(6) The OECD index is:

$$\sum_{i=1}^{n} \left| 1 - \frac{\frac{W_i}{T_i}}{\frac{W}{T}} \right| \frac{T_i}{T}$$

(7) The OECD-index is standardized for structural change by using final year occupational structure as weights in the index. It thus only shows changes in segregation due to changed sex composition of the occupations. See next section.

(8) To my knowledge no study, aside from the one included in chapter 5, written by Karen Schober, in Reubens (1979), is available for Germany.

(9) Good reviews of economic approaches to occupational segregation are included in Kahne (1975), Blau and Jusenius (1976), Lloyd and Niemi (1979) and Polochek (1979). For recent evaluations of these hypothesis see Beller (1982), England (1982).

REFERENCES

Beller, A. (1982) "Occupational Segregation by Sex: Determinants and Changes". Journal of Human Resources, Summer.

Blau, F.D. and Hendricks, W.D. (1979) "Occupational Segregation by Sex: Trends and Prospects". Journal of Human Resources, Spring.

Blau, F. & Jusenius, C. "Economists' Approaches to Sex Segregation in the Labour Market: An Appraisal", in Blaxall, M. & Reagan, B. (eds.); Women and the Workplace: The Implications of Occupational Segregation. Chicago, 1976.

Duncan, O.D. and Duncan, B. (1955) "A Methodological Analysis of Segregation Indexes". American Sociological Review 20, April.

Economic Report of the President (1973), Washington: US Printing Office.

England, P. (1982) "The Failure of Human Capital Theory to Explain Occupational Sex Segregation". Journal of Human Resources, Summer.

Fuchs, V. (1975) "A Note on Sex Segregation in Professional Occupations". Explorations in Economic Research 2, Winter.

Gross, E. (1968) "Plus ca Change...? The Sexual Structure of Occupations Over Time". Social Problems 16.

Hakim, C. (1979); Occupational Segregation. Research Paper no. 9. London: Department of Employment.

Kahne, H. "Economic Perspectives on the Roles of Women in the American Economy"; Journal of Economic Literature, Vol. XIII, no. 4, 1975.

Lloyd, C. & Niemi, B. The Economics of Sex Differentials, New York, 1979.

OECD (Organization for Economic Cooperation and Development) (1980); Women and Employment. Paris.

O'Neill, J. and Braun, R. (1981); Women and the Labor Market: A Survey of Issues and Policies in the United States. Washington: The Urban Institute, mimeo.

Oppenheimer, V. (1970); The Female Labor Force in the United States: Demographic and Social Factors Governing Its Growth and Changing Composition. Population Monograph Series, Number 5. Westport, Conn: Greenwood Press.

Petterson, M. (1981) Deltidsarbetet i Sverige, Stockholm: Arbetslivscentrum.

Polachek, S. "Occupational Segregation Among Women: Theory, Evidence and a Prognosis", in: Lloyd, C., Andrews, E. & Gilroy, C. (eds.); Women in the Labour Market. New York, 1979.

Reubens, B.G. (ed.) (1983); Youth at Work: An International Survey. Totowa, N.J.: Allenheld & Osmun (forthcoming).

Roos, P. (1981); Occupational Segregation in Industrial Society: A Twelve-Nation Comparison of Gender and Marital Differences in Occupational Attainment. Doctoral Thesis, UCLA.

SCB (Central Bureau of Statistics), Folk och Bostadsräkningen 1960, 1970 and 1975 (Population and Housing Census 1960, 1970 and 1975). Stockholm.

Stevenson (1975) "Relative Wages and Sex Segregation by Occupation" in: Lloyd, C. (ed.); Sex Discrimination and the Division of Labor. N.Y.: Columbia University Press.

4 EARNINGS DIFFERENTIALS: EMPIRICAL EVIDENCE AND CAUSES

JUNE O'NEILL

1. INTRODUCTION

During the past thirty years women in western industrialized countries have greatly increased their labor force participation. Yet women's earnings are still substantially below those of men. Women's earnings expressed as a per cent of men's earnings are shown in Table 1 for five countries. In 1980 the female-male ratio was roughly around 70 per cent, except in Sweden where it ranged from 72 per cent to 90 per cent, depending on the particular measure of earnings used (1). In four of the countries women's earnings appear to have risen relative to men's over the past two decades; but there has been virtually no increase in the United States. The United States, however, was one of the first countries to adopt equal pay and equal employment legislation.

The seemingly large differential in pay between women and men has been a source of frustration to feminists, many of whom interpret it as evidence of persistent and undiminished discrimination. The differential has also been a puzzle to economists and sociologists who have tried to explain it.

The existence of a pay gap, however, does not in itself prove the existence or extent of discrimination. Women and men may differ in labor market productivity because of cultural differences which affect the acquisition of work experience and work-related skills. This paper first discusses the underlying determinants of earnings and of male-female earnings differences. Empirical studies of the pay gap are then reviewed. Because occupation is also an outcome of human capital investments and may also be a mechanism through which discrimination operates, the determinants of occupation and the relation

Table 1

Women's Earnings as a Percentage of Men's in Several Countries, 1955-1982

	Britain a)	France b)	Germany (Federal Republic) c)	d)	e)	Sweden f)	g)	United States h)	i)
1955	60.5	65.4						63.9	
1960	60.4	64.3	65.4	58.0				60.8	
1965	59.3	64.1	68.1	60.2		74.9		60.0	
1970	59.9	66.7	69.2	61.2		80.0		59.4	67.9
1975	67.8	68.4	72.3	63.6	74.0	84.8		58.8	67.6
1978	72.7	70.6	72.9	64.5	79.8	88.4		60.0	66.9
1980	71.4	72.4	72.3	64.4	81.2	89.8	72.3	60.2	68.7
1981	70.1								70.4
1982	67.8								70.7

a) Average hourly earnings of adult full-time manual workers.
b) Annual earnings of full-time employees in the private, non-agricultural sector.
c) Gross hourly wage rate of industrial workers.
d) Gross monthly income of salaried employees (technical and business administration) in industry and trade.
e) Annual earnings, full-time, year-round workers, 20-64.
f) Hourly wages of workers in manufacturing.
g) Monthly salary for full-time white collar workers in manufacturing and in wholesale and retail trade.
h) Annual earnings of year-round workers who mainly work full-time.
i) Weekly earnings adjusted for hours worked.

Source: Britain (Joshi, Layard and Owen, 1983); France (Riboud, 1983); Germany (Franz, 1983); Sweden (Gustafsson and Jacobsson, 1983); United States (O'Neill, 1983).

between occupation and earnings is also emphasized.

2. DETERMINANTS OF THE EARNINGS GAP

Three broad factors may contribute to differences in wages: human capital investments, non-wage job characteristics and discrimination.

2.1 Human Capital Investments and Productivity

True worker productivity is difficult to observe or to measure. A large volume of theoretical and empirical research has, however, identified many of the characteristics associated with higher pay, and, presumably, higher productivity. Many of these characteristics involve investments in "human capital" which improve the worker's market value.

Human capital theory stresses that individuals make schooling, training and other investment decisions on the basis of their perceptions of the costs of the available options and of the expected benefits associated with each (Becker, 1975; Mincer, 1962). Men and women may evaluate such options differently, however, because of differences in anticipated lifetime work patterns stemming from different roles in the family. Thus, if women expect to assume primary responsibility for child care and home maintenance, they would invest less in market skills and their earnings would be commensurately lower during periods of employment. At the same time, if men are expected to provide the bulk of the family's money income, they would have a strong incentive to invest in market skills, the returns to which would accrue over a long working life resulting in higher earnings for men.

Why is the responsibility for home and children usually assigned to women? One hypothesis is that the division of labor in the home is a response to discrimination in the labor market which reduces women's earnings relative to men's. However, one can point to compelling economic and biological factors that would have led to gender differences in the division of labor in the past. At one time high rates of child mortality and the function children performed of providing economic security to their parents in old age required a large number of births, and the bearing and nursing of infants was time consuming enough to give women the job advantage in home work. These considerations, however, have become less relevant over time. The actual bearing of children when small families are desired no longer need require any considerable time out of the market; and modern contraceptives enable women to plan the number and timing of births. Moreover, technological change in the production of home goods has greatly reduced the time required to do household chores and has also reduced the specialized skills required of the homemaker. (For example, the laundering of wash and wear products requires less skill than the laundering of goods requiring ironing; preparing frozen foods requires less skill than "home cooking.")

The gains to be made from the traditional division of labor in the home have diminished over time with the rise in the market wage, the decline in family size and the continuing availability of low cost substitutes for labor in the home. Although the care of children has shifted somewhat to the market (through earlier school starting ages, more use of group day care arrangements) it is still perhaps an open question whether the desired quality of care

71

can be fully provided in the market. However, it is no longer clear that it is the mother who has the natural advantage in childrearing (2). Changes in the underlying economic and demographic factors point to a convergence of the roles of women and men in the coming decades.

The average woman of today, however, is still more likely to have spent many years out of the labor market attending to home responsibilities; as a result, women have accumulated fewer years of market work experience than men. Data for the United States from the National Longitudinal Survey (NLS) show that, on average, white women age 40 to 49 in 1977 had spent only half of the years since leaving school in the labor market (O'Neill, 1983 b). Women who were employed in 1977 were likely to have had more lifetime work experience than the average woman. Employed white women age 40 to 49 had worked in the market for 61 per cent of the years since leaving school. (For black employed women this statistic was 68 per cent.) Data from other countries do not report the information on lifetime work experience in precisely the same way, but the comparison is of interest. Data for France (Riboud, 1983) suggest that the average French married woman in 1977 had spent 56 per cent of the years since school working in the market; but among employed married women in 1977, the proportion of years worked was considerably higher - 80 per cent. In Sweden, the ratio of employed women's to employed men's years of work experience was 75 per cent in 1981 (Gustafsson and Jacobsson, 1983). If men are in the labor force continuously after leaving school, this ratio would roughly represent the proportion of years worked by women since leaving school.

What effect does women's smaller amount of work experience have on their earnings? The relationship between women's work experience, market investments and earnings has been examined in a series of articles by Mincer and Polachek (1974 and 1978) and Mincer and Ofek (1982). Theoretically, years of work experience are expected to increase earnings in part because a substantial amount of training occurs on the job (Becker, 1975; Mincer, 1962) (3). During the training period wages are expected to be lower to compensate for the employer's monetary investment; after the training period the worker's new skills command a higher wage. Other investments that enhance earnings are also associated with time in the labor force: job search may lead to information about higher paying job opportunities; job experimentation provides the worker and the employer a way to better match the worker's talents and tastes with the job and the firm.

In addition to the number of years in the labor force several other aspects of women's work experiences are relevant for understanding the extent to which women's work experience is converted into higher pay. One factor is that women's employment has been characterized by periods of work alternated with periods of labor force withdrawal. Periods of work interruption are associated with depreciation of those skills that may have been accumulated (Mincer and Polachek, 1974). Using actual longitudinal observations on earnings in the period before a work interruption and earnings after reentry, Mincer and Ofek find a significant decay in earnings associated with career breaks.

Another factor is that women who eventually spend a considerable number of years in the labor market did not anticipate that they would do so. Data from the National Longitudinal Survey (NLS) illustrate the unrealistically low work expectations of women in their developing years. In 1968, only 32 per cent of a panel of women age 20-24 indicated they expected to be in the labor market when they reached age 35; but more than 60 per cent were in fact in the labor force ten years later when the group reached age 30-34 (O'Neill, 1983 a). The work experience of young women, however, appears to be catching up to reality. By 1973 when they were 25-29 years old, 57 per cent of the cohort expressed the intention of working at age 35. More recent cohorts express even higher expectations. Thus, among the group who reached age 25-29 in 1978, 77 per cent responded that they intended to be in the labor market at age 35.

If human capital investments are based on future work expectations, even women who eventually accumulate considerable work experience may have invested little because at younger ages they anticipated they would primarily be homemakers. Expectations have been changing, however. Younger cohorts of women are more likely to anticipate a market career and have also shown signs of an increased rate of human capital investment. Women's enrollment in college has been increasing more rapidly than men's, and women appear to be choosing more vocationally oriented training - medicine, the law, business and engineering.

A third factor that may affect the extent to which women invest on-the-job is that some women may find it advantageous to continue working while their children are young, but at jobs offering less demanding work, flexible schedules or other characteristics compatible with home responsibilities. This is discussed in the next section. Discrimination is another possible reason why women would have less investment in human capital than men since employers may exclude women from opportunities for training that would enhance earnings. This topic is also discussed below.

The way in which women's patterns of work investment, and career interruptions may influence earnings is summarized in Figure 1. Line AB portrays the growth rate of wages for a continuous worker who had always planned to work continuously. A worker who plans an interruption might take a job with initially higher earnings but with a lower training component so that the slope is flatter (CD). After a work interruption (EF) earnings grow rapidly as in (GH). One may note that in a statistical analysis of the effect of experience on earnings where some continuous workers with profiles like AB are mixed with large numbers of workers with interrupted profiles like CDEFGHI, the effect of experience variables on earnings will not be fully comparable to that estimated in an equation for men who are virtually all continuous workers. The slope coefficient of experience for men will always be derived from an equation where increases in age and experience coincide, while the experience coefficient for women will be derived from an equation where age and experience interact in diverse ways depending on the pattern of interruptions.

Perhaps a better comparison of men's and women's earnings would restrict the analysis only to those women with continuous participation. However, there are two reasons why such a comparison may not fully adjust for differences in earnings growth based on differences in voluntary investment. As noted, one reason is that some women who work continuously did not plan to do so initially. Thus, some women may expect to spend some time out and start along a career path such as CDP, but with a change in marriage plans or other plans remain in the labor force. Although investment activities may increase at point P when expectations are adjusted, and follow the path PQ, it may be too late to ever attain the earnings of the planned continuous worker, AB. The second reason is that women who are balancing home and career may choose jobs with less of an investment component. In this case earnings may follow a

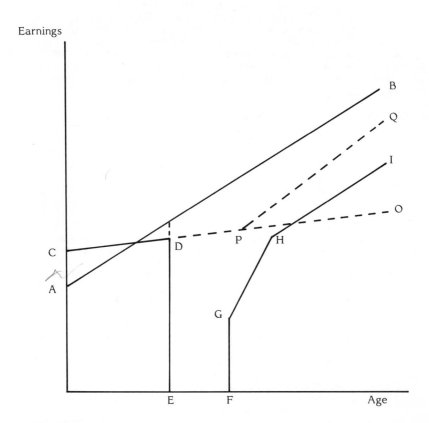

Earnings

Age

Figure 1

74

course such as CDPO. As will be shown below, however, less investment by women may in part be the result of labor market discrimination - a factor which further complicates the analysis.

2.2   Tastes, Home Responsibilities and Job Characteristics

Many women continue to be responsible for a disproportionate share of household maintenance and child care even after they enter employment. Data from U.S. time budget studies show that in 1975-76 married women holding full-time jobs spent about 25 hours a week on household work whereas married men spent 13 hours a week on home tasks. Married women working part-time spent 33 hours a week in home-related chors and full-time homemakers averaged 41 hours a week (Hill, 1981). For this reason women may also evaluate certain job characteristics differently than men and this could have implications for their occupational choices as well as for their earnings (4). For example, some women may place a premium on a job with a workday and calendar year corresponding to the time children are in school or on flexible hours in more informal work settings. A shorter work day may make a long trip to work a poor investment; women working part time may therefore place a premium on work located closer to home. In addition, the burden of household responsibilities may deter women from taking jobs requiring a considerable commitment of responsibility. In a study of the determinants of the male-female earnings differential in the Sovjet Union (based on a sample of Soviet emigrees), Ofer and Vinokur (1981) concluded that it was the extremely uneven division of household work between husbands and wives that led Soviet wives into relatively undemanding and lower paying occupations, even though their labor force participation appears to be almost as high as that of men.

Tastes and physical and personality characteristics may also differ between men and women and create differences in occupational choice and possibly in earnings. An extensive psychological and physiological literature has explored sex differences in behavior manifested in childhood arising from a combination of genetic endowment and social conditioning. In a review of studies (mostly of children) in the psychological literature, Maccoby and Jacklin (1974) found support for greater visual-spatial and mathematical abilities, energy expenditure, and agressive behavior among boys, and for greater verbal ability among girls. Evidence is also found for parental encouragement of sex-typed activities and behavior, ranging from choice of dolls and play activities to occupational aspirations. And sex-typed vocational aspirations have been found frequently among children (Papalia and Tennent, 1975; Scheresky, 1976; Hewitt, 1975).

These differences have been reflected later on - during high school and college - by significant differences in the choice of subject matter (5). Physical differences (e.g. in weight and height) between men and women are likely to have been more important in influencing occupational differences in the past than they are today because of the lesser importance of manual labor in the economy.

What effect would differences in tastes and responsibilities have on earnings and the pay gap? Differences in tastes related to job characteristics would influence wages if workers on balance found particular job characteristics to be desirable or undesirable and if employer costs would rise to provide a desirable work situation or to remedy an undesirable one. Some studies have attempted to estimate the magnitude of any "compensating wage differential" for such characteristics but with mixed results. Thaler and Rosen (1975) found evidence of a premium paid for hazardous work. O'Neill found that among blue collar occupations those requiring lifting, outdoor work or noisy conditions tended to pay more, other things the same, but the results were not as consistent as one might wish (O'Neill, 1983 a). This study did find, however, that men were much more likely to be in jobs with these characteristics than women.

The payoff to effort, motivation or responsibility has proven difficult to measure, although one expects these factors to be important.

2.3   Discrimination and Labor Market Barriers

Discrimination against women can lead to lower pay for women and higher pay for men even if men and women had identical productivity. The theory of labor market discrimination developed by Gary Becker (1957) demonstrates that discrimination may arise even in competitive markets if employers are so strongly prejudiced against a group that they would employ them only at a discount equivalent to the employer's "taste for discrimination" - the employer's disutility or psychic cost from employing the worker at all, or in a particular capacity.

Discrimination is not costless to the employer, however. If the group that is being discriminated against - suppose it is women - is equal in productivity to the preferred group - suppose it is men - an employer would increase the firm's money profits by hiring more women, since women would have a lower wage rate. The "taste for discrimination" would therefore have to be strong for employers to continue indulging their prejudices. If more and more nondiscriminating employers were to enter the market, the wage of women would eventually be bid up and the gap due to discrimination would close. It is perhaps because market forces do tend to erode discrimination that societies have sought to institutionalize discrimination against particular groups through legislation. For example, at one time in the United States, state laws restricted the economic and social mobility of Blacks, and kept women from working long hours, lifting heavy weights on the job, or pursuing occupations designated as hazardous. Thus, unprejudiced employers were prevented from freely employing Blacks and women.

In Becker's model, co-workers and customers may also be the source of discrimination, even if employers themselves have no prejudices. If male workers demand a premium to work with women, however, unprejudiced employers would have an incentive to run segregated establishments since integration would be more expensive (6). In this case the wages of women and men with the same productivity would tend to be equalized, though they would work in different establishments. Consumer prejudice could lead to discriminatory pay differentials if consumers, for example, were willing to pay a premium for a male doctor, lawyer, automobile salesperson. Again, if women and men were equally productive in these tasks, consumers would have an incentive to switch to a woman, thereby increasing the demand and the pay of females in these jobs.

Although Becker's theory allows for discrimination in competitive markets   it also suggests that competition would tend to reduce discrimination in the long run. To explain the persistance of a wage gap, some authors have developed the idea of statistical discrimination where employers may not be prejudiced, but treat individual women as having the average characteristics of all women (Phelps, 1972; Arrow, 1973). Thus, if women on average are believed to have lower productivity than men, employers might deny opportunities to individual women who are potentially more skilled than the average (and presumably the reverse for those less skilled). The implicit assumption is that the cost of obtaining information about individuals would exceed the gain from better matching workers to jobs. Aigner and Cain (1977) question the empirical validity of this assumption. They also point out that if the employer's assessment of average female productivity is correct, then employers are not discriminating in an economic sense if they pay women less as a group. Moreover, if employers have mistakenly underestimated the average women's productivity, competition would favor those employers who did not make the mistake and eventually eliminate the practice.

The acquisition of skills is to some extent under the control of employers who offer on-the-job training. Arrow (1973, 1976), Blau (1977, 1983) and others have developed a theory of feedback discrimination, where employers, by denying women training, insure that women will in fact exhibit the characteristics that they believed women to have. Thus, if women are restricted to low-level jobs they will have high turnover, confirming the employer's prejudice. While this feedback or "vicious circle" theory could explain why competitive forces might take longer to erode discrimination it does not really explain how discrimination could be perpetuated indefinitely. If women did not in fact differ from men in work expectations, motivation and stability, employers who trained women would gain at the expense of discriminating employers, and again competition would eventually raise women's pay to the level of men's.

Theoretical arguments suggest, therefore, that in basically competitive markets, forces are at work to erode discrimination. The extent to which this occurs depends, however, on how widespread is the "taste for discrimination." It also depends on the strength of noncompetitive forces. Monopolies could use their monopoly profits to pay for discriminating tastes. Monopsony - the case of a single dominant employer in the labor market - is not considered to be empirically important in modern times. Discrimination can be enforced through legalized or institutionalized barriers to entry into particular occupations. As noted, overt barriers restricting women's choices were evident in the past, but have largely been eliminated. Thus, the economic theory of discrimination provides a reason why discrimination might persist for a while, but it also provides reasons for optimism about the eventual erosion of discrimination, once legalized or institutionalized discrimination is eliminated. The length of the transition is, however, an empirical question.

3.   EMPIRICAL EVIDENCE ON THE WAGE GAP

A growing body of literature has investigated the extent to which differences in human capital investments and other characteristics can account for the earnings gap. Table 2 summarizes the results of several econometric studies. Although most refer to the United States, studies of the wage gap in Sweden and the Soviet Union are also included.

Table 2
Summary of Recent Research Findings on the Male-Female Earnings Gap

Author	Population and Data Source (1)	Chief Explanatory Variables		Unadjusted Wage Gap (2)	Adjusted Wage Gap (3)	Percentage Reduction in the Gap (4)
Astin and Bayer (1972)	College and university teaching faculty, 1969, U.S. (Carnegie-ACE)	Rank, institutional type, degree, research output, field		.22	.13	41
Blinder (1973)	Employed, white men and women, 25 years and over, 1969 U.S., (PSID)	Age, education, parental income and education, health, local labor market conditions, siblings, migration		.46	.46	0
M.Corcoran and Duncan (1979)	Married men and not their wives, 1975, U.S. (PSID)	Work history, labor force attachment, education, city size, region	White women: White men	.36	.22	39
			Black women: White men	.43	.32	26
Fuchs (1971)	1960 Census, U.S. (1/1000 sample) nonfarm persons	Age, race, education, marital status, city size, class of worker, length of trip to work		.40	.34	15
Gustafsson (1979)	White collar workers, private sector, Sweden, 1974	Schooling, work history, age		.33	.20	39
Gustafsson and Jacobsson (1983)	Panel of men and women, "Level of living investigation," Sweden:	Schooling, work history				
	1968	Same		.28	.25	11
	1974	Plus government		.25	.21	16
	1981	Plus government		.17	.15	12

73

Table 2 (continued)
Summary of Recent Research Findings on the Male-Female Earnings Gap

Author	Population and Data Source	Chief Explanatory Variables	Unadjusted Wage Gap (2)	Adjusted Wage Gap (3)	Percentage Reduction in the Gap (4)
Johnson and Stafford (1973)	Ph.D.s in six fields by sector, 1970 (U.S.) (NSF)	Years since receipt of doctorate, field, sector, degree	By Years since Ph.D. 0 yrs. .07 10 yrs. .15 20 yrs. .20 30 yrs. .51	.07 .07 .07 .07	0 53 65 86
Malkiel and Malkiel (1973)	272 professional employees of a single corporation, 1971, U.S.	Education, work experience, degree, research output, absences; with and without job level	.35 with job level	.12 .01	66 97
Mincer and Polachek (1974)	White married and single women 30-44; white married men, 30-44, 1967, U.S. (NLS, SEO)	Schooling, years of experience since completion of school, current job tenure	White, married:.34 White, single: .14	.22 .13	35 7
Oaxaca (1973)	Urban whites and blacks, 16 and over, 1967, U.S. (SEO)	Age, education, health, hours, migration, marital status, children, size of urban area, region, with and without occupation and industry	White: .35 with industry and occupation Black: .33 with industry and occupation	.28 .24 .32 .22	20 31 3 33

Table 2 (continued)

Summary of Recent Research Findings on the Male-Female Earnings Gap

Author	Population and Data Source (1)	Chief Explanatory Variables	Unadjusted Wage Gap (2)	Adjusted Wage Gap (3)	Percentage Reduction in the Gap (4)
Ofer and Vinokur (1979)	1016 Soviet emigrant families, based on last year in Soviet Union, urban European sectors, 1972-74	Hours, education, work experience, age, broad occupation and industry	.36	.26	28
	-- university grads		.30	.16	47
	-- secondary professional		.38	.20	47
	-- general schooling or less		.36	.28	22
O'Neill (1983a)	Women and men age 24-34 in 1976-78, U.S. (NLS)	Education, work history job characteristics, major industry (also percent female in worker's occupation)	White: .34	.20	41
			--with percent female	.12	65
			Black: .18	.16	11
			-- with percent female	.09	50
Sawhill (1973)	Wage and salary workers, U.S., 1966	Race, education, age, hours per week, weeks worked per year	.54	.44	19
Strober and Reagan (1977)	Sample of 580 economists, 1974-75, U.S.	Experience, research output, institutional characteristics, quality of grad school, age at whether in administrative work	Academic:.19	.10	47
			All .16	.08	50

(1) Abbreviations for data sources are: National Longitudinal Survey (NLS), Carnegie Commission on Higher Education-American Council on Education (Carnegie-ACE), Survey of Economic Opportunity (SEO), Panel Study of Income Dynamics (PSID), National Science Foundation Register (NSF), Current Population Survey (CPS).

(2) Unadjusted wage gap = $\dfrac{M - F}{M}$, where F = observed female wage, M = observed male wage.

(3) Adjusted wage gap = $\dfrac{(M - F)^*}{M}$, where $(M - F)^*$ is the wage differential adjusted for male-female differences in characteristics. Where the adjustment is derived from separate wage equations for men and women, the female coefficients are used. See note below for definition of wage.

(4) [(Unadjusted wage gap - Adjusted Wage gap) ./. Unadjusted wage gap] x 100.

Note: The wage is expressed as hourly earnings except for: Astin and Bayer, institutional salary controlling for months of work; Johnson and Stafford, 9-month salary; Malkiel and Malkiel, annual salary for full-time workers; Ofer and Vinokur, monthly earnings; Sawhill, annual earnings; Strober and Reagan, annual income including salary, consulting fees, royalties, etc.

The studies reviewed use different data sources, refer to different populations and control for many, but not always the same set of variables. The unadjusted or gross earnings gap - defined as the difference between men's and women's earnings expressed as a percentage of men's earnings (before adjusting for skill and other factors) - also varies from study to study, ranging from 5 to 54 per cent, depending on the type of population considered as well as on the measure of earnings used. Studies based on national samples of the entire working population most often show an unadjusted hourly wage gap of about 35 per cent. The smaller gross wage gap in Sweden and between black men and women in the U.S. are notable exceptions. The gross wage gap is larger in the Sawhill study because it used total annual earnings which were not standardized for hours or weeks worked during the year. Studies based on more homogeneous populations selected on a basis which narrows the skill range tend to start out with smaller gaps even before adjustment. Thus, the unadjusted differential is smaller among college faculty (Astin and Bayer), economists (Strober and Reagan), and persons with recent doctorates (Johnson and Stafford).

After accounting for the effects of male and female differences in the various explanatory variables, the earnings gap generally narrows. The percentage reduction in the gap as a result of these adjustment ranges from about 15 to 65 per cent, although there are a few extremes - Blinder explains virtually nothing and Malkiel and Malkiel almost everything. The factors accounting for the effects are reviewed below.

3.1   Work Experience

Sex differences in work experience have been found to contribute significantly to the wage gap. However, those studies that do not have an observed measure of women's work experience and try to infer it by estimates of potential experience (for example, by using age or age of school leaving subtracted from current age) find little or no effect of "work experience" on the wage differential (Blinder, 1973; Oaxaca, 1973; Fuchs, 1971). But this method of accounting for work experience guarantees the outcome because in most countries women's actual work experience falls short of potential experience. The wage gap is reduced substantially in those studies in which longitudinal or retrospective information was used to determine actual years of labor market experience, the pattern and length of career breaks and current job tenure (Mincer and Polachek, 1974, 1978; Corcoran and Duncan, 1979; O'Neill, 1983 a; Strober and Reagan; Gustafsson, 1979).

Some studies (Mincer and Polachek, 1974, 1978; O'Neill, 1983 a; Ofer and Vinokur, 1979) also find that the wage gap would be further reduced if account were taken of differences in the effect of work experience on wages - the coefficients of the work experience variables in wage equations (7). In these studies men's earnings rise more rapidly per year of experience than women's suggesting that women invest less intensively in on-the-job training, job search, and other investments. It has been argued, however, that such differences in investment rates are measures of labor market discrimination, not of voluntary investment decisions (Blinder, 1973; Gronau, 1982). Thus, employers may deny women entry into training programs or fail to promote them to higher levels of supervisory responsibility. If women were restricted to jobs where advancement is unlikely, the observed lower investment would be a form of discrimination.

It is difficult to prove or disprove whether lower investment rates reflect discrimination or voluntary decisions. Some circumstantial evidence suggests that women who are likely to have a stronger motivation to work do invest more. Thus, investment rates vary at different stages of the life cycle in ways that are compatible with changes in home responsibilities. Investment rates are lower at ages corresponding to childbearing years or years when children are young, but investment rates are high for married women after a return to the labor force (Mincer and Polachek, 1974; Mincer and Ofek, 1980; O'Neill, 1983 a). Those who return to the labor force when they are more mature are more likely planning a sustained period of work and invest accordingly, whereas plans are likely to have been more uncertain in early years. Stronger work motivation may also be expected among those who have already made extensive investments in work-related schooling and other training. Thus, higher work experience coefficients have been found for college educated women than for those with 12 years or less of schooling (O'Neill, 1983 a; Mincer and Polachek, 1974). More direct evidence on the relation between work motivation and investment rates has been found by Sandell and Shapiro (1980) who show that women who planned to work at a younger age had steeper wage-experience profiles later on.

3.2   Schooling

Although the overall level of schooling does not differ significantly between women and men, most of the studies reviewed did find that the distribution of schooling differed by sex. A common pattern found is that women are less likely than men to leave school before completing high school, but are also less likely to complete college and university training. Thus women are more concentrated at the high school graduate level. However, several studies have found that women obtain a higher rate of return to college and university training than men, while men obtain a higher return to schooling than women at levels below college (Smith, 1977; Ofer and Vinokur, 1979; O'Neill, 1983). It is likely, however, that these are not true return to education per se but also reflect selectivity factors for women. Women who expect careers are more likely to attend college (8). So a higher education variable in an earnings function for women is likely to be capturing motivation to some extent (9). At education levels below high school, selection factors could be operating as well if only high ability women with low levels of education participated in the labor force. The high returns to women that have been found to accrue in job training programs have long been recognized as contaminated by selectivity bias (see, for example, Kiefer, 1979; Bassi, 1982). Differences in field of study in school may also be important although the data needed to establish this are not commonly available. One study did find that women majoring in science at the college or university level received considerably higher earnings than other women (O'Neill, 1983 a).

3.3   Occupation and Non-Wage Characteristics

There is ample documentation of the extreme differences in the occupational distributions of men and women in many countries. To what extent do these differences actually affect earnings? Since occupation is an outcome measure like earnings it is expected that many of the factors determining earnings will also influence occupation, such as the quantity and quality of schooling and training. However, some studies have found that even after controlling for the effect of human capital variables, occupation or job level appears to have an independent effect on earnings and that sex differences in occupation can account for an additional component of the wage gap (Malkiel and Malkiel, 1973; Oaxaca, 1973; Ofer and Vinokur, 1979; O'Neill, 1983 a).

The meaning of an occupational adjustment is open to question. Such an adjustment may be regarded with suspicion if occupational assignments are a mechanism for discrimination. However, as noted, there is also good reason to suppose that women would choose different occupations than men because of differences in the priority placed on earning an income versus home responsibilities. In addition women and men may evaluate job characteristics differently because of differences in culturally determined attitudes and in physical ability for performing certain tasks.

It is difficult to obtain quantitative measures of discriminatory barriers to entry into occupations or of the nonwage characteristics of jobs and the attitudes of individuals. Some data on attitudes are available from the National Longitudinal Survey which has questioned the same panel of women about their occupational and work expectations at different points in time. The effect of prior expectations on eventual outcomes can therefore be examined. Analysis of the NLS data suggests that there is a strong element of personal choice in the occupations held by women (O'Neill, 1983 a). A strong positive relation was found between those reporting they wished to be a homemaker at age 35 and those actually holding a more typically female job five years later. (The women were at ages 19 to 29 years at the time of the question). Moreover, those who planned to be working at age 35 and indicated a preference for a typically male occupation were in fact more likely to be in male occupations later on, while those indicating a preference for typicyally female work were much more likely to enter such occupations.

The relation between actual (as opposed to expected) work experience was more complex. Analysis of the NLS data showed that married women who worked more continuously were more likely to be in female occupations. One explanation for this relation is that female occupations are characterized by features that make it easier to combine home responsibilities and work. Consistent with this explanation is the observation that work experience was only positively related to being in a typically female occupation for married women, not for nonmarried women.

Data also show that predominantly female occupations are much more likely to offer part-time work and less likely to require a work week of excessively long hours. Direct measures of stressful work, job responsibility or the actual effort and motivation of individuals are understandably more difficult to obtain and do not seem to have been incorporated into any studies of occupational choice or the wage gap.

Evidence on environmental job characteristics shows that predominantly female occupations are less likely to have characteristics that would more commonly be considered a disutility - exposure to hazardous work, heavy lifting, excessive noise and outdoor work. These characteristics, however, were found to be only weakly related to earnings, and, therefore, contributed only a small share to the measured wage gap. Because of the inherent difficulties of measuring nonwage job characteristics, these results were not regarded as conclusive (10).

In sum, women and men may evaluate job characteristics differently because of differences in their roles in the home. Characteristics related to the full time and energy demands of jobs have been difficult to quantify. Thus, a variable denoting occupation or job level may serve as a proxy for these intangible characteristics. Although there is some evidence that women choose occupations, a role for discriminatory behavior of employers cannot be ruled out. If women's access to certain occupations was restricted because of discriminatory hiring and promotion policies, women's choices would likely be affected. It is difficult, however, to see how barriers that depend on elusive employer prejudices can be maintained for long when employers would have a real pecuniary gain from accepting women and women would have a real gain from entering the occupation. Borrowing from U.S. history one can in fact find several examples of job categories that changed sex over time. At one time secretary, bookkeeper and telephone operator were "male jobs". High school teaching appears to have been switching from a male to a female job. Numerous occupations have gone from predominantly male to mixed: accountant, real estate broker, and more recently lawyer, judging from law school enrollments. In the Soviet Union medical doctor has become a predominantly female occupation (11).

4.   CONCLUDING COMMENTS

A large share of the gross earnings gap between men and women stems from differences in lifetime labor market experience, both in terms of the sheer amount of hours and weeks spent in the labor force and in the amount of planned investment made in acquiring labor market skills and information. Even after controlling for these and other measurable characteristics that affect earnings, an unexplained residual remains of about 10 to 25 per cent. As Mincer has noted (1979), the residual should be viewed "as a measure of our ignorance".

Identifying the villain in this gray area is difficult to do with available data and the usual tools of the economist. Some or all of the unexplained differential may be attributable to discriminatory treatment of women in the labor market. Moreover, some of the explained portion, such as labor market experience, may also be attributed to discrimination if women's work incentives have been affected. On the other hand, women, on average, may not view labor market activities the same way as men if they retain primary responsibility for maintaining the home and child rearing. Thus in a study of the wage gap in a single firm, Malkiel and Malkiel (1973), found that a variable denoting job level could explain virtually all of the remaining 12 per cent difference in pay between women and men (after accounting for a wide array of human capital variables). But it could not be determined whether women voluntarily chose jobs with fewer demands or were barred from jobs with greater responsibility.

The uncertain results of the studies leave an uncertain role for policy. Overt discrimination in pay and promotion is susceptible to change through legislation. Women who believe they have been unfairly treated do have legal recourse in many countries. Barriers to advancement that operate in a more elusive way - for example, through harassment or through exclusion from informal interaction - are more difficult to remedy through legislation. Efforts by government to monitor all hiring and promotion would impose intrusions that free societies would have difficulty accepting. However, as discussed, competition in the economy imposes financial costs on prejudiced employers, so that there are self-correcting mechanisms at work.

Some signs of change have been observed in the past decade with respect to women's earnings prospects. Women have been increasing their schooling at the college and university level and have been marrying later and working longer. The wage gap has perceptibly declined in Sweden and appears to be narrowing in Britain, France, West Germany, and among persons under the age of 35 in the United States. There is also evidence in the United States of an increase in the rate of return women receive from work experience, suggesting that a narrowing in the wage gap should occur over the next decade.

NOTES

(1) It should be noted that earnings are not measured in the same way in each country and in some cases more than one measure is given for a country. Unfortunately, the ratio of women's to men's earnings differs depending on the measure used and also on the particular subgroup of workers used. So caution must be observed in drawing comparisons.

(2) Fuchs (1983) suggests that mothers have stronger feelings for their children than fathers. But this may simply be the consequence of mothers having spent more time with their children rather than a genetic difference.

(3) Earnings may also increase with job tenure because of institutional arrangements - or contracts between employer and employee - made within the firm.

(4) For an analysis of the allocation of energy among activities, the sexual division of labor and implications for the sex difference in earnings see Becker (1983).

(5) Although women have been greatly increasing their representation in non-traditional college subjects such as business, engineering and law they are still disproportionately overrepresented in education, English and nursing. At the high school level, women are overrepresented in vocational courses such as secretarial subjects and home economics while men specialize in trade and industrial arts. There is less sign of change at the high school level (O'Neill and Braun, 1981).

(6) In practice, however, this could be difficult to implement if women are a small component of the relevant labor market. For example, the formation of all-female construction crews would be difficult to implement if only few women were willing and able to perform the necessary construction crafts and jobs.

(7) The results shown in Table 2 are given only for an adjustment which accounts for the difference in years of experience (and other measurable characteristics) and not for the difference in coefficients. In other words, the estimates show what women's wage rates would be if they had men's characteristics but obtained the female increment in pay for a given change in the characteristic.

(8) The National Longitudinal Survey young women's panel shows that among employed women 24 to 34 years of age in 1978, 50 per cent of those with 12 years of schooling or less five years earlier had indicated that they expected to be a homemaker at age 35; the figure was only 27 per cent for college graduates.

(9) Among women who are not married (compared to married women), education coefficients are considerably higher in the range up through high school and much closer to the coefficient for college graduates (O'Neill, 1983). Since most nonmarried women are in the labor force, selectivity factors would be less important for them.

(10) In this study (O'Neill, 1983a) job disutilities were measured by the U.S. Department of Labor's ratings of an individual's 3-digit occupation, which only imperfectly measures the actual work situation the individual confronts. Hence, one would not expect very strong results.

(11) Ofer and Vinokur note that medicine is public in the Soviet Union and that the burdens of the job are considerably lower there than in the West. They suggest that the medical profession was adapted to the needs of Soviet women and the pay reduced accordingly.

REFERENCES

Aigner, Dennis J. and Glen C. Cain. 1977. "Statistical Theories of Discrimination in Labor Markets", Industrial and Labor Relations Review, Vol. 30, No. 2 (January).

Astin, Helen S. and Alan E. Bayer. 1972. "Sex Discrimination in Academe", Educational Record, Spring.

Arrow, Kenneth J. 1973. "The Theory of Discrimination", in Orley Ashenfelter and Albert Rees, eds., Discrimination in Labor Markets. Princeton University Press, Princeton, N.J.

Arrow, Kenneth J. 1976. "Economic Dimensions of Occupational Segregation: Comment" Signs, 1, 3, Part 2 (Spring).

Bassi, Lauri J. "Estimating the Effect of Training Programs With Non-Random Selection", Review of Economics and Statistics, forthcoming.

Becker, Gary S. 1957. The Economics of Discrimination, Chicago: University of Chicago Press.

Becker, Gary S. 1975. Human Capital, New York: Columbia University Press.

Bergmann, B. 1974. "Occupational Segregation, Wages and Profits when Employers Discriminate by Race or Sex", Eastern Economic Journal, Vol. 1, April/July.

Blau, Francine D. 1977. Equal Pay in the Office, Lexington, Mass.: D.C. Heath and Co.

Blau, Francine D. 1983. "Discrimination Against Women: Theory and Evidence", forthcoming in William A. Davitz, Jr., Labor Economics: Modern Views, Boston: Martinus Nijhoff.

Blinder, Alan. 1973. "Wage Discrimination: Reduced Form and Structural Estimates", Journal of Human Resources, Vol. 8.

Corcoran, M. and G.J. Duncan. 1979. "Work History, Labor Force Attachment, and Earnings Differences Between the Races and Sexes", Journal of Human Resources, Vol. 14, Winter.

Franz, Wolfgang. 1983. "An Economic Analysis of Female Work Participation, Education, and Fertility: Theory and Empirical Evidence for the Federal Republic of Germany", paper presented at Conference on Trends in Women's Work, Education and Family Building, The White House Conference Center, Chelwood Gate, Sussex, England, June, 1983.

Fuchs, Victor. 1971. "Differences in Hourly Earnings Between Men and Women", Monthly Labor Review, May.

Fuchs, Victor. 1974. "Recent Trends and Long-Range Prospects for Female Earnings", American Economic Review 64.

Fuchs, Victor. 1983. How We Live, Cambridge, Massachusetts: Harvard University Press.

Gregory, R.G. and P. McMahan and B. Whittingham, Women in the Labor Force: Trends, Causes and Consequences in Australia, paper presented at Conference on Trends in Women's Work, Education and Family Building, The White House Conference Center, Chelwood Gate, Sussex, England, June, 1983.

Gustafsson, Siv. 1981. "Male-Female Lifetime Earnings Differentials and Labor Force History" in Eliasson, Holmwood, Stafford, Studies in Labor Market Behavior in Sweden and the United States, IUI, Stockholm.

Gustafsson, Siv, and Roger Jacobsson. 1983. Trends in Women's Work, Family Formation and Earnings in Sweden, paper presented at the Conference on Trends in Women's Work, Education and Family Building, The White House Conference Center, Chelwood Gate, Sussex, England, June, 1983.

Hewitt, L.S. 1975. "Age and Sex Differences in the Vocational Aspirations of Elementary School Children", The Journal of Social Psychology 96.

Hill, Martha S. 1981. Patterns of Time Use, Survey Research Center, University of Michigan (mimeograph).

Joshi, Heather and Richard Layard and Susan Owen. 1983. Why Are More Women Working in Britain? paper presented at Conference on Women's Work, Education and Family Building, The White House Conference Center, Chelwood Gate, Sussex, England, June, 1983.

Kiefer, Micholas M. 1979. "Training Programs and the Employment and Earnings of Black Women". in Cynthia B. Lloyd, Emily S. Andrews, and Curtis L. Gilroy (eds.), Women in the Labor Market, New York: Columbia University Press, 1979.

Leibowitz, A. 1974. "Home Investments in Children", Journal of Political Economy 82 (2/2).

Leibowitz, A. 1977. "Potential Inputs and Children's Achievement", Journal of Human Resources 12(2): 242-49.

Maccoby, E. E. and C. M. Jacklin. 1974. The Psychology of Sex Differences, Stanford University Press.

Masters, J.C. and A. Wilkinson. 1976. "Consensual and Discriminative Stereotype of Sex-Type Judgments by Parents and Children", Child Development, 47.

Papalia, D.E. and S. Tennent. 1975. "Vocational Aspirations in Preschoolers, A Manifestation of Early Sex Role Stereotyping", Sex Roles, Vol. 1, No. 2.

Phelps, Edmunds. 1972. "The Statistical Theory of Racism and Sexism", American Economic Review, Vol. 62, 4, September.

Riboud, Michelle. 1983. Women in the Labor Force in France: Trends, Causes and Consequences, paper presented at Conference on Women's Work, Education and Family Building, The White House Conference Center, Chelwood Gate, Sussex, England, June, 1983.

Sandell, S.H. and D. Shapiro, "Work Expectations, Human Capital Accumulation, and the Wages of Young Women", Journal of Human Resources, Summer 1980.

Scheresky, R. 1976. "The Gender Factor in Six to Ten Year Old Children's Views of Occupational Roles", Psychological Reports 38.

Smith, James P. 1979. "The Convergence to Racial Equality in Women's Wages", in Cynthia B. Lloyd, Emily S. Andrews, and Curtis L. Gilroy (eds.), Women in the Labor Market, New York: Columbia University Press.

Thaler, R., and S. Rosen. 1975. "The Value of Saving a Life: Evidence from the Labor Market", in N.E. Terleckyj (ed.), Household Production and Consumption, 1975.

5 EQUAL OPPORTUNITY AND THE LAW IN THE UNITED STATES

RACHEL EISENBERG BRAUN

1.   INTRODUCTION*

Many of the economic gains made by American women since World War II have come about with the encouragement and statutory protection of federal and state governments. In this chapter I will describe the formal legal structure supporting American women in the fight for economic equality. Recent changes introduced by the Reagan Administration will be discussed, and controversial issues surrounding equal opportunity legislation will be considered.

The Constitution of the United States did not always guarantee equal rights to women. At the end of the Civil War, two amendments to the Constitution specifically abolished slavery and extended voting rights to blacks. A third, the Fourteenth Amendment (1868), provided that "No State shall make or enforce any law which shall abridge the privileges or immunities of citizens of the United States; nor shall any State deprive any person of life, liberty, or property, without due process of law; nor deny to any person within its jurisdiction the equal protection of the laws." These amendments were construed as providing full equality for men, but not, however, for women.

An additional amendment was required to ensure women the right to vote, and it was not adopted until 1920. Moreover, "equal protection of the law" did not apply to women's economic rights. States could still deny women a license to pursue particular occupations such as law, or could establish so-called "protective legislation" which limited hours women could work and barred women from jobs where heavy lifting and other such conditions prevailed.   Although much of this legislation may have been well intended, it eventually served to keep women out of a range of occupations and firms.

2. LEGISLATIVE LANDMARKS

Since 1963, the United States government has been committed to eliminating sex discrimination in employment, housing, credit and education with the enactment of various anti-discrimination laws. Those aimed at ensuring equality in employment and pay, backed by the regulatory authority of enforcement agencies, have brought change as well as controversy. In this section I will briefly review the history of equal employment opportunity legislation and litigation in the U.S. (1).

2.1 The Equal Pay Act

The Equal Pay Act (EPA) of 1963 (2) prohibits sex discrimination in salaries and covers state, local, federal government and private sector employees. Unlike subsequent provisions, EPA is concerned solely with compensation. It requires that men and women employed in the same establishment receive equal pay for equal work, that is, for jobs that are substantially (not identically) equal in skill, effort, responsibility and working conditions. Wage differentials based on the factors of (1) seniority (2) merit (3) quantity or quality of production of (4) any other factor other than sex are permitted. The Act also provides that employers may not reduce the wages of any employee in order to comply with its provisions.

While the EPA has been used effectively to remedy wage inequalities within an establishment and to award back pay to aggrieved employees, it can not be used to raise the wages of women who work in predominantly female occupations or in establishments which employ too few men for comparison. It was not the legislative intent of the Congress to provide equal pay for "comparable" work, rather than for equal work as stated in the Act (3). Hence, the legal interpretation of the EPA has involved determining what "equal work" is.

In Schultz vs. Wheatson Glass Co. (Third Circuit Court, 1970), the court ruled that male and female packer-inspectors worked at "substantially equal" jobs although the male employees performed additional insignificant tasks, and that the ten percent pay differential between them was in violation of the EPA. Similarly, in Brennan vs. Owensboro-Davies City Hospital (Sixth Circuit, 1975) the court ruled that the female nurses' aides and the male orderlies had substantially equal duties because the extra tasks assigned orderlies, such as setting up traction and assisting in removing casts, were performed too infrequently to justify the existing wage differential.

Under the Equal Pay Act, employers cannot justify pay differences on the basis of job descriptions or classifications, but only on the basis of actual work done. Hence, an employer may not inflate male wages relative to female wages by requiring the men to have additional education if it is not, in fact, related to job performance. Also, women are not be paid less based on an employer's argument that they will work for less than men.

2.2 Title VII of the Civil Rights Act of 1964

Section 703(a) of Title VII of the Civil Rights Act of 1964 (4) forbids employers

> "(1) to fail or refuse to hire or to discharge any individual, or otherwise to discriminate against any individual with respect to his compensation, terms, conditions, or privileges of employment, because of such individual's race, color, religion, sex, or national origin; or
>
> (2) to limit, segregate, or classify his employees or applicants for employment in any way which would deprive or tend to deprive any individual of employment opportunities or otherwise adversely affect his status as an employee, because of such individual' race, color, religion, sex or national origin."

Title VII is the most far-ranging and comprehensive federal law prohibiting discrimination, covering all aspects of employment such as firing, hiring, compensation, terms, conditions, privileges of employment, training, retraining and apprenticeship. As amended in 1972, Title VII applies to employees in federal, state and local governments, in educational institutions, and in establishments with fifteen or more full-time workers, including labor unions and employment agencies. Those exempt from coverage include elected officials and their staffs, certain appointed government officials, employees of bona fide private membership clubs (except labor unions), religious institutions, Indian tribes and government-owned corporations. Employers may use sex, religion or national origin - not race - as a bona fide occupational qualification (BFOQ) if it is reasonably necessary to the normal operation of the enterprise. In their interpretation of Title VII, the courts have allowed sex as a BFOQ in very limited circumstances, as in the employment of actors and actresses, lingerie fitters and restroom attendants who are present when the restroom is in use.

2.3 Executive Orders 11246 and 11375

Executive Order 11246 (5), issued in 1965, is a presidential order requiring that federal contractors not discriminate in all aspects of employment on the basis of race, color, religion and national origin. Three years later, it was amended by Executive Order 11375 (6) to include discrimination on the basis of sex. It is unique in that it sanctions federal fund cutoff if a violation is found and in that it requires contractors to have an "affirmative action" program that actively recruits and promotes women and minorities.

2.4 Title IX of the Education Amendments of 1972

Title IX (7) is an important piece of legislation bearing on the education of women. It bans sex discrimination in the treatment of both students and employees in any academic, extracurricular, research, occupational training or other education program, from preschool to postgraduate, that is operated by an organization receiving federal aid. Certain exemptions are provided, among which are military schools, religious schools where Title IX compliance conflicts with religious practices, membership policies of single-sex, tax-exempt youth service organizations such as Boy Scouts and Girl Scouts, and university-based sororities and fraternities.

General provisions of Title IX include the requirement that recipients of federal education aid evaluate their current policies and take steps necessary to end discrimination. They must adopt and publish grievance procedures to resolve complaints, and issue notice of their nondiscriminatory policies to students, parents, applicants, employees and others. In the event of non-compliance, the government can delay awards of federal contracts, terminate current contracts or debar the institution from receiving future awards. The Department of Justice can bring suit, which may be filed on a class action basis.

2.5　　　　Pregnancy Discrimination Act of 1978

The Pregnancy Discrimination Act (8) is an amendment to the Civil Rights Act of 1964 requiring that women affected by pregnancy, childbirth or related medical conditions be treated on the same basis as other employees, including receipt of fringe benefits. It stipulates that employers may provide abortion benefits in health insurance plns, but are not required to do so except where the mother's life is endangered by pregnancy or childbirth or where medical complications have resulted from an abortion.

Congressional passage of this amendment followed an unfavorable ruling in a 1976 Supreme Court case, General Electric vs. Gilbert. In that case, the employee charged that a violation of Title VII of the Civil Rights Act had occurred because General Electric excluded pregnancy-related disabilities from coverage under its employee benefit plan. The Court indicated that pregnancy is sui generis, and differential treatment because of pregnancy does not constitute sex discrimination.

With the passage of the Pregnancy Discrimination Act, a woman who is unable to work due to pregnancy is entitled to the same disability benefits or sick leave as employees who are unable to work for other medical reasons, and health insurance provided by her employer must include coverage for pregnancy-related expenses. Under federal guidelines, Title VII had already prohibited an employer from firing, refusing to hire or promote a woman of pregnancy. It is also required that the employer provide the same benefits for those on leave due to pregnancy-related conditions as those on other disability leaves, including retention and accrual of seniority, continued payments to a pension plan, continuation of life, health and disability insurance, etc. Also, an employer cannot prohibit a woman from returning to work for a predetermined length of time following childbirth (9).

2.6　　　　Equal Rights Amendment

In 1972 Congress approved the passage of the Equal Rights Amendment (ERA) which states that "equality of rights under the law shall not be denied or abridged by the United States or any State on account of sex." The amendment required ratification by 38 state legislatures in order to become part of the U.S. Constitution. By June 1982, the deadline for its passage, the ERA had won the approval of only 35 state legislatures and did not become part of the Constitution. The ERA was reintroduced in both Houses of Congress in January 1983. Should the legislation be passed, the state-by-state ratification process will begin again.

The ERA would essentially nullify all state and federal laws and regulations that provide unequal treatment of men and women. Changes that could take place include elimination of all remaining sex-related differences in state and federal laws concerning jury service, social security, age at marriage, and those that place restrictions on married women with regard to property or legal domicile. State labor laws that protect or restrict one sex in wages, hours worked, or working conditions would have to be nullified or have pro-tection extended to both sexes.

Critics of the ERA oppose the amendment on a number of grounds. Some labor organizations argue that it would eliminate necessary protective legislation; religious and "pro-family" groups charge that it would uproot the traditional family; others oppose it on the grounds that it would require women to be drafted into the armed services if a draft were instituted. Even some who de-sire an equal role for women oppose the ERA, charging that the Civil rights Act, which specifically addresses sex discrimination, and the Fourteenth Amendment to the Constitution, which guarantees "any person...the equal protection of the laws" are sufficient to override any existing discriminatory laws. Proponents argue that the presence of the ERA would facilitate suits to change discriminatory laws and that the courts and the legislatures need a continuing mandate - the ERA - to ensure adequate legal protection of women. They also point out that the Fourteenth Amendment, adopted in 1868, did not in fact apply to women in such areas as suffrage, property rights and other legal treatment. Perhaps most importantly, the ERA has great symbolic value in upgrading women's opportunities and status. Proponents of women's rights also fear that the failure to adopt the ERA in 1982 was a signal that our society is not ready or willing to guarantee complete equality of opportunity for women.

3.   ENFORCEMENT AND IMPLEMENTATION OF FEDERAL LAWS
        AND GUIDELINES

The major responsibility for enforcing federal laws prohibiting sex discrimi-nation in the labor market resides with the Equal Employment Opportunity Commission (EEOC) and the Office of Federal Contract Compliance Programs (OFCCP) within the Department of Labor.

3.1   Title VII

Title VII is administered by the EEOC, consisting of five bipartisan presidential appointees. Initially the powers of the EEOC were limited largely to investiga-tion and conciliation, but were expanded in 1972 and 1978 to strengthen enforcement. The EEOC investigates complaints of discrimination, attempting to resolve them by "conciliation and persuasion." Failure to resolve the case results in judicial action, and either the EEOC or the aggrieved parties may file suit. The EEOC also conducts compliance investigations on its own initiative, and requires firms to document their employment practices in order to detect noncompliance. If a case is brought to court and discrimination is found, the court is empowered to grant relief, including reimbursement for legal expenses. Class action suits may be brought under Title VII and they are believed to be particularly effective.

Charges of discrimination on the basis of sex, minority status or age are first processed through the 22 district and 27 area EEOC offices which are located in areas with high concentrations of potential charging parties. The district offices house legal and administrative staff that provide both compliance and legal services. Attorneys and investigators in the district offices work together on the Early Litigation Identification Program, which identifies the more difficult cases at intake or from the backlog of cases. This recently implemented program is designed to improve the quality of EEOC litigation by ensuring a close partnership between attorneys and investigators. Investigators at the area offices are responsible for charge intake and for the Rapid Charge Processing System focusing on early fact-finding and attempts at settlements. This system of processing complaints identifies charges inappropriate to Title VII litigation and allows new cases to be processed quickly, before investigations become dated and while the parties are amenable to out-of-court settlements (10).

Potentially greater leverage under Title VII is associated with a shift in the definition of discrimination in 1972 when the concept of <u>systemic</u> discrimination was introduced. When Title VII of the Civil Rights Act was enacted in 1964, discrimination was perceived as consisting of intentional, overt employment policies that excluded certain individuals or treated them unfairly on the basis of race, color, sex, religion and national origin. Thus, elimination of discrimination would entail redress for the aggrieved individuals and cessation of the unfair employment practices.

In 1972 the EEOC moved away from the requirement of showing individual intent to discriminate by stating:

> "The most pervasive discriminatory practices now are recognized to result from seemingly neutral policies and practices within basic employment <u>systems</u>. However neutral they appear, however neutral and benign in intent, these systems produce highly discriminatory <u>effects</u>; neutral practices also <u>perpetuate discriminatory effects</u> of past discriminatory practices." (11).

This new thinking was reflected in the Equal Employment Opportunity Act of 1972 which broadened the definition of unlawful discrimination to include the consequences of employment practices which affect a class of persons and, therefore, an individual, even if no intent against the particular individual was evident. The landmark case that established this legal definition of discrimination was Griggs vs. Duke Power Company (Supreme Court, 1971). Griggs charged that the company's requirements - written tests and a high school diploma - adversely affected blacks but were not a business necessity. The court declared that employment practices, procedures, and tests that were neutral in appearance and/or intent, but operated to exclude a class of individuals and showed no relation to job performance were prohibited.

Such "systemic discrimination" is established by the review of statistics, conducted by the EEOC, indicating that a class of individuals have been excluded by a particular employment practice, such as a height-weight requirement. The burden of proof shifts to the employer, who must show that the practice in question is a business necessity that is job-related and has no reasonable alternative.

3.2   Equal Pay Act

Since 1978, enforcement of the Equal Pay Act (EPA) has been organizationally shifted to the EEOC from the Wage and Hours Division of the Department of Labor. Under the EPA, employees may sue for back wages, double damages for willful violations, and attorney fees and court costs, although no class action suits may be brought. In addition, compliance investigations may be brought even without a specific employee complaint.

One of the more important and well-publicized settlements obtained in part under the EPA involved the American Telephone and Telegraph Company (AT&T), which signed a multimillion dollar consent agreement with both the EEOC and the Department of Labor. AT&T agreed to substantial wage adjustments and back pay awards, and adopted new hiring and employment policies in the treatment of women and minorities. The cost was estimated at well over $ 60 million over a five-year period (12).

3.3   Executive Orders 11246 and 11375

The Office of Federal Contract Compliance Programs (OFCCP) in the Department of Labor oversees compliance with these Executive Orders and establishes policy, though individual government agencies are responsible for enforcing the Executive Orders in industries with which they do business. OFCCP conducts compliance reviews routinely as well as responds to individual complaints. In the extreme, OFCCP may delay or actually cancel contracts and debar a contractor from receiving future federal contracts, though these tactics are rarely used. While the threat of loss of federal contracts is believed to be a potent tool, the OFCCP's resources with which to pursue compliance reviews have often been limited. On a number of occasions, the OFCCP has been taken to court for failing to enforce the law forbidding sex discrimination.

Besides the direct sanction in the form of loss of federal funds, the Executive Orders differ from Title VII or EPA in that they require federal contractors to develop detailed affirmative action plans with targets for female or minority representation. The paperwork involved has been a constant source of complaints by firms, and changes in regulations have been suggested by the Reagan Administration.

3.4   Enforcement Problems

If intent to discriminate can be detected, it generally is not difficult to re-solve a court case and obtain redress for the aggrieved parties. Under the systemic discrimination model, intent to discriminate need not be demon-strated, but a particular employment practice that is not a business necessity must be shown to have an adverse impact on, or operate to exclude, a class of individuals.

Adverse impact is initially established by presentation of statistics showing that the composition of a firm's workforce is not representative of that of the available workforce. While they are not conclusive proof, such statistics are taken as "prima facie", that is, initial evidence that discrimination exists, and the employer must then justify the policies responsible for the exclusion of the particular class of individuals. For example, the Surpreme Court found that the State of Alabama's height-weight requirements operated to exclude women from employment as correctional counselors (State of Alabama vs. U.S., 1962), noting "Statistics tell much and the courts listen."

All of this complicates the working of the courts, as both sides of a case have come to rely increasingly on the testimony of statisticians and economists who provide multiple regression analyses to prove or disprove discrimination. Judges vary in their ability to weigh the statistical and technical arguments that are offered in discrimination cases, as well as in other areas where experts are invited to testify, such as antitrust and school expenditure cases. Federal district judge Fred Winner has been quoted as saying "judges are quite handi-capped in trying to understand this testimony...all a trial judge whose statistics course dates back 45 years can do is to try to use his limited knowledge of this quasi-mathematical approach to a problem and then temper the argued for results with a pinch of common sense" (Padilla, 1981).

3.5   Enforcement Under the Reagan Administration

Under the Reagan Administration, funding for civil rights enforcement has dropped, and now constitutes approximately 0.07 % of the federal budget. Ac-cordingly, the ability of federal agencies to conduct compliance reviews, in-vestigate complaints, and engage in other activities to eliminate systemic dis-crimination has been sharply curtailed.

The EEOC has experienced cutbacks in both staffing and budget. Clerical staff and field office attorney positions are most heavily affected, slowing the pro-duction of documents needed for legal cases. Reductions in funding have also affected EEOC's litigation activities, with less money available for expert witnesses, special studies and data processing. The systemic discrimination program, which requires considerable data to develop evidence of discrimi-nation, has received less attention as limited resources are devoted to handling individual complaints and eliminating the considerable backlog of cases. In 1978, the EEOC was given authority to coordinate enforcement activites among government agencies, reducing costly duplication of effort. However, the number of employee slots devoted to coordination has also been reduced.

Staffing has also been cut back in the OFCCP, resulting in more limited   compliance reviews, fewer negotiated settlements and less relief for victims of discrimination. By focusing its limited resources on compliance reviews, OFCCP has accumulated a backlog of individual complaints (13).

Beginning in 1981, OFCCP undertook to relieve the paperwork burden of smaller firms with the publication of new regulations on affirmative action requirements. At the time of this writing, the final regulations have been issued (14), but have not yet been made official via publication in the Federal Register.

The regulations would essentially excuse smaller firms that contract with the federal government from developing written affirmative action programs (AAPs). All firms having at least 100 employees and a $ 100,000 contract would be required to develop AAPs. Firms with 100 to 250 employees and contracts between $ 100,000 and $ 500,000 would be responsible for short form AAPs. Those with more than 250 employees and more than $ 500,000 in government business would continue to file detailed AAPs. Under this new rule, an estimated 25,699,843 workers remain covered, compared to 26,244,330 under the old rule. The estimated number of covered firms, however, drops by thirty percent, from 16,353 to 11,438 (15).

Other proposed changes greatly weaken OFCCP's ability to prevent and redress discrimination. Under the new regulations, all third-party charges alleging systemic discrimination must identify the individual employees who have complained of discrimination. While OFCCP acknowledges that this raises the risk of retaliation by contractors against individual complainants, it promises to vigorously enforce new provisions against intimidation and retaliation. Despite the OFCCP's promise of protection, this change will certainly discourage systemic suits.

Back pay awards are limited under the new regulations to <u>identifiable</u> (i.e., individual) victims of discrimination, rather than to classes of employees who have faced discrimination. Pre-award compliance reviews, which were considered to be especially effective in obtaining prompt remedies for civil rights violations, would be eliminated. Some firms would be allowed to produce five-year, rather than annual AAPs, during which time OFCCP would not conduct compliance reviews. Finally, the goal of 6.9 % female representation in the construction industry is retained, but cnanged from a trade-by-trade basis to an aggregate basis.

4.   SOME CONTROVERSIAL ISSUES IN EQUAL OPPORTUNITY
        POLICIES

4.1   Affirmative Action

Affirmative action "refers to the concept that discrimination can be eliminated when employers take positive steps to identify and change those policies, practices and any other institutional barriers that cause or perpetuate inequality," (Sandler and Dunkle, 1980: 25). Detailed requirements for affirmative action were described in Executive Order 11246 and in EEOC guidelines. These requirements entail among other items:

- self evaluation to determine whether discrimination exists

- dissemination of non-discriminatory policies (identifying the firm as an equal opportunity employer in recruitment)

- advertising all positions

- eliminating sex bias in job advertising, as in sex-segrated want ads

- active recruitment of women and minorities

- developing numerical hiring goals and timetables

Of all these requirements, the last, having "numerical goals" is perhaps the most controversial. Critics charge that goals amount to quotas or "reverse discrimination," and hence are inconsistent with the intention of the 1964 Civil Rights Act. Opponents fear that constant surveillance of firms, no matter how worthy the goal initially, can set a precedence for repressive intervention. Moreover, the cite the high costs of compliance with regulation that a) necessitate the compilation of detailed statistics on the firm's work force and on the labor market and b) may require unproductive firm practices, if the firm must hire or promote less skilled individuals to meet goals and timetables. Finally, some opponents believe that women and minorities who gain employment under an affirmative action plan may be stigmatized in the eyes of themselves and others by the appearance that preference rather than strict merit obtained their jobs or promotions (16).

Proponents of affirmative action argue that goals are targets designed to overcome previous and continuing exclusion. They are neither permanent nor absolute but are designed, based on employer work force analyses, to reflect the sex-race composition of the qualitified workforce available, not the general workforce. Furthermore, the goal should not require the selection of unqualified persons. Once a charge of discrimination has been proven, however, the court has the power to order more stringent targets which require the offending employer to hire a certain number of women for a limited period of time or to hire a certain proportion of women for a given number of new jobs openings. Supporters of affirmative action also contend that the principle of merit is consistent with and requires equal employment opportunity (17).

The legality of affirmative action has been upheld in court decisions, although a clear case may not yet have been decided. The Supreme Court's 1979 decision in United Steelworkers of America vs. Weber, regarding the placement of minorities in training programs, upheld the EEOC's position that no evidence of a violation of Title VII is required to justify adoption of an affirmative action plan. In Bakke vs. Regents of the University of California (1978), a bitterly contested case concerning minority admissions to medical school, the Supreme Court upheld the constitutionality of affirmative action programs as a legitimate method of remedying past discrimination, but denied the use of inflexible quotas.

The Supreme Court recently refused to rule on what would have been the most unambiguous case testing affirmative action, Boston Firefighters Union et al. vs. Boston Chapter, NAACP et al. (1983). In that case, unions and the federal government both argued against affirmative action programs. The case stemmed from a 1981 fire department layoff order, in which the city of Boston, Massachusetts laid off white workers with greater seniority in order to preserve gains made by blacks and Hispanics under an affirmative action order. Because the two issues in conflict, seniority versus discrimination remedies, are both considered worthy, this case was particularly difficult. The Supreme Court declared the case moot since the layoffs had been rescinded.

The Boston case marks the first time that an administration has intervened on behalf of whites in a major "reverse discrimination" case at the Supreme Court. Although both the EEOC and the U.S. Civil Rights Commission asked the government to side with the minorities in this case, a "friend of the court" brief was filed by the U.S. Solicitor General charging that the laid off whites were a new class of victims. Most recently, William Bradford Reynolds, chief of the Justice Department's Civil Rights Division, called racial quotas "morally wrong" and said that the Reagan Administration would not seek nor accept them as a remedy for racial discrimination or school segregation (18).

4.2   "Comparable Worth"

The Equal Pay Act requires that men and women receive equal pay for equal work, where the work must entail equal skill, effort and responsibility and be performed within the same establishment. Four "affirmative defenses" were established to justify inequalities in pay, including (1) seniority, (2) merit, (3) quantity or quality of production, and (4) any factor other than sex. The courts have interpreted "equal work" to mean substantially equal.

When the more widely reaching Civil Rights Act was passed, Congress attempted to resolve possible tensions between the Equal Pay Act and Title VII by incorporating the Bennett Amendment, which states:

> It shall not be an unlawful employment practice under this title for any employer to differentiate upon the basis of sex in determining the amount of wages or compensation paid or to be paid to employees of such employer if such differentiation is authorized by the provisions of section (d) of the Fair Labor Standards Act of 1938, as amended 29 U.S.C. 206(d) (i.e., the Equal Pay Act) (19).

That is, the Bennett Amendment permitted wage differentiation between men and women if the difference was "authorized" by the Equal Pay Act. An emerging debate centers on whether the authorization provided by the Bennett Amendment applies to just the four affirmative defenses listed above or to the equal work standard of the EPA as well. If the former case holds, another standard for evaluating jobs, "comparable work" rather than "equal work", may be permitted under Title VII.

The "comparable worth" concept, which apparently has eluded any workable, practical definition, arises from the contention that classes of jobs traditionally held by women, such as nursing and clerical work, are undervalued relative to their true worth (20). Proponents of comparable worth argue that the labor market is discriminatory because it forces women into a few low wage occupations, so pay systems which are a product of the labor market are also discriminatory. What is needed instead, it is argued, are "bias-free" job evaluation techniques that can provide a standard for comparing men and women in dissimilar occupations. The comparable worth issue has recently attracted the attention of the EEOC.

Opponents of the comparable worth concept argue that the administrative dimensions and implications of such a program entail a mammoth regulatory job and could only be undertaken in a planned economy. Furthermore, the concept violates fundamental notions about how a market system determines the "worth" of a job, which traditionally is measured by its marginal product as reflected approximately in the market wage its performance commands. Also the market system would determine or tend toward an efficient allocation of workers and skills. The alternative system, based on job evaluation, would be based on subjective determination of job characteristics such as skill, responsibility, and working conditions and could not balance the supply of labor for a job with the demand for it. Hildebrand (1980) argues that implementation of comparable worth would likely harm women, because the forced rise in the cost of low-productivity workers would encourage firms to substitute capital for labor, resulting in declining employment possibilities for women. Some feminists also stress that comparable worth would increase occupational segregation since women would have no incentive to train for or to seek to enter non-traditional jobs (Killingsworth, 1981).

The courts have almost consistently rejected the comparable work concept up to now. For example, the court dismissed a Title VII salary discrimination claim in Orr vs. Frank R. MacNeill & Son, Inc. (Fifth Circuit, 1975), where the plaintiff claimed that her job as a department head was "just as important" as those of male department heads, even though the work content was different. One of the most important comparable worth cases, also dismissed, was County of Washington vs. Gunther, argued before the Supreme Court in June 1981. In that case, four female jail guards argued that they were substantially underpaid relative to the male guards. The Supreme Court simply agreed that comparable worth claims could be brought under Title VII, but left many issues unresolved. For example, the Court did not determine under what circumstances a claim of comparable worth was properly raised, nor whether it was necessary to show intent to discriminate (21). Of course, job evaluation schemes that merely label "substantially equal" jobs differently in order to pay women less have been and may be challenged under Title VII of the Civil Rights Act.

5.   CONCLUSIONS

In a weakened economy and with an unsympathetic Administration, equal opportunity policies have come under increasing attack. Women are less likely to be hired and more apt to be laid off in a recession, due to a variety of factors such as shorter labor market tenure, stereotypes favoring men, discrimination and less seniority. Without vigorous enforcement of equal opportunity legislation, women stand to lose many of the gains made in the last two decades.

---

* I am indebted to June O'Neill and Günther Schmid for helpful comments, and to Bobbie Mathis for capable technical assistance.

NOTES

(1) For other reviews of U.S. legislation and litigation, see Greenberger, 1980; Sandler/Dunkle, 1976; and particularly Thomas, 1982.

(2) 29 U.S.C. sec. 206(d).

(3) See Williams/McDowell, 1980. This point is disputed by others; see Livernash, 1980.

(4) 42 U.S.C. sec. 2000e.

(5) 32 Fed. Reg. 12319.

(6) 32 Fed. Reg. 14303.

(7) 20 U.S.C. sec. 1681-86.

(8) Pub. L. 95-555.

(9) U.S. Equal Employment Opportunity Commission (EEOC), 1979: A-48 - A-49.

(10) U.S. EEOC, Annual Reports, various years.

(11) U.S. EEOC, 1979: II-3.

(12) See Shaeffer, 1980 and Greenberger, 1980 for further discussion. The EEOC reported (Annual Report, 1980) that in 1980, over $ 20 million had been obtained in monetary relief in litigation activities by its district offices. This figure also includes suits brought under the Age Discrimination in Employment Act.

(13) For further discussion of federal civil rights enforcement, see U.S. Civil Rights Commission, 1982 and Women Employed, 1982.

(14) The regulations have been published in the Daily Labor Report, 1983, "Final OFCCP Regulations on Affirmative Action Requirements."

(15) Estimates were made available by the Division of Program Policy, OFCCP.

(16) See, for example, Hatch, 1980; Welch, 1981; Glazer, 1975.

(17) See, for example, Loury, 1981; U.S. EEOC, 1979 and U.S. Civil Rights Commission, 1977.

(18) Mr. Reynolds was quoted in The Washington Post, April 30, 1983, p. A1, "Top Justice Aide Calls Race Quotas 'Morally Wrong'."

(19) 42 U.S. sec. 2000e-2(h), sec. 703(h).

(20) See Livernash (1980) for further discussion of comparable worth.

(21) Gasaway (1981) discusses many of the legal implications of this case.

REFERENCES

Babcock, Barbara Allen, Ann E. Freedman, Eleanor Holmes Norton, and Susan C. Ross. 1975. Sex Discrimination and the Law: Causes and Remedies, Little, Brown and Company, Boston. 1975.

Dunlap, Mary C. 1977. "The Legal Road to Equal Employment Opportunity: A Critical View", American Women Workers in a Full Employment Economy, a compendium of papers submitted to the Subcommittee on Economic Growth and Stabilization of the Joint Economic Committee. Washington, D.C.: U.S. Government Printing Office.

"Final OFCCP Regulations on Affirmative Action Requirements." 1983. Daily Labor Report No. 54, Section D. March 18.

Gasaway, Laura. 1981. "Comparable Worth: A Post-Gunther Review." Georgetown Law Journal, Vol. 69, No. 5, June.

Glazer, Nathan. 1975. Affirmative Discrimination. New York: Basic Books.

Greenberger, Marcia. 1980. "The Effectiveness of Federal Laws Prohibiting Sex Discrimination in Employment in the United States," in R.S. Ratner, ed., Equal Employment Policy for Women. Philadelphia: Temple University Press.

Hatch, Orrin. 1980. "Loading the Economy". Policy Review, Spring.

Hildebrand, George. 1980. "The Market System." in E.R. Livernash, ed., Comparable Worth: Issues and Alternatives. Washington, D.C.: U.S. Equal Employment Advisory Council.

Killingsworth, Vivienne. 1981. "Labor: What's a Job Worth?" The Atlantic Monthly, February.

Livernash, E. Robert, editor. 1980. Comparable Worth: Issues and Alternatives. Washington, D.C.: U.S. Equal Employment Advisory Council.

Loury, Glenn C. 1981. "Is Equal Opportunity Enough?" American Economic Review, Vol. 71, No. 2, May.

Nicholas, Susan Cary, Alice M. Price and Rachel Rubin. 1979. Rights and Wrongs: Women's Struggle for Legal Equality. New York: The Feminist Press.

Padilla, Art. 1981. "The Earnings Gap." University of North Carolina (mimeograph).

"Quotas Under Attack." 1983. Newsweek, April 25.

Sandler, Bernice and Margaret Dunkle. 1976. "Achieving Equal Employment Opportunity for Women." Prepared for the Organization for Economic Cooperation and Development (mimeograph).

Schaeffer, Ruth Gilbert. 1980. "Improving Job Opportunities for Women from a U.S. Corporate Perspective." in R.S. Ratner, ed., Equal Employment Policy for Women. Philadelphia: Temple University Press.

Thomas, Claire Sherman. 1982. Sex Discrimination in a Nutshell. St. Paul, Minn.: West Publishing Co.

"Top Justice Aide Calls Race Quotas 'Morally Wrong'." 1983. The Washington Post, April 30, p. Al.

U.S. Civil Rights Commission. 1976. A Guide to Federal Laws and Regulations Prohibiting Sex Discrimination. Clearinghouse Publication 46. Washington, D.C.: U.S. Government Printing Office.

U.S. Civil Rights Commission. 1977. Statement on Affirmative Action. Clearinghouse Publication 54. Washington, D.C.: U.S. Government Printing Office.

U.S. Civil Rights Commission. 1982. The Federal Civil Rights Enforcement Budget:Fiscal Year 1983. Clearinghouse Publication 71. Washington, D.C.: U.S. Government Printing Office.

U.S. Equal Employment Opportunity Commission. 1979. Eliminating Discrimination in Employment: A Compelling National Priority. Washington, D.C.

U.S. Equal Employment Opportunity Commission. Annual Report. Washington, D.C.: U.S. Government Printing Office, various years.

Wallace, Phyllis. 1973. "Employment Discrimination: Some Policy Considerations." in O. Ashenfelter and A. Rees, eds., Discrimination in Labor Markets. Princeton, New Jersey: Princeton University Press.

Washington Council of Lawyers. 1983. Reagan Civil Rights: the First Twenty Months. Washington, D.C.

Welch, Finis. 1981. "Affirmative Action and its Enforcement." American Economic Review, Vol. 71, No. 2, May.

Williams, Robert E. and Douglas S. McDowell. 1980. "The Legal Framework." in E.R. Livernash, ed., Comparable Worth: Issues and Alternatives. Washington, D.C.: U.S. Equal Employment Advisory Council.

Women Employed. 1982. Damage Report: The Decline of Equal Opportunity Enforcement Under the Reagan Administration. Chicago, Illinois.

Women's Legal Defense Fund. 1981. "Reagan's EEOC Transition Team Report and WLDF's Response." Newsletter, Vol. V, No. 8, March.

6 THE EFFECTS OF STATUTORY EMPLOYMENT POLICIES ON WOMEN IN THE UNITED KINGDOM LABOUR MARKET

PAULINE GLUCKLICH

1.   INTRODUCTION*

In Britain, as elsewhere, the post-war period has witnessed a substantial growth in women's employment (See Table 1). Yet despite this increased participation, women still compete in the labour market on unequal terms with men. They continue to hold a 'subordinate' position within the labour force and are often treated as 'marginal workers'. In Britain, women also represent a majority amongst the low paid. Despite the Equal Pay and Sex Discrimination Acts, women's earnings are still significantly lower than men's (See Table 2). One of the factors which helps to explain this continuing labour market disadvantage for women is the concentration of their employment in a narrow range of industries and occupations, in which pay and conditions are poor for both men and women (See Tables 3 and 4). This occupational and industrial segregation can mean that, even if policies such as the Equal Pay Act succeed in equalising the pay of men and women in the same jobs, women's average earnings overall will remain lower than men's. This being the case, two types of measure may be more appropriate than equal pay legislation to improve the pay and conditions of women workers. The first is those policies concerned with the improvement of opportunities for women to enter better paid jobs and industries through removal of various form of discrimination. The second type of measure is those policies intended to improve pay and conditions of work generally in those jobs and industries in which women are concentrated. An important element in such a policy might be legislation on minimum wages.

Incomes policies too are of relevance to a discussion of women's pay and employment. Whatever the primary purpose of incomes policies, they have been generally presented as a means of improving the position of the low paid. The effect of incomes policies on the wages council and public sector in particular need to be examined in order to assess their likely impact on women.

In this paper the policy instruments introduced specifically to improve the pay and position of women in the labour market are examined, followed by a consideration of the extent to which minimum wage legislation and incomes policies have an impact on women's pay and jobs.

2.   OVERALL EFFECTS OF THE LEGISLATION

Seven years after the legislation came onto the statute book, there is increasing evidence to show that the Equal Pay and Sex Discrimination Acts have not achieved equal pay or opportunity in the wider sense. However the legislation does appear to have had some impact, particularly in relation to equal pay. National figures show (See Table 2) that women's hourly average earnings rose from 63 % of men's hourly average in 1970 to 75 % in 1977, though from 1978 they have fallen to 73.3 %. Research evidence (Snell, Glucklich, Povall 1981) shows that the implementation of equal pay resulted in considerable and sometimes dramatic narrowing of differentials between the basic rates of manual and non-manual women and those of men. This narrowing was considered to be greater than could be attributed solely to the pay policy which was in operation at the time.

The Sex Discrimination Act also appears to have had a limited effect. As a result of the Sex Discrimination Act most forms of overt discrimination in employment disappeared and some job opportunities formerly closed to women were subsequently opened to them. Moreover the laws appear to have brought about a change in the climate of public opinion by giving an official seal of approval to the idea that women and men should have equal pay and opportunity, and by giving encouragement to people to change their behaviour and attitudes (Robarts, Coote, Ball 1981). McIntosh (1980) concludes that legislative action has had some positive results, not only in largely eliminating inequality of pay rates in unisex jobs, but in the fact that employers are less prone to the kind of sex stereotyping which was common at the beginning of the decade.

Yet the overall impact of the legislation has been limited. In 1980, the Equal Opportunities Commission (EOC 1981) reported that no further progress could be made to the Equal Pay and Sex Discrimination Acts without 'substantial amendment to enable them to give better effect to Parliament's intention'. In proposing a number of amendments to both statutes, the Commission considered there to be a possibility of growing disenchantment with the relevance of such legislation, unless strengthened along the lines they suggest. Evidence from other sources supports this view. The survey of employers referred to earlier(McIntosh 1980) showed that progress had been disappointingly slow. The authors of the report (IIFF Research 1980) conclude that both statutes have had a very modest effect in breaking down inequalities between the sexes at the place of work, and that the provisions of the legislation were being observed, in the great majority of establishments, in letter rather than spirit. The LSE study (Snell, Glucklich, Povall 1981, op.cit.), whose research findings are heavily drawn on later in the chapter, came to similar conclusions.

3. LIMITATIONS OF THE STATUTES IN RELATION TO THEIR SCOPE AND IMPLEMENTATION

Why has the legislation had such a limited effect on women's position in the labour market? A combination of factors, rather than a single cause, provide explanations for its ineffectiveness. The Equal Pay Act failed to lift women out of low paid work for two main reasons:

1. many women, regardless of their skill level or the industry in which they worked, did not receive their entitlements under the Act because the employers did not comply with the legislation or took actions to reduce their obligations under the Act;

2. the Act was not intended to overcome the fact that women are concentrated in low paid industries and/or predominantly female jobs. Each of these factors is considered in turn.

3.1 Implementation of the Equal Pay Act

The LSE research findings (Snell, Glucklich and Povall, op. cit.) show that the way in which employers complied with the legislation, and the strategies they used, seriously limited its impact. Many women, regardless of skill level or industry, received less than they might have done; less than their skills and jobs levels merited; or less than a comparable man would have been paid, because of actions taken by employers to minimise their obligations under the Act. Such actions took many forms.

For example men and women were moved out of jobs, or job content was changed to prevent equal pay comparisons; new grading schemes were introduced so that women ended up on lower, and often all - female rates or grades regardless of their skill level; job evaluation factors were altered to favour men; and the lowest male rate was depressed, relative to the skilled rate, over the period of implementation to reduce the amount of women's equal pay increases.

Many of these actions, had they been taken after 29 December 1975 would have been unlawful. But taken before the Act came into force, they enabled employers to comply with the law whilst reducing the amount of pay to which women would have been entitled.

There were considerable differences in the extent and frequency with which certain types of actions were taken, both within, and between organisations. Some organisations merely made minor adjustments to anomalous situations (for example, amending job evaluation results for isolated individuals), whereas others showed both a consistent and pervasive pattern of reducing obligations which affected many men and women rather than odd individuals. These actions affected basic pay structures and occurred in both white collar and manual areas. A disturbingly high number of such actions were found in the engineering industry, particularly affecting low paid women in the industry.

Moreover, although cases of employer's clear non-compliance with the statute were relatively few, they mostly affected the low paid. Such cases involved

109

small groups of cleaners, canteen or warehouse-workers and outworkers who had not been given equal pay with men, although employers were aware of these anomalies. For example, twenty cleaners employed in a large engineering company were paid less than the lowest male rate of the collective agreement, as were twenty women warehouse workers in another company. In a small company, all 56 women were paid below the lowest male rate, and separate male and female pay structures still operated 2 years after the Act came into force. Explanations for minimising actions or non-compliance, ranged from those employers who wished to avoid resentment on the part of male workers or potential union conflicts, to those who maintained they had done all that they felt was necessary.

In addition, cases of possible non-compliance were found in over half the organisations studied. These cases were considered borderline because the evidence itself seemed more likely to be disputed or open to different interpretations at an industrial tribunal, chiefly because most of these cases involved the identification of like work. This meant that even where women did possess skills which were broadly similar to those of men, these were not recognised or rewarded. Often this happened in industries not normally associated with the low paid, such as in engineering.

In some cases action was taken to compensate men and restore differentials rather than to minimise employers' responsibilities to women. Often compensatory actions for men went hand-in-hand with minimising strategies. Some of these actions were taken by employers to prevent women in semi-skilled jobs claiming equal pay with similarly skilled men, but much of the compensatory action was concerned with preserving pay levels for unskilled male jobs, especially those of male labourers. Such action included giving additional fork lift truck driving duties to male labourers, upgrading male labourers for a willingness to clean toilets, putting male labourers on a bonus scheme to protect their earnings, and 'red circling' (2) the pay of unskilled men. In some instances low paid men also suffered under equal pay implementation. In several organisations, increases to low paid men were deliberately kept lower than those of other male workers whilst women were being brought up to the lowest male rate. There is evidence too that in some industries the differentials between low paid men were also compressed.

3.2   Scope and Objectives of the Legislation

The second main reason why the Equal Pay Act failed to tackle the question of low pay was the limitations of both the Equal Pay and the Sex Discrimination Acts. Even if all women had received full entitlements under the statutes, the majority would continue to be low paid, because the legislation was limited in scope and objectives.

Limitations in the scope of the Equal Pay Act were two-fold. The first was a practical limitation in application rather than a limitation in objectives. The provisions of the Act did not cover certain groups of workers, who either fell outside collective agreements or employers' pay structures or who were employed in totally female areas of work where there was no comparable man. In manual areas of employment, such groups were found in canteen and cleaning work, mainly in the engineering industry. The greatest incidence, however, was amongst white-collar women in private manufacturing. In most cases these were women working in traditionally female jobs such as secretaries, typists, industrial nurses and receptionists, who were not covered by collective bargaining proceses and who were either part of an all-female pay structure or not covered by a formally designated pay structure.

Although the numbers of women who fell outside the provisions of Equal Pay Act altogether were not high, such groups were found in 15 of the 26 organisations studied. Furthermore, it has been estimated that 44.5 per cent of all full-time women fall outside collective agreements (Alison Mitchell, 1976). This suggests a lack of coverage on a very large scale. These women, almost by definition, tend to be those least likely to have the bargaining power or the numbers needed to win higher increases. And, not surprisingly, in the industries studied, they were often the very lowest paid workers.

The second limitation arises from the objectives of the Act and the fact that it was not designed to tackle the wider questions of the nature of women's employment and the differences between men's and women's work. Firstly, the Act was concerned only with equal pay within establishments and not between organisations and industries. In practical terms this limited the Act's effectiveness for many women, particularly those in low paid industries, for it meant that at best low paid women were equalised with low paid men. In this respect it is likely that alternative approaches such as the 'fair wages' claims under Schedule II of the 1974 Employment Protection Act (enabling workers to claim the recognised rate of pay for their job - a provision which was abolished in 1980), a continued flat rate incomes policy or a national minimum wage, could have been potentially more effective in bringing up the general level of pay within localities and industries in a way which was just not possible within the terms of the Equal Pay Act.

Secondly, both the individual and collective provisions of the Act were limited in the context of the divisions which exist within the labour market. The extent of segregated work meant that many women were in areas of work and in pay structures which were totally female and where it was not possible to find a comparable man. Thus the like work provisions of the Act could not be used to obtain equal pay. Furthermore, many women, particularly in manual work, were not covered by job evaluation. The requirements, under Section 3 of the Act, to bring women covered by collective agreements, employers' pay structures or wages council orders, up to the lowest male rate was meant to ensure that such women received at least some increase under the Act. In this respect of the Act was largely successful. It almost certainly brought millions of women within the scope of the Act who might otherwise not have had a claim to equal pay.

But under Section 3 (S3) employers were not obliged to pay women according to their skill level nor the value of their work. Nor were employers required to examine the job content of men and women's work as was necessary under the like work or work of equivalent value provisions. As a result, in a number of organisations where S3 was used for implementation, large groups of women in semi-skilled jobs such as machine operator, assembler, packer or inspector were lawfully paid on or just above the unskilled rate. In some industries female rate differentials based on skill differences were compressed and lost in bringing women up to the lowest male rate. This was a particular feature of national level implementation in two of the low paid industries studied by the

LSE research team.

3.3   Implementation and Scope of the Sex Discrimination Act

The Sex Discrimination Act also had little impact on the extent of sex segregation found within organisations, and the occupational distribution of women remained unchanged. The introduction of the legislation was intended to improve women's opportunities to enter higher graded work by making discrimination in employment unlawful, and by the promotion of equal opportunities generally, but the LSE research team found, that, for a combination of reasons, this was not so.

Changes in working practices, as a result of the Act, were few. Most personnel policies and practices were assumed by employers to meet the requirements of the law and to provide equal opportunities for all employees, although clear differences in job distribution remained. As a result most employers did not carry out a systematic examination of their personnel practices in the light of the provisions of the Act. There was little change to training and promotion procedures and practices, and no use, by employers, of the provisions of the Act which allowed positive discrimination in training, for jobs which have been largely the preserve of one sex. In the main, women were concentrated in low paid jobs, in low paid, often predominantly female, occupations and industries. In many cases job segregation was the outcome of the way in which established structures, practices and attitudes interacted to restrict women's opportunities, indirectly and often unintentionally, rather than as a result of unlawful behaviour.

Furthermore the LSE research study showed that in most organisations one or more members of management, concerned with hiring, training or promotion, said that they were discriminating or intending to discriminate against women in making future employment decisions. Most of these instances involved direct discrimination in recruitment or promotion, where a suitable women (or man) had been, or would have been, refused a job because of their sex. In addition the research team found a number of instances of possible indirect discrimination. These were cases where a condition or requirement for a job was such that a considerably smaller proportion of women than men could comply with it and where the team felt that the requirements might not be justified in terms of the job itself. These included lifting requirements which effectively excluded many women from jobs and promotion; apprenticeship requirements where the jobs involved did not appear to need the skills; age restrictions for entry to certain jobs; and restriction of part-time workers to clerical grades.

Thus, the Sex Discrimination Act, which it had been hoped would eliminate discrimination in employment, has also proved too limited in scope. The removal of overtly discriminatory practices or procedures alone is unlikely to lead to a significant reduction in job segregation in the near future. Without more positive measures to overcome the effects of past discrimination and to break down the more subtle barriers which limit women's opportunities at work, women are likely to remain in low paid, lower grade jobs.

The structure of the labour market was also clearly a major factor in limiting the effectiveness of both the Equal Pay and Sex Discrimination Acts. Because women were, in the main, concentrated in low paid industries and, within industries, in lower graded and low paid jobs which were totally or predominantly female, equal pay often meant equally low pay, or no change in pay at all.

3.4   Employment factors which limited the effectiveness of the statutes

A number of factors in employment interacted with the Equal Pay and Sex Discrimination Acts to limit their effectiveness; in particular, the low level of priority attached to both pieces of legislation by management and the widespread lack of detailed knowledge of the provisions of the statutes, particularly amongst women. The role of unions at local level, as both a positive and negative force in equal pay implementation, and their failure to exert pressure on employers with regard to sex discrimination, was also clearly a crucial factor. Similarly, women's lack of participation in unions and in pay determination contributed to their low awareness of equal pay, and allowed employers and male trade unionists to neglect or actively override the interests of women both on pay and access to jobs. Above all, the extent of job segregation of women in low paid and less skilled jobs both contributed to the limited effectiveness of the statutes and failed to be disturbed by them in operation.

Three factors specifically affected the Equal Pay Act. Employers implementation strategies have been shown to be critical. When the first Act came onto the statute book it was estimated that only 10 % of women hd equal pay. How much action by employers was necessary, was partly determined by the existing methods and levels of pay determination in the organisations and how these interacted with the different requirements of the Act. In the event most employers opted for the least costly and disruptive method of dealing with equal pay. However, a number of issues influenced employers' strategies both positively and negatively. Some, such as the cost of equal pay, hostility to the notion of equal pay and fears of reactions from men, played a part in causing employers to adopt negative strategies. Lack of positive guidance and direction from employers' federations at industry level was another reason for employers' late and often negative actions. By the time the majority of employers took action (from 1973-1975) they could see that it was possible to reduce their responsibilities under the Act, without breaking the law, or to opt for methods of implementation which contravened the spirit if not letter of the law. Other motives, such as the desire to maintain well-established, orderly pay systems, encouraged employers to take positive action. A major influence in this process was the move in many organisations to more rational and acceptable payment systems. The growth of job evaluation, particularly for white collar staff, was only partly because of equal pay, but it contributed significantly to the Acts' effectiveness when carried out and implemented properly.

The second major factor which critically influenced the implementation and effects of the Act was union attitudes and actions at establishment level. Lack of pressure from unions was one reason for many employers' failure to take earlier and more positive action on equal pay. This lack of pressure, which often contrasted with the situation at the national level, was sometimes due to lack of knowledge or involvement in pay determination at a local level. This was particularly true where pay negotiations were carried out at a national   or head office level or where union organisation was weak. In some organisations white collar unions were engaging for the first time in collective bargaining, and that lack of experience, was an added handicap.

But lack of pressure was also the result of a lack of real commitment to the concept of equal pay. For most local union representatives and officials equal pay was a minor issue, peripheral to their central concerns and worries. Increasing unemployment, inflation and recession gave rise to fears of redundancies, and on-going changes to pay structures and to the organisation itself, presented more pressing problems. Other new legislation, particularly the Employment Protection and Health and Safety Acts, were seen as more important. In the absence of pressure from women members, and of firm direction and detailed guidelines from union Head Offices, little real support and weight was given to implementation by many local union representatives. In some cases, union representatives and many of their members were actively hostile to equal pay; it was seen as a threat to men's pay and jobs. The attitudes of the union representatives were crucial in all those organisations where a persistent tendency to minimise was found. The worst examples of such action appear to have been taken not only with union knowledge but in certain cases with union collusion and pressure.

Third, and most important, women's conspicuous failure to put pressure on management and unions for equal pay clearly contributed to the ease with which employers were able to minimise their obligations under the Act, and to the neglect by unions of the interests of their women members. In the organisations studied by the LSE project team, women made almost no demands on management at the stage of implementation, did not resist minimising actions when they occurred and did not, on the whole, take up cases of non-compliance and unequal treatment which they encountered.

There appeared to be a number of reasons why women were so undemanding and acquiescent on issues which so directly affected them. First, their level of involvement in pay matters generally was low. Only a handful of women were involved in pay negotiations as employee representatives. Where women were shop stewards they were rarely on negotiating committees. This absence of women from pay bargaining meant that they were not in a position to safeguard their own interests but had to rely, as they had traditionally done, on their fellow male representatives. For women, pay generally - and equal pay in particular - was something which happened to them but in which they had little say. Even where they were involved in pay determination, they had often seen themselves as representing other women. As a result, they often had little or no knowledge of men's pay and earnings. Second, women's lack of bargaining strength with respect to equal pay reflected their lack of bargaining power generally with respect to pay. Whether mens actions were taken with the intention of preserving differentials with women or not, it is clear that men were more likely than women to get increases in pay.

Third, women's failure to take up cases of unequal or unfair treatment was mainly due to their failure to recognise non-compliance and minimisation. Women's knowledge of the Equal Pay Act and their rights under it, was found to be very limited and vague. Although the Act was pased in 1970, there was only limited publicity aimed directly at women until the Act came fully into force in December 1975. The LSE research findings indicate that both government and union bodies failed to reach women at an early enough   stage   with

114

the kind of detailed information they would have needed to recognise what was going on and take action. Women also failed to recognise inequalities in pay because they were not aware of men's jobs and the pay levels associated with them. The high degree of job segregation meant that many women were not familiar with the content of men's jobs.

The employment factors which limited the effectiveness of the Sex Discrimination Act appeared to be structural and organisational as much as attitudinal. First, a number of job and promotion criteria were found to act as barriers to women's opportunities. Such barriers, although considered to be legitimate and justifiable, were also found to be a matter of convenience or tradition or to reflect male career patterns. Many barriers were specific to particular jobs or industries, but many were common. For example, lifting requirements prevented women in many organisations from moving into better paid jobs or into jobs which traditionally led to higher graded jobs. Management and unions tended to assume that many jobs were too heavy for women, without actually examining the content of such jobs. The hours of work which many women worked also acted as a barrier to many jobs. Women's reported inability and unwillingness to do shift or overtime work was often given as the reason why women did not move into better paid jobs. While this was often true there was considerable evidence that some women wanted or needed to work longer and different hours.

Traditional promotion paths and promotion criteria often limited women's job opportunities. In many organisations women do not have access to traditional promotion paths. For example, it is common in engineering to select supervisors from setting and from time-served jobs, which women have not done in the past, often because of discrimination. Similarly, promotion to supervision and management is often from technical and shop floor jobs rather than from the clerical and administrative side.

In addition personnel practices and policies in many organisations were found to limit womens opportunities at work, often indirectly or unintentionally. For example, in many organisations, line managers or supervisors often have the final say in selection procedures. Given their attitudes, their low level awareness of what constituted discrimination, and the fact that the personnel department's role was often only advisory, both intentional and unintentional discrimination seemed likely to continue. Furthermore, many organisations lacked certain kinds of personnel procedures, particularly with respect to training and promotion, a lack which negatively affected womens opportunities. In many organisations the research team found a lack of formal appraisal procedures where employees could discuss their career aspirations and problems systematically with their supervisors.

A number of organisational and structural factors also appeared severely to limit women's employment prospects. In several organisations, attempts were being made to professionalise supervision and management by introducing, or raising qualifications required. As a result, women who, with training, might well have moved into supervisory and management positions, were finding their paths blocked by young male and (a few) female graduates. Age and career structures in some industries were also found to reflect male career patterns and make careers for women difficult, while redeployment and redundancy decisions taken in some organisations also affected women more negatively than men. In one industry, manual men whose jobs were lost due to restructuring, were made supervisors in related clerical areas. Thus, posts, into which women were poised to move, were closed to them. In another organisation the decision to close a number of smaller units, resulted in several of the very few women managers being made redundant. Traditionally women had reached managerial status only in the small units.

Attitudes to women at work, and towards the legislation itself were also crucial in limiting the effectiveness of the Sex Discrimination Act; they showed little change after the Sex Discrimination Act came into force. There continued to be widespread acceptance of job segregation in manual jobs, and strong views on the suitability of certain jobs for men (those involving lifting or mechanical tasks) and for women (those involving dexterity or monotonous work). Attitudes to the legislation were also an important factor. The two most frequently encountered attitudes in response to the legislation were that the legislation was irrelevant because "we already have equal opportunities", and that where an organisation was discriminating, such discrimination was generally accepted by management and in some cases by unions and male employees.

4.   MINIMUM WAGE LEGISLATION AND THE EMPLOYMENT OF WOMEN

It is clear that statutory policies aimed at removing discrimination from the labour market, though limited in scope and objectives, have not achieved their statutory objectives. It is also clear that little further progress is likely as a result of the legislation, without some further intervention to stimulate action. It has been argued that an alternative approach to improving womens pay and employment conditions is minimum wage legislation. The effects of that legislation in the United Kingdom as it operates through the wages council machinery are now considered.

In Britain, many of the industrial sectors which have a high proportion of women workers are subject to minimum wage regulation operated through the wages council machinery. The effectiveness of this machinery is therefore important in determining the incidence of low pay amongst women and their overall earnings relative to men's. Although the wages councils were established to provide some minimum protection against wage exploitation, the incidence of low pay in this sector is high. The Royal Commission on the Distribution of Income and Wealth reported that, although the councils accounted for only 6.7 per cent of manual and 4.1 per cent of non-manual men in 1977, 12 per cent of manual and 10 per cent of non-manual low paid men were found in this sector. The wages council industries employed 23 per cent of manual and 17 per cent of non-manual low paid women, even though they accounted for only 18 per cent and 9.4 per cent respectively of the whole labour force. (Royal Commission on the Distribution of Income and Wealth, Report No 6, HMSO, Table M23).

There is widespread agreement in Britain that the wages councils have failed to fulfil the original objectives of eradicating low pay and encouraging voluntary collective bargaining in the industries in which they operate; there is however less agreement as to the appropriate response to this failure. Much of the reason for the persistence of low pay and the absence of voluntary collective bargaining can be found in the economic and industrial factors at work in these sectors which the wages councils are ill-equipped to tackle; much is due to the structure of the labour force itself. But there are also important institutional factors in the workings of the wages councils themselves which should be considered, and which directly affect the position of women in employment.

First, the level of minimum rates set by the Councils is low (3). A comparison between the legal minima and the actual level of earnings reveals that the average earnings of female employees fall closer to the minimum rates than do male earnings. The actual earnings of female workers in wage councils exceed the average Statutory Minimum Rate by only around 25 per cent. Male workers on the other hand, tend to exceed the SMRs by nearly 100 per cent. Minimum rates, therefore, are more important to women workers since they constitute a much greater proportion of actual earnings than is the case for men. (E. MacLennan, 1980). A comparison of earnings and minimum rates in selected wages council industries, for 1979, illustrates the point. (See table 5). Second, despite the low level of minimum rates, wages council employees are subject to a high and increasing level of illegal underpayment below these minima. During 1980, the Department of Employment found that 35.1 per cent of the employers inspected, were paying below the legal minimum rates. This compares with 31.5 per cent in 1979 and with 14.8 per cent in 1971. The rate of illegal underpayment increased dramatically during the early 1970s, reaching a peak in 1977 of 37.4 per cent of all establishments inspected. The Labour government responded by increasing the number of wages inspectors, by increased publicity and by instituting 'saturation' inspections of selected towns.

These revealed rates of underpayment as high as 45 to 60 per cent of employers in some parts of the country. The result of these initiatives by the Department of Employment was to reduce the rate of underpayment in 1978 and 1979. However, the saturation inspections were abandoned with the change of government in 1979 and the size of wages inspectorate was reduced by a third.

The problem of illegal underpayment is of particular importance to women. In Table 5, actual earnings are shown to be much closer to the statutory minima for women than for men. Their vulnerability is reflected also in a higher incidence of underpayment. The Department of Employment does not publish a breakdown of underpayment by sex, but in their 1974 investigation of retail distribution, the Commission for Industrial Relations (CIR) found that while 2.4 per cent of full-time adult male employees were paid less than the Statutory Minimum Rate, (SMR) as many as 9.5 per cent of full-time adult females were underpaid. Similarly in the clothing trade, the Commission found that 4 per cent of adult males were underpaid but the proportion of females paid less than SMR was 8 per cent, and rose again to 24 per cent amongst juvenile females. The Commission warned that part of the workface should be regarded as a 'vulnerable minority' earning less than ten per cent above the SMR and not covered by adequate voluntary collective bargaining, whose living standards therefore depended heavily on the wages council rates. While 6 per cent of adult males fell into this category, it included 15 per cent of adult females and 23 per cent of juvenile females. (CIR, 1974, and Clothing Wages Councils, 1974).

Moreover certain groups amongst the female labour force, young people, homeworkers and part-timers in particular, are especially vulnerable to illegal underpayment. The CIR, report on retailing, cited above, found that while 16.8

per cent of female adult full-time shop assistants were underpaid, the proportion amongst part-timers rose to 28.9 per cent. In a recent investigation of the Toy Manufacturing Wages Council (ACAS 1978 Report No. 13) ACAS found that 80 per cent of homeworkers were paid less than the statutory minimum rates.

4.1   Minimum Wages for Women: Abolition or Improved Protection?

The failure of the wages council system, either to encourage the development of voluntary collective bargaining, or to eradicate low pay, is clear. There is more agreement about the failure of the councils than about what should be done. The late sixties and early seventies witnessed increasing pressure from the trade union movement for complete abolition of wages councils, reflecting a belief that the very existence of the councils had inhibited the development of voluntary arrangements. This was also the approach of official bodies such as the National Board for Prices and Incomes (NBPI) and CIR, referred to earlier. However, the CIR and the Advisory Conciliation and Arbitration Service (ACAS) which succeeded it, both warned of the existence of vulnerable minorities, mainly women, who would suffer from the withdrawal of statutory protection. Nevertheless, the 1974-79 Labour government introduced procedures intended to accelerate the disappearance of individual councils, and their replacement by voluntary collective bargaining.

Arguments for the maintenance of minimum wage protection are regaining currency in Britain. ACAS has recently referred to "the continuing need for statutory protection for the lowest paid workers", and has recommended the introduction of a new council to cover contract cleaning staff - the first such proposal since 1965. (ACAS 1981). It has also proposed the extension of minimum wage protection for workers in launderettes. And in its investigation of Toy Manufacturing, ACAS commented:

> "In an industry where the average size of establishment is small and the turnover is high, the position of the lower paid workers in smaller establishments is not likely to improve and may not even be maintained. For homeworkers in particular, where the constant over-supply of willing labour mentioned to us by employers is a natural downward force on market rates of pay, the prospects without statutory protection are bleak."

The British government, however, is opposed to the further extension of minimum protection. Indeed the complete abolition of the system is under consideration.

Given the importance of the wages councils in determining women's earnings, and given the additional vulnerability of groups such as part-timers and homeworkers, it is clear that their abolition would be extremely detrimental to the interests of Britain's women workers. For the same reason, more effective minimum wage machinery would be expected not only to reduce the extent of low pay amongst the women concerned, but also to raise women's earnings as a whole relative to men's. A number of proposals as to how this might be done have been put forward in various publications by the Low Pay Unit. They include an increase in the minimum rates to more adequate   levels;   further rationalisation of the structure of wages councils; simplifications of the Wages Orders so that they are more comprehensible to employers and workers; and better enforcement of the minimum rates. Other measures, including the proposal for a "trade union development fund" and time off during working hours for participation in trade union meetings, would help to improve the coverage of voluntary collective bargaining in this 'sector'. (For a fuller discussion of these proposals see E. MacLennan, 1980 and S. Crine, 1980).

However, while these measures would undoubtedly improve the relative earning of women they would not, in themselves, be sufficient to eradicate low pay. One of the difficulties is that wages councils represent a selective approach to minimum wage protection. They are therefore poorly adapted to take account of changes in the size and scope of the secondary employment sector. Industries which were once prosperous may sink into the secondary sector because their technology ages or their market decline. Yet without a continually changing wages council system, minimum protection cannot be extended to these groups. Among the few other countries who have a selective, industry-based minimum wage system of this type, an increasing number are adopting a more general approach to legal minimum wages, applied to all workers (G. Starr, 1980). Resistance to such an approach in Britain appears to be less pronounced than during the 1970s. The Equal Pay Act was introduced in 1970 against a background of discussions concerning the need for a National Minimum Wage. At the time, the Equal Pay Act appeared to be more attractive on grounds of costs. (A. Mitchell, 1976 op. cit.). It may be that an effective national minimum wage would have resulted in a more lasting improvement in women's earnings.

5.   INCOMES POLICIES AND THEIR EFFECTS ON WOMENS PAY

Britain has operated some form of pay policy, almost continuously, since the mid 1960s. With the exception of the period June 1970 to November 1972 such a policy was in operation for virtually every year between 1965 and 1979. Even after 1979, a policy of wage restraint was applied to those in the public sector. The purpose of such policies has been principally to restrain the growth of wages as a means of controlling inflation, improving the balance of payments or shifting resources to corporate sector.

Yet whatever the primary purpose of such policies during the late 1960s and throughout the 70's, they were generally presented as means of improving the relative position of the low paid. Since women form a majority of the low paid, we might expect them to have been the main beneficiaries.

The policies which have operated since 1965 may convienently be grouped together into three periods: - from 1965-70 when low paid workers - those deemed by the Prices and Incomes Board to have earnings "too low to maintain a reasonable standard of living" - were to be allowed increases above the norm; from 1972-74 when exceptional rises were allowed to certain groups of workers where the Pay Board believed this would "facilitate an improvement in the relative position of the low paid" (the later stages of this policy also influenced flat rate elements thereby providing larger percentage increases for the low paid), and the third period (1974-1978) when the policy was initially explicitly equalising. (See C. Playford, 1980)

Throughout the period, therefore, pay policies were presented as providing special treatment for the low paid. The experience was disappointing however. Considering the effects of pay policy up to 1970 the National Board for Prices and Incomes concluded: "what little improvement took place in the relative position of the low paid in the earlier years of the prices and incomes policy was later lost" (NBPI, HMSO 1971). As table 6 demonstrates, the relative earnings of the lowest paid men were little different at the end of the period considered, compared with the beginning - their earnings increased by less than one per centage point. However, this masks some important changes within the period. Between April 1973 and April 1977 the lowest decile earnings increased significantly. This was a period which included three stages of formal pay policy, each with a flat-rate element, and one stage of free collective bargaining, subject to a minimum wage target for the low paid. As might be expected the transition to policies having mainly a percentage limit to pay rises was reflected after 1977 in a deterioration in the relative earnings of the low paid men.

The pattern of changes in the relative earnings of low paid women was slightly different. Over the entire period there was a considerable improvement - of over 5 per centages points - in the relative earnings of low paid women. In this case, relative earnings began to rise in April 1973 but not as fast as was the case with low paid men. Low paid women workers caught up only between April 1976 and April 1977. But whereas the male low paid found their position deteriorating after 1977, that of low paid women continued to improve. This perhaps is a surprising result, since the period after 1977 contained no pay policy elements which would have given rise to an improvement in the relative position of the low paid. Part of the explanation may be found in Table 7 which shows how women's average earnings changed, relative to men's. This table shows that, whether measured in terms of weekly or hourly earnings, women's average relative earnings increased significantly, from only 63 per cent of men's to 71 per cent. However, this improvement can be almost wholly accounted for by changes between April 1973 and April 1976. In part this may be explained by employers' attempts to 'catch up' at the last minute on their obligations under the Equal Pay Act, which came fully into force at the end of 1975. On the other hand, as we have seen, this was also a period in which the structure of pay policies would have led us to expect an improvement in the position of the low paid of which the majority are women.

From 1978, it appears progress towards equal pay evaporated. Since that date women's relative earnings have declined slightly. This may reflect the limitations of the Equal Pay Act in overcoming differences in pay which are due to occupational and individual segregation. The apparent improvement in the earnings of low paid women may therefore be a deceptive reflection of the decline in those of the average women against which they were compared.

Clearly, it is difficult to distinguish the effects of pay policy, from those of the Equal Pay Act. Throughout most periods of pay policy, increases in pay for women necessary to move towards equal pay were allowable in full. One recent analysis attributed most of the change in women's relative earnings between 1970 and 1975 to flat-rate pay policies. Chiplin, Curran and Parsley estimated that women's relative earnings over this period increased by about eight percentage points but that six percentage points of this change was due to flat-rate pay policies. P. Sloane (ed.) 1980). This calculation, however, assumes that in the absence of the incomes policy there would have been no increases in pay. Hence it clearly overstates the likely impact of pay policies. (See C. Playford 1980 op. cit.).

As Glucklich and Snell note in their study of women and low pay,

> "The effects of pay policy should not be overestimated...although it is true that pay policy benefitted women generally, our findings suggest that, as many women were in any case entitled to equal pay increases, the main function of flat-rate increases was to speed up the movement to equal pay. Where pay policy undoubted did help was through specific exemptions of equal pay payments from incomes policy. Because equal pay payments could be made separately from pay policy increases and there was little room for negotiation anyway, normal bargaining over shares in the 'kitty' and potential conflicts between men and women were forestalled and reduced". (Glucklich and Snell, 1982).

6.   WOMEN'S EARNINGS AND TRADE UNION GROWTH

In the discussion so far there has been an implicit assumption that the improvement in women's relative earnings between 1970 and 1977 was the result of the Equal Pay Act, incomes policies or both. However, this may overlook an important factor which might be more important than either of these legislative measures - the growth in female trade union membership (see Table 8 Hunt and Adams 1980).

This suggests that neither the Equal Pay Act nor incomes policies were in themselves the decisive measure in such an improvement over the period. It may have been the case, instead, that these facilitated but did not cause the improvements which were the result of the increased union strength of women workers. This conclusion accords well with the fact, noted earlier, that under periods of flat-rate policies (or those specifying minimum wage targets) the unionised low paid fared rather better than those who were less well-organised. The evidence of the effect of incomes on women workers is ambiguous. During periods of flat-rate pay policies, or where minimum wage targets are pursued, women seem to have fared rather better than in periods of percentage limits, along with the rest of the low paid. However, these gains were somewhat ephemeral. Moreover, the experience of low paid women in the private sector (principally wages councils) may have differed from those in the public sector. The pattern was not consistant; in some years the public sector low paid did relatively well; in others they received less than their private sector colleagues.

This suggests than an important contributory factor to the improvement in women's earnings may have been the growth in female unionisation during the 1970s. This may have enabled women workers through the collectiv bargaining power of the unions to make better use, both of incomes policy norms and the Equal Pay Act than would otherwise have been the case.

7. CONCLUSION

A combination of factors, arising from the nature of employment and from the statutory policies themselves, appear to be responsible for the limited effectiveness of the Equal Pay and Sex Discrimination Acts in improving womens pay and their concentration in low paid jobs. Other statutory policies which might have had a beneficial effect on the position of women in the labour market, have also had little effect. Minimum wage legislation - as it currently operates through the Wages Council machinery - appears to be a partial, and in many respects, an ineffective strategy, and it is difficult to separate the beneficial effects of pay policies on women's pay from their effects on the low paid in general.

What kind of policies and policy-mix, therefore, might be effective? What kind of strategies are needed to bring about real and lasting improvements? Overall the evidence suggests that more than one starategy is needed to overcome low pay amongst women workers. It suggests that additional legislative and voluntary strategies are needed. Although there is considerable debate about the way forward, it does seem clear that action is needed which is directed at the problems of women as workers as well as at low pay. Furthermore action is needed which recognises and addresses the questions of women's role in the home, action which will attack the root causes of womens position in the labour market. It has been suggested (Glucklich & Snell op. cit.) that action directed at women as workers should be aimed primarily at breaking down segregation and at enabling women to combine family responsibilities with working. Their specific recommendations include: - (i) action aimed at strengthening the existing equal pay and sex discrimination legislation by tackling discrimination more systematically and by positive action aimed at bringing women into traditional male job areas thus overcoming the effects of past dicrimination; (ii) changing the structures and patterns of industries and careers to take into account the different work and career patterns of women; (iii) increasing facilities to enable parents to raise children and continue working (the facilities they list include: extending maternity and paternity leave, better day-care facilities for children, the right to work shorter hours, access to better paid and more responsible jobs on a part-time or job-sharing basis). Finally they recommend that action should be aimed at increasing collective bargaining and trade union initiatives at both national and local level to introduce positive action programmes, to bring more women into pay bargaining, to widen collective bargaining strategies to cover the needs of women workers and to organise many more women in low paid industries into unions.

However, action aimed at low pay itself and in particular at the problems of the low paid industries is also needed. It seems unlikely that contracting or bankrupt industries will be able to provide higher wages and improved opportunities for women. Nor would it be acceptable merely to maintain the existing earnings ladder and improve women's position on it at the expense of men. Clearly women would be the major beneficiaries of most policies aimed at the low paid general. In particular, improvements in the effectiveness of the wages council system could have a significant effect on the relative pay of women workers (see E. MacLennan, op. cit.). A national minimum wage could also benefit women workers disproportionately as would a trade union development fund to help unions reach potential members in poorly organised workplaces. But as Glucklich and Snell conclude "until women have the genuine opportunity to move into better paid jobs and industries, and thus no longer constitute a pool of easily exploitable and cheap labour, there is likely to be little real improvement to the position of those on the bottom of the ladder, be they men or women" (Glucklich, Snell 1982).

But finding an appropriate policy mix, finding the right balance between the voluntary and legislative approaches, between voluntary action within legislative frameworks, and increased statutory intervention and enforcement, is a central issue for those involved in the study of policy and should be of concern to policy-makers if real and lasting change in the position of women in the labour market is to be achieved.

Table 1
Activity Rates for Males and Females aged 16 and over in Great Britain: 1951-1979

(Per cent) (including students)	1951	1961	1966	1971*	1976	1979	1986**
Males	89.0	88.6	87.4	85.8	83.8	82.2	80.4
Married Females	21.7	29.7	38.1	42.3	49.0	49.6	49.9
Non-married Females	56.8	54.5	55.0	51.5	50.4	50.7	51.1

Sources: Department of Employment Gazette, December 1975, Table 5, and April 1981, Table 4.

* Estimates for the period from 1951 to 1971 are derived from the Census of Population while those for the later years are derived from Labour Force Surveys and estimates of the working population published in the Gazette. The figures include students as economically active.

** Projected.

Table 2
The Earnings of Men and Women, 1970-1980

APRIL	1970	1973	1975	1977	1980	1982
Average Gross Weekly Earnings (including Overtime) (£'s)						
Men	29.7	41.9	60.8	78.6	124.5	154.5
Women	16.2	23.1	37.4	51.0	78.8	99.0
Womens earnings and a % of mens	54.4	55.1	61.5	64.9	63.3	64.1
Average Gross Hourly Earnings (excluding Overtime) (pence)						
Men	67.4	91.6	136.6	177.4	280.7	364.6
Women	42.5	60.3	98.3	133.9	206.4	262.1
earnings as a % of mens	63.1	66.8	72.1	75.5	73.5	71.8

Source: Equal Opportunities Commission, Fifth Annual Report, Table 4.3 and New Earnings Surveys, 1980-1982, Part A, Table 1.

Table 3
Full-time women's average hourly earnings (excluding overtime)
as a percentage of men's, by industry 1970 and 1980

	Manual		Non Manual	
	1970 %	1980 %	1970 %	1980 %
All industries and services	61.7	70.9	52.5	61.1
Food, drink and tobacco	62.4	74.5	n. a.	57.6
Chemical and allied industries	59.1	68.3	42.9	52.0
Metal Manufacture	n. a.	67.8	n. a.	56.6
Mechanical engineering	62.8	75.0	46.9	56.5
Instrument engineering	63.6	74.1	n. a.	54.8
Electrical engineering	64.5	72.8	44.0	57.4
Vehicles	63.4	77.3	47.5	58.7
Metal Goods	60.4	72.0	n. a.	54.1
Textiles	67.3	73.1	n. a.	50.2
Woollen and Worsted	70.3	78.7	n. a.	n. a.
Clothing and footwear	62.7	73.3	n. a.	n. a.
Clothing	65.7	76.4	n. a.	n. a.
Bricks and Rottery	66.3	71.1	n. a.	58.1
Timber and furniture	n. a.	n. a.	n. a.	55.9
Paper & printing	54.0	66.9	n. a.	63.3
Other manufacturing	59.8	69.5	n. a.	57.4
Gas, electricity and water	n. a.	n. a.	50.8	55.7
Transport and communication	79.0	81.7	59.1	65.1
Distributive Trades	62.8	75.8	45.6	56.1
Retail distribution of food and drink	63.4	78.3	n. a.	57.9
Insurance and banking	n. a.	n. a.	43.2	51.3
Professional and scientific services	65.6	79.0	57.1	66.3
Catering	56.0	81.8	n. a.	73.7
Miscellaneous services	59.3	74.7	53.6	68.6
Public Administration	71.4	81.2	61.3	64.9
Local Government Service	72.5	78.9	62.9	63.4

Source: New Earnings Survey 1970, tables 18-21; New Earnings Survey 1980, tables 54-57, part C.

Table 4 a
Women as a % of industrial labour force, April 1980

	%
Agriculture, Forestry, Fishing	16.6
Food, Drink and Tobacco	39.5
Chemicals and Allied Industries	26.0
Metal Manufacture	12.2
Mechanical Engineering	15.1
Instrument Engineering	33.3
Electrical Engineering	35.0
Vehicles	11.5
Metal Goods not elsewhere specified	26.2
Textiles	42.4
Clothing and Footwear	74.5
Bricks, Pottery, Glass, Cement, etc.	25.5
Timber, Furniture, etc.	20.5
Paper, Printing and Publishing	30.6
Other Manufacturing Industries	35.4
Transport and Communication	18.7
Distributive Trades	53.4
Insurance, Banking, Finance and Business Services	51.2
Professional and Scientific Services	68.5
Miscellaneous Services	53.9
Public Administration	40.9
All Industries Total	39.4

Table 4 b
Women as a % of occupational labour force, April 1980

Non Manual	%
Managerial (General)	7.6
Professional and related	14.2
Prof and related in Education, Welfare and Health	65.5
Literary, Artistic and Sports	24.6
Prof and related in Science and Similar fields	7.7
Managerial (excluding General Management)	12.9
(part) Clerical and related	75.6
(part) Selling	60.0
(part) Security and Protective Service	7.7
Manual	
Catering, Cleaning, Hairdressing etc.	76.3
Materials Processing (excluding Metal)	24.8
Making & Repairing (excluding Metal and Electrical)	35.8
Processing, Making, Repairing & related	5.3
Painting, Repetitive Assembling, etc.	48.0
Transport Operating, Materials Moving etc.	5.5
Total Manual and Non-Manual	39.4

Source: Dept. of Employment, New Earnings Survey 1980, Part E.

Table 5
Wages Councils — actual gross weekly earnings compared with
statutory minimum remuneration, full-time male and female workers
excluding those whose pay was affected by absence, April 1979, £ per week

Wages Council (a)	WOMEN Average Earnings	SMR. (b)	MEN Average Earnings
Dressmaking & Women's Light Clothing (E&W)	49.20 M	34.60	—
Ready-made and Wholesale Bespoke Tailoring	48.30 M	42.00	—
Made-up Textiles	52.80 M	38.00	—
Retail Food (E&W)	48.60 M/N	41.70	85.40 M/N
Retail Bread and Flour (E&W)	48.30 M/N	42.00	—
Retail Drapery	52.60 M/N	38.10	88.20 M/N
Retail Furnishing	49.60 M/N	42.00	78.80 M/N
Licensed Res Est	45.00 M	40.40	63.30 M
Licensed Non Res Est	43.20 M	41.00	68.00 M
Unlicensed Place of Refresh	44.90 M	34.92	—
Hairdressing	41.60 M	31.35	—
All Wages Councils:			
1. Manual	47.70	—	72.50
2. Non-manual	49.80	—	86.10
3. Average SMR (b)	—	39.00	—

(a) Those for whom NES data exists.

(b) For those settlements operative or proposed on 30.4.79.

M — Manual

N — Non manual

Source: New Earnings Survey April 1979, Part B, Tables 30 and 31; and wages council settlements published in IDS
Report No. 301, March 1979, and IDS Report No. 307, June 1979.

Table 6
Lowest decile as a percentage of corresponding median earnings

	Men (1) All	Women (2) All
	%	%
1970	65.4	64.2
1971	66.1	65.0
1972	65.5	65.6
1973	65.6	67.4
1974	66.8	67.7
1975	67.0	67.4
1976	67.6	66.1
1977	68.1	68.6
1978	66.8	69.1
1979	66.0	69.4
1980	65.9	68.4
1981	65.6	68.0
1982	64.5	66.9

(1) Full time, over the age of 21, pay not affected by absence.

(2) Full time, over the age of 18, pay not affected by absence.

Source: NES 1982, Part B, Table 30.

Table 7
Average female earnings as a percentage of average male earnings

	Weekly Earnings (including overtime) %	Hourly Earnings (including overtime) %
1970	54	63
1971	56	64
1972	56	64
1973	54	64
1974	56	66
1975	61	70
1976	64	74
1977	65	74
1978	63	73
1979	62	71
1980	63	72
1981	65	73
1982	64	72

Source: NES, Part B, Tables 30 and 31.

Table 8
Unions with largest increases in women's membership

	1968 000's	1978 000's	Increase 000's	Per cent Increase
National Union of Public Employees	136.0	457.4	321.4	236
National and Local Government Officers Association	132.1	318.8	186.7	141
Transport and General Worker's Union	194.7	317.9	123.2	63
Confederation of Health Service Employees	38.9	159.4	120.5	310
National Union of General and Municipal Workers	199.9	318.2	118.3	59
Union of Shop, Distributive and Allied Workers	155.6	270.5	114.9	74
Association of Scientific Technical and Managerial Staffs	9.4	77.2	67.8	721
Civil and Public Services Association	100.0	158.8	58.8	59
Amalgamated Union of Engineering Workers (Engineering Section)	97.4	148.3	50.9	52
Association of Professional, Executive, Clerical and Computer Staff	38.7	83.7	45.0	116

Source: Hunt, J. and Adams, S., Op. Cit., page 14.

NOTES

* This paper has been prepared from the United Kingdom report "Women in the Labour Market. A study of the impact of legislation and policy towards women in the UK Labour market" by R. Elliott, P. Glucklich, E. MacLennan, C. Pond.

(1) The 1970 Equal Pay Act came into force, after a five year implementation period, on December 29, 1975, the day on which the Sex Discrimination Act came onto the statute book.

The Equal Pay Act's main objective was to provide for equal treatment in contractual terms between men and women. Specifically, it laid down that women were entitled to equal pay with men if they were doing the same, or broadly similar, work, or if their jobs had been rated as of equivalent value under a job evaluation exercise. In addition to the individual provisions of the Act, the collective provisions laid down that collective agreements or pay structures were to be non-dicriminatory. The 1975 Sex Discrimination Act makes it unlawful to discriminate on grounds of sex against a person in relation to employment and other fields. Although the Act is drafted in terms of discrimination against women, its provisions apply equally to discrimination against men and, in the employment field only, to discrimination against married persons. The Act defines two kinds of discrimination, direct and indirect discrimination. It also has special provisions in relation to certain kinds of statutory exceptions and in relation to positive action by training bodies and employers in specific circumstances. As with the Equal Pay Act, an individual has the right to take her (or his) case to an Industrial Tribunal. The Act also provided for the setting up of the Equal Opportunities Commission (EOC), a body whose statutory duty is to promote equality of opportunity for women and to enforce the legislation in certain circumstances.

(2) Red circle cases are defined as Equal Pay cases where a pay differential exists for reasons personal to the holder, i.e. where an employee has moved from a higher paid post to a lower paid post, (for example, for health reasons), but retains their previous salary. (Equal Opportunities Commission, (1982) Towards Equality,Glossary page 127).

(3) In Autumn 1981 the adult minimum rates ranged from Ł 39 a week in hairdressing to Ł 59 a week for shopworkers. The median wages council rate currently stands at Ł 54.20. The level of these rates may be compared with the official definitions of 'poverty' in Britain. At rates applicable from November 1981, a typical family (married couple with two young children) would be entitled to a minimum income under supplementary benefit - unless the head of household was employed full-time - of Ł 60.02 per week (including averaging housing costs). Where the head of households was employed full-time (30 hours or more per week) this family would be entitled to claim Family Income Supplement until their earnings reached Ł 64.50 per week. By comparison the current minimum adult rates established by the wages councils are shown in Table 5.

REFERENCES

Advisory, Conciliation and Arbitration Service (1981). The Contract Cleaning Industry. Report No. 20.

Advisory, Conciliation and Arbitration Service (1978). Toy Manufacturing council. Report No. 13.

Chiplin, B., Curran, C., Parsley, C. (1980) "Relative Female Earnings in Great Britain and the Impact of Legislation",(Chapter 3). P. Sloane Ed.Women and Low Pay. MacMillan London.

Clothing Wages Council (1974), Report No. 77 , HMSO. London.

Commission for Industrial Relations (1974), Retail Distribution Report No. 89 HMSO London.

Crine, S. (1980), Legal Minimum Wages, Studies for trade unionists. Workers Educational Association.

Equal Opportunities Commission (1981), Fifth Annual Report 1980, Equal Opportunities Commission (1982), Towards Equality. A casebook of decisions on Sex Discrimination and Equal Pay, 1976-1981.

Glucklich, P. and Snell, M., Women and Low Pay, Low Pay Unit, Discussion Series. No. 2.

Hunt, J. and Adams, S. (1980), Women, Work and Trade Union Organisation. Studies for Trade Unionists. Workers Educational Association.

IFF Research Ltd. (1981), Women and Under-achievement at work, Research Bulletin No. 5, Spring 1981.MacLennan, E. (1980), Minimum Wages for Women, Equal Opportunities Commission/Low Pay Unit.

McIntosh, A. (1980). IFF Research Ltd. "Women at Work: A survey of Employers." Department of Employment Gazette, November 1980.

Mitchell, Alison (1976), "The consequences of the Equal Pay Act" Field F (Ed) Are Low Wages Inevitable? Russell Press.

National Board for Prices and Incomes (1971). General Problems of Low Pay Report No. 169. HMSO 1971.

Playford C. (1980) Low Pay Policies. Low Pay Unit Report No. 2. Low Pay Unit.

Robarts, S. with Coote, A. and Ball, E. (1981). Positive Action for Women: The next step in Education, Training and Employment NCCL.

Royal Commission on the Distribution of Income and Wealth (1978), Lower Incomes Report No. 6, HMSO London.

Starr, G. (1980), Minimum Wage Fixing. International Labour Office, Geneva.

Snell, M.W., Glucklich, P., and Povall, M. (1981), Equal Pay and Opportunities Research Paper No. 20: Department of Employment.

7 EQUAL OPPORTUNITY POLICIES IN SWEDEN

SIV GUSTAFSSON

1.   INTRODUCTION

There are a large number of policies and instruments directed to promote equality between men and women in Sweden. Sweden has previously stressed social policy instruments rather than antidiscrimination rules. It was not until 1980 that the Act on Equality between men and women at work was passed.

Among the important social policy means should be mentioned separate taxation of earnings of husband and wife which has the effect of increasing the payoff to more equal distribution of paid work. Paid parental leaves for childcare not only for mothers but also for fathers is believed to be important. State subsidized daycare centers have been built. Supply of places at daycare centers does however not meet demand.

Some facts are still very discouraging for proponents of equality between men and women in Sweden. Other facts are more heartening. Among the more encouraging of these is the development of labor force participation. Swedish women have a labor force participation rate that is rapidly approaching that of men. Women make up 46 per cent of the total labor force. In 1982 the male rate of labor force participation for ages 16-64 was 86.3 per cent and the female rate was 76.9 per cent. The highest labor force participation rate of women is in the age group of 35-44 where it is 87.3 per cent. The corresponding male rate in this age group is 96.3 per cent. Women have entered the labor force and the trends show no sign of levelling off in spite of the decreasing level of economic activity in recent years. In 1980 about 37 per cent of the total wage and earnings bill was paid to women. Men consequently earned   63 per cent of total Swedish labor income (1). One of the most important reasons for this is the large proportion of part time workers among women. In 1982 46.6 per cent were part time workers. In addition to the large share of part time workers it is important to note that because of generous leaves of absence in connection with childbirth the absentee rate has increased in Sweden. At the time of childbirth and care of newly born infants, Swedish mothers continue to be employed but on leave, whereas in countries with less generous parental leave mothers give up their jobs and are considered out of the labor force.

One of the most discouraging facts is that sex segregation by occupation is very pronounced. Occupational segregation is dealt with more in detail in Christina Jonung's chapter of this volume. In addition to occupational segregation within the same occupation women have the less prestigious positions. 34.5 per cent of the men in the private sector who have a degree in business administration have managing positions while only 8.5 per cent of women do so (2). Of all managing directors mentioned in an industry directory only 28 out of 2 341 were women (3). The same pattern applies to the government sector. In spite of the fact that women make up 60 per cent of all school teachers their share among heads of schools is only 14 per cent (4).

The purpose of this chapter is to describe equal opportunity policies in Sweden. Those interested in the development of labor force participation and earnings of Swedish women are referred to other chapters of this volume and other work (5).

The outline of the chapter is first to give a description of some of the most important social policy instruments that have been used in the work for equal opportunity for women and then describe the anti-discrimination legislation.

2.   SOCIAL POLICIES TOWARD EQUALIZATION

2.1   Education and Occupation

The first prerequisite in the road towards equality between men and women in the labor market is to open all education and occupations to women.

We do not have to go back far in Swedish history to find that occupational and educational choices for women were restricted. Until the middle of the 19th century women lacked legal capacity. They were supervised by their husbands if married and by their fathers or brothers if unmarried. They could not sign any contracts; that is to say, no work contracts could be concluded. Restrictions were gradually abolished. In 1958 an unmarried woman was made legally responsible automatically at the age of 25. Demographic changes led to a much larger proportion of adult unmarried women (6). According to Gunnar Qvist (1978) it was not desirable to emancipate women but rather to diminish economic burden for brothers and fathers that made the parliament take the decision to extend freedom of trade to unmarried women in 1846. Public employment was opened to women for the first time in 1858 when women were allowed to teach the first years of elementary school.

Some restrictions were introduced to protect women from danger. In 1901 there was a ban on women working underground in mining and quarrying, in spite of the fact that the ban was opposed to by women active in the labor movement. This restriction was later removed and no work is now legally considered for women, with the exception of many military occupations. In 1958 a law was passed to admit women into the "state church" of Sweden. This could be done only after allowing those ministers who had "confessional doubts" to refuse working with female colleagues.

Beginning in the middle of the 19th century the Swedish people's school (folkskola) system was developed to teach elementary reading, writing and Bible studies to everyone's children, boys as well as girls (7). Parallel to this, secondary schools were developed for boys only (realskola and gymnasium). The student could graduate from the realskola after 4+5 years of schooling or continue in the gymnasium. After 4+4+4 years of schooling in folkskola, realskola and gymnasium respectively, the student got the "studentexamen" certificate and qualified for university studies (8).

During the 1860's a separate school system for girls was developed, the girls school (flickskola). The "flickskola" was a kind of secondary school that had as much training as the secondary schools for boys (realskola) in the humanities but much less in the natural sciences and mathematics (Kyle, 1979). Girls entered the "flickskola" after the fourth grade in the elementary school, and it took seven years to finish. "Flickskolor" existed as separate schools until the beginning of the 1960's (9).

The parallel system was abolished beginning in 1950 with the decision to gradually extend compulsory schooling to 9 years and from 1962 the "grundskola" was introduced, meaning that the "folkskola", the "realskola" and the "flickskola" were integrated into a single school. The idea behind the comprehensive grundskola is that more equality and understanding between people is achieved if children are not segregated at an early stage in life.

The Swedish equality concept emphasizes the individual as opposed to the family. Today young women have the same opportunities as men to participate in any education including university studies. Very important in this respect is that students loans and subsidies are not made dependant on parent's income, but the individual young man or woman is considered solely on the basis of his or her own income. This means that parents cannot exclude daughters from higher studies even if they favor and subsidize such for their sons.

Sweden has a policy of no tuition at all for any kind of schooling. For financing costs of living of university students, state-subsidized students loans with a grant part are available. In the Swedish system parents do not have to carry a heavy financial burden that is concentrated in a few years; individuals do not depend on their parents for receiving a higher education (10).

Student loans were long dependent on the spouse's income. Often married women who are in low paid jobs want to increase their earning power by acquiring new education after their children have grown up. If student loans are dependent on husband's earnings, the wife cannot leave her job in order to go to school because her earnings are needed to meet the costs of the family. In 1980 student loans were made indepent of the spouse's income, resulting in better opportunities for adult women to participate in re-education. In Table 1 the educational distribution of the Swedish population in 1980 is given. There are much bigger differences between age groups than between men and women when the educational achievements of different demographic groups are compared. Within the group of people with secondary training men have received longer training than women. The proportion of university trained men with the longest education is also larger than the corresponding proportion for women. The main impression is, however, that women have about the same amount of education as men.

Table 1

Distribution by educational level of the Swedish population in 1981

	20—24		25—34		35—44		45—54		55—64	
	f	m	f	m	f	m	f	m	f	m
Compulsory										
less than 9 yrs	3.1	4.0	12.9	14.1	33.2	36.7	52.9	52.2	67.0	62.2
9 years	21.9	23.8	18.0	17.1	13.7	9.1	9.0	5.9	8.7	4.7
	25.0	27.8	30.9	31.2	46.9	45.8	61.9	58.1	75.7	66.9
Secondary										
1 year	10.9	6.5	15.8	6.9	16.2	7.3	13.5	7.9	8.3	7.7
2 yrs or more than one	30.4	35.5	15.7	20.8	11.7	11.4	8.5	9.1	4.7	6.8
more than 2 yrs	17.4	21.1	11.8	19.1	7.1	14.7	3.8	11.0	3.6	8.8
	58.7	62.1	43.3	46.8	35.0	33.4	25.8	28.0	16.6	23.3
University										
less than 2 yrs	12.0	6.5	11.5	8.4	7.3	5.4	4.9	4.4	3.3	1.8
more than 2 yrs	4.1	2.2	14.0	12.6	10.1	13.9	7.0	7.8	3.7	7.0
	16.1	8.7	25.5	21.0	17.4	19.3	11.9	12.2	7.0	8.8
Total population	99.8	98.6	99.7	99.0	99.3	98.5	99.6	98.3	99.3	99.0

Source: Labor Force Surveys ("Arssysselsättningen 1980 och Utbildningsnivan februari 1981, Tilläggsfragor till Arbets-kraftsundersökningen, AKU, i februari 1981"), investigation, education and retrospective survey. National Central Bureau of Statistics, SCB.

2.2   Maternity Protection and Parental Leaves

Maternity protection has existed since the beginning of the industrialization (11). In the year 1900 an employer was forbidden to put a woman to work earlier than 4 weeks after childbirth. This restriction was extended 2 weeks before and 6 weeks after childbirth in 1912. The right to leave of absence before childbirth was extended in 1931 and again in 1948 when there was a right to leave 6 weeks before birth and it was made unlawful to employ a woman earlier than 6 weeks after birth.

However, women were often dismissed when they married or became pregnant. In 1939 a law protecting women from dismissal because of childbirth or marriage was introduced. It stated that the woman had a right to be absent 12 weeks without being dismissed. In 1945 this period was extended to 6 months. Not until 1962 was this 6 months leave of absence turned into a paid leave of absence.

The law of 1945 was effective until the first law of parental leave   was   instituted in 1974. It was in the act of 1974 that parental leave was introduced. It gave parents a choice so that either the mother or the father could stay home from work without being dismissed.

In 1975 a second kind of childcare leave was introduced, called leave for "occasional care". Parents got the right to stay home from work to take care of the children when they got sick. At introduction there was a maximum of 10 days per child per year allowed but it has later been extended to 60 days per child per year. Fortunately, Swedish children are not often sick. The average number of days used per child is 5.5 as shown in table 2 B.

In 1978 a third kind of child care leave was introduced, called the "special child care leave". This last reform can be used in a number of different ways. It can be used to lengthen the period of leave absence in connection with childbirth. It can also be used to take leaves of absence at special periods in your child's life when there is extra need for such, i.e. during the first school year. The allowance is 180 days of which the frist three months are given full earnings compensation and the next three months a per diem allowance equal for all of SEK 37 (12) is provided. In 1979 in addition to all this, either of the parents were given the right to shorten work hours without compensation to six hours a day until the child is 8 years old.

The Swedish law on parental leaves distinguishes four different rights to child care leave:

     1) leave to care for the newborn
     2) occasional care for sick children
     3) special child care leave to be used with great flexibility
     4) the right to reduced working hours.

A special paid leave has been introduced (havandeskapsledighet) for mothers, whose work is too hard for a pregnant woman to perform, to compensate for the fact that such mothers otherwise must take time before birth. The right to this leave is given only for special circumstances and if the employer is unable to offer lighter work during pregnancy.

The earliest regulations on rights to leaves of absence were not connected with any kind of economic subsidies. The first maternity allowance introduced in 1937 included only mothers who were in need of economic assistance. In 1954 the maternity allowances were connected to the mandatory national health insurance system.

The subsidies are paid out of tax money and not by the employer. An employee must qualify for the rights to parental leave by having worked with the firm for 6 months during the year or 12 months altogether during the past two years. Exempted from this work requirement is leave of absence for occasional care of sick children and 6 weeks before and after birth for the mother. The employer must also be given notice two months in advance, if a parent is going to take advantage of the leave of absence. The notice is necessary since paid parental leaves include fathers and also include adopted children.

The regulations of the Swedish maternity and parental leave make it economically very important to first be established in the labor market and then have a child. The benefits are paid to compensate for loss of income. A woman who gets a child directly after school or while in school does not have

Table 2 A
Per cent absent of employed due to child care leaves in Sweden 1980

Both Sexes	Paid parental leave at child's birth	other including occasional care	Unpaid child care leave	Own sickness	Vacation	Total absence[a]
Men and women	1.3	0.2	0.2	4.3	9.0	17.8
Men	–	0.3	–		8.6	15.6
Women	2.7	0.2	0.5	4.7	9.4	20.5
Women with children under 7	12.6	1.1	2.4	3.9	8.8	31.7

a   Forms of absence not separately shown are leaves for studies (1.2 per cent of all employed), week off schedule (1.1 for all employed), military service (0.9 per cent of employed men equals 0.5 for all employed).

Source: Tables 4 and 5 of RRV 1980: 1242.

Table 2 B
Days paid parental leaves subsidies

	At child's birth		Occasional care		
	Thousand days per year[a]	% used by men	Thousand days per year[a]	% used by men	Average number of days used[c]
1974	16 726	0.5	689	39.9	3.9
1975	15 980	1.2	958	40.4	4.1
1976	15 781	1.7	1 076	40.6	4.1
1977	16 185	2.7	1 850	46.3	5.0
1978	18 075[b]	4.8[b]	2 416	53.3	5.4
1979	20 107[b]	5.1[b]	2 855	52.8	5.5

a   Total number of days in all Sweden used during the year.
b   Days used for "special child care leave" whether used at child's birth or later available from 1978 have been included in column 1 by adding two columns of table 17 in the primary source.
c   Per year per parent who used parental leave for occasional care, i.e. for caring for sick children.

Source: Tables 17 and 18 of RRV 1980: 1242.

an income to be compensated for. Unless the mother finds a job shortly after delivery, the opportunity to share parental leave between father and the mother is also lost.

It is apparent from table 2 that fathers take quite a small share of the parental leave except for the days of occasional child care where the men take more than half of the 5.5 days used on average per child per year. Also many fathers use the special child care to stay home 10 days when mother and child come home from the maternity hospital.

2.3 Separate Taxation of Income

A tax system that makes it profitable for spouses to equitably divide work between them so that both spouses work in the market and in the household is a preferable system from the point of view of equality between men and women. Not only does it give the woman an income of her own in the present but also helps to build up her human capital so that she becomes more competitive in the labor market in the future. Furthermore it gives her a pension of her own that can support her in old age or in the case of divorce.

The combination of a high marginal tax with separate taxation of income often induces additional work from the wife. The correct comparison to make is if the husband by increasing his work hours can increase his net income more than the wife can increase her net income by a similar increase in hours. If there are children, it is very important to the net family income if they have places at a government subsidized daycare center or not. The parent's fee is dependent on income and increases with the level of income. This creates marginal effects. There is, furthermore, a housing subsidy dependent on income which also creates marginal effects.

The average and marginal tax rates for one earner and two earner families have been calculated by Lybeck (1981) and are reproduced in tables 3 A and 3 B. It is evident that both marginal and average tax rates are higher for the one-earner family than for the two earner-family (13).

Comparing the one-earner family with the two-earner family at SEK 70 000 taxable income per year shows that the average tax is equal but the marginal tax is 90 per cent for the one-earner family as compared to the two-earner family. This is a case where it is more profitable for a wife to start working even a limited number of hours per week rather than increasing the husband's work hours from full time work. The income brackets shown in the calculation are ordinary Swedish earnings. Therefore the calculation shows the amount of income Swedish taxpayers pay to the public sector. A fulltime industrial worker would in 1981 earn about SEK 70 000. Since parttime work is often more than half time SEK 40 000 per year is not an unusual income for a part-time working woman. The calculation of who shall increase work hours in order to increase family net income is complicated by the fact that mortgages payments are deductable. For homeowners it might be more profitable to increase gross income by a high wage earner. This effect is not included in table 3 A and 3 B since the calculation is based on net taxable income after deductions.

Table 3 A
Average and marginal taxes for a one earner household with two young children

Taxable income SEK	State tax SEK	Local community tax, SEK	Housing Subsidy SEK	Average tax percent	Marginal tax percent
30 000	(-1 432)	7 092	10 920	– 18	45
50 000	(– 86)	13 002	9 120	8	73
70 000	4 586	18 912	5 136	26	90
90 000	11 960	24 822	336	41	78
110 000	21 274	30 732	–	47	(81) 80
130 000	31 574	36 642	–	52	(83) 80
150 000	42 174	42 552	–	56	(83) 80
170 000	52 774	48 402	–	60	(87) 80
190 000	64 174	54 372	–	62	85

Table 3 B
Average and marginal taxes for two earner households with two children, one spouse assumed constant income at SEK 40 000

Taxable family income, SEK	State + local community tax, SEK	Housing Subsidy SEK	Parents fee at daycare center SEK	Average tax percent	Marginal tax percent
70 000	17 780	5 136	5 760	26	68
90 000	25 036	336	7 200	35	62
110 000	35 618	–	8 640	40	74
130 000	48 902	–	10 080	45	81
150 000	64 126	–	11 040	50	(84) 82
170 000	80 336	–	11.520	54	(84) 80
190 000	96 846	–	11 520	57	80

Note: There is a rule that marginal income taxes should not exceed 80-85 per cent. This rule disregards day care fees and housing subsidies. The bracketed figures in the last column would apply in the absence of this rule.

Source: Lybeck, 1981.

2.4 Daycare for Children

We have seen that the Swedish society has greatly enabled working women to have children through paid parental leaves of absence. Moreover, we have described above how there are strong economic incentives for women to work after childbirth. The most important concern for parents when both want to work, is how to arrange daycare for their children. Without daycare there can be no working for one of the parents, usually for the mother.

In Sweden there has been extensive involvement in building daycare centers for children during the past 10 years. Whereas in the 1960's there were daycare centers only for a minority of children, the 1970's have seen a rapid increase in the number of places.

In table 4 some facts about the Swedish day care system are given. The proportion of children 0-6 years old who have a place at the day care center has increased from 5 per cent to 20.5 per cent. In addition to this 13.4 per cent had a subsidized place with a day care mother. In 1981 there is an estimate of the proportion of children who have a mother that either works or studies more than 20 hours per week. This estimate is 53.8 per cent of the children. From this can be concluded that there is an excess demand for day care at the price paid.

The day care centers are built and run by the communities. There are extensive public subsidies for day care. It is evident from table 4 that the cost for a place at the day care center has greatly increased. Parental fees made up only 8.8 per cent of total costs in 1982 whereas half of the total costs are covered by a state subsidy and the remainder is borne by the community.

Since only a small proportion of the cost of a place at a day care center is paid by the parents it is very interesting to try to estimate the social effectiveness of day care centers. Jönsson (1970) came to the conclusion that the communities paid too large a proportion of the costs of day care. Because they lost money in this area, they had little incentive to increase the number of places.

One issue in calculation of costs and benefits of day care was raised by Gustafsson (1978). Since individuals invest in their human capital not only through schooling but also through on-the-job-training, labor force withdrawals carry costs in the form of labor force interruptions. From a theoretical point of view such costs can arise because of two reasons: First there is no opportunity to make further inestments in job related activities when the mother cares for the children at home. Second the possibility exists that labor force withdrawals will also carry a cost of depreciation of human capital (Mincer and Polachek, 1974). For these two reasons we might expect human capital or earnings capacity to be smaller for women with interrupted careers than for those with continuous careers. Since the human capital is smaller, their productivity in the labor market is also lower. The effect of this can be observed in smaller earnings after returning to the labor market.

The long run costs and benefits of day care have been estimated by Gustafsson (1978) using salary data for about 32 000 salaried employees in the private sector of Sweden (14). The results of the calculations can be interpreted in the following way: Lifetime earnings of fulltime working women without labor

Table 4
Public day care

YEAR	Per cent children 0-6 with subsidized day care		Per cent children 0-6 needing a place [1]	Total cost of a place at a day care center in SEK	Per cent paid by parents	Per cent paid by central government	Per cent paid by local government
	Day care centers	Day care mothers					
1971	5.0	4.6					
1972	6.1	4.4					
1973	7.1	4.7					
1974	7.9	5.6					
1975	8.6	6.5		20 675	11.5	38.2	50.4
1976	10.1	7.8		23 540	10.4	33.5	56.1
1977	10.8	9.0		26 960	9.9	51.6	38.5
1978	13.7	9.7	48.8	31 460	9.8	50.1	40.1
1979	16.3	10.9		34 505	9.6	52.5	38.0
1980	18.4	12.9		38 590	9.1	51.2	39.7
1981	20.5	13.4	53.8	42 700	8.3	49.8	41.9
1982				45 300	8.8	49.6	41.6

1 "need" is calculated on the basis that the mother of the child either works or studies more than 20 hours per week.

Sources: Columns 1 and 2: SOS, Socialvården 1980 and Befolkningsförändringar.

Column 3: Socialstyrelsen, Barnomsorgen i siffror.

Columns 4, 5, 6 and 7: Svenska Kommunförbundet.

interruptions are on average big enough to pay for 4.4 places at day care centers during 7 years of full day care and an additional 4 years of after school care estimated at half the cost of full day care. Compared to a life-time career as a housewife the break-even point is more than 4 children.

Jönsson and Paulsson (1979) recalculate social costs and benefits of day care. One of the calculations shows that women with children at pre-school age who entered the labor market during the past 10 years and working at least half-time have increased GNP by an amount twice as big as the cost of the places at day care centers for the children of these women. Even if these calcu-lations are good arguments for arranging day care for children, they tell us nothing about who should pay for it. Parents who have places at day care centers receive a large allowance. Whether the system should be developed into a cost-free one like the public school system is today or if fees should in-stead be increased is a political question. The financial situation in Sweden has slowed down the increase in the number of places of day care centers. Today social losses from lack of day care places must be weighted against social losses from increasing already large budget deficits.

2.5   Labor Market Policies

It is one of the goals of Swedish labor market policy to promote equality between women and men in the labor market. A program entitled: "Equality on the Labor Market" - a task for the labor market authorities, was accepted in plenum by the National Labor Market Board (AMS for Arbetsmarknadsstyrelsen) in 1977. This program starts by stating the goal as laid out in a Swedish Government report to the United Nations from 1968: "Every individual irrespective of sex shall have the same practical opportunities not only for education or employment but also in principle the same responsibility for his or her own maintenance as well as shared responsibility for the upbringing of children and the home making". It means that time devoted to market work and unpaid home work should be distributed equally between spouses and it would not be consistent with this goal to have more equal distribution across families with some women assuming the traditional male role and some men the traditional female role. The AMS program for equality states this idea of equality to be the universally accepted official Swedish view. This is however much too optimistic in view of reality (15).

The common aim of labor market policies, general economic policy and demand management is to reduce unemployment. Labor market policy is often restricted to mean policies financed through the budget of the AMS. Labor market policies are important in terms of the number of people being enrolled and the share of GNP spent on programs. In the budget year of 1977/78 labor market programs amounted to 9 per cent of government expenditure and 3 per cent of GNP.

Since 1972 more people have been in labor market programs as an annual average than in open unemployment (see Stafford, 1981 and Johannesson, 1981). In 1981 the open unemployment rate was 2.5 per cent of the labor force and the proportion of people in programs 2.7 per cent.

This emphasis on labor market programs as the main way of helping people who risk unemployment as opposed to helping them only by cash payments is known as the work principle as opposed to the cash principle. The priorities for the employment offices are: 1) job placements, 2) labor market training, 3) relief work.

To be eligible for unemployment benefits there is a member requirement and a work requirement. The person must have been a member in an unemployment benefit society run by unions and subsidized by the government for 12 months and have worked for 5 months during the last year. Membership is most often gained in connection with the first job when the person is recruited into the union. In order to insure those who do not fulfill the member requirement another subsidy called the cash labor market assistance (KAS) was introduced. The work requirement was retained but an exception was made for persons who came directly from schooling or labor market training and who had already been unemployed for 5 months. The unemployment insurance is paid for a maximum of 300 days and the KAS for 150 days if the person is younger than 55 years. For older persons the limits are 450 and 300 days respectively. The unemployment benefit is about the same size as the wage of a low level industrial job and the cash labor market assistance provides a smaller subsidy.

The large increase in the female labor force participation rate for Swedish women has been helped by the fact that in the 1960's and early 1970's there was an excess demand for labor in Sweden. Much of this excess demand was met by immigration or, as it was called at that time, "imported labor". However the AMS was early in trying to meet demand for labor by also motivating married women to enter the labor force (16). In the 1960's 100 "activation inspectors" were recruited to the employment offices of the AMS with the special purpose to "activate" women into entering the labor force. A well-known project carried out in 1974 in Kristianstad later on resulted in a regular course given on entry and re-entry of women to worklife and education (ALU-kurs). Since 1974 there has been a sex quota in the regional policy subsidy given to firms that increase employment in the regionally subsidized areas of Sweden. The sex quota stipulates that at least 40 per cent of the increase in employment must be by the "underrepresented sex", which has always been the women. There is also an "equality grant" which can be applied for by an employer who educates women into male dominated occupations. This grant has seldom been used which is believed to be caused by the fact that the firms think there is too much bureaucracy involved for too little money.

For most job applicants, men and women, the services of the employment office in matching the job applicant with available vacancies should be more important than different kinds of subsidies and quotas. In this respect the easily accessible information on vacancies from all occupations and regions by computerization has been considered very important. It is held to be easier to carry out guidance talks and show on the computer terminal how the number of possible vacancies increases if the applicant is less rigid and considers change of occupation and regional mobility.

Schooling for the unemployed has existed since the end of the second world war. Originally the students of labor market training were refugees and handicapped and those were the only persons eligible for economic subsidies during training. Today there are education benefits for all students in the labor market training equal to the unemployment benefits and an additional per diem of SEK 10 called "stimulation addition" to induce people to go to labor market training rather than just receiving the unemployment subsidy. In 1980 the training of the handicapped was delegated to a special organisation called the Employability Assessments Institutes (AMI). Most of the labor market training takes place in special schools the AMU-centers available in 120 places all over Sweden. The training is mostly vocational but some labor market training has been in the ordinary school system.

To qualify for labor market training the person must be 20 years old, be unemployed or risk unemployment or apply for education into a shortage occupation. During the fiscal year 1979/80 the number of persons starting labor market training was about 86 500, of which 49 per cent were women. Only 12 per cent of those going to labor market training in manual industrial work were women, which is about the same proportion as in 1969 and a decrease from 1974 when 26 per cent were women. Women make up 74 per cent of those going to courses in service work (17).

Attempts to create employment by relief work was started already in 1914 by the State. In 1933 relief works became a regular countercyclical and a special authority was instituted called the "Unemployment commission" (AK-kommissionen). In 1948 the active labor market policy was born and the unemployment commission was reorganized into the labor market board. Wages paid to persons in relief work are equal to market wages. Traditionally relief work had been arranged in typical male areas of employment but in recent years   relief work are equal to market wages. Traditionally relief work had been arranged in typical male areas of employment but in recent years relief work has also been created in e.g. hospitals. The proportion of women in relief work increased from 12 per cent in the fiscal year 1972/73 to 41 per cent in the fiscal year 1979/80.

3. THE ACT ON EQUALITY BETWEEN MEN AND WOMEN AT WORK
    (18)

3.1 The Background of the Act

In 1972 an Advisory Council to the Prime Minister on Equality between Men and Women was instituted and active policies to improve situations of women on the labor market were initiated. In 1976 it was transferred to the Government Department of Labor and reformed into a committee.

The Advisory Council of the Social Democrat government did not propose an Act on Equality between men and women at work. The Confederation of Swedish Trade Unions (LO) held that equality issues should be dealt with by collective bargaining and not by legislation. Since this opinion was shared by the employers organizations (SAF) as well as the organization of white   collar workers (TCO) there was a strong opinion against legislating equality issues and it was held that issues on equality should be dealt with by negotiation and not by legislation. This idea was consistent with the earlier pattern of the Swedish bargaining system. In 1960 a central agreement between SAF and LO was reached about equal pay for equal work and the special women's wages were abandoned by 1965.

In the Swedish constitution of 1974 there are several statements implying that nobody can be discriminated against because of sex. These statements maintain that the norm in the exercise of public power should be equality between men and women (Constitution § 1:2 = RF 1:2), that objectivity and impartiality should be observed in the exercise of public authority which means that sex discrimination is not objective conduct and not permitted under the Constitution (RF 1:9). The principle of equal treatment in the legislation process is stated: "Laws and other regulations must not entail that any citizen is discriminated against on grounds of sex." (RF 2:16). There are three exceptions to this 1) provisonal exceptions based on today's reality 2) military service 3) active efforts to promote equality.

The constitution also states that appointments to positions in the government sector must be based only on material qualifications such as merits and aptitude. In practice this means number of years of experience and qualifications suitable for the job such as education, whereby sex is not a ground for appointments.

One of the major issues of the Liberal Party (Folkpartiet) in the election of 1976 was an Act on Equality between Men and Women at work. When the Folkpartiet was part of the government coalition an Act was finally suggested in 1978 and became effective from January 1st 1980. The regulations of the enforcement institutions and on affirmative actions had been opposed by the unions. Anita Dahlberg (1983) observes that later when the Act has come into effect and the Equality Ombudsman has started to work the contacts between unions and the Equality Ombudsman have been positive and directed towards cooperation.

3.2   The Main Content of the Act

The Act applies to all kinds of employment, both in the public and 'in the private sectors and aims at the employers. Many of its rules also relate to how prospective employers treat job applicants. An Equality Ombudsman is responsible for insuring compliance with the Act.

In the motives for the Act on equality positive values for both men and women are emphasized. Both men and women are considered to be gaining from the equal society. The attitude is that both sexes are disadvantaged by inequality. In the unequal society men have less rights to their children and feelings. Women have less rights to work. They work shorter hours at lower wages, have less selfdetermined jobs with lesser career prospects. They have more responsibility for their homes and children.

The Act consists of three parts:

1) ban on discrimination
2) request to the employer to actively promote equality at work
3) regulations on the Equality Ombudsman and the Equal Opportunities Commission (19).

The first two parts constitute measures against offensive treatment by employers on the basis of sex and the third part pertains to enforcement of the Act.

3.3   Ban on Discrimination

The ban on wage discrimination is valid both for equal work and work of equal value. Equal work can be defined in collective agreements. These cannot differentiate between men and women. In this respect the law merely codifies what has been achieved by agreement between the parties of the labor market already in 1960 when the special women's wages were abandoned in the SAF-LO agreements.

Work of equal value is less well defined. It is probably difficult for someone to prove that she is paid less in spite of the fact that she performs work of equal value. The employer can try to prove that differences in wages are due to differences in the objective qualifications of the woman compared to the man or that the differentials are not determined on the basis of sex.

Sex discrimination in job placement exists when an employer choses one person in preference to another person of the opposite sex, despite the fact that the disadvantaged person is objectively better qualified according to the third section of the Act. This means that a woman who has qualifications equal to those of a man cannot claim that she has been discriminated against if the man is hired. She must be better qualified in order to   prove   discrimination against her.

In order for a woman to sue an employer in the Labor Court the woman has to prove that she has better objective qualifications. If she can prove this there is an offense against the ban on discrimination. However, the employer has the right to prove that his decision was not made because of the woman's sex or that it was a measure taken to improve the sex ratio among the employees. Some employers have interpreted the second possibility to appoint men to leading positions where there are only women among the employed. One case is a head of the personel at school lunches, another is a head of the budget department of a community government.

The Labor Court is obliged to look into what is usually considered to be objective qualifications in the industry where the plaintiff works or is a job applicant. In the private sector "suitable personal characteristics" can be an objective qualification. This means that in the private sector, in spite of the ban on discrimination, women can be discriminated against because they lack "suitable personal characteristics". In one court case, the Labor Court stated that second hand undocumented statements on a person's behaviour could not be the basis for favoring a man who is otherwise objectively less qualified. As pointed out before, in the government sector there are more formal grounds laid down in the Constitution for appointing somebody when there are several applicants. The person should be appointed on the basis of capability and performance. Inferences about these grounds are often drawn on the number of years in qualifying work.

3.4   Affirmative Actions

Employers are demanded to take active measures to promote equality according to the Act. The rules are organized in the form of a stated goal towards which different activities lead. The goal is equality at work. In a shorter perspective the goal is to actively promote equality at work. In the Act different examples are given on what the employer can do. Both work environment and organization should be so adapted that both women and men can work there. The employer should try to ensure that vacancies are sought by members of both sexes. By means of training and other appropriate measures, the employer shall also promote an even distribution between   sexes (at least 40 % of each sex) in different types of work and in various categories of employees. When recruiting, the employer must make special efforts to get applicants from the underrepresented sex.

The examples given in the Act are only examples of what can be done. No actions have to be taken before there is a collective agreement between employers and employee organizations. Such agreements have now been concluded for the different sectors of the labor market.

Dahlberg (1983) observes that the collective agreements about equality have been very general and in some instances less precise than the examples given in the Act. Nowhere in the agreements do any time schedules exist on what the employer has to do when. The Act is also constructed in such a way that when there is a collective central agreement as there is now (1983) on most of the labor market, the Equality Ombudsman no longer has any right to enforce compliance to the Act in regulations of affirmative action. The ban on discrimination cannot be negotiated. Christensen (1979) remarks that in spite of the revolutionary goal of the Act of equality between men and women at work there will be no revolution as a consequence of the Act because there are no enforcement possibilities. If the opinion on both sides of the labor market is that nothing must be done to actively promote equality, then nothing will be done.

3.5   The Equality Ombudsman

It is the task of the Equality Ombudsman to ensure that the Act is observed. In the first place the ombudsman shall try to persuade employers to comply voluntarily with the rules of the Act. Her means are advisory services, information and negotiation. Not until it is found that such reminders have no effect does the ombudsman take other measures. The ombudsman may appear on behalf of an individual employee or job applicant in a discrimination dispute before the Labor Court.

The ombudsman can speak for the plaintiff only if the woman who has been discriminated against allows it and her union does not wish to speak on the plaintiff's behalf in court.

Furthermore, the ombudsman is responsible for information to the general public and for taking other appropriate actions to contribute towards the promotion of equality. The ombudsman thus has an important role to play in the mobilization of public opinion. This means for instance, that the ombudsman must keep in constant touch with the organizations on the labor market and with the institutions and public bodies on the labor market, as well as with other organizations concerned with equality issues.

3.6   Cases Brought Before the Equality Ombudsman

During the first one and a half years there were 233 cases brought before the ombudsman. They were distributed among private and public employers in the following way. There were 98 cases concerning private employers and 135 concerning public employers. The State was responsible for 75 and the Local Communities for 60 cases. Most of the cases fell under the ban on sex discrimination (146 cases), but a third of the cases fell under the headline of affirmative actions, most of which were offenses against sex neutrality in "help wanted" advertisements. Out of the 98 cases of the private sector, as many as 74 were complaints about advertisements. The remaining few cases were on sex discrimination.

Anita Dahlberg (1983) speculates that the reason there are more cases concerning public employers' offense of the ban against sex discrimination in appointments than against private employers is that events in the public sector are much more visible than that which happens in the private sector. It is indicative that most of the cases brought to the Equality Ombudsman from the private sector are from highly visible activity there that is advertisements for help wanted.

4.   Concluding Remarks

In a short period of time the Swedish society has a transformation into almost universal labor force participation of women. In spite of this change, there has been little effect on the sex segregation of the labor market. Most women work in occupations different from men and a large part of the increase in female labor force participation has been due to expanded employment of women in the public sector. It remains to be seen if the introduction of an act against sex discrimination in the labor market will have any effect on the traditional division of labor between men and women.

NOTES

1) Calculated from income statistics in 1980 according to the following formula from SCB, "Statistiska meddelanden, serie N".

$$\frac{\overline{Y}_m \cdot n_m}{\overline{Y}_m \cdot n_m + \overline{Y}_k \cdot n_k} \quad \text{and} \quad \frac{\overline{Y}_k \cdot n_k}{\overline{Y}_m \cdot n_m + \overline{Y}_k \cdot n_k} \quad \text{respectively}$$

where $\overline{Y}_m$ = average wage income for men, n_m = number of male wage earners, $\overline{Y}_k$ = average wage income for women, n_k = number of female wage earners.

2) These figures have been calculated from salary statistics covering the total population of private sector white collar workers. There is for this sector a job classification system classifying jobs according to degree of difficulty. The proportions of people classified at highest level 2 (1 does not exist) for men and women with a degree in business administration is given in the text.

3) Arrived at by simply counting female and male first names in the Directory of Industry (Sveriges Industrikalender), 1980.

4) See SOU 1980:19. The proportion of female teachers refers to April, 1978, whereas heads refers to March, 1977, (Heads equals "studierektor" and "rektor").

5) Among those who were early to contribute in this field is Jonung (1974) in Swedish. Surveys available in English include Jonung (1979 and 1980). Earnings differentials between men and women have been analyzed by Gustafsson (1976 and 1981) and trends in labor force participation by Gustafsson (1980) and Gustafsson & Jacobsson (1983). The development of parttime work has been analyzed by Pettersson (1981).

6) See Carlsson, Sten, 1977.

7) A description of the development of the Swedish educational system is given in Sohlman, 1981.

8) Second and third opportunities to pass the entry requirements to realskola and gymnasiums were given resulting in longer time spent in school for some students like 6+5+4 years in folkskola, realskola and gymnasium respectively.

9) I myself went to gymnasium 1958-1962 in Västeras, a city with a population of 100 000 people to the west of Stockholm. Most of the girls came from the "flickskola" to the gymnasium. It meant that they lost two years compared to the boys who came from the "realskola". The "realskola" was open to girls but tradition was strong and it was considered more appropriate for girls to go to the single sexed "flickskola".

10) The maximum allowance for students in the spring semester of 1982 was a low interest loan of SEK 11.375 for half an academic year. In addition there was a subsidy of SEK 1.089. An additional loan amount for the semester of SEK 2.227 per child was allowed studying parents. If the student were to have no other income then students loans during the whole year it would be about 35 per cent of a fulltime full year industrial workers earnings.

11) Eklund, R., 1981, gives a historical description of the development of maternity and parental leaves legislation.

12) A description of the laws now in effect is given in Bylund and Wiklund, 1980.

13) The calculations in table 3A and 3B are taken from Lybeck, 1981, in an editorial to Ekonomisk Debatt, a journal that presents economic research in a popular form and is read by practically all Swedish economists. The issue of the editorial is that we cannot lower marginal tax rates unless we are willing to make housing subsidies and daycares fees independent of family income.

14) A fuller description of the calculations is given in Gustafsson (1978) mimeo and Gustafsson (1979) printed in Swedish.

15) It has been vividly demonstrated to me that this idea of equality is not universally accepted. In a seminar discussion with male economists, they stated that equality of time devoted to market work and household work within the family would be economically very inefficient. There must be room for specialization and economics of comparative advantage. People holding this view often accept the idea that women should not be discriminated against and often want their daughters to do well in their careers. However many think that if some women are more intelligent than the average men (like their own daughters presumably) they will succeed in adopting the traditional male role and have their husbands do the home work.

16) The actions taken by AMS and the economic situation of Sweden at the time of the Kristianstad project are described in Jonungs's and Tordarsson's (1980) paper on policies directed to reintegrating women into the labour force. In the report on equality between men and women in the labor markets of the Scandinavian countries from the Nordiska ministerradet NU A 1979:2. (also available in English). Labor market policies to promote women are compared for Sweden, Norway, Denmark and Finland.

17) AMS has put together a 27 pages mimeo on Statistics on Equality in the Labor Market in 1980 from which these figures have been taken.

18) This section draws heavily on a manuscript by Anita Dahlberg (1983) on the Act on Equality. An earlier shorter version is available in English, Anita Dahlberg (1982).

19) There are rules in the Act on an Equality commission to be appointed by the Government and entrusted with imposing fines to employers who do not take active measures to promote equality. The Commission is to act after suggestions from the Ombudsman. The Commission is to be chaired by an experienced court lawyer and consists of persons with good knowledge of conditions on the labor market and experience of work to further equality, together with representatives of the main organisations on the labor market. The Commission has however not yet been put into effect (1983).

REFERENCES

Bylund, B., Wiklund, L., 1980, Föräldraledighet och föräldrapenning (Parental Leave and Parental Compensation), Tidens Förlag, Stockholm.

Carlsson, Sten, 1977, Fröknar, mamseller och jungfrur. Ogifta kvinnor i det svenska standssamhället (Unmarried Women in the Swedish Society of Estates). Studiae Historica Upsaliensia 90.

Christensen, A., 1979, Proposal on the Act of equality between women and men at work, in Forskning för jämställdhet (Research for Equality). A report from a symposium, RJ 1979:3, Riksbankens Jubileumsfond.

Dahlberg, Anita, 1982, The Equality Act, in Nielsen, Ruth ed. Women's law in Scandinavia, Copenhagen.

Dahlberg, Anita, 1983, Om Jämställdhet - aktivt jämställdhetsarbete och diskrimineringsanmälningar i kommuner och landsting, Arbetslivscentrum, 318 pp.

Eklund, R., 1981, Ledighetsregler i lag och kollektivavtal, framväxt, motivkrets och deskription (Regulations on Absence from Work in Law and Collective Agreements - Development, Motives and Description), SNS, Occasional paper no. 12, 1981.

Gustafsson, Siv, 1976, Lönebildning och lönestruktur inom den statliga sektorn, in Swedish with a summary in English. Determination and Structure of Salaries in the Public Sector of Sweden, IUI, Stockholm, 266 pp.

Gustafsson, Siv, 1978, Cost-Benfit Analysis of Early Childhood Care and Education, Commission for the OECD, mimeo.

Gustafsson, Siv, 1979, a Arbetskraftsutbud och jämställdhet mellan kvinnor och män (Labor Supply and Equality between Women and Men), in Utrikeshandel, Inflation och arbetsmarknad (Foreign Trade, Inflation and the Labor Market), special studies for the medium term forecast of IUI, 1979, part I, Axell-Gustafsson-Holmlund-Horwitz, IUI, Stockholm.

Gustafsson, Siv, 1980, Lifetime patterns of labor force participation, forthcoming in Burton A. Weisbrod and Helen Hughes ed. Human Resources Employment and Development, Volume 3. The Problems of Developed Countries, Mac Millan.

Gustafsson, Siv, 1981, Male-Female Lifetime Earnings and Labor Force History, in Eliasson, Holmlund and Stafford eds. Studies in Labor Market Behavior: Sweden and the United States, IUI.

Gustafsson, Siv and Jacobsson, Roger, 1983, Trends in Women's Work, Family Formation, Education and Earnings in Sweden, mimeo.

Johannesson, Jan, 1981, On the Composition of Swedish Labour Market Policy, in Eliasson, Holmlund and Stafford eds. Studies in Labor Market Behavior: Sweden and the United States, IUI.

Jonung, Christina, 1974, Kvinnorna i Svensk Ekonomi, 2: a reviderade upplagan i Södersten, Bo, red. Svensk Ekonomi, Stockholm, 3:e uppl., 1982.

Jonung, Christina, 1979, Policies of Positive Discrimination in Scandinavia in Respect of Women's Employment, Research Series of the International Institute for Labor Studies, Geneve, No. IV.

Jonung, Christina and Thordarsson, Bodil, 1980, "Sweden" in Alice Yoholem red. Women Returning to Work, Allenheld Osmond Montclair, N.J.

Jämställhetssavtalnt Mellan SAF-LO/PTK (The Collective Agreement on Equality between SAF-LO/PTK).

Jönsson, B., 1970, Daghem och samhällsekonomi (Economics of Public Child Care), Prisma in cooperation with LO.

Jönsson, B., Paulsson, A., 1979, Daghem och samhällsekonomi, (Economics of Public Child Care). Prisma in cooperation with LO.

Kyle, Gunhild, Gästarbeterskai Manssamhället. Studier om industriarbetande kvinnors villkor i Sverige. Publica Liber Förlag, Stockholm.

Lybeck, Johan, 1981, Vet du din marginalskatt? (Do You Know Your Marginal Tax Rate?), editorial in Ekonomisk Debatt no. 1981:2.

Mincer, Jacob and Polachek, Solomon, 1974, Family Investments in Human Capital Earnings of Women, Journal of Political Economy, part 2, March/April, 1974.

Pettersson, Marianne, 1981, Deltidsarbetet i Sverige. Deltidsökningens orsaker. Deltidsanställdas levnadsförhallanden. Arbetslivscentrum, Stockholm.

Qvist, Gunnar, 1978, Konsten att blifva en god flicka/The Art of Becoming a Good Girl), Kvinnohistoriska uppsatser (a collection of research papers in feminist history), Liber Förlag, Stockholm.

RRV 1980: 1 242 Franvaron i arbetet - omfattning, utveckling, kostnader (Absence from Work, Trends and Costs).

SCB (National Central Bureau of Stistics) 1982:2, Statistika meddelanden/Statistical reports.

SFS 1980:412, Jämställhetslagen (The Act of Equality between Women and Men at Work).

Sohlmann, A., 1981, Education, Labour Market and Human Capital Models, Swedish Experiences and Theoretical Analyses, Stockholms Universitet, GOTAB, Stockholm, 1981.

SOU 1980:19, Flera kvinnor som skolledare (More women as heads of schools!). Report from the investigation on Female Heads of Schools.

Stafford, Frank, 1981, Unemployment and Labor Market Policy in Sweden and the United States, in Eliasson, Holmlund and Stafford eds., Studies in Labor Market Behavior - Sweden and the United States, IUI, Stockholm.

8 EQUAL OPPORTUNITY POLICIES FOR WOMEN IN THE FEDERAL REPUBLIC OF GERMANY

HEIDE M. PFARR AND LUDWIG EITEL

INTRODUCTION

It is an undisputed fact that there is discrimination against women in society and, in particular, in employment in the Federal Republic. What follows is therefore not a description of the various forms of discrimination or an analysis of the causes, though the importance of investigating the forms of discrimination against women - which are often covert and difficult to detect - should not be underestimated. The complexity of the problem and its close links with historical and social processes exceed the limits of jurisprudence and call for a multidisciplinary approach. Furthermore, it is not intended to convoy the impression that discrimination against women can be eliminated by legal means alone. Still, it is claimed that it is both necessary and possible to improve the situation of women by legal instruments and by utilizing the capacity of the courts for solving conflicts.

Discussion on ways and means of eliminating discrimination is not new, although it has recently intensified. Parliament and the courts have also had to deal with these issues and continue to do so.

The first section (I) provides a brief summary of rules and regulations aimed at ensuring equality of status for women in employment, past experience in putting the relevant norms into effect, and recent trends in their practical implementation and court rulings. The second section (II) deals with the current discussion on an anti-discrimination-law for the Federal Republic. The final section (III) presents some considerations for future equal rights policy for women.

I.   PREVIOUS LEGISLATION AND ITS PRACTICAL EFFECTS

1.   CONSTITUTIONAL BANS ON DISCRIMINATION

1.1   Article 3, paragraph (2) and Article 117, paragraph (1) of the Basic Law

Equality of status for women has the best conceivable legal basis in the Federal Republic of Germany. Article 3, paragraph (2) of the Basic Law, the Federal Republic's constitution adopted in 1949, states: "Men and women shall have equal rights." Moreover, Article 3, paragaph (3) contains the prohibition that "no one may be prejudices or favoured on account of sex...". When the Basic Law was drawn up, Article 3, paragraph (2) was discussed at great length (1), but there was general agreement - across party lines - that equal rights for women should go beyond the field of civil rights and that women should be equal to men in both civil and labour law, and also in every-day life (2). This consensus was apparent when the Basic Law was adopted in a plenary meeting of the Parliamentary Council, the representatives of the people charged with drawing up a constitution, which unanimously approved Article 3, paragraph (2) (3).

That the members of the Parliamentary Council were aware of having initiated real changes is documented by Article 117, paragraph (1) of the Basic Law: "Law which conflicts with paragraph (2) of Article 3 shall remain in force until adapted to that provision of this Basic Law, but not beyond 31 March 1953."

The constitutional requirement that men and women are to have equal rights is valid without reservation for all spheres of social life; it has direct validity for the legislature, the courts and the executive and it is also valid, at least in-directly for private relations between citizens (4).

Yet, it is impossible to overlook the continuing discrimination against women, which has even increased in some fields. There are many reasons for dis-crepancy between the intent expressed in the constitution and social reality, some of which will be considered in greater details below.

1.2   Constitution of the Laender

Since its establishment after the Second World War, the Federal Republic of Germany has been a "democratic and social federal state" (Article 20, paragraph (1) of the Basic Law), divided into ten Laender and the Land Berlin (West) with a special legal status. These Laender adopted their own consti-stutions, in some cases even before the Basic Law came into force. Most of these constitutions also include provisions aimed at ensuring the equality of men and women, dealing in particular with the issue of equal pay for equal work. The prevalent view today is that the provisions of the Laender consti-tutions - to the extent they go beyond Article 3, paragraph (2) of the Basic Law - are merely high-sounding principles and not legal rules with any practi-cal effect (5).

1.3 International Agreements

In addition to these constitutional norms there are a considerable number of provisions in international agreements and treaties which are concerned with the status of women in employment and which are applicable to the Federal Republic. These treaties and agreements are quite varied. One, however, merits particular attention because of its importance for contemporary discussions: The Council of the European Community issued a binding directive on the realization of the principle of equal treatment for men and women with respect to access to employment, vocational training and occupational advancement as well working conditions (6). It obligated the Federal Republic to issue by August 1978 the necessary legal and administrative regulations for its implementation. Under external pressure the law transforming the EC labor law directive into national law (The Equal Treatment Act of 1980) was finally passed with some delay in August 1980 (see I.4 below). This EC directive is of special importance because related cases from German courts are at the present time awaiting consideration by the European Court of Justice; the issue to be clarified is whether the EC directive has the force of law in the Federal Republic and whether the 1980 law transforming the EC directive into national law fulfills the requirements of that directive (7).

2. PROHIBITION OF DISCRIMINATION IN THE WORKS CONSTITUTION ACT

2.1 Effects of Basic Rights on the Employer's Behaviour

In the classical sense of the term, basic rights are first and foremost rights aimed at protecting the citizen from government encroachment. In labour law, a "relative third-party effect" of basic rights is today no longer contested, but its range and the legal consequences are still being discussed (8). In the field of labour law, the courts and prevalent opinion have evolved a "principle of equal treatment", which is essentially based on the general principle of equal treatment stated in Article 3, paragraph (1) of the Basic Law and on the ban on preferential treatment and discriminatory treatment contained in Article 3, paragraph (3) of the Basic Law and which is considered merely a ban on arbitrariness (9). Pursuant to this principle, an infringement of basic rights only occurs in relations between individuals if, "when adopting an approach geared to justice", there is no objective reason for the unequal treatment of equal circumstances, viz. of unequal circumstances subject to the ban on discrimination. Invoking such an "objective reason" can be an effective means of invalidating basic rights, especially if, at times of economic crises, the particular economic strains caused by laws protecting employees (10) or other "pressing company demands" are interpreted as legitimate interests of the employer and thus, as "objective reasons", become recognized restrictions of basic rights (11).

The equal rights principle set forth in Article 3, paragraph 2 of the Basic law goes much beyond the general principle of equality in Article 3, paragraph (1). It forbids every differentiation based on sex. In contrast to the general principle of equality in Article 3 paragraph (1) of the Basic Law, which would permit sex-based distinctions bordering on arbitrariness, Article 3, paragraph (2) is more far-reaching and tends toward permitting every sex difference to be considered non-essential unless ignoring it would constitute arbitrariness (12).

In contrast to the general prohibition of arbitrariness of Article 3, paragraph (1) of the Basic Law, objective reasons are not of themselves sufficient to justify different treatment which is related to sex differences; compelling reasons are required. This is applicable to both direct discrimination as well as to indirect discrimination, whereby formally sex-neutral requirements or conditions have in fact a discriminatory effect. The absolute ban on sex discrimination would be in practice annulled if requirements and conditions with a discriminatory effect could be justified by objective reasons which would not represent a justification in the case of direct discrimination.

2.2   The Prohibition of Discrimination Contained in Section 75, Subsection (1) of the 1972 Works Constitution Act (13)

Section 75, subsection (1) of the "Works Constitution Act" provides for an end to all discriminating treatment on the ground of sex. Accordingly, it is the joint duty of the employer and the works council to ensure that all the employees of the company are treated in accordance with the "principles of law and equity".

(1) The works council and the employer must endeavour to respect these principles in their own spheres of activity, actions and decisions.

(2) The works council must fulfil its duties and exercise its co-determination rights in a way which accords with the principle of law and equity and respects the ban on discrimination.

(3) The same also applies to the employer, who must ensure non-discriminatory behaviour, not only in the exercise of executive functions, but also in organizing company activities in general.

(4) Entitled to non-discriminating behaviour are not only employees already working in the company, but also job applicants - an opinion now also supported in most of the relevant literature. In support of this view, reference is also made to the act transforming the relevant EC directive in the field of labour law into national law (see also I.4 above). Accordingly, the bans on discrimination set forth in that law are not considered as privileges of those employed in the company but as the application in practice of Article 3, paragraph (2) of the Basic Law to employer-employee relations, thus covering also those who are not yet employed in the company or have already left.

(5) The equal treatment requirement is applicable, in particular, to the voluntary granting of benefits by the employer (collective agreements, agreements with the works council, individual employment contracts, company practices). Employees are entitled to equal treatment and can not be excluded from these benefits without an "objective reason".

(6) With respect to promotions, the prevalent opinion in the relevant literature is that section 75, subsection (1) of the Works Constitution Act does not entitle a female employee who has been discriminated against to a better position (14).

(7) It is now generally accepted that the equal treatment requirement laid down in section 75, subsection (1) of the Works Constitution Act also

obliges the employer, as a "general principle of labour law", to treat his employees equally in companies without works councils (15).

2.3   Non-Discriminatory Personnel Policy

Other provisions of the 1972 Works Constitution Act aim at ensuring a personnel policy which is just and free from arbitrary decisions by linking the exercise of the employer's rights to the works council's co-determination rights (16).

(1) Section 99 of the Works Constitution Act makes the effectiveness of any appointment, transfer, classification or re-classification dependent on the approval of the works council. The circumstances in which the works council can refuse to approve individual measures concerning personnel are limited, and they are interpreted restrictively by the courts and by the relevant literature. However, it is not disputed that, under applicable law, an infringement of the equal treatment requirement constitutes a valid reason for withholding such approval (17).

(2) Section 95 of the Works Constitution Act considerably restricts the employer's "freedom of contract". Pursuant to this provision, guidelines concerning the selection of staff in connection with appointments, dismissals, transfers and re-classification require the approval of the works council. In companies with more than 1,000 employees the works council can even enforce the adoption of such selection guidelines. Provisions of this kind must comply with the equal treatment requirement (18).

Any infringement of such guidelines entitles the works council to withhold its approval (19).

2.4   Comments of the Works Constitution Act

(1) The principle of equal treatment stated in section 75, subsection (1) of the Works Constitution Act is inadequate. It would therefore be desirable, for instance, for section 80 of this act, which lists the functions of the works council, to assign another - mandatory - function to this body, namely the task of initiating measures to further the equal treatment and promotion of female employees and of monitoring their implementation.

(2) In spite of section 15, subsection (2) and section 62, subsection (3) of the Works Constitution Act which concern the composition of the works council and of the body representing young employees and which provide that account should be taken of the "ratio of women", women are almost invariably underrepresented, especially on works councils of the parent company or concern. These sections therefore need to be amended.

(3) Practice has shown that works councils only make inadequate use of the rights available to them to enforce non-discriminatory decisions in personnel matters, which in many cases can doubtless be attributed to the fact that the works councils (composed mainly of men) are also prejudiced against women or are in any case ignorant of their specific problems. To remedy the situation, the works council should consider the   possibility   of

159

setting up committees charged with seeking to achieve equal status for women.

(4) Furthermore, additional rights for works councils should be included in the Works Constitution Act, in particular co-determination in vocational training, participation in developing and implementing plans aimed at achieving equal status for women, participation in legal proceedings instituted on account of discrimination, an explicit right to withhold approval in personnel measures involving discrimination, the duty of the employer to inform rejected applicants if the works council refuses to approve the employer's proposal, more rights for part-time employees, and the introduction of co-determination both in the assignment of the area of work and in the planning of selection guidelines.

3. LABOR LAW: THE EXAMPLE OF EQUAL PAY (20)

The new constitutional order of the Federal Republic established the equality of men and women as a generally applicable constitutional legal principle, and a number of Land constitutions stipulate the right of women to equal pay (21). Already previously recognized in the court interpretations of the Federal Republic, the Law on Equal Treatment, which came into force in August 1980 (22), incorporates the basic principle of equal pay for the same or similar work in the Civil Code.Nevertheless, this principle of equal pay is clearly not reflected in the everyday experience of work life.

Comparative data on pay for men and women in the Federal Republic in October 1981 were as follows: The average gross monthly pay of female employees in industry, banking and trade was 64.5 per cent of that for males; the average gross hourly earnings of female industrial workers was 72.6 per cent of that for males; the average gross weekly compensation of female industrial workers was 68.3 per cent of that for males (23).

3.1 The Concept of "Equal Pay"

There are two fundamentally different aspects to be borne in mind when considering the demand for the realization of equal pay for men and women: on the one hand there is a continuing lack of equality of opportunity for women in employment which - directly or indirectly - has consequences for pay levels (24). On the other hand, even when they perform the same or equivalent work as their male colleagues in the same firm, women are paid less (25). The lack of equal opportunity is apparent, for example, in the considerably limited occupational spectrum for girls and young women: of the ca. 450 possible recognized apprenticeships in the Federal Republic ca. 46 per cent of all female apprentices are sales clerks, hairdressers, office clerks or physician's assistants; 75 per cent of all girls who find an apprenticeship at all are trained in only 9 occupations, and 86 per cent of all female apprentices are registered in 22 "typical female occupations" (including, in addition to those mentioned above, legal secretaries, housekeepers, florists), while the remaining 14 per cent are distributed over more than 300 diverse occupations (26). Thus among industrial fitter apprentices, for example, there were 41,500 males nationwide in 1978 compared to only 85 females, i.e. only 0.2 per cent (27). In 1973 there

160

were 312 different types of apprenticeships available for boys and only 170 for girls under the same conditions. No apprenticeships at all were available for boys in five types of apprenticeships, while none were available for girls in 109 (28). With the entry into regular employment after the completion of vocational training a selection often takes place in which men are placed in jobs with prospects for advancement and women in dead end positions. Moreover, the percentage of girls receiving occupational training is considerably lower than that for boys, although there is a "surplus of women" among school leavers. In 1977 60 per cent of the adolescents without an apprenticeship were gilrs (29). One result, among others, is a higher percentage of women in unskilled and low paying jobs (30).

Ninety per cent of part-time employment in the Federal Republic is accounted for by women (31), and usually combined with a renunciation of career and further education and lower paid than comparable full-time employment.

"Typical female occupations" are on the average lower paid than "typical male occupations." For example, industrial workers in Food, Drink and Tobacco (1981, North Rhine-Westphalia) received only 73 per cent of the average hourly earnings of comparable workers in the Energy and Water sector (32).

So far unequal treatment of this sort has been insufficiently researched, and there are no signs of efforts to deal with this problem. Quick solutions are not to be expected, especially where there are strong traditional conceptions of male and female employment. In the long run legal and other governmental measures have to provide the basis for change. The reduction of differences between "typical" male and "typical" female occupations is mainly the task of collective agreements between management and labor, however, it is doubtful that they will take action on a voluntary basis. It may be inferred from their economic interests that employers are not striving for an upward adjustment of low paid "women's work" in times of large labor surplus. The unions still face the problem of a continuing entanglement in traditional role assignments and prejudices. Even though the offical policy pronouncements have undergone a favorable change during recent trade union congresses, there has been, as of yet, little practical effect on the negotiation of collective agreements. In addition to the factors mentioned above there are a number of others related to the nature of employment structures, which result in considerably lower average wages for women (32a); a detailed discussion of these is not possible here.

Direct discrimination in pay occurs when pay is different for the same or equivalent work under comparable working conditions. The concept of "compensation" should be understood comprehensively and includes every compensation furnished by the employer in connection with the employment relationship: wages and salaries, special payments, meal allowance, premiums, reimbursement for expenses, benefit outside the company and payments other than for time worked (e.g. for vacation, illness, "Housework days" and other paid leave) and payments made when leaving an employer (severance pay, payments under a "welfare plan", or company pensions) (33).

A central problem in the discussion on equal compensation is still the precise meaning of the concept of "same", "similar", "equivalent" or "recognized as equivalent" work (34). In order to examine whether equivalent works is performed meaningful schemes for the analysis of work have to be developed and applied which make it possible to evaluate whether, for   example,   there   are significant differences in the totality of job operations that can be externally observed, considering previous knowledge, training, effort, responsibility and learning conditions; or whether - and that is the most difficult case - although externally different work is performed, jobs are to be classified as similar or equivalent because active and passive job requirements are on the whole equal.

The forms of discrimination in pay are manifold. Relatively easily recognizeable and as such simple to prove are those open discriminations which contain different regulations for men and women without compelling reasons or unequal treatment of men and women due to family status. More difficult to recognize and generally to accept as discrimination are the forms of hidden, indirect discrimination (35), which takes place, for eyample, when regulations or conditions are not explicitly formulated with reference to sex and family status, but which in their practical effect discriminate against women.

3.2   The Development of Court Interpretation

(1) It was not until 1955 that the Federal Labor Court (36) had for the first time to decide four cases with respect to the "wage reduction clause" which was then usual in collective agreements. This clause in collective agreements stated, for example, that "women receive 75 per cent of the male wage" (37). The Federal Labor Court declared such provisions to be unconstitutional, although it did suggest that "some reordering of the wage structure in collective agreements" (38) might be undertaken in order to avoid the feared rise in wage costs as a result of its ruling. This suggestion resulted in the introduction of female wage groups and light work wage groups. While the latter was formulated in sex-neutral terms, its rules for classifying work in fact designated not only the lowest wage groups but also created female wage groups. It was not until 1973 that the Federal Government could report that these two forms of collective agreement provisions were no longer being used (39).

(2) In the period after 1955 the Federal Labor Court dealt with a series of cases involving discrimination in compensation. In addition to the pay differential clauses, sex-specific regulations were also declared unconstitutional, for example, in company pension plans, in the conditions for the receipt of housing allowances, in the allocation of Christmas bonuses, in special child and family allowances and in certain unexplained payments made only to men (40).

(3) Althouh the 1st Senate of the Federal Labor Court (41) expanded the term "equal" work to "equivalent" work in 1955, and introduced for the assessment of the equivalent work the argument of "objective criteria of scientific job analysis", what this means and who is entitled to decide it was not explained (42).

(4) With the coming into force of the Equal Treatment Act implementing the EC labor law directive (43) a further issue was clarified: the principle of equal pay is also applicable to individual work contracts.

(5) In the last two years courts have contributed to a further reduction of discrimination in some spectacular cases: In its opinion on the "Heinze Women" the 5th Senate of the Federal Labor Court again found that even

the granting of special payments, in individual work contracts, in exess of the provisions of collective agreements has to conform to the principle of equal treatment (44).

(6) In the case of the "Triumph-Adler Women" before the Frankfurt Labor Court, the court ordered the employer to pay equal pay retroactively to female assembly line workers. For the same work men were paid according to wage group 5, while women only received wage group 2, a difference of about 200 DM a month. The firm initially appealed the courts decision but then withdrew its appeal in October 1982 so that the decision could go into effect. Of the original group of 32 women, 4 still worked for Triumph Adler in December 1982. According to a newspaper report on the case: "Scattered among different jobs, isolated from one another, seldom having the possibility of talking among themselves during breaks, their communication impeded by national differences, and as foreigners burdened by double problems, many of the women have left the firm." (45)

(7) In the case of the "Schickedanz-Women" (46) the Federal Labor Court again found that the employer had also to adhere to the principle of equal treatment as regards compensation in excess of the provisions of collective agreements. This was also applicable to unexplained special payments. However, this decision also opened another flank for unequal treatment: In this case the Federal Labor Court expressed the view that a "labor market special payment" paid only to men was permissible if "certain jobs could not otherwise be filled." The special payment would only be impermissible when it was made "when men were not ready to work for the same wage as the women who were employed at the same job under the same conditions." (47)

(8) The Third Senate of the Federal Labor Court (48) decided in 1978 that the basic right of equal treatment between men and women is also violated if the minimum and the regular retirement age in a company pension plan is less favorable for women than for men.

(9) The Third Senate of the Federal Labor Court (49) also made an important ruling in 1982 on the treatment of part-time work. According to this opinion less than full-time work is not alone sufficient to justify the exclusion from certain benefits (this case concerned the regulation of retirement benefits). The opinion also found that it constituted a hidden case of discrimination against women when the exclusion of part-time employees from certain benefits "predominantly disadvantaged female employees."

4.   THE 1980 EQUAL TREATMENT ACT (50)

The law concerning equal treatment of men and women in employment came into force on 21 August 1980. The new regulations which are of interest here were inserted into the part of the Civil Code headed "contract of employment" as sections 611a, 611b, 612, paragraph (3), and 612a.

An external impulse was needed for the Federal Government to take the initiative of passing the Equal Treatment Act. In 1975 and 1976 the EC Council of Ministers had issued binding directives concerning the application of the principle of equal pay for men and women and for putting in effect the principle of equal treatment of men and women with respect to employment, training, promotion, and working conditions (51). These provisions also obliged the Federal Republic of Germany to enact the legal and administrative regulations needed to translate them into effect. The bill was severely criticized even while the bill was being considered, but without effect. Critics maintained that the new legislation would have no effect on the reality of working life with its manifest forms of discrimination against women (52).

4.1 The Blanket Clause (Section 611a, Subsection (1), First Sentence of the Civil Code)

Under the blanket clause contained in section 611a, subsection (1), first sentence of the Civil Code, the employer is forbidden to take any discriminatory measures or issue any discriminatory instructions in recruitment and hiring or as regards the promotion or dismissal of employees; thus, all relations and situations with which labor law is concerned, are covered. The employee discriminated against has a right to demand that the discrimination be ended (Exception see 4.3).

4.2 The Equal Pay Rule (Section 612, Subsection (3) of the Civil Code)

The employer may not make any differentiations on the basis of sex in the level of wages paid for the same or equivalent work; forbidden in particular are agreements on a lower rate of pay for employees enjoying special protective rights (e.g. maternity leave).

4.3 Indemnity Rule in the Case of Refusal of Employment or Promotion on the Ground of Sex (Section 611a, Subsection (2) of the Civil Code)

If a woman is refused employment or promotion because of her sex to which she has no other legal claim (e.g. reinstatement after maternity leave), the employer is obliged only to compensate her for the loss resulting from her good faith assumption that she would not be discriminated against.

4.4 Reversal of the Burden of Proof (Section 611a, Subsection (1), Third Sentence of the Civil Code)

Section 611a, subsection (1), third sentence of the Civil Code provides for a reversal of the burden of proof. In the case of litigation the employee must merely furnish satisfactory evidence that she was discriminated against on the ground of sex. If she is successful, the onus subsequently lies with the employer: It is up to the latter to prove that there were objective, sex-related reasons which justified the contested action or that a particular sex is an indispensable requirement for the work in question.

4.5 The Directory Provision that Job Advertisements should not be Sex-Specific (Section 611b of the Civil Code)

Public or internal advertisements of vacancies by the employer <u>should</u> not be sexspecific, i.e. they should not be addressed exclusively either to men or to women, unless a particular sex is an indispensable requirement for the work in question. This rule is no more than a directory provision; failure to comply has, therefore, no legal consequences and non-specific job advertisements cannot be enforced by legal means.

4.6 The Ban on Victimization (Section 612a of the Civil Code)

The ban on victimization makes it illegal for the employer to discriminate against an employee because the employee has exercised her rights in a permissible way.

4.7 Criticism of the 1980 Act Implementing the Relevant EC Directive International Law (53)

(1) The act implementing the relevant EC directive into national law clarifies the controversial legal situation and states that the requirement of equality laid down in Article 3, paragraph (2) of the Basic Law also applies to the individual legal relationship between employer and employee or job applicant.

(2) The exception to the ban on discrimination contained in section 611a, paragraph (1), second sentence of the Civil Code - different treatment is permitted if an agreement or measure concerns the type of work to be carried out by the employee and if a particular sex is an indispensable requirement for the activity in question - has not been formulated with sufficient precision and is open to differing interpretations. Moreover, the third sentence contains, surprisingly enough, yet another restriction: in connection with the rule concerning the reversal of the burden of proof, the term "objective reason" is introduced as an additional, vague exception. From this it might be concluded that there is another exception to the ban on discrimination contained in the first sentence which is not mentioned in the second.

(3) Although the directive of the EC Council of Ministers on the subject of equal treatment explicitly permits measures to ensure <u>positive unequal treatment</u> if they are capable of eliminating market sex-specific inequalities in employment, there is no mention of this in the act. Company initiatives in this direction (e.g. minimum employment quotas etc.) could even appear to contravene the requirement of equality contained in section 611a, subsection (1), first sentence of the Civil Code. The act could prove in this respect to be more of a hindrance.

(4) There is no mention either of the problem of "indirect discrimination" which occurs whenever measures or regulations are <u>phrased</u> without specific reference to either sex but, in practice, cannot be carried out or complied with by women on account of their general circumstances, or only to a

lesser extent than by men, without there being compelling reasons for laying down such conditions in the first place. An explicit provision in the law was needed for precisely these cases.

(5) Under the act any violation of the ban on discriminatory treatment through unilateral acts of the employer such as instructions, dismissals or other measures results in these actions being void. Where an employee is not promoted or a contract of employment not concluded for discriminatory reasons, the law only provides for compensation of the costs of the unsuccessful application (see also 4.8).

(6) The fact that the legal consequences of discrimination in respect of the conclusion of contracts of employment or promotion are restricted to compensation for the loss suffer as the result of abuse of trust is allegedly due to the need to maintain the principle of freedom of contract. Convincing arguments have been advanced against this viewpoint, in particular that the 1972 Works Constitution Act provides for comparable restrictions of the freedom of contract without these provisions having given rise to serious legal misgivings.

(7) The "reversal of the burden of proof" provided for in section 611a, subsection (1), third sentence of the Civil Code is in fact rather weak. The employee must still "furnish satisfactory evidence of facts which lead to the assumption of sex-based discrimination", which suggests that the women concerned must prove, at least in outline, and in accordance with the applicable rules of civil procedure, the facts supporting her claim, i.e. the occurence of both dicrimination and loss, whilst the employer has to provide counter-evidence of the exceptions justifying the discriminatory measure or measures in question.

(8) The principal of equal pay stated in section 612, paragraph (3) of the Civil Code sanctions the existing legal situation and makes it clear that the equal pay requirement also applies to individual agreements. However, there is no mention of the claim, recognized by the courts, of underpaid employees to retroactive pay.

(9) The new acts lacks a stipulation that the systems used for job classification, as provided for, for example, in collective agreements, should preclude the possibility of sex-based discrimination, even though Article 1, paragraph (2) of the EC directive explicitly refers to such a stipulation. Thus, there is the danger that discrimination in rates of pay may occur, for example, as a result of the classification of "typically female" occupations, which are characterized by a high degree of monotony, concentration and dexterity as well as by short operation cycles, as "easy work" rating lower pay than "typically male" jobs.

(10) The ban on victimization contained in section 612a of the Civil Code simply restates the self-evident fact that employees exercising their rights in a permissible way may not be disadvantaged. A ban on victimization can, however, only become effective if it is coupled with a reversal of the burden of proof worthy of the name or if it is combined with a general legal presumption. It is difficult for an employee who has exercised her rights in a permissable way and is subsequently affected by measures taken by the employer with a negative impact on the employment relationship to establish, let alone prove, the existence of a real but not immediately apparent connection between the exercise of her rights and the   employer's

action.

4.8   Experiences Gained to Date with the 1980 Equal Treatment Act

(1) While it was still in power the Social Democratic/Liberal coalition government announced the preparation of a report which was to document the effects of and experiences gained to date with the act implementing the
relevant EC directive. So far (February 1983), this report has not yet been
published. Thus, an appraisal of the practical implementation of the law
must remain limited to only a few aspects.

(2) The directory provision contained in the 1980 Equal Treatment Act that job
advertisement should not be sex-specific has had no apparent effect. Employers - in the public sector too - still publish sex-specific advertisements.

(3) As yet, the courts have only had to deal with a few lawsuits invoking the
new act, which for the most part confirm the criticism of the law's effectiveness expressed here.

In one of the cases which provoked a lively public discussion (54) (see the
"Frankfurter Rundschau" of 6 June 1982) a commercial firm repeatedly refused
to employ a woman, arguing the first time that the position had hitherto only
been held by men. The proceedings instituted by the woman against this discrimination were successful: the court declared that, in accordance with applicable German law, were she was entitled to compensation: DM 1,80 for
postage for the letter of application; DM 0,47 for the envelope, and DM 0,08
for two sheets of paper, i.e. compensation amounting to altogether DM 2,35
(55).

Both this case as well as a second one (56) have now been submitted to the
European Court of Justice to decide whether the sanctions provided for in the
act transforming the EC directive into national law are adequate and to
clarify the sanctions provided in the EC directive itself. Moreover, the
European Court of Justice is to clarify to what extent the EC directive is
self-executing law in the Federal Republic of Germany.

5.   THE FAMILY LAW REFORM OF 1976

Although, as shown above, the authors of the Basic Law in 1949 only foresaw a
limited period for the adjustment of existing legislation to the constitutional
requirement of equal rights for women in Article 3, paragraph (2), it was not
until 1976 that the First Law for the Reform of Marriage and Family Law was
passed, which came into force on January 1, 1977. This reform dealt with such
areas as marriage, the family name, married life, marital property, divorce
and its consequences. The extent to which these changes in law can alter the
actual social situation of women in the Federal Republic remains to be seen.
However important such reforms may be, one should not expect any
fundamental changes in the near future. This is especially true with respect to
the employment situation of women. Although the reforms were urgently
necessary, the area of family law is least susceptible to real changes through
legislative intervention. Traditional values are particular strong in this area.
Shaped by ideology and historically evolved role perceptions, they do not lend

themselves to direct change through legislation. Furthermore, it is quite difficult to formulate desirable modes of behavior in legislation and implementation is frequently difficult, particularly in the intimate sphere of the family
which eludes the forms of legal controversy.

The family reform law of 1976 abandons the model of the housewife and
leaves the allocation of household duties to the married couple. In place of the
traditional image of the housewife, the new legislation now assumes that the
married couple should decide freely and equally among themselves how they
wish to shape their intimate sphere. 'Free and equal' means that the decision
is not influenced through the "pressure of external arguments." However,
"external arguments", i.e. factors which lie outside of the marriage, are not
amenable to change through a reform of family law: the worse working conditions, training and pay of women, which on the average are worse than for
men, permit only a very limited "free and equal decision" as to whether the
husband or the wife should work, if, for example, because of the lack of child
care facilities, or their costs, only one of the spouses can work. Thus a reform
of family law which merely creates a new formal basis of equality remains
necessarily insufficient.

6.   AN EXAMPLE FROM TAX LAW: INCOME-SPLITTING METHOD

Income splitting is provided for under tax law and results in special tax
concessions for married couples if only one spouse is gainfully employed or, if
both spouses are gainfully employed, there are differences in their income
levels. To calculate the income tax payable, the incomes of both spouses are
added together and divided by two. Income tax is then payable on the income
determined by this method. As a result the tax-free allowance (57) is doubled
for married couples (if only one spouse is gainfully employed) and their joint
income is taxed at a lower rate, the advantages of which increase as income
rises. The maximum benefit accrues to couples with only one gainfully employed spouse and a taxable annual income of DM 260,000 and amounts to DM
14,837 (58). In 1980 married couples availed themselves of these tax concessions (or, as they might also be called, revenue shortfalls) to the tune of
some DM 32.2 (59) to DM 35 billion (60), according to various estimates. The
criticism of the income-splitting method singles out mainly two aspects:

(1) Income splitting as practised today benefits married couples more, the
    higher their income (the maximum benefit accrues at approximately DM
    22,000 income per month) and the greater the difference between incomes
    (the maximum benefit therefore accrues with only one spouse being gain-
    fully employed). Firstly, couples in the income brackets in which, for
    economic reasons, both spouses need to work are disadvantaged. Secondly,
    income splitting is an incentive for only one spouse to work - practically
    always the man (who earns more) - if the couple's financial situation makes
    this possible.

(2) Income splitting does not take into account the existence of children.
    Childless couples enjoy the tax advantage denied to single parents (those
    widowed, divorced, living separately or those unmarried) (61).

    Opponents of income splitting as practised to date have describes the
    special benefits involved as "an anti-social, annual premium for a marriage
    certificate which is unjustified from the point of view of family policy"
    (62).

In 1982 the Federal Constitutional Court(63) ruled that the tax discrimination against single parents as compared with married couples constitutes an offence against tax equity and is therefore contrary to the Basic Law. The relevant provision must be amended by 31 December 1984 at the latest. Although the Federal Constitutional Court did not hold that the princip of splitting could be applied unchanged to single parents, it did recognize that present tax practice did not take adequate account of the more limited resources of gainfully employed single parents as compared with married couples, who can compensate for the time spent looking after their children and the expense incurred either by more leisure time or by a higher income. The Federal Constitutional Court did not prescribe how the offence against tax equity is to be stopped, but ruled that the amended tax regulations must take into consideration the actual amount of time and money which single parents spend looking after their children. However, the new legal arrangement must not place single parents in a better position from the point of view of taxation than couples.

7. INSTITUTIONALIZED EQUAL OPPORTUNITY POLICIES

Since the beginning of the 1970s there have been a increasing number of initiatives to establish official institutions to represent and study the concerns of women (64). Although the usefulness, the actual powers and the level at which such institutions are established is still quite controversial, those who favor such institutions have been sucessful in influencing government authorities and ministries in many Laender of the Federal Republic. The effectiveness of the offices that have been established is controversial and depends, inter alia, on the tasks and authority which they are given, the extent to which they are independent in their relations with the public and the media as well as on the personnel and other resources provided (65).

Thus far these institutions have been created largely through simple administrative actions of the executive, and their responsibilities have not been determined by law. Their scope of activities is thus limited: they lack, inter alia, the possibility of issuing binding decrees, initiating investigative procedures, independently assessing fines, or initiating or intervening in judicial proceedings. The spectrum of institutions thus far established ranges from a women's office in a ministry to an "equal opportunity office" consisting of several sections with its own director and directly subordinate to the head of the Land government.

7.1 Existing Institutions

The institutions which have been thus far established at the federal and Land levels have had very different organizational models based on conflicting assessments of the necessity of such offices. They can be roughly divided into two structural types. In some cases women's issues are either not handled separately or merely in a special but subordinate office, usually in the ministry for social affairs; in other cases such issues are regarded as having been neglected in the past and there have been efforts for a number of years to give them more emphasis, both substantively and organizationally, and to elevate them in importance.

(1) Since 1979 there has been a "working group on women's issues" within the Federal Ministry for Family, Youth, and Health which developed out of the women's office that was established in 1972. Its involvement in legislation is assured through the terms of internal rules of administrative procedure (66). The ministers of all other government departments in the previous SPD/FDP government had committed themselves to insuring that the working group would be given sufficient notice of all projects pertaining to women. In addition to conducting research on the situation of women, its other most important tasks are carrying out model projects, public information activities, conducting scientific and applied research and functioning as a contact point for interest groups, churches, unions and other organizations. In 1982 the working group presented a report on its activities up until that time. A "Commission on Women and Society" created by the Bundestag has now completed its report (67). However, the role of the commission under the new CDU/CSU/FDP government is not yet clear.

(2) In Baden-Württemberg women's affairs are included within the advisory office for family policy of the Ministry for Labor, Health and Social Affairs. There has been for some time a proposal to establish a separate office for women's issues in family life, employment, and in society. Matters affecting women are also dealt with by various other government departments (68).

(3) In Bavaria matters specifically affecting women are dealt with within the Ministry for Labor and Social Affairs. It special competence in such issues is not, however, fixed by internal rules of administrative procedures. The Land Women's Committee, which has a merely advisory function, is also located within this ministry (69).

(4) In Berlin the office for women and family policies is under the Senator for Family, Youth and Sport. There is also, in addition, a "Working Group on the Employment and Career Policy Interests of Women" subordinate to the Senator for Labor and Social Affairs. There is thus far no formal delimitation of the competence of these institutions in internal rules of administrative procedure, which, for example, would allow them to influence legislation. At present an attempt is being made to establish a equal opportunity office modeled after that in Hamburg. A hearing on this topic took place on march 4, 1983 the results of which are not yet known. On June 26, 1980, during the previous SPD/FDP government, the Berlin parliament decided to commission a "Report on the Situation of Women in Berlin" (70). The new CDU Senate accepted this report on February 2, 1982 and, after some controversy, it was made available to the public.

(5) In Bremen women issues were until 1981 the responsibility of the office for Family Policy within the Department for Social Affairs, Youth and Sport. Since that time Bremen has established a "Central Office for the Realization of Equality for Women". As described in the governmental program of the Hanseatic City of Bremen on December 12, 1979: "It has the task of supporting the Senate's legislative activity and administrative measures promoting equality for women and of contributing to the realization of this constitutional right in society at large. Its goal is to increase awareness of the situation of women in our society and, where necessary, to contribute to its improvement" (71).

(6) Hamburg has had since 1979 a "Central Office for the Promotion of Equality for Women" in the executive office of the Hamburg Senate, which is directly subordinate to the mayor. The "Hamburg model" has served as an example for similar innovations in other Laender of the Federal Republic. Not only its high institutional position but also the functions of the Hamburg office are regarded as being especially advanced. It supposed to be involved in the plans of the Senate in a timely manner by the lead agency or competent office of the Senate. In the case of major legislative proposals the Hamburg office is supposed to be informed during the initial stages of the preparation of legislative proposals. If it is not informed, or informed too late, the draft legislation is stopped until it has had an opportunity to present its comments (72). The Hamburg Central Office published its first report in 1981 (73).

(7) In Hessen a "Central Office for Women's Affairs" was established in the state chancellery in 1979 and is thus directly subordinate to the minister president of the Land government. The Central Office has direct access to the minister president. It examines and comments upon all cabinet business, proposed legislation, and regulations of the Federal government and of the Land Hesen with respect to their implications for women. The views of the Central Office are presented in the cabinet by the minister president. There is a designated official in every principal administrative office of the Land government who is the contact person for the Central Office and responsible for informing it about all measures (74).

(8) In Lower Saxony the Office for Women's and Family Affairs is located in the Ministry for Social Affairs and has interdepartmental responsibilities. In principle the office has the right to participate in the development of legislative initiatives, and especially to examine them with respect to possible discriminatory elements. There is, however, no supportive provision to this effect in internal rules of administrative procedure. In July of 1981 the Land government announced the establishment of a research institute, "Women and Society" to investigate the situation of women in the family, employment, and in public life. It is to carry out information gathering tasks and to develop training and retraining methods for women (75)

(9) North Rhine-Westphalia created the office of a "Commissioner for Women's Issues" in 1975 within the state chancellery and thus directly subordinate to the minister president. In 1976 this office was transferred to the Ministry for Federal Affairs, where a working group on "the general affairs of women" was established. It has originated two important new initiatives: the program "Opening New Careers for Girls" and the suggestion that the Land statistical office undertake an analysis with the title "The Situation of Women in North Rhine-Westphalia." The Minister for Labor and Social Affairs is, since 1978, the commissioner for women's affairs of the Land government. Women's issues are handled by the four offices in the working group General Women's Affairs, Family Assistance, Kindergarten, etc. of the section "Social Affairs, Family and Youth" in the Ministry for Labor, Health and Social Affairs. A role in legislation through a change in internal administrative procedures is planned, but has not yet been implemented (76). The current report on women of the Land government was published at the beginning of 1983 (77).

(10) In Rhineland-Palatinate the Office for Basic Questions of Women's Policy is a part of the section Women, Family, and Youth of the Ministry for Social Order, Health and Environment. The office is supposed to become

involved at an initial drafting stage in any governmental actions bearing on subjects of particular concern to women. Participation in the preparation of legislation is likewise foreseen. Since 1976 there has been a Women's Advisory Council in Rhineland-Palatinate, which has the task of advising the Land government in social, legal, economic and cultural matters of special importance to women. In particular the Council is expected to make suggestions and recommendations to the Land government and, at its request, to provide expert advice (78). In August 1982 the Minister for Social Affairs, Health and Environment presented a "report on women between family and career" with the title "More Freedom of Choice for Women" (79).

(11) In the Saar the Office for Family and Women's Questions is located in the Ministry for Family, Health and Social Affairs. There is no provision in the internal rules of administrative procedure for its participation in the legislative process; this occurs at the discretion of the responsible minister. An effort to promote the establishment of an equal opportunity office modelled after that in Hamburg has thus far been rejected by the government as unnecessary, since, in its opinion, "all offices of the Land government are concerned in the course of their official duties with the achievement of equal rights for men and women and the reduction of any shortcomings which may exist" (80).

(12) In Schleswig-Holstein the Office for Family and Women's Issues is located in the Ministry for Social Affairs. The parliamentary secretary for family and social affairs also primarily deals with women's issues. Moreover the Ministry for Social Affairs has announced the establishment of a "Commission for Women's Issues", which will have as its principal task the systematic investigation of situations which violate the equal rights principle of Article 3, paragraph (2) of the Basic Law, report to the Land govenment about problems found and develop of remedial proposals (81).

(13) In Cologne the first official municipal equal opportunity office was established in 1982 (Bremen, Berlin and Hamburg have the constitutional status of "Laender"). The office is directly subordinated to the head of the city administration (82).

7.2   Comments on the Performance of the Equal Opportunity Offices

There are two principal arguments against equal opportunity offices. First, the fear that the women's issue may become bureaucratized (83) and, in particular, that equal opportunity policy may be excluded from other government departments under the pretext that it is the responsibility of the equal opportunity office. Secondly, it is argued that equal opportunity offices may become "reservations for women" (84) and thus particularly unsuitable for effective action against sex discrimination. In spite of these reservations, and the critique above of their limited authority and the deficient implementation of their role in internal administrative procedures, the equal opportunity offices have already achieved a whole series of successes. They have been especially effective in the area of public relations in which they have contributed significantly to increased public awareness of discrimination against women. A further achievement is the now almost comprehensive reporting available on the situation of women in the Federal Republic of Germany. Even though the various reports may be of uneven quality, altogether   they   constitute   a documentation of discrimination which makes it now impossible to avoid the issue of sex discrimination by reference to the lack of adequate data. The function of the equal opportunity offices in transforming "individual injustices" into a political cause celebre with intense public interest should also not be underestimated (85).

II.   DISCUSSION OF AN ANTI-DISCRIMINATION LAW (86)

During the previous social democratic-liberal coalition government the Ministry of the Interior developed a draft text for an anti-discrimination law which has not yet been published and is presumably no longer under active consideration. The draft text was, however, discussed at a hearing held, in accordance with the "mandate of the government's policy statement of November 24, 1980, to examine whether the situation of women could be improved through an anti-discrimination law" (87).

The draft anti-discrimination law was not itself the object of the hearing. Rather the legal experts, women's groups, labor unions, employers' associations and political parties invited to testify were presented with a set of questions on a general clause applicable to private legal relations with emphasis on questions pertaining to employment. In addition to constitutional and procedural problems, other topics treated were the burden of proof in legal disputes; the specification of relevant facts; the legal consequences in cases of discrimination; quotas for training, hiring and promotion, in particular within the public service; and a number of other topics. It does not seem likely that this text will be the basis for any future legislative initiatives, since the Christian Democrats (CDU) as well as the Christian Social Union (CSU), the two largest parties in the present coalition government, rejected any proposal for an anti-discrimination law in their testimony at the hearing. Nevertheless, we shall consider here some of the problems which were dealt with in this text because they are significant in themselves.

1.   ELEMENTS OF AN ANTI-DISCRIMINATION LAW

A number of basic problems of anti-discrimination legislation were raised by the draft text, although the actual contents of the proposed regulation left much to be desired.

1.1   The General Clause

A general clause in the anti-discrimination draft law prohibits discrimination on account of sex in legal relations regulated by civil law, with the exception of relationships characterized by "extremely personal circumstances." The general clause does not, however, mention any legal consequences which result from a violation of the prohibition of discrimination. It can be doubted whether a general clause can actually change anything, since the obligation of Article 3, paragraph (2) of the Basic Law has existed for more than thirty years and there are also enough general clauses present in existing legislation. The evident shortcomings in equal treatment for women can not be attributed to the lack of a general clause, which in itself is without effect. At a minimum, the legal consequences of a violation of a general clause must be clearly specified, and they must be more than merely "contestable" or compensation of damages incurred in good faith. A general clause should contribute to the realization of a basic right by stimulating the adoption of measures to favor and promote women in order to reduce existing inequalities.

1.2   Misdemeanor/Fines

In order to strengthen the 1980 Equal Treatment Act's prohibition of "demeaning advertising" and similar layouts of the cover pages of publications, the draft law defines violations for which fines can be levied. The low effectiveness of fines as sanctions in civil law, especially in employment situations, is well known. For this reason fines should only be resorted to as sanctions when other possibilities either do not exist or offer little hope of success. Fines are just no substitute for the right to require that the violation cease, although there can be no objection to fines as an additional measure.

1.3   Quotas/State Benefits

The provision of public benefits, "which are not matter of right" such as subsidies, credits, and favorable tax treatment can, according to the draft, be linked by federal agencies to the fullfillment of certain quantitative conditions (quotas), i.e. "until the target figure is reached members of the underrepresented sex are to be hired and promoted when they have equal qualifications." Firms which wish to take advantage of subsidies or are government contractors are to be required to develop and to implement "equal opportunity plans" as a condition of obtaining state benefits or as part of their contractual obligations. If the equal opportunity plans are not in fact implemented and there are no extenuating reasons, the public funds must be repaid, or the firm will no longer be considered for public contracts or a contractual penalty would be due.

1.4   Quotas/Public Employment

The draft law contains a provision empowering the Federal Interior Minister to issue regulations establishing quotas for hiring and promotion in government employment. All measures which have been proposed for the private sector can also be implemented in the public sector. There is an important additional factor pertaining to equal opportunity policy in the public sector: employers in the private sector assess intensified measures to achieve equal status for men and women in employment especially from the point of view of the costs which they entail. Moreover, state regulations which infringe upon the freedom of action of firms are constantly confronted with the charge of "state intervention" in the private sphere. The resistance to anti-discrimination regulation on the part of those who are its immediate object, the employers, is not lessened, and understanding for such measures is not increased, when the "state" is unable to effectively implement equal opportunity policies in public employment. Thus public employment has the role of a "positive model", a role which, considering the situation of women in public employment, it clearly has

174

not fulfilled.

1.5 Parties/Candidates for Office

A non-binding provision in the draft text calls upon political parties to give appropriate consideration to women in selecting candidates for German federal elections and for the elections to the European parliament, i.e. corresponding to their share of the membership in the Land organization of the party selecting candidates.

A whole series of arguments were made against such a regulation. Nevertheless, it remains a fact that, in thirty-five years without quotas, the parties have neither been able to achieve an appropriate level of female participation in internal party structures nor among party candidates. The internal party situation is beyond the scope of state regulation; however, changes could certainly be brought about in candidate selection through "positive motivation", without direct intervention in internal party decision-making. It would be possible, for example, to conceive of a quite effective regulation which would make the reimbursement of election costs (paid in the Federal Republic to the parties by the state according to the number of votes received) dependent upon the extent to which women are appropriately represented among party candidates.

1.6 Equal Rights Commission

The draft law proposes the establishment of a seven person commission, four of which would be women. The federal parliament, the federal council (the representation of the Laender) and the federal government would each select one member of the commission; four other members would be designated by the federal government on the basis of persons nominated by the national organizations of the local governments, the employers' associations, the trade unions and the women's organizations. According to the draft text, the commission would have broad powers to issue warnings, make violations public if they are repeated, as well as the right to intervene in all court proceedings. The commission would also have the right to enjoin further violations in cases of sex discrimination in job descriptions and demeaning advertisements. Further tasks of the commission would be to undertake analyses of the causes of the unequal status of women, to develop programs to promote equal opportunity, to carry out experiments with model programs, to advise and support public agencies, and to present an annual report to the German federal parliament. It would also have the right to require information and the right of access to records backed up by fines for noncompliance. The usefulness of such a commission is a subject of controversy. Against the view that a control agency at the federal level, whatever its powers, would be superfluous, it can be countered that past efforts which focused on the firm or affected individual were inadequate. Furthermore, collective bargaining agreements over the past thirty years have not been able to achieve the elimination of discrimination in employment. Against the charge that the creation of legal possibilities for state intervention endangers the autonomy of collective negotiations, it can be countered that this autonomy does not give employers and unions the right to legalize discriminatory practices and that they have a duty to act in confirmity with the constitution. There are recent cases in which courts have examined collective agreements in order to determine their conformity with the constitution and, as the case may require, declared them to be null and void (88).

It is doubtful that an equal rights commission which includes all important social groups can lead to any progress. Such a commission may possibly do more harm than good because the interests represented will be too willing to accept any compromise for the sake of agreement and such a commission can not be very effective because it lacks real executive authority. Similar reservations are applicable to the proposal to name a "parliamentary commissioner" for this subject. It seems, therefore, preferable to create an "agency" which might be usefully organized in a federal structure parallel to that of the West German state and reaching down to the municipal level. The greatest possible independence would be indispensable, which means that the new agency should not be incorporated as a subordinate division of any existing government agency so that it can carry on its work without hindrance. The task of such agency would be to supervise enforcement of the anti-discrimination law. It should possess its own powers of investigation, be able to issue directives and oversee compliance, and to enforce them with compulsory administrative measures. Such an agency should not become involved at all in the central tasks of trade union activity nor should it merely serve an alibi function for inactive public policy. It should collect and publicize information, receive complaints and assume a leading role in their further prosecution. It should also bring problems to the attention of a broader public and promote possible solutions. Legal aid remains the responsibility of the trade unions, however the agency should have the right to intervene in all relevant judicial proceedings as well as to bring suit itself in order to enjoin violations.

2.   FURTHER PROPOSALS FOR ANTI-DISCRIMINATION LAW

An effective anti-discrimination law, especially one for the purpose of achieving equal opportunity in employment, has to deal comprehensively with all areas affected by discrimination:

2.1   Quotas for Apprenticeship Programs

It is necessary to prescribe certain targets for employers in the area of training and employment in order to achieve a reduction in existing inequalities, particularly the underrepresentation of women in certain occupations, occupational groups and career levels. Rigid quotas are necessary in the area of training, except for those occupations for which sex is an unavoidable prerequisite. There is a need for legislation which conditions the validity of an apprenticeship contract on the approval of the labor office. Placement in apprenticeship should be based on quotas established by the labor office according to the number of school leavers in a region. If the employer rejects one referral, then another would be referred by the labor office.

2.2   Obligatory Vocational Education

Since the number of apprenticeships available is less than the number of school leavers and, as a result sex specific selection, many more young women than young men fail to find an apprenticeship, it would be desirable to make it obligatory for employers to offer apprenticeships. This change could be so designed that youth under the age of 18 could only be employed eiher as apprentices or after the completion of an apprenticeship. This form would also permit, in addition to apprenticeships in a narrow sense, further schooling as well as special training programs or vocational education in public institutions.

2.3 Job Descriptions

A general prohibition (also binding third persons) of either internal or external vacancy announcements that are for men or for women only is urgently needed, since the duty imposed by the 1980 Equal Treatment Act has had no significant impact.

2.4 Guidelines for Work Organization

In addition to the areas of training, hiring and promotion, guidelines should also apply to jobs, work organization and the work environment. The employer should be obligated to shape them in such a way that they can be performed by women as well as by men. It would be preferable to incorporate this obligation as an express component of the prohibition of discrimination in section 611a of the Civil Code.

2.5 Supportive Measures

In order to prevent a stagnation at the level of participation which has been thus far typical, e.g. certain occupations or career levels, positive supportive measures are necessary which give preference to previously disadvantaged groups. An express provision making this possible is required, which could be based on the formulation in Article 2, paragraph 4 of the EEC-Directive L 39/40 of 14.2.1976.

A preference, for example, in hiring in the case of "equal qualifications" would not be sufficient, since the discriminatory reality of the work situation could supply many "objective reasons" as pretexts for attributing higher "general qualifications" to men. Possible circumvention of the regulation could be avoided if such a preference was already permissible when the female applicant could show "sufficient qualifications" for the job.

2.6 Obligation to Report Works Council Agreements

Frequently instances of discrimination remain unknown because the regulations in terms of which it occurs are not made public, and thus effective legal counseling can not take place. Discrimination against women is frequent in company level agreements (e.g. in rules for hiring and firing, methods of determining pay or in corresponding provisions of collective agreements). In order to be able to discover such violations an obligation to report local agreements analogous to that for collective bargaining agreements in Article 7 of the Law on Collective Labor Agreements (TVG).

2.7 Obligation to Report Rejections

A reporting obligation should be introduced which requires that the employer inform the rejected female applicant when a male applicant was hired or promoted instead. Certainly a reporting obligation should be introduced for cases in which the works council or staff council rejects an individual personnel measure because of a violation of the ban on discrimination.

2.8 Shifting the Burden of Proof

The complete shifting of the burden of proof to the side of the employer is indispensable. The requirement that the existence of discrimination must first be established is, on the one hand, from the point of view of legislative drafting inconsistent and, on the other hand, highly impractical. One particular case of shifting the burden of proof should be provided for explicitly: When a job is filled in an area in which women are underrepresented and for which women have applied whose qualifications for the job are not clearly deficient, in such cases there should be a presumtion that the rejection of the female applicant constitutes a case of direct or indirect discrimination.

2.9 Prohibition of Victimization

The anti-discrimination law must also include a prohibition of any retaliation by the employer for invoking it. A reversal of the burden of proof should be the core of such a prohibition. The employer should be required to bear the burden of proof that no disciplinary punishment has taken place when there is a temporal coincidence between a complaint of discrimination or invocation of a right under the act and a measure of the employer with negative effect for the work relationship.

2.10 Right to Initiate a Complaint

The right to initiate a complaint should be expanded beyond the individual immediately affected in order to remove some of the pressure from the individual woman in a given situation as well as in order to promote clarification of issues of principle. In particular works councils or staff councils as well as trade unions and - outside of the work context - interest groups must be given an independent right to initiate complaints under the law.

III. THOUGHTS ON FUTURE EQUAL OPPORTUNITY POLICY

The above description and critique of equal rights measures introduced thus far has shown some of the shortcomings of equal opportunity policies in the

Federal Republic. The existing discrimination against women affects nearly all areas of social life. A listing of all the affected circumstances and relationships would be merely a complete list of social situations and relationships. Instead of listing the areas not yet discussed, it appears more sensible to make some comments on the structures and conditions which will basically influence all future equal opportunity policies:

1.   THE SOCIAL CONTEXT

Legislation in the pluralistic-parliamentary system is usually the result of interest alliances and socio-political compromises which are dependent upon the given power constellations. The achievement of legislation and the implementation of laws is dependent in practice, inter alia, on whether and how sucessful the organized and unorganized interests which support or oppose it, with their influence and alliances, are able to prevail; what accompanying situations develop as a result of political and economic circumstances; and what changes the principles adopted undergo during the phase of implementation as a consequence of changed interest constellations or court interpretation. The elimination of discrimination through law today is, moreover, not primarily a legal expression of a change in social consciousness but rather a contribution to bringing about this change in consciousness. This circumstance is the source of many dangers which may not be neglected when designing anti-discrimination laws. Such legal initiatives can only be successful when they relate to attitudes already extant in the society and are based on an existing readiness to regard discrimination against women as unjust. Furthermore, the recognition that the implementation of anti-discrimination measures is a social process means that the elimination of discrimination must be achieved step by step. Every change in social structures collides with existing interests and values and it must survive this challenge. At the same time it is itself, in a dialectical process, a contribution to the transformation of social values and majorities. This step-by-step process of change must not, however be focused exclusively or primarily on "values" and "consciousness", but must concentrate on the related underlying and supportive modes of behavior. If one relates to concrete interest constellations and aims step-by-step to achieve changes with limited goals in certain modes of behavior, then one can intervene in social processes and, through a gradual change in the social structures, prepare the ground for a far-reaching change in values, accelerating a process which is already underway.

2.   THE EFFECT OF LEGAL PROHIBITIONS

Thus far the law with respect to equal rights for men and women has merely been developed to the point of prohibiting discrimination. This negative, proscriptive approach has three implications:

(1) Prohibitions are directed against already existing practices of discrimination. As can be easily demonstrated by the example of unequal pay, prohibitions are circumvented and illegal behavior is replaced by other types of behavior which are not, or not yet, proscribed and which serve the same purpose. Legal prohibitions always lag behind the actual social process; they are, when one considers the cumbersomeness of legislation and legal processes, an instrument which represents related and defensive inter-

179

vention rather than positive formation of the development of society.

(2) Prohibitions first become effective when the rights of an individual are violated and a complaint is made. The individual woman effected is not only subjected to the risk of court proceedings; she is also involved in a procedure which lasts a long time, frequently requires her to stand alone and often requires a significant capacity to engage in conflict. The individual women is usually only inadequately or not at all prepared for this situation. She is faced with the choice of either enduring a high degree of individual stress or giving up her legal rights.

(3) Approaching the problem only in terms of the discriminated individual makes the structures, the organization of work life, jobs, and the labor market, constants. Laws are supposed to enable women to enter into jobs that were denied them in the past, and they have to adjust themselves to the requirements of these jobs. At this point the critical question must be posed as to whether this is the right approach. Do we want to insert the individual woman into a system which remains otherwise unchanged - simply subordinating her to what are often male-oriented job structures and conditions, or do we want to transform occupations, job structures, working conditions, work organization and working time so that women can and want to get these jobs? If we are not prepared to make these changes, equality for women will mean an integration into inhumane working conditions and into job structures that are hostile to the family and working hours which are not oriented toward the needs of persons who live in a family with children but rather, for example, presuppose a traditional division of labor in the family.

The ineffectiveness of the legal forms which have thus far been utilized is evident. The mere expansion of a catalog of prohibitions can not promise any substantial improvement in the real situation of women. It is therefore necessary to discover and enact into law norms which are aimed at improving the social situation of women through positive measures that effectively compensate for the existing unequal treatment. In particular women must be able to determine their own behavior - their thought and their decisions - in a genuine climate of real equal opportunity.

3.   THE NECESSITY OF SUPPORTIVE MEASURES

Law which seeks to eliminate discrimination must, in addition to prohibitions, also strive to change contextual conditions and not forget that equality for women can not be directed toward their selective participation in privileges reserved in the past for men. The change of existing structures through law also encounters other problems, in addition to those described above, e.g. the fixation in the past on a formal equality, which in some areas led not to the elimination of discrimination against women but to its reinforcement. In such cases only those laws which intervene in the existing conditions of unequal treatment by treating the sexes unequally, at least until the constitutional requirement of equal rights has been realized, can fulfill the constitutional commandment of equality.

4. EMPHASIS ON LABOR LAW

A further consideration with respect to efforts to achieve equality between men and women is the degree to which different areas of social life are susceptible to change by external intervention, for example, by means of laws and regulations. Furthermore, different areas have a different impact and different significance for change in the general situation of women in society. One has, therefore, to concentrate primarily on those areas which are really susceptible to external regulation and which have major significance for the larger process of change. As was already mentioned above, the family is a quite unfavorable point of intervention, although it must be admitted that, in many respects, the basis for equal treatment of men and women has yet to be created in this area.

A strengthening of the position of women in employment will contribute, through the demonstration of their ability to earn their own living outside the home and through active involvement in productive social processes which transcend the sphere of the family, to the strengthening of self-confidence, increased capacity to deal with conflicts, broadening of horizons, an increased feeling of independence and of being taken seriously, etc., which will also affect other social relations. The achieved standard of equal rights for women is easiest to measure in the area of employment; progress as well as reversals are quantifiable and hence the effects of legal regulations can be assessed - at least more easily than in other areas.

It is thus in no way arbitrary when labor law is given a special emphasis in anti-discrimination policy. The particular aspects of legal reforms in the area of labor law have already been indicated:

- going beyond mere prohibitions,

- positive discrimination in favor of women by regulations until equality has been achieved,

- a scope which includes not only individual problems but also change in the general conditions of work life,

- militant enforcement agencies,

- strengthening of the plant-level interest representation.

5. THE EMPLOYER AS OBJECT OF REGULATION

The object of regulations to eliminate or prevent discrimination is necessarily the person who potentially discriminates, i.e. the employer, since he alone is in a position to create discriminatory structures and make discriminatory individual decisions. He is thus also in a position to abstain from discrimination. Directing attention to the employer also makes it possible for the plant-level interest representation or state agency empowered to take legal action to undertake preventive measures. The obligation to engage in conduct free of discrimination under the watchful attention of the public, the works council and the trade unions, and additionally, for example, linked to conditions for the receipt of public subsidies, puts the employer under pressure to conduct himself in accord with the law which is quite different from that of the possible recourse of a discriminated women to the courts in order to secure equal treatment in her individual case.

6.   CLOSING REMARKS

There will be considerable resistance to such legislation, and not only from employers and firms. Since the elimination of discrimination against women affects their position not just in one area but in society as a whole, what is in fact being sought is a new und unprecedented form of social life. For the individual, in particular for the individual women, this means that the general direction in which further progress is to be sought is known, not, however, the particular forms and content of life in a society with equal rights and equal duties. A struggle for equal rights which is limited merely to a changing the roles of women to be like those of men would be destined to fail for a number of reasons. Such a goal would leave existing social structures unaffected, in spite of their inherent elements of inhumanity and domination, as an inevitable and seemingly optimal social order. More importantly, the male role always incorporates discrimination of women. Thus the redefinition of one role necessarily entails the redefinition of the other. This fundamental process of transformation, which must be the ultimate meaning of the emancipation of women, explains not only the widespread resistance of men, but also that of many less discerning women. The replacement of accustomed modes of behavior by new and untried ones, which provoke conflict with those who have to give up their privileges and are accompanied by confusion and failed experiments, creates widespread insecurity. If on the one hand there is widespread dissatisfaction with the current situation of women, one frequently also finds that the same people are, in spite of all criticism, reluctant to give up what they are accustomed to, which is perceived as being safe or at least calculable, for a situation full of insecurity which certainly also requires a measure of social and individual costs.

If the reasons for the resistance of some women are understandable, this resistance is still not an argument against further progression toward the elimination of discrimination, even with the aid of legislation and legal procedures. The individual steps of reform must however be carefully calculated and integrated in a long-term perspective. Legislation as well as the practical policies of the state, political parties and trade unions have to be more strongly based on the self-initiatives of women in order to learn from practical experiences.

NOTES

(1) For the history of Article 3 Paragraph 2 of the Basic Law see: Reich-Hilweg, Männer, p. 17 ff.; Matz, Entstehungsgeschichte, p. 66 ff.; Pfarr/Bertelsmann, Lohngleichheit, p. 24 ff., and the references included therein.

(2) Matz, Entstehungsgeschichte, p. 71 f.

(3) Beitzke, Gleichheit, p. 201.

(4) See I. Maier, Rechte, p. 124 ff.

(5) Pfarr/Bertelsmann, Lohngleichheit, p.30; Nipperdey, RdA 1950, 127.

(6) Amtsblatt der Europäischen Gemeinschaft Nr. L 39/40, 2.14.1976, reprinted in: Renger, Chancen, p. 150 ff.

(7) See below section "I.4.8 Experiences..."

(8) See I. Maier, Rechte, p. 126 ff.

(9) Däubler, Arbeitsrecht II, p. 154 f.

(10) See Pfarr, Arbeitnehmerschutzrechte, p. 259 ff.

(11) See Hanau/Adomeit, Arbeitsrecht, p. 39.

(12) Dürig, Art. 3 Abs. 2 GG.

(13) On the following see Dietz/Richardi, Betriebsverfassungsgesetz, § 75 Rn. 1 ff.; Gnade/Kehrmann/Schneider/Blanke, Betriebsverfassungsgesetz, § 75 Rn. 2 ff., Rn. 17 ff.

(14) See Pfarr, Kritik, p. 20 on this point.

(15) See Pfarr, Kritik, p. 20, and the references included therein.

(16) Pfarr, Kritik, p. 21.

(17) Gnade/Kehrmann/Schneider/Blanke, Betriebsverfassungsgesetz, § 99, Rn. 67.

(18) Pfarr, Kritik, p. 21; Gnade/Kehrmann/Schneider/Blanke, Betriebsverfassungsgesetz, § 95, Rn. 1.

(19) Pfarr, Kritik, p. 21.

(20) Vgl. Däubler, Lohngleichheit; Pfarr, Lohn; Pfarr/Bertelsmann, Lohngleichheit; Pohl, Frauen; Wolter, Probleme.

21) For historical background see Pfarr/Bertelsmann, Lohngleichheit, p. 24 ff.; Wolter, Erfahrungen, p. 68 ff.

22) See below section 4a "The 1980 Treatment Act".

(23) Calculated from dpa/vwd data, in: Frankfurter Rundschau, 2.3.1982.

(24) See Pfarr/Bertelsmann, Lohngleichheit, p. 35 ff.

(25) See Pfarr/Bertelsmann, Lohngleichheit, p. 50 ff.

(26) Data for 1977, Source: Bundesministerium für BIldung und Wissenschaft, reported in: BMJFG, Frauen '80, p. 9.

(27) Source: Statistisches Bundesamt, reported in: BMJFG, Frauen '80, p. 10; see also Braun/Gravalas, Benachteiligungen, p. 11.

(28) See Klimpe-Auerbach, Diskriminierung, p. 56.

(29) Source: Bundesanstalt für Arbeit, reported in: BMJFG, Frauen '80, p. 8.

(30) See Däubler-Gmelin, Frauenarbeitslosigkeit, p. 53 ff.

(31) See Table 14, in BMJFG, Frauen '80, p. 19.

(32) Statistisches Landesamt (Düsseldorf), reported in: Süddeutsche Zeitung v. 28.4.1982.

(32a) See Pfarr/Bertelsmann, Lohngleichheit, p. 37 ff.

(33) Pfarr/Bertelsmann, Lohngleichheit, p. 49 f.

(34) On this and the following see Pfarr/Bertelsmann, Lohngleichheit, p. 50 ff.

(35) Pfarr/Bertelsmann, Lohngleichheit, p. 59 f.

(36) BAG v. 15.1.1955, AP Nr. 4 zu Art. 3 GG; BAG v. 2.3.1955, AP Nr. 6 zu Art. 3 GG; BAG v. 6.4.1955, AP Nr. 7 zu Art. 3 GG; BAG v. 20.5.1955, - 1 AZR 137/54. (BAG = Bundesarbeitsgericht).

(37) Bertelsmann/Pfarr, Gleichbehandlung, p. 86.

(38) So Wolter, Probleme, p. 132.

(39) Wolter, Probleme, p. 132, Fn. 50.

(40) References in Bertelsmann/Pfarr, Gleichbehandlung, p. 86, more than 100 court rulings on the problem of discrimination in pay are documented in Pfarr/Bertelsmann, Lohngleichheit.

(41) BAG v. 6.4.1955, AP Nr. 7 zu Art. 3 GG.

(42) Bertelsmann/Pfarr, Gleichbehandlung, p. 86.

(43) See below section I.4, "The 1980 Equal Treatment Act".

(44) See BAG AP Nr. 117 zu Art. 3 GG.

(45) Frankfurter Rundschau 12.19.82.

(46) BAG v. 25.8.82 = RdA 1983, 66 ff.

(47) Hereto Bertelsmann, Lohngleichheit, p. 29 f.

(48) BAG v. 31.8.1978 - 3 AZR 313/77.

(49) BAG v. 6.4.1982 = ZIP 1982, p. 866 ff.

(50) "Gesetz über die Gleichbehandlung von Männern und Frauen am Arbeitsplatz und über die Erhaltung von Ansprüchen beim Betriebsübergang vom 13.8.1980", BGBl. I p. 1308.

(51) Excerpts from the most important regulations are reprinted in Pfarr, Kritik, p. 18 ff.

(52) See Blinkert, Probleme; Hanau, Zugang; Hohmann-Dennhardt, Antidiskriminierungsgesetz; Pfarr, Kritik; Slupik, Entwurf; Trieschmann, Gleichbehandlung.

(53) See Pfarr, Kritik; Rust, Vertragsverweigerung; additional references in footnote 52.

(54) E.g. Frankfurter Rundschau, June 6, 1982.

(55) Arbeitsgericht Hamburg, Aktenzeichen: 8 Ca 124/81.

(56) Arbeitsgericht Hamm, 12.6.1982, Aktenzeichen: 4 Ca 1076/8.

(57) See Wehner, Begrenzung, p. 489 f.

(58) Wehner, Begrenzung, p. 489.

(59) BMJFG, Frauen '80, p. 23.

(60) Hempel-Soos, Prämie.

(61) Tax revenues lost as a result of income "splitting" by married couples without children is estimated at seven billion DM per year, Hempel-Soos, Prämie.

(62) The national vice-chairman of the Arbeitsgemeinschaft sozialdemokratischer Frauen, Christine Schmarsow, quoted in Hempel-Soos, Prämie.

(63) Decision of the Bundesverfassungsgericht, 11.3.1982, = NJW 1983, p. 271 ff.; see also Knapp, Alleinerziehende.

(64) A summary can be found in Kühling, Modelle, with additional references.

(65) See Pfarr, Gleichstellung, p. 88 f., and Herstellung, p. 271 f.; Slupik, Verrechtlichung, p. 361, see also section II.6. below.

(66) After the change in § 23 Nr. 2 Ziffer 9 GGO II of June 1979 the Federal Minister for Youth, Family and Sport also participates in the preparation of draft legislation when matters of policy toward women are affected. See Kühling, Modelle, p. 40, Note 23.

(67) Enquête-Kommission, Bericht der Enquê te-Kommission Frau und Gesellschaft gemäß Beschluß des Deutschen Bundestages vom 25. Mai 1977 - Drucksache 8/305.

(68) Kühling, Modelle, p. 28 f.

(69) Kühling, Modelle, p. 29 f.

(70) Der Senator für Gesundheit, Soziales und Familie, Bericht über die Situation der Frauen in Berlin, 1981.

(71) Regierungserklärung des Senats der Freien Hansestadt Bremen vom 12.12.1979, edited by Pressestelle des Senats, p. 42.

(72) Bürgerschaftsdrucksache der Freien und Hansestadt Hamburg 9/142, p. 168 f.

(73) Bürgerschaftsdrucksache der Freien und Hansestadt Hamburg 8/3582, 4.11.1978.

(74) Kühling, Modelle, p. 42 ff.; see also: Hessischer Landtag, Bericht der Hessischen Landesregierung über die Arbeit der Zentralstelle für Frauenfragen, Drucksache 10/542 of 3.9.1983.

(75) Press release of Lower Saxony Government, 7.3.1980, see Kühling, Modelle, p. 34.

(76) See Kühling, Modelle, p. 45 ff.

(77) See Voss, Farthmann.

(78) Ministerium für Soziales, Gesundheit und Umwelt, Wahlfreiheit, p. 103.

(79) Ministerium für Soziales, Gesundheit und Umwelt. Mehr Wahlfreiheit für Frauen - Bericht über Frauen im Spannungsfeld Familie und Beruf, 2 Vols., Mainz 1982.

(80) Communication of the Saar Land government of Dec. 12, 1980 to the Chairman of the Arbeitsgemeinschaft saarländischer Frauenverbände and the Chairman of the Saar Land district of the German Federation of Labor, quoted in: Kühling, Modelle, p. 35; see also Hempel-Soos, Taubheit.

(81) See Kühling, Modelle, p. 36 ff.

(82) See Hempel-Soos, Kölsch.

(83) Wex/Kollenberg, Frau, p. 216 f.

(84) I. Maier, Amt, p. 12.

(85) See Kühling, Modelle, p. 53 ff.

(86) See Janssen-Jurreit, Frauenprogramm, especially p. 333 ff., p. 391 ff.

(87) See Minutes of Hearing, Bonn 1983; Slupik, Verrechtlichung, p. 363 ff.

(88) BAG v. 13.10.1982 - 5 AZR 370/80 (= ArbuR 1983, S. 121).

Thanks go to Hugh Mosley who translated a great share of the article from German into English.

REFERENCES

Beitzke, G. "Gleichheit von Mann und Frau". Neumann/Nipperdey/Scheuner, <u>Die Grundrechte - Handbuch der Theorie und Praxis der Grundrechte</u>, Berlin 1954.

Bertelsmann/Pfarr. "Gleichbehandlung von Frauen und Männern bei betrieblichen Zulagen." <u>Arbeit und Recht</u> 1982, p. 86 ff.

Binkert. "Konzeptionelle Probleme bei arbeitsrechtlichen Teilreformen." <u>Juristen-Zeitung</u> 1979, p. 747 ff.

BMJFG (Bundesminister für Jugend, Familie und Gesundheit), <u>Frauen '80</u>, Bonn 1980.

Braun, F./Gravalas, B., <u>Die Benachteiligung junger Frauen in Ausbildung und Erwerbstätigkeit</u>, Munich 1980.

Däubler, W., <u>Das Arbeitsrecht</u>, Vol. 2, Reinbek 1979.

Däubler, W. "Lohngleichheit von Mann und Frau als Rechtsproblem", <u>Arbeit und Recht</u> 1981, p. 193 ff.

Däubler-Gmelin, H., <u>Frauenarbeitslosigkeit - oder: Reserve zurück an den Herd!</u>, Reinbek 1977.

Dietz/Richardi. <u>Betriebsverfassungsgesetz, Kommentar</u>, 6th ed., 1981.

Dürig, in: Maunz/Dürig/Herzog, <u>Grundgesetz-Kommentar</u>, München, as of 9/1980.

Enquête-Kommission. <u>Bericht der Enquête-Kommission Frau und Gesellschaft gemäß Beschluß des Deutschen Bundestages vom 25. Mai 1977</u>, Drucksache 8/305.

Gnade/Kehrmann/Schneider/Blanke. <u>Betriebsverfassungsgesetz - Kommentar für die Praxis</u>, 2nd ed., Cologne 1983.

Hanau, P. "Der gleiche Zugang zur Beschäftigung in der Privatwirtschaft nach deutschem Recht." Gamillscheg et.al. (eds.), <u>In Memoriam Sir Otto Kahn-Freund</u>, Munich 1980.

Hanau/Adomeit. <u>Arbeitsrecht</u>, 3. ed., Frankfurt am Main 1972.

Hempel-Soos, K. "Viel Kölsch und ganz viel Frauen." Vorwärts, December 2, 1982.

Hempel-Soos, K. "Eine Prämie fürs bloße Verheiratetsein." Vorwärts, March 4, 1982.

Hempel-Soos, K. "Gegen die Taubheit in Männerohren." Vorwärts, March 3, 1983.

Hohmann-Dennhardt. "Antidiskriminierungsgesetz contra Grundgesetz." Zeitschrift für Rechtspolitik 1979, p. 242.

Janssen-Jurreit, M. (ed.). Frauenprogramm - Gegen Diskriminierung, Reinbek 1979.

Klimpe-Auerbach, W. "Diskriminierung der Frauen beim Zugang zu den Berufen, bei Einstellung und Kündigung." Posser/Wassermann, Von der bürgerlichen zur sozialen Rechtsordnung, Heidelberg/Karlsruhe 1981.

Knapp, U. "Jetzt müssen "Alleinerziehende" steuerlich entlastet werden." Frankfurter Rundschau, November 4, 1982.

Kühling, U. Modelle und Konzeptionen in der Antidiskriminierungsdebatte, Diplomarbeit, Hannover 1981.

Maier, I. "Mit einem Amt für Frauenfragen lassen sich Interessen nicht durchsetzen." Informationen für die Frau, Sonderheft 3, 1979 (edited by the Deutschen Frauenrat).

Maier, I. "Gleiche Rechte, gleiche Chancen - Konsequenzen aus Art. 3." M. Weber (ed.), Probleme der Frauen - Probleme der Gesellschaft, Köln/Frankfurt am Main 1976.

Matz, W. "Entstehungsgeschichte der Artikel des Grundgesetzes." JöR (NF) 1 (1951), p. 66 ff.

Ministerium für Soziales, Gesundheit und Umwelt. Mehr Wahlfreiheit für Frauen - Bericht über Frauen im Spannungsfeld Familie und Beruf, Vol. 1, Mainz 1982.

Nipperdey, H.C. "Gleicher Lohn der Frau für gleiche Leistung - Ein Beitrag zur Auslegung der Grundrechte." Recht der Arbeit 1950, p. 121 ff.

Pfarr, H.M. "Besondere Arbeitnehmerschutzrechte zwischen sozialpolitischer Zielsetzung und arbeitsmarktpolitischer Dysfunktionalität." Kittner (ed.), Arbeitsmarkt - ökonomische, soziale und rechtliche Grundlagen, Heidelberg 1982.

Pfarr, H.M. "Gleichstellung der Frau im Arbeitsleben - Vorschläge zur Rechtsreform." Posser/Wassermann (ed.), Von der bürgerlichen zur sozialen Rechtsordnung, Heidelberg/Karlsruhe 1981, p. 75 ff.

Pfarr, H.M. "Herstellung und Sicherung von Chancengleichheit durch Recht - dargestellt am Beispiel der Frauen." Hassemer/Limbach/Hoffmann-Riem, Grundrechte und soziale Wirklichkeit, Baden-Baden 1982, p. 255 ff.

Pfarr, H.M. "Zur Kritik des Entwurfs eines Gesetzes über Gleichbehandlung von Männern und Frauen am Arbeitsplatz." Blätter für Steuerrecht, Sozialversicherung und Arbeitsrecht 1980, p. 17 ff.

Pfarr, H.M. "Gleicher Lohn für gleiche Arbeit." WSI-Mitteilungen 1981, no. 4, p. 269 ff.

Pfarr/Bertelsmann. Lohngleichheit - Zur Rechtsprechung bei geschlechtsspezifischer Entgeltdiskriminierung, Stuttgart/Berlin/Köln/Mainz 1981.

Pohl, S. "Frauen und Lohndiskriminierung - Haben die Gewerkschaften versagt?" Blätter für deutsche und internationale Politik 1981, no. 1, p. 65 ff.

Reich-Hilweg, I. Männer und Frauen sind gleichberechtigt - Der Gleichberechtigungsgrundsatz (Art. 3 Abs. 2 GG) in der parlamentarischen Auseinandersetzung 1948-1957 und in der Rechtsprechung des Bundesverfassungsgerichts 1953-1975, Frankfurt am Main 1979.

Renger, A. Gleiche Chancen für Frauen? - Berichte und Erfahrungen in Briefen an die Präsidentin des Deutschen Bundestages, Heidelberg 1977.

Rust, U. "Die Vertragsverweigerung als Verstoß gegen das Benachteiligungsverbot des § 611a BGB und der Anspruch auf Einstellung." Blätter für Steuerrecht, Sozialversicherung und Arbeitsrecht 1982, p. 337 ff.

Slupik, V. "Verrechtlichung der Frauenfrage - Befriedungspolitik oder Emanzipationschance?" Kritische Justiz 1982, no. 4, p. 348 ff.

Trieschmann. "Gleichbehandlung von Männern und Frauen am Arbeitsplatz." Recht der Arbeit 1979, p. 407 ff.

Voss, R. "Fahrtmann: Frauen droht Rückkehr ins Biedermeier." Frankfurter Rundschau, January 11, 1983.

Wehner, H.-G. "Was heißt Begrenzung des Splittingvorteils auf 10.000 DM?" Die Quelle 1982, no. 9, p. 489 f.

Wex/Kollenberg. Frau und Industriegesellschaft, Cologne 1979.

Wolter, H. "Erfahrungen aus dem Kampf um Lohngleichheit." Arbeitsrecht im Betrieb 1982, p. 68 ff.

Wolter, H. "Probleme der Lohngleichheit zwischen Männern und Frauen." Arbeit und Recht 1981, p. 129 ff.

9 POLICIES AND IMPLEMENTATION OF ANTI-DISCRIMINATION STRATEGIES

CHRISTINE JACKSON

1.   INTRODUCTION

How can discrimination against women in employment be eliminated? What strategies - legal, penal, persuasive - are most effective and most appropriate? This paper attempts to define and examine the merits of various kinds of strategies which have been proposed, tried or developed in various countries.

First, I wish to define three models:

- anti-discrimination legislation,

- positive discrimination or affirmative action, and

- equal opportunity policies.

By <u>anti-discrimination</u> legislation I mean specific laws (as distinct from constitutional safeguards) which make it unlawful to treat men and women differently in their access to, terms and conditions, and remuneration in employment. Discrimination may be defined, as it is in the British and American legislation, in a sophisticated way to include 'indirect' discrimination: usually motiveless or unintentional discrimination whereby a rule or qualification is imposed equally but has an unequal impact, because only one sex or predominantly only one sex can comply (for example, a rule that police constables must be two metres tall).

Secondly, I draw a <u>distinction between positive or reverse discrimination on the one hand, and affirmative or positive action</u>, on the other. Positive discrimination means giving preference to women. Affirmative or positive action means giving special encouragement and providing special programmes to try to correct or redress the imbalance between men and women in their access to employment - an imbalance which has occured because of past discrimination or because of current inequalities arising from their different roles outside the workplace.

Equal opportunity policies are defined as those which intend to raise the level of women's qualifications for entry into the labour market and to improve the compatibility of paid employment with domestic responsibilities. I use the term social policy initiatives to include equal opportunity policies. My definition of social policy initiatives is provision by the State, educators, employers and trade unions which facilitate the entry of women into employment without detriment to their domestic responsibilities, or, to state it more positively, which enable the better management and sharing of work and home resposibilities by women and men.

I shall attempt to describe the potential effectiveness of these different strategies in eliminating discrimination against women in employment. I shall then go on to suggest that the ideal policy-mix is a combination of limited but powerful anti-discrimination legislation along with social policy initiatives, a combination of essentially related strategies. I will argue that the strategy of positive or reverse discrimination should not be followed because it is or would be socially and politically unacceptable, and because it is incompatible with anti-discrimination legislation. However, I shall suggest that much of what is called positive or affirmative action consists of little more than good equal opportunity employment practices, which do not contravene anti-discrimination legislation and which might as well be described as social policy initiatives. They are positive or affirmative in that they are not passive.

2.   THE BRITISH ANTI-DISCRIMINATION LEGISLATION: ITS DEVELOP-
        MENT AND IMPACT

The British anti-discrimination legislation is perhaps the most sophisticated, wide ranging and thorough that exists in Western Europe. It has its inadequacies (and its extensiveness may be one of them), but I suggest it is a more useful model for Europe than the American one, because of fundamental differences between Europe and America in relation to legal frameworks and procedures, trade union organisation and, regrettably, the degree of seriousness with which sex inequality is regarded on either side of the Atlantic. The British Parliament 'borrowed' much from the greater and longer American experience in equal opportunity experiments. They could not however borrow commitment to the achievement of equal opportunities for women along with the legislative and administrative tools which they copied so assiduously!

Briefly, the British Sex Discrimination Act 1975 makes discrimination on grounds of sex unlawful in a number of different circumstances in relation to employment, education, and access to housing, credit and other services. It provides a means of redress for individuals through Industrial Tribunals (labour courts). In the first six years of operating, 434 cases were brought by individuals, of whom 104 (just under 25 %) won their cases; but most of these received derisory compensation from their employers. For example, in the first months of the legislation coming into force, in March 1976, an Industrial Tribunal found that a Mrs. McLean had been discriminated against because she

192

was sacked when she married a colleague: the company had a policy of not employing married couples. She lost her job and was awarded Ł 317 damages (1). Some years later in July 1980, a Mrs. Wallace failed to be considered for a job as a projectionist on a ship because the company said they did not have suitable accommodation. The Tribunal found that she had been discriminated against on the grounds of sex and awarded her Ł 10 for injury to feelings (2).

The Act established the Equal Opportunities Commission to monitor the Act and the Equal Pay Act which came into force simultaneously (3). The Equal Opportunities Commission (EOC) has a duty to "promote equality of opportunity" and "work towards the elimination of discrimination between men and women generally". It also has considerable enforcement powers. It can conduct a 'Formal Investigation' into a company or organisation it believes to be discriminating and if that discrimination is proved, it can issue a Non-Discrimination Notice. If the 'offender' does not comply with that Notice in the following five years, the Commission can apply to a court and the court may fine the offender for non-compliance with the Order.

The EOC has issued one Non-Discrimination Notice in the last six years (the Commission for Racial Equality which has identical powers arising from the Race Relations Act has issued ten Non-Discrimination Notices). No employer has been fined by a court for non-compliance with a Notice. The point or relating this is not to imply that the EOC itself has failed, which many critics allege, but to suggest that, regardless of the EOC's ability or determination, the powers it has been given are largely unuseable and that the sanctions it could impose on offenders are too inoffensive to have any effect.

It must be said that the EOC preferred to adopt a persuasive rather than a punitive approach in its early years; that it was nervous of the powers with which it found itself vested; and it was and is under-resourced. Furthermore, the EOC is a 'quango' - a quasi autonomous non-governmental organisation, a public body financed by government but constitutionally separate from it. This indeterminate status means that the relationship of the EOC to any 'constituency' and to government itself is unclear. The leadership of the EOC - the 14 or 15 Commissioners - are appointed under a system of government patronage. Individually some represent a clear interest group, in particular three from the Trades Union Congress and three from the Confederation of British Industry. But collectively they are not accountable in any direct way to anyone. The 'political' mix which exists (and changes as their terms of office come to an end) means that consensus is the order of the day and a consensus between such diverse interests does not produce courageous or dynamic action. Moreover the procedures the EOC has to adopt in order to conduct a Formal Investigation are lengthy and tedious, and give so much protection to the company or organisation being investigated at every stage (far more than would be available to a defendant in a criminal court) that clear, exemplary exposure of discriminatory practices is almost impossible to achieve. Furthermore, the EOC has learned a hard lesson from the Courts in its support of individual cases. The British judiciary is naturally conservative and, not surprisingly, has shown itself far from progressive on the question of sex discrimination. It is unlikely that offending employers will ever be penalised heavily. Besides which, any penalties which might be imposed would be so deferred in time from the original offending action that the relationship between the two is likely to be forgotten.

Even if this analysis is too pessimistic, there is little evidence that the existence of anti-discrimination legislation and an agency with statutory duties to enforce that legislation has had a fundamental impact on the low status, low paid and marginal position of women in the labour market in Britain. The segregation of jobs by sex in most jobs, and the invisibility of women in the higher echelons of those occupations were job segregation is not so all-pervasive - so adequately documented in the area studies - is still the dominant picture.

However, the legislation is an unequivocal statement of public policy and its use has had an educative effect. It also provides an orderly method for the resolution of individual grievances. And there have been some improvements. There are no longer advertisements in newspapers under separate columns for male and female jobs. Some important individual cases have been won, one or two through the European Court. For example, in July 1977 Belinda Price brought a case against the Civil Service Commission alleging that an upper age limit of 28 on entry to the Executive Officer grade in the Civil Service indirectly discriminate against women since fewer women could comply with such a requirement than men, since many in their twenties were otherwise engaged in bearing or bringing up children. Although she lost at the Industrial Tribunal, with the support of the EOC, her appeal was allowed. As a result entry to this grade was opened up to any women over the age of 28. This case, therefore, had the effect of a 'class action' in the American sense in that a whole category of women were affected by the ruling (4). A straightforward case of direct discrimination was proved by a Mrs. Hurley who was dismissed after one day's work as a waitress by an employer who had a policy of not employing women with children (5).

Some employers are beginning to think that equal opportunity policies may be good for their public image (6). The trade union movement, in response to pressure from its growing female membership, is beginning to look beyond tokenism. The legislation has provided a necessary under-pinning to prevent blatant, deliberate and insulting discrimination practices. The fact of the legislation has made equal opportunities for women respectable, albeit as yet unacceptable. The EOC, through its numerous publications and promotional activities, has described and exposed the problems and suggested remedies. Without its financial backing, many important cases woud not have been fought. The Commission has also been most vociferous in drawing attention to the many aspects of discrimination which were deliberately excluded from the ambit of the Sex Discrimination Act - social security, taxation, nationality and immigration, retirement age - which, although tangential to the central problem of inequality in employment, are important contributing factors in their impact on women's financial status, independence, and self respect. In a period of recession and with a monetarist Government, perhaps the attack on women's right to work has been less than might have been expected because of the legislation.

3.   TOWARD AN EFFECTIVE ANTI-DISCRIMINATION POLICY. FIRST
         REQUIREMENT: CHANGE OF THE TRADITIONAL LABOUR
         DIVISION

It is clear in Britain, and both the Swedish and German studies underline this, that however good effective anti-discrimination legislation may be, no equality will be real whilst it is assumed that women's main responsibility is to care for their dependants (children, husbands, the elderly and handicapped) and   the home. So long as this assumption prevails, any measures taken towards promoting equality for women will entail attempting to fit women into employment patterns which have developed out of a traditionally male way of life, and will therefore, inevitably, have limited success.

The Swedish researchers quote what they describe as the official view: "The aim of long-term programmes for women must be that every individual, irrespective of sex, shall have the same practical opportunities, not only for education and employment but also in principle the same responsibilities for his or her own maintenance as well as a shared responsibility for the upbringing of children and the upkeep of the home" (7). The German study notes that even though family size has decreased, even though improvements in technology have reduced the level of time and work necessary for domestic tasks, "the division of labour within the family still remains as unequally divided between the sexes as before" (8). And American research asserts: "Men no longer monopolise gainful employment outside the home even in theory. But while this change has become firmly established, women have retained an unwilling monopoly on unpaid labour within the household" (9). Equality for women at work therefore depends on breaking down inequality in the home. Any anti-discrimination strategies which eschews this problem as a private one which individuals have complete freedom to resolve as they wish, must have the effect of perpetuating the belief that the care of dependants and the home is the prime responsibility of the woman. It must perpetuate the habits, attitudes, social expectations and institutional practices which derived from a time when the role of women was narrowly circumscribed by the German concept of Kinder, Küche and Kirche. All of the area studies emphasise the dicriminatory effect of 'neutral' social policies based on this assumption. Obviously little can be done to directly affect the private arrangements individuals make within their own homes, but a great deal can be done to change the nature of the relationship between home and work, to affect the way in which women and men manage their paid employment in relation to their domestic responsibilities.

Adequate collective day care during the working day for children under school age, and after school and holiday provision for older children is, in my view, essential; but it is a relatively short-term and limited solution to this problem. Women are expected to - and do - invest a great amount of time outside normal working hours in the care of their children: and they are also expected to - and do - take the primary responsibility for caring and maintaining the domestic arrangements within the household. Even good maternity provisions in the workplace (pay, leave, and right to return to work) do little to alleviate this double burden. All the area studies reveal patterns of low pay, low status, part-time working and occupational segregation which have persisted in spite of reasonable, if not good, maternity provisions in those countries.

There must therefore be a fundamental change in the norm of the working day, week and life. At present this is a male norm, based on a model of continuous employment for five days a week, for 48/49 weeks a year, from leaving school to retirement. This model is central to most wage determination, to the provision of many State benefits (particularly in relation to retirement), and to the availability of training and promotion in employment. Its pervasiveness also inhibits the possibility of men participating fully in their domestic role, even if they want to. The period in their working lives when men are expected to be most mobile, to work their hardest and for long hours covers precisely those years when they are most likely to have a young family.

It is essential that alternative working patterns are established for both men and women to enable the better, compatible management of work and home responsibilities. This means flexible working hours, shorter working hours, the provision of part-time work at all levels, the extension of job sharing (as distinct from work sharing). It also means the removal of the many structural barriers which prevent individuals from leaving and re-entering the labour force at different times in their lives: on the one hand, the emphasis on seniority and length of service as a qualification for training and promotion, and on the other, the lack of credit given to experience gained when not in paid employment - domestic management, voluntary activity, etc. Also, at least in the UK, the inflexibility of occupation pensions for those who leave and reenter the labour force or merely change jobs inhibits the free flow of labour between work and home.

Employment patterns which are predicated on the assumption that nearly every worker is a parent and that the parental role is a valuable and important one, would not only enable women to enter and participate in the labour force as equals with men, but would also enable men to share in their domestic responsibilities. Such patterns would also, incidentally, create much greater flexibility for the education, training and retraining of adults throughout their working lives, a growing need in an era of high unemployment, a decline in manufacturing industries, and technological change.

4. SECOND REQUIREMENT: AFFIRMATIVE OR POSITIVE ACTION

However, even if such social policy initiatives became common, the effects of past discrimination against women in employment would still prevail. There must also therefore be positive action by employers and by trade unions where they effectively control entry to and promotion within certain occupations. There must be a move from employment policies which fit people into existing structures according to existing assumptions about their abilities, to policies which enable the development of potential and skills. Positive action is a means to this end, and is a natural and necessary adjunct to anti-discrimination legislation. Within an individual company or organisation, such a policy requires the exercise of professional personnel practices conducted with a commitment to the achievement of equality between the sexes.

It might include

- declaring publicly, and to its own workforce, that it is an equal opportunity employer

- analysing the workforce to identify the actual and relative position of men and women (this stage is essential for later monitoring of the policy)

- examining job definitions and requirements to ensure that the qualifications expected for each job are actually job related, that is, are necessary to the performance of the job (some of the criteria which may indirectly discriminate against women are physical characteristics, length of service, geographical mobility, hours, shift work, maximum age bars, union membership, inflated formal qualification)

- introducing alternative working patterns in all jobs

- opening up recruitment sources by ensuring that all responsible - from the gatekeepers and receptionists to private or public hiring agencies - know that female candidates will be considered for all jobs, adopting strategies to encourage female applicants by visits to all-girl schools, advertisements in women's magazines, etc.

- ensuring that the criteria by which candidates are to be judged are job related and that no extraneous criteria are introduced which might prejudice women's chances (particularly questions about domestic circumstances) by training recruiters, examining selection tests for possible bias, and including both sexes on interviewing panels

- appraising managers on the basis of their equal opportunity performance

- ensuring the promotion and training procedures are examined by the same criteria as recruitment procedures

- setting targets and monitoring the programme according to those targets.

5.   THE LIMITATIONS OF QUOTA RULES

Many of these processes form the core of affirmative action programmes in the United States. The point at which such programmes incorporate positive discrimination is the last stage: setting goals or targets which are interpreted as quotas. A quota system means keeping people out of jobs, regardless of their suitability, whereas the seting of targets or goals means making efforts to include people in a workforce who have previously been excluded. Attempts to set quotas in the State have met with considerable resistance. Two major cases have been tested in the courts which raise doubts about the legality of positive discrimination.

The first concerned Alan Bakke, who had applied for entry to a medical school of the university of California and had been turned down on two subsequent occasions in 1973 and 1974. He later found out that in the same years, ethnic minority group students who were less well qualified than himself had been admitted in order to fill sixteen places set aside for them as part of an affirmative action plan. The Supreme Court ruled that the medical school had been wrong to adhere to a rigid quote system, and, by a narrow majority, ruled that affirmative action programmes were not illegal, but race or sex should not be used as the sole factor in admitting to a college or recruiting to a job. Essentially, the judgement meant that all other criteria being equal, a protected person should be given preference over a white male. This judgement lessened the scope of affirmative action plans to some extent but, as the judges kept the judgement relevant to that case alone, it did not have the sweeping effect it could have had.

The second case was that concerning Brian Weber, a white semi-skilled laboratory technician, who applied unsuccessfully for regrading training. However, he discovered that among the five who were selected there were two blacks who were less senior than himself. He sued Kaiser, the firm involved, alleging that it was illegal under the Civil Rights Act to use race rather than strict seniority as a basis for selection. The Supreme Court judges decided in July 1979 that the intention of the Civil Rights Act was to eliminate discrimination and therefore ruled that race conscious   steps   taken   in   order   to eliminate manifest racial imbalances in traditionally segregated job categories were not illegal, as they concurred with the spirit of the law and were of a temporary nature.

A third case in 1973, that of American Telephone and Telegraph (AT&T), clarified the matter further. It was agreed by the court that in a situation where an adequately qualified woman or minority (black) male was competing with a better qualified more senior white male, in order to reach the goals which had been set, the woman or minority male must be promoted. It was assumed that this would be a temporary expedient, that the 'affirmative action override' as it was called, would be unnecessary when the goals had been achieved.

The affirmative action override is clearly a form of positive or reverse discrimination, as is Section 6 of the new Swedish legislation which, as I understand it, allows an employer to give preference to a person of the underrepresented sex with merits of lower standards than those of a person of the opposite sex, on condition that this is part of a conscious effort to promote equality. It is obviously too early to judge the Swedish model but in the States, positive discrimination has been bitterly opposed by the labour unions and has given rise to a public backlash which has, in my view, reduced the overall impact and acceptability of the move towards equality of opportunity for blacks and women. As the Dean of Faculty at San Jose State University has said: "Under the guise of enforcing an executive order and through ....manipulation of the concepts of 'discrimination' and 'equal opportunity', the affirmative action policy has transformed a legitimate order to ensure equal treatment into a wilful command to hire more members of the preferred groups. Affirmative action is simply and overall a preferential policy of proportional employment" (10). It has also been suggested that it has caused rather than healed racial tensions. Furthermore, reverse discrimination might also have the effect of shifting discrimination from one social group to another which, in many circumstances, will be socially and politically unacceptable. It is designed to disregard the qualifications and interests of other groups. It is also alleged that minimum quotas soon become maximum quotas. That is to say, that when a commitment to hire 10 % of women in a particular job is achieved, no further effort is made. Quotas introduce a form of compliance with the law which pays minimal attention to the letter of the law but none to the spirit. But a more important consideration is that establishing quotas as the solution to inequality means in practice slotting women into male patterns of employment. It is essentially tokenist and conservative because it merely attempts to fit women into patterns designed for men. What is needed is a change in those patterns, a reorganisation of work which would make such tokenism redundant.

6.   ENFORCEMENT STRATEGIES OF ANTI-DISCRIMINATION POLICIES

Important improvements in the position of women in employment in the State are, I suggest, due to the success of the cases of discrimination which have been brought against employers, and the punitive financial damages which many have suffered. When a corporation has to pay out $ 38 million in back pay (as AT&T did), it plans to prevent that happening again. Even if the terms of the legal settlement outside or inside the court do not formally commit the company - as they usually do in the States - to adopting an affirmative action plan for a period of years, I believe that the threat of real financial sanctions against those shown to be discriminating will soon persuade employers to examine their practices.

During the first years of the experiments in affirmative action programmes in the USA many of those involved realised that the cost of the programmes was the cost of creating a professional personnel function. This point is central to my argument that equal opportunity policies in employment mean good general professional personnel practices which are good for business. The interests of employers lie in the most rational distribution of man or woman power, in the most efficient and cost effective way of making profits. It is sensible for them to ensure that the talents and skills of all workers, regardless of their sex or race, are fully realised. Affirmative action programmes are not very expensive: their absence may be. Furthermore, most companies or organisations are concerned with their public image and will avoid the publicity attached to anti-discrimination legal suits against them, was well as the costs of such actions and the possibility of heavy fines.

I think this is as true with regard to class actions or the British Formal Investigation procedures, as it is with individual actions. In other words, equal opportunity policies will automatically arise to solve problems which arise within the workforce and in order to prevent individual suits being brought.

The Swedish legislation imposes an obligation on employers to take active measures to promote equality, but the Swedish researchers suggest this will be ineffective because there are no sanctions against those who ignore it. Such clauses can be helpful; but they will be effective when employers find it is in their financial interest to comply.

The British legislation makes provision for special training (but not hiring) of one sex, if it can be shown that in the previous twelve months very few members of that sex were engaged in that training, or for special courses for that sex (usually women) returning to the labour force after a period when "they have been discharging domestic or family responsibilities." This facility for positive action has been little used, as the British research team notes. Many of the courses 'designated' under this provision (twelve as at 25 November 1981) have been what we call 'new opportunities for women' (NOW) courses which attempt to encourage women and give them confidence and social, technical or professional skills in order to re-enter the labour force or education. One Industry Training Board pioneered two special courses for girls in engineering. Their endeavour is to be applauded but, unfortunately, it was remarkable only because of its uniqueness. However, the Manpower Services Commission is now taking initiatives in this field, particular training women in traditionally male jobs. This form of special separate training for women is to be welcomed but unless employers are seriously engaged in equal opportunities, they will not go out of their way to hire women trained on such courses. But when access to employment is opened up by positive action, education and training for jobs will have to adapt to meet that need.

In my view, anti-discrimination legislation which imposes fixed and serious financial sanctions on offenders is an essential pre-requisite for the creation of equality in employment. Such legislation, I suggest, and the enforcement which would flow from it, would detonate social policy initiatives both because employers would have to adapt to meet the challenge and because public consciousness of discrimination would be heightened and give rise to   demands for such initiatives to ensure women's equal access to the labour market. As the Chairperson of the American Equal Employment Opportunities Commission said of the AT&T lawsuits, "they are designed to turn the ripples into waves where necessary".

NOTES AND REFERENCES

(1) Law Report (1976) IRLR 202: London IT case no. 4767/76/E.

(2) London (Central) IT case no. 31000/79/A.

(3) I shall make little reference to the Equal Pay Act in this paper, because I believe that wage discrimination is explained more as a result of sex-specific allocation and qualification than as the original cause of unequal treatment in employment, or to the non-employment elements of the Sex Discrimination Act because the central concern of this reader is the labour market.

(4) Law Reports (1978) ICR 27; (1977) IRLR 291; (1978) IRLR 3.

(5) Law Reports (1981) ICR 490, IRLR 209.

(6) Although a recent piece of research on companies which had declared an equal opportunity policy found that the Personnel Departments in most of them were unaware that such a policy existed.

(7) Renate Weitzel, Labour Market Policies Related to Women and Employment in the Federal Republic of Germany, Manuscript, Berlin: International Institute of Management, May 1982.

(8) Lillemor Gladh und Siv Gustafsson, Labor Market Policy Related to Women and Employment in Sweden, Manuscript, Berlin: International Institute of Management, Dezember 1981.

(9) June O'Neill and Rachel Braun, Women and the Labour Market: A Survey of Issues and Policies in the United States, Manuscript, Berlin: International Institute of Management, November 1981.

(10) Robert F. Sass, 'Affirmative Action and the Principles of Equality', Studies in Philosophy and Education, Spring 1976, p. 283.

10 LABOUR MARKET POLICY IN FOUR COUNTRIES: ARE WOMEN ADEQUATELY REPRESENTED?

EMMA MACLENNAN AND RENATE WEITZEL

1.   INTRODUCTION

A growing body of social research has been developed to analysis of the disadvataged position of women in the labour market. Those factors which restrict the availability or limit the entry of women into certain types of employment are well known. As pointed out by the OECD: "The main responsibility for the care of children is usually borne by women, whether or not they work outside the home. The constraints that this tends to impose on their labour market activity is an important cause of their inequality of access to employment." (1) Although overt discrimination against women occurs, there is a general recognition that indirect constraints upon women's employment prospects can be equally damaging. Prominent among these is the inadequacy of childcare provision. The need to tailor employment to fit into a domestic schedule of childcare and other commitments is a determining factor in women's employment patterns, particularly in western industrialized countries were despite those domestic duties the employment of mothers with young children has been increasing dramatically. Nevertheless these constraints still affect their employment prospects in a more qualitative respect.

Other features of women's employment which have often been described by social researchers include their segregation into certain types of jobs, especially in the service sector and in unskilled grades. Women make up a majority of the low paid, and are more likely to work in part-time, seasonal or temporary employment. Although the rate of women's unemployment has been increasing, women are also more likely than men to fall among the unregistered unemployed, or to be discouraged workers.

These aspects of women's employment have been described by many. In this paper we will not be concerned with tracing the pattern of women's employment, but with the way in which women's position in the labour market affects their access to basic unemployment benefits and inclusion in labour market policies. In the four countries examined - Britain (U.K.), the United States (U.S.), West Germany (FRG) and Sweden - women's employment disadvantage persists despite greatly divergent approaches to policy and obvious social and economic differences. This paper aimed at pinpointing common features in labour market regulation which serve to perpetuate this disadvantage.

In this context we have chosen pragmatic definitions of discrimination: If women are underrepresented among recipients of benefits according to their share of the unemployed we suggest this as an indicator for indirect discrimination of the insurance systems. Furthermore, if women are equally treated in participation and eligibility criteria for labour market policy schemes, although their preconditions and characteristics of employment differ, we assume an indirect disadvantage for women. This is due to the fact, that equal treatment of unequal groups consequently leads to a prolongation of the gap in inequality.

In chapter 2 we begin by considering the treatment of women under unemployment insurance systems. In each country there exist a number of regulations concerning liability to unemployment insurance which prevent more women than men from being covered. Furthermore the receipt of benefit during periods of unemployment is dependent upon numerous rules and eligibility tests. As we will show, there is a tendency for these rules and regulations to exclude women from eligibility. Moreover, the contributory nature of most unemployment insurance schemes can deny benefit to those most vulnerable to unemployment, and often requires a greater contribution from low paid workers, relative to their income, than from the highest earners. Apart from these issues, where women benefit to a lesser extent under unemployment insurance systems they are less likely to register for benefit and thus are less accessible as a target population for policy measures.

These policy measures and the targeting of women within them are examined in the chapter 3 and 4. While women's underregistration in unemployment insurance reduces their 'visibility' as a target group, other features of women's domestic and employment patterns also tend to exclude them from the scope of policy countercyclical in approach concentrate on the registered unemployed and core groups in the labour market to the relative exclusion of women and more marginal workers. However, as we shall show, even where women are specifically targeted as a priority group their position in the labour market may not be greatly affected if the policy instrument itself is only marginal and limited in scope. Chapters 3 and 4 therefore include a critique of existing measures as far as they influence the pattern of women's employment, and overcome some of the constraints under which women work.

2. THE UNEMPLOYMENT INSURANCE SYSTEMS: REQUIREMENTS AND BENEFITS

2.1 Introduction

At one time, to be unemployed in the four countries included in our analysis was tantamount to a criminal offense. Lack of employment or other means of support was considered a consequence of being either 'workshy' or 'unemploy-able' due to personal deficiences. Then during the period of recession and high unemployment of the 1930's it was no longer possible to explain away unem-ployment in such terms. Systems for insuring the 'genuinely' unemployed were thus developed, while safeguards were erected to prevent abuse by 'malingerers'.

For these reasons in all four countries a contributory system of benefits was preferred to one financed out of general taxation. Those individuals whose at-tachment to the labour market could be demonstrated either through their own contributions to a benefit scheme or through employers' contributions on their behalf would be eligible to claim financial support during unforeseen and temporary interruptions in employment. An essential feature of these systems was the requirement that a claimant be available for work, and registration with an employment office was made mandatory. This linkage between the provision of unemployment benefits and job placement services emphasized the payment of financial aid during a period of job search, rather than the al-leviation of need. All four countries therefore developed separate social wel-fare systems which were meanstested to provide for those in poverty.

In this chapter we shall show how the 'contributory principle' underlying unem-ployment insurance and the non-contributory tests which are intended to pre-vent abuse of the systems indirectly discriminate against women. In doing so detailed comparisons of the four countries will not always be possible due to the enormous complexity of their respective systems. However in the interest of clarity some description of specific insurance rules will be necessary.

2.2   Framework of the Insurance and Contribution Systems

The contributory principle in unemployment insurance had some precedents in voluntary arrangements developed by labour organizations in the four countries. In Britain, for example, 'friendly societies' established for collec-tively insuring workers against illness, accident or unemployment were the pre-cursors of modern trade unions. In Sweden unemployment insurance has re-tained this connection with voluntary collective arrangements in that it is run by the trade unions and has a voluntary membership. Members must pay con-tributions to these unemployment benefit societies according to their earnings and which vary from one society to another. But far from being self-financing private schemes, the State makes a substantial contribution to the societies' unemployment insurance funds, comprising over 90 per cent of the average benefit paid out by all societies in 1980 (2). For those who are unemployed but not covered by a benefit soiety there is also a safety net in the form of 'cash labour market assistance' (Kontant Arbetsmarknatsstöd or KAS) payable at a lower rate than unemployment benefit. From July 1981 government subsidies make up 45 per cent of KAS funds, with the remainder financed by an em-ployers' payroll tax of 0.8 per cent - also used to finance active labour market policies (3). However the majority of the Swedish labour force are insured by benefit societies (73 per cent in January 1981) (4), while only 17 per cent of the unemployed were in receipt of KAS in 1980 (5).

The polar opposite to Swedish voluntarism is the American system of unem-ployment compensation which functions like a compulsory payroll tax. Em-ployers are liable for a tax of 3.4 per cent on each employees' earnings up   to a contribution ceiling (currently $ 6,000 p.a., or 44 per cent of average earnings in December 1981) (6). Of this, 2.7 per cent is offset for contributions to State unemployment programmes and the remaining 0.7 per cent goes to the federal government. In practice employers' contributions to State unemployment insurance range from 0.7 per cent to 4.2 per cent depending on the employer's 'experience rating'; the average rate is around 2 per cent. Thus an employer whose firm has experienced frequent redundancies is liable to a higher rate of tax than a more stable employer. Apart from this variable, the low level of the tax ceiling in relation to average incomes makes the employers' contribution a virtual flat-rate payment for each employee.

Unemployment insurance schemes are also compulsory in the United Kingdom and the FRG, and require contributions from both employers and employees. In each country there is a lower earnings limit for contributions, and these currently fall between 18-23 per cent of average male manual earnings (in 1981, 18.6 per cent in the FRG; 22.4 per cent in the U.K.). In the U.K. no contributions are called for below this limit, but once the limit is breached become payable on the whole of an employee's income. In the FRG the employer and employee equally share liability above the limit, but below the limit the employer bears the full cost. Both countries also operate a ceiling on contributions similar to that in the United States, but in each case the ceiling is much higher in relation to average earnings (at roughly two times the average wage).

Despite the apparent differences in these four schemes, all have certain features in common. They each use the concept of the insurance principle, though none of the schemes functions in the way of a private insurance scheme: Actuarial survivals are not taken into consideration, rates of benefit are subject to State manipulation and are dependent on State subsidies, and many who participate in the schemes are ineligible to benefit in spite of their contributions. However, the contributory principle remains central, and all four countries operate contribution ceilings in recognition of the ceiling on benefit payments. With respect to contributions alone unemployment insurance schemes are due to the ceilings regressive in that the highest earners pay a smaller proportion of their incomes than low earners; nevertheless, in absolute terms contributions rise with rising income. In the case of employers' contributions in the United States, high earners are a lesser burden on employers' payrolls. The contributory principle means, of course, that benefit paid is related to contributions. As contributions are generally earnings-related, on an individual level the system could be seen as equitable.

In many ways this basic feature of unemployment insurance has consequences for women's employment. In the United States the flat-rate nature of employers' contributions could be a disincentive for hiring part-time workers, most of whom are women, as the fixed cost is the same as for a full-time employee. In contrast in the United Kingdom a part-time employee whose earnings fall below the lower earnings limit for contributions is cheaper for employers, who are then not liable to pay the employers' national insurance contribution (currently 12.2 per cent of wages).

2.3   Liability for Contributions

The first test in a succession of eligibility requiremens for the receipt of   unemployment insurance in the four countries is whether or not one is liable to contributions.

In Britain until 1977 it was possible for married women to opt out of the unemployment insurance system by paying a reduced rate contribution. The reasoning behind this option was that, as unemployed or retired men can receive an additional allowance for a dependent spouse, a married woman was already 'covered' by her husband's insurance. Of course, during their own spells of unemployment married women were ineligible for benefit in their own right, though savings made by paying a lower rate of contribution were tought to compensate for the loss of married women's earnings (presumed to be 'secondary' to their husbands'). Since April 1977 this option has been phased out, so that at present only married women who were paying the reduced rate before that date (and have not changed jobs since) can continue to do so. In the past this has meant that a large proportion of married women were ineligible for benefit: In 1970, some three quarters of all married women were paying the reduced rate (7). By the year 1980 this proportion had dropped to 50 per cent, and in 1982 an estimated 45 per cent of all married women in employment are still on the reduced rate. As the years go by the numbers of married women affected by this option are progressively reduced, though other eligibility requirements continue to exclude women.

In Sweden with its voluntary benefit societies there is no liability as such, apart from the employers' contribution towards KAS. In its strictest application the Swedish system makes no provision for the self-employed, who must voluntarily choose to join a benefit society in order to be covered by unemployment insurance. In all of the other three countries the self-employed are simply excluded from coverage. The sole consequence this may have for women is in the case of the homeworkers, who are often technically self-employed and are almost women. This may be more a problem of defining employment status than a restrictive aspect of the insurance systems (8).

In addition to the self-employed, civil servants are exempt from liability in the FRG because they receive - formally - alimentation, not salaries, and other arrangements are made with the employer (i.e. the government) in the case of redundancies. In the U.S. at a federal level government employees are also excluded, as are agricultural workers, domestic workers, railway workers and ex-service people. Nevertheless, for the most of these groups of employees are covered by special schemes or occupational insurance. Additional State provisions may extend coverage, though only eight American States insure all local government employees, only four States cover domestic employment and only two, farmworkers. Of these groups, the exclusion of domestic employment is of the most significance to women, as over one million women in the United States were classified as private household service workers in 1979, comprising 2.6 per cent of all female employment (9).

But the exclusion of specific occupations from liability is not in general as important for women workers as other apparently more technical qualification conditions. In the FRG, for example, there is an explicit minimum requirement concerning weekly work time before an employee becomes liable for contributions. This minimum of 20 hours per week excludes a rather high percentage of female part-time workers: In 1979 around 40 per cent of all female part-timers were thus not liable for unemployment insurance (10). In addition the existence of a lower earnings limit in the FRG and U.K. serves to exclude many women from coverage. In the FRG, where the lower limit is 470 DM gross per month, 20.3 per cent of women workers earned less than 600DM net per month in 1980 compared to only 7.3 per cent of men (11). In the U.K. it is estimated that one-third of all part-time workers in 1980 earned less than the lower earnings limit for national insurance contributions (12). As we shall see, contributory tests for the receipt of unemployment benefit serve to further exclude many unemployed women.

2.4   Eligibility: Contributory Tests

Once an employee has passed the test of liability for contributions it is still necessary to meet certain contributory conditions in order to receive unemployment benefit. In all four countries the amount of benefit paid is also dependent upon contribution records, except under the KAS system in Sweden. Two significant variables exist which determine the payment and level of benefits: an employee's earnings and/or duration of employment. In respect of both these two variables women are at a disadvantage.

Three of the four countries set explicit minimum work requirements with respect to duration of employment prior to redundancy for the receipt of unemployment benefit.In the FRG, apart from the 20-hours rule already described, a claimant must have been in insured employment for at least twelve months out of the three years prior to claiming in order to qualify for the minimum duration of unemployment benefit. There is also a meanstested payment for the unemployed termed 'unemployment aid' for which the minimum work requirement is 150 days (or the receipt of unemployment benefit in the last twelve months). In the United States minimum work requirements vary by State, but range from 15-20 weeks of employment. In Sweden membership of a benefit society is mandatory for a period of twelve months prior to qualification, and theoretically anyone, whether employed or not, can join and contribute to a benefit society. However during that twelve month period a claimant must have been in paid employment for a minimum of five months.

Duration of employment is also significant in the U.K., though only indirectly. In Britain eligibility for benefit is based upon the lower earnings limit below which no contributions are chargeable. This limit serves as a measure of entitlement to benefit in a way which demands a longer qualification period from low earners than high earners. In order to be eligible for the full rate of benefit an employee must have paid or been credited with (e.g., while on an approved training course) contributions on income equivalent to fifty times the lower earnings limit in the relevant contribution year. Thus, someone whose weekly earnings are equal to the lower earnings limit would have to work for 50 weeks in order to be eligible for the full rate of benefit, whereas an employee who earns five times the lower limit every week need only work for ten weeks to meet the requirement. Moreover, the relevant contribution year for the calculation of benefit entitlement is the last completed 'insurance' year (running from April to March). Thus, depending upon the date of the claim, a claimant's entitlement may rest upon contribution paid as much as 23 months prior to unemployment. This method of calculation adversely affects women workers, who on average have lower earnings and experience higher rates of labour turnover than men. A reduced rate of benefit is payable, however, to claimants who have paid contributions on income equal to 25 and 37 1/2 times the lower limit, at 50 per cent and 75 per cent of the full rate of benefit. In this way many part-year workers receive, if any, a lower rate of benefit.

Minimum earnings requirements also exist in the U.S.. These vary from one State to another, but typically refer to 'high quarter wages' (i.e., the claimant's maximum quarterly income) during the first twelve of the 15 month preceding the claim for benefit. An example of this is the State of Idahoe which in 1980 specified a high-quarter earnings minimum equivalent to $ 70.00 a week, or about 46 per cent of the average weekly wage in the retailing industry (13). Those whose earnings fall below this level are ineligible for unemployment compensation; a requirement which must particularly affec part-time workers.

In the FRG there is a minimum earnings requirement of 470 DM per months which is relatively low, and the level of benefit paid is directly related to earnings: Unemployment benefit and unemployment aid are fixed at 68 per cent and 58 per cent of previous net earnings, respectively. In contrast in Sweden the relationship between earnings and benefit under unemployment insurance is much more complex, and varies considerably between the 43 different societies. In 1981 there were basically thirteen classes of benefit ranging from a daily benefit payment of 90 to 210 Sw.kr. Most societies, however, apply only a few of these classes to their members (14). Contribution towards these benefits are generally earnings-related, and in 1980 ranged from 1.5 Sw.kr. to over 17.00 Sw.kr. per day. In the same year, while 84 per cent of all benefit recipients paid contributions of less than 9.00 Sw.kr. per day, 88.6 per cent were in receipt of the maximum rate of benefit (15). Thus. a claimant with relatively low earnings may still receive the highest rate of benefit subject to a legal limit of eleven/twelfths of the claimant's previous earnings. However, only low earners receive low rates of benefit.

Qualification conditions which specify minimum earnings are equally discriminatory against women. This is most true in the United States, where the earnings required can be as high as 50 per cent of median earnings. In the U.K. the lower earnings limit is currently (1982) around 30 per cent of median female earnings, but still excludes approximately one-third of all part-time workers, or over ten per cent of the female working population (16). Finally, contribution rules which reward lower or less frequent contributions with lower rates of benefit in all four countries normally mean that women receive less benefit than men. In any insurance system based on a contributory principle this is bound to be the case.

So far there has been no detailed mention of eligibility tests under the system of 'cash labour market assistance' (KAS) in Sweden. KAS is remarkable for its absense of restrictions, and thus provides a model for a non-contributory alternative to the other systems of unemployment insurance. Although there is a requirement that claimants should have been employed for at least ten days or 70 hours per month in five out of the twelve months preceeding unemployment to be eligible, such activities as caring for sick relatives are counted as work. Moreover, the requirement is waived for anyone who is a registered jobseeker for at least three months thus enabling re-entrants into the labour market or those excluded from unemployment insurance to receive some financial assistance. This is particularly important for women, who in 1980 were 53 per cent of the unemployed in Sweden but only 50 per cent of unemployment insurance recipients. Among KAS recipients, however, women were over 64 per cent (17). It must be noted, though, that the rates of benefit paid are low in relation to unemployment insurance benefits.

Simply being in insured employment and having a satisfactory contribution record is not in itself sufficient proof of eligibility for unemployment benefit in the four countries. All lay down certain non-contributory tests for eligibility and grounds for disqualification which can be classed under three headings: 1) Availability for work, 2) involuntary unemployment and 3) misconduct. The precise definitions of these criteria and penalties for failure vary, but the principle that more is required from the unemployed than insurance hold true in all of the systems.

Availability for work is the most crucial non-contributory test to be satisfied. As a minimum for eligibility all countries require registration with the employment service, although in the U.K. this was made voluntary in 1982. Instead, other stricter availability tests are applied in the form of a questionnaire, which concentrates on such factors as the availability of alternative childcare arrangements (a stumbling block for many female claimants). Availability for work in general means that there are no factors which prevent a suitable job offer from being taken up, and that the claimant is willing to take up "adequat" work. In the U.K. this must be full-time work, a requirement which is particularly unfavourable for women who more often seek part-time work for reasons of childcare. Full-time in Britain is defined as 30 hours or more per week, and in September 1982 a total of 48.900 women in Britain who would otherwise be eligible were excluded from benefit because they were seeking part-time work only. The extent to which this is a discriminatory requirement is illustrated by the fact that only 2,900 men were thus excluded from unemployment benefit (18).

In the FRG and Sweden there are also rules which define availability by the number of hours one is prepared to work every week. In the FRG until March 1982 it was possible for a claimant to register as available for either full-time or part-time work, though only partial benefits were paid in the latter case. However, in the context of recent amendments to the Employment Promotion Act this option will be limited to persons who are responsible for children under age sixteen or who are looking after a sick relative at home. It is estimated that around 40 per cent of all women searching part-time employment may no longer do so according to the new regulation. All other claimants will be required to register and look for full-time work. In Sweden a claimant must be prepared to work a minimum of three hours per day or 17 hours per week. Even this relatively generous restriction may pose difficulties for women with childcare problems.

The requirement that a person be prepared to work for a certain number of hours per week would not in itself be such a barrier to eligibility for benefits if there were some provisions made for childcare in those circumstances. In general, inadequate childcare provisions act as a barrier to both finding employment and obtaining benefit when unemployed. Until recently it was the practice of the German employment services to demand the signature of someone who would be prepared to look after the children of a claimant should the claimant be offered work, but this practice has been abandoned (19). However, the employment services still maintain the right to restrict eligibility where there are 'serious doubts' about the availability of alternative childcare arrangements. As the ratio of public daycare places to the number of small children (aged zero - three) who might require them was 1/64 in 1979 (20), and as private provision is not much more abundant, then this test could be diffi-

209

cult for many women to satisfy. Exempting persons with children from the necessity to demonstrate availability for full-time work should at least lessen the impact of these rules.

In the U.K. it is also necessary to demonstrate the availability of childcare, and in future this test will be stringently adhered to as one of the stricter availability tests replacing the requirement to register for work. Furthermore, as evidence of alternative childcare arrangements it is now necessary to submit a signature of someone prepared to fulfill this role. The consequences for women of stricter adherence to this test are likely to be severe: A 1974 survey by the Office of Pupulation Censuses and Surveys found that in Britain only one-third of all women wanting day care for their children were able to find any (21). Women who are at home are not a priority group for places with the scarce, public day care facilities, so that most unemployed women would need to have recourse to either relatives or childminders in order to satisfy this condition. But private childminders are not legally allowed to care for more than three children at one time, and holding a place open for a mother whose prospects of employment may be poor is not normally possible.

Where availability for work is dependent upon the availability of childcare a viscious circle is established which can exclude many unemployed women from benefit: On the one hand a woman may be prevented from making childcare arrangements through lack of income, and on the other be prevented from seeking or taking up gainful employment through lack of childcare provision. In Sweden this is exacerbated by the fact that many communities do not allow parents to keep their places at public daycare centres when they become unemployed. In future there are plans to regulate this, however, with legislation requiring that priority be given in providing daycare places to children whose parents have found re-employment (22).

In the United States a different stance is taken towards part-time work, and some extent, childcare constraints. Instead of penalizing the unemployed who seek part-time work, part-time employment is encouraged as a means of reducing unemployment overall. In most States, a claimant who accepts part-time work as an alternative to unemployment is entitled to receive an allowance to compensate for the difference between his or her wages and the level of unemployment benefit he or she would otherwise be entitled to. An additional allowance is usually added to persuade workers to prefer a part-time job to unemployment. For those who claim welfare benefits (Aid to Families with Dependent Children), there is also provision for childcare or daycare for inform relatives if such responsibilities are a constraint upon jobseeking. This should not be overly emphasized, as these arrangements are discretionary and are attached to a package of requirements (including compulsory counselling and training) for welfare recipients. But the general approach of encouraging part-time employment and the recognition made of family constraints is a contrast to eligibility tests which rule out part-time employment and inhibit childcare arrangements.

Apart from availability tests, in all four countries a precondition for the payment of unemployment benefit is that a claimant has not become voluntarily unemployed or does not voluntarily choose to remain so. Disqualification from benefit due to voluntary unemployment may occur, for example, because a claimant has refused the offer of a 'suitable' job without 'good cause' or has quit employment due to family reasons. The refusal of full-time work or work which clashes with one's domestic routine is not considered 'good   cause'   for job refusal in any of the four countries, excepting the special treatment given to persons with duties of care in the FRG. It is also not 'good cause' to refuse a job which is far from one's home, and as women tend to choose jobs which are in close proximity to home (again for domestic reasons) this requirement would affect more women than men. However, with present high rates of unemployment the infrequency of job offers makes these problems less likely to arise.

A claimant may also be deemed to be voluntarily unemployed if he or she has left his or her previous job without good cause. Some reasons for leaving one's employment which are not considered 'good cause' include the illness of a family member, the demands of childcare (e.g., during school holidays), and the decision to follow a spouse who has moved to a different area, perhaps due to a job change. Women would tend to fall foul of the first two causes because of social roles, and as married women's employment is generally less remunerative and more impermanent than that of their spouses, it is most often the wife who follows her husband if he changes jobs or move elsewhere. Only the Swedish system provides eligibility for a person who follows a spouse to a different area and therefore becomes unemployed.

A final criterion for the payment of unemployment benefit in the countries we examined is that a claimant's unemployment must not have occured through his or her own misconduct. Dismissal due to theft, sexual misbehaviour or disloyalty to one's employer are all grounds for disqualification under this rule. Although women workers are no more likely than men to be dismissed for such reasons, they may be more prone to dismissal due to tardiness or absenteeism where the employer has an inflexible work schedule. Again, the burden of responsibility for childcare and care of the sick is often at the root of such problems.

Penalties for infringement of these rules vary, most involving a disqualification from benefit for a limited period (ranging from two to eight weeks). In the FRG the duration of disqualification is related to the offence; two weeks for failure to register for employment, four weeks for a second failure to register and eight weeks for refusal of a 'suitable' job or training offer or other infringements. However, if disqualifications amount to a total of sixteen weeks or more then permanent disqualification ensues (23).

But the most punitive system exists in the United States, whereby a claimant is not only disqualified from benefit during unemployment, but upon eventually obtaining employment must work in insured employment for a specified amount of time in most States before 'requalification' is granted. Only then do further insurance tax payments begin to count once again towards eligibility for benefit. For many women workers who do temporary jobs, this system of re-qualification must be particularly hard.

2.6 Amount and Duration of Benefits

Our concern in examining unemployment insurance systems has so far been with entitlement to benefit and the way in which apparently 'sex-neutral' rules can discriminate against women. Once an unemployed person has negotiated the various eligibility rules, however, there are still features of the insurance systems which are less favourable to women workers.

211

In each of the four countries there is a <u>maximum duration</u> for the payment of benefits which cease whether or not employment has been found. To this extent, then, unemployment benefit is independent of employment status. But within this limitation some systems pay out benefits of uniform duration once eligibility is established, and others pay benefits of variable duration according to the individual concerned. As described by the U.S. Department of Labour, the first approach..."is based on the concept that once a worker achieves 'insured status' he is entitled to the same income maintenance protection as all other insured workers. It embodies the idea that the <u>length of time</u> required to find work should be the determining factor rather than <u>how long</u> (the claimant) worked..." (24).

Unemployment insurance in the <u>United Kingdom</u> is the best example of payment according to 'insured status' among the countries we examind. Once contribution and other conditions have been met, benefit is of uniform duration and lasts a maximum of one year. The recent abolition of the earnings-related element in benefit payment means that the rates of benefit paid are also virtually uniform; the sole exception being the payment of 50-75 per cent of the full rate in cases where contribution records do not entitlement a claimant to a full rate of benefit (as described earlier). As we have seen, this exception disproportionately affects low earners and temporary workers, and the minimum contribution conditions alone exclude large numbers of female part-time workers from eligibility. But once these conditions have been met treatment is similar for low and high earners, and the emphasis is on income support rather than earnings replacement (which distributes greater resources to the well-paid). It must be noted, however, that the rates of benefit paid are low in absolute terms.

In the <u>United States</u> most States operate unemployment insurance systems of variable duration. The maximum length of payment is normally 26 weeks, although due to the present high rates of unemployment an extended benefits programme was initiated by the federal government in the 1970's which allows for an extension of the duration of payment by 13 weeks in States with particularly high rates of unemployment. Within this maximum, duration of payment is "based on the <u>individual</u> worker's experience. <u>The longer</u> he worked or the <u>more</u> he earned - the longer duration" (25). This is because of the way that benefit is calculated, which in most States allows each individual to receive in total a set proportion of 'base period' (yearly) earnings in unemployment compensation. This proportion varies, but is typically around one-third of annual earnings. The weekly rate of benefit paid is also earnings-related (usually 50 per cent of weekly wages) and is based upon 'high quarter earnings' in the insurance year. The duration of benefit is a function of these two factors: The total allowance divided by the weekly benefit amount yields the number of weeks' payment. Thus the amount and duration of benefit is determined on an entirely individual basis, with low earners and temporary workers receiving both less and shorter unemployment compensation.

These calculations are bounded, however, by a floor and ceiling on benefit payments. In 1980 the minimum benefit payable ranged from $ five to $ 38 according to State, and the maximum payment ranged from $ 80 to $ 160 per week (26). This maximum payment is normally linked to average earnings in some way; for example, at 66 2/3 per cent of average State earnings in Arkansas in 1981 (27). Unemployment compensation is therefore earnings related within a certain range of income only: The lowest earners are excluded by the minimum earnings requirement for qualification or else receive the minimum level of benefit, while highest earners receive the flat-rate, maximum benefit payment.

In both the FRG and the Swedish benefit societies the amount of unemployment compensation is also individually determined and to some extent earnings-related, subject to a floor and ceiling on payments. Duration of benefit under both systems is related to duration of employment or society membership, although in Sweden the variation in requirements from one society to the next is considerable. The maximum under Swedish unemployment insurance is 300 days, paid on a daily basis for up to five days weekly. In the FRG there is a maximum duration of 312 days if the claimant has been in insured employment for at least three out of the four years prior to unemployment. For those in insured employment for only one year out of the last three years, the duration of benefit is 104 days. Payment of unemployment aid is not limited if the claimant is in need of support, but is formally given for a maximum of one year.

In Sweden, as we have seen, there are thirteen classes of benefit each of which is paid on a flat-rate basis to all who qualify. Qualification for a particular class of benefit is in general dependent on the level of·past contributions, which are earnings-related. But there is some flexibility within this and, as mentioned earlier, individual societies may set lower than normal contribution rates while paying out a high level of benefit. There is an absolute maximum on benefit payments which is specified by the government, and no claimant may receive more than eleven/twelveth of previous earnings as compensation for unemployment. The vast majority of benefit recipients, though, are paid benefit at the maximum benefit class level.

In the FRG benefit levels are more directly earnings-linked, with compensation set at 68 per cent of previous net wages. Contribution conditions for qualification effectively set a floor to benefit payments at 68 per cent of the minimum earnings requirement, and there is a benefit ceiling which in 1982 was 4,700 DM monthly. The meanstested unemployment aid is also earnings-related, at 58 per cent of previous income.

Finally, the KAS system in Sweden, though catering for a minority of benefit claimants, is the most open of all systems and makes no demands in terms of either contributions or minimum earnings. For re-entrants to the labour market duration of employment is also immaterial, the only requirement being a three-months period of registration for work. Others have a very low work requirement to meet - 70 hours per month for five months - and some domestic duties can be offset against this. The full rate of benefit is low in relation to what one would receive under benefit society schemes, and at 75 Sw.kr. per day (1981) is less than the lowest benefit class rate. Interestingly, 'insured status' is not fixed, but rather dependent upon one's employment intentions: A claimant seeking part-time work is eligible for benefit in proportion to the number of hours he or she is available for work. The maximum duration of benefit is 150 days for most claimants, although longer periods are allowed for the older unemployed (e.g., 300 days for those aged between 55 and 60).

Contributory tests, particularly those which specify a minimum earnings level, exclude many women who have low wages due to their part-time or low paid employment. Eligibility tests which necessitate a long employment record are also discriminatory in that the higher incidence of temporary work and labour turnover among women makes them less likely to qualify. Once qualifying   for benefit, women's lower earnings and shorter job tenure continue to be a disadvantage under insurance systems which stress past employment records in setting the amount of compensation.

The indirect discrimination against women due to the eligibility rules may be demonstrated by the proportion of female unemployment benefit recipients: In the United States between 1973 and 1978 women comprised around 40 per cent of all benefit recipients (28), whereas they made up nearly half of all the unemployed. Among all Swedish recipients the female share was 50 per cent (29), while their share among the unemployed was 53 per cent (1980). In the United Kingdom women comprised one third of all the unemployed (1980) but only 28 per cent (in November 1981) (30) of all those who were in receipt of unemployment benefit. In the FRG 66 per cent of the male unemployed received unemployment benefit or aid but only 60 per cent of the female unemployed were recipients (31). These figures give the average share of benefit recipients by sex: It is likely that, if characteristics such as age, family status and number and age of dependent children were considered, even more pronounced differences between male and female eligibility for unemployment benefit would be found.

Table 1
Women as percentage of the unemployed, and benefit recipients, 1980

	Women as a % of all unemployed	Women as a % of all unemployment benefit recipients	Women as a % of all unemployment aid recipients 3)
FRG	52	54	32
U.K. 1)	30	29	25
SWE	53	50	64
U.S.A. 2)	49	39	- 4)

1) On the basis of the averages of the months May and November 1980.
2) 1979
3) U.K.:Supplementary benefit. Note: Supplementary benefit is meanstested, and must be claimed by the man in a married couple. SWE: KAS.
4) There is no comparable benefit in the U.S.

Source: Gruppe Politikinformationen, Chronik 11, January 1983.

The effect of these indirect constraints is to deny unemployment benefit to some women, particularly part-time workers, who may have been in continuous employment for a number of years. Moreover, qualification conditions which make childcare arrangements or availability for full-time work a pre-requisite for the receipt of benefit may exclude even fully-insured women who satisfy all the contributory requirements. If unemployment benefits are viewed as financial assistance during a period of job search, women are at a disadvantage compared to unemployed men who otherwise face the same or similar reemployment difficulties. It follows that a system of unemployment compensation in which these elements do not feature would include more unemployed women within its scope, and re-distribute resources in their direction. A possible model for such a system will now be considered.

2.7   An Open Model of Unemployment Compensation

The contributory principle in unemployment insurance has certain attractions. Unemployed individuals who claim benefit draw upon funds which they and/or their employers have contributed towards to insure against such an eventuality. A claimant may therefore feel 'entitled' to such benefits without the stigma which is attached to other, meanstested state support. A contributory insurance system is ideally self-financing, and at times of high unemployment this aspect may become paramount to governments seeking to cut public expenditure.

But contributory systems are also by definition 'closed' systems, insuring only those whose insurance has been paid for. Those who are thereby excluded are labour market re-entrants, individuals who are vulnerable to unemployment due to lack of skills or other labour market disadvantage, employees in industries which are subject to a high degree of demand fluctuation and labour turnover, and those whose family commitments prevent them from full participation in employment. In short, those groups which should be most targeted for labour market policies are those most excluded from unemployment insurance, and women figure prominently among them. In the United States, for example, "unemployed women have benefited less than men from unemployment insurance. Despite their growing participation in the labour market, the majority of women continue to fill jobs which are less well covered by insurance. This is confirmed by the fact that they represented almost two-thirds of the recipients of SUA (32) (Special Unemployment Assistance, E.ML./R.W.) in 1975" (33).

This relative exclusion of women is of concern for two reasons: First, because it means that they are at a financial disadvantage to men when unemployed. It would be argued that the lack of unemployment compensation is immaterial for many women, who may at any rate rely on the income of their husbands or fall back upon meanstested benefits for subsistence. However, married women whose husbands are in employment are not normally eligible to receive such meanstested benefits on their own behalf. For those with young children, the absence of financial aid during unemployment may also inhibit job search, and may even prevent them from taking up employment through lack of finance for alternative childcare arrangements.

Second, the more that women are excluded from benefit, the less will be their propensity to register with the employment service. In the U.K. one survey found that only 59 per cent of women seeking work in 1978 were in fact registered for employment. In contrast, Department of Employment registration figures actually over-represented male unemployment, as many men are registered who are close to retirement age and not seeking work (34). Similarly in the FRG at least 7.5 per cent of all employed women are not covered by social insurance due to part-time employment and therefore have no incentive to register, because they are not liable to unemployment insurance (35). In

Sweden 'hidden', unregistered unemployment comprises individuals who would like to work but are not seeking work because they feel their prospects of finding a suitable job are poor or because they are constrained in some way (including the lack of childcare) from doing so. Over twice as many women fall under this heading as men, though because of the KAS system registration is relatively high (36). Finally, in the United States some 17 per cent of female unemployment is accounted for by 'discouraged' workers who do not register, compared to only eight per cent of male unemployment (37). This under-registration of women in all countries means that they receive less counselling and direction in their job-seeking. Also it means that women benefit to an even lower degree than the official registration statistics show.

It is possible to conceive of a system of unemployment insurance which would not exclude women and other disadvantaged groups from the benefit of financial aid during job search. Such a system could not, for reasons given, be contributory, so that some other means of defining eligibility would be neces-sary. We have commented on the ways in which existing availability tests dis-criminate against women in calling for evidence of alternative childcare ar-rangements and, with some exceptions, in requiring availability for full-time work. But such discriminatory requirements are not necessary. In principle availability for work or training as a condition for the receipt of unemploy-ment benefit is a self-evident requirement. Allowances can be made for those who desire part-time work, and it would be equally possible to provide support for those who are constrained by child care or other family commitments. Re-designing availability tests would necessitate some thought in order to meet standards of fairness and non-discrimination. But the existence of the KAS system in Sweden shows that more 'open' access to unemployment benefit is possible.

The major obstacle to instituting a more open alternative to present unemploy-ment insurance systems - at least in Britain, the U.S. and the FRG - is finance. At present the emphasis in all three countries is towards restricting claims upon the benefit funds by even fully insured individuals. This is particu-larly true in the United States, where once 'supersolvent' State trust funds are now over-subscribed and require heavy subsidy by the Federal government (38).

The failing of the contributory system is that at such times of high unemploy-ment there are fewer contributors to finance benefits and, worse still, fewer of the unemployed are able to meet the contributory tests. A non-contributory system financed out of general taxation would at least escape this second fail-ing. Furthermore, a progressive 'unemployment tax' could redistribute the costs of unemployment in a way that a contributory system by definition could not: In all four countries those most likely to suffer unemployment are those least able to contribute. There is no reason why tenured groups (such as the civil servants in the FRG) and those in a more privileged position should not help to support those who are less protected. The institution of a steeply pro-gressive 'solidarity' tax in Belgium to share the costs of unemployment proves that such a proposal is possible in practice (39). A system like this would make the targeting of so-called problem groups in the labour market clearer. It would also give women who are among the 'hidden' unemployed a better chance of financial aid and counselling during their job search.

3. TRAINING AND RETRAINING OF ADULTS

3.1 Introduction

In the last chapter we have shown the way in which the payment of unemployment benefit or compensation is linked to registration for employment and availability for work in the four countries examined. There is also a connection between unemployment insurance systems and participation on further training or other labour market programmes. Because of their under-representation among the registered unemployed, women in all four countries are less evident and accessible as a target group for policy measures, and are also less likely to receive counselling and advice in employment decisions from the state employment services. In some cases, those factors which tend to exclude women from eligibility for unemployment compensation also serve to exclude them from participation in labour market programmes. Indeed, the more the application of policy measures is tied to the unemployment insurance system, the more selectivity works to the disadvantage of women.

As described by the OECD, labour market policies can have two distinct aims: "to cut the social cost of unemployment by providing the unemployed with public employment, and to reduce structural employment, which mainly affects those at the biggest disadvantage on the labour market by providing them with opportunities for training and their first work experience. While the second type of action is, therefore, intended to be selective, the first seems very clearly designed as a cyclical regulator of the labour market" (40).

As disadvantaged groups are likely to be over-represented among the unregistered and long-term unemployed, these two aims are not mutually exclusive. However, where targeting is based on registered unemployment countercyclical policies which aim to reduce 'visible' unemployment can ignore the needs of women. Furthermore, counterstructural policies which may concentrate more effort on disadvantaged groups have also been known to give priority to the more 'serious' problem of male unemployment. Neither approach has been very successful in changing the pattern of women's employment in any of the countries, although as we shall show, an emphasis on countercyclical measures has a lesser impact than specific targeting.

In this chapter we will discuss the participation of women in selected instruments of labour market policy. If targeting for labour market programmes is based on criteria of income support, improving skill levels or equal employment opportunity, women should claim a high priority in all of the countries examined. In each country women make up a majority of low paid, unskilled workers, and are far more likely to maintain a family on a poverty income than men. In terms of equity women's segregation in traditional areas of employment persists. Such widespread inequality in employment requires an approach which does more than merely reduce unemployment and which is on a larger scale than most targeted measures for women. In our critique of existing policy measures we shall therefore attempt to highlight those policies which seem to point in a more successful direction, and pose some questions for the future.

3.2 Aims and Administration

Adult training and retraining opportunities have a particular importance for women. In all four countries most women enter the labour market with skills which are fitted to traditionally female employment, and which may yield a slight wage advantage in initial income (41). However, women's earnings in traditional work tend to flatten over time, and the relative absence of women in higher levels of employment is evidence that in all countries opportunities for promotion are fewer than for men. In addition, many women leave the labour market during the first years of child-rearing, and the longer the period of absence the more difficult it is to gain adequate re-entry into employment. For these reasons adult training and retraining could provide a means of improving income and employment prospects for unskilled or low paid women, and could help to reintegrate women who have left the labour market to raise families.

In all four countries there are legal prescriptions concerning the training of women. In the FRG, section two of Employment Promotion Act (EPA) specifically concerns "the occupational integration of women who have difficulty in view of the normal labour market conditions, either because they are married, or because of their family ties", and section 43 stipulates that one of the aims of further training should be the promotion of women's entry and re-entry into employment (42). The body concerned with carrying out these duties is the Federal Employment Agency, which administers labour market policy and oversees placement services. Interestingly, the FEA is mainly funded through unemployment insurance contributions, though this is supplemented by tax revenues when contributions are inadequate during times of recession. But in Germany the conceptual link between training, placement and insurance is thus particularly strong: On the one hand, those who are fully insured and meet eligibility requirements have a legal right to training. On the other hand, even insured applicants may find themselves ineligible for training and training allowances. This may be explained by reference to the German way of financing labour market programmes. With the introduction of the EPA in 1969 it was the first time that a legal right to occupational training was provided for, but no extra financial resources were written in to cover the costs of the expanding demand for these training schemes. At that time the act did not set out any special requirements concerning insured employment prior to further training or following training schemes. But since 1969 the EPA has undergone seven amendments and the addition of several more detailed regulations which increasingly restricted the eligibility criteria for occupational training to a reduced and selected group of insured persons and the unemployed. This occured due to the budgetary problems of the FEA, arising from the necessity of financing increasing levels of unemployment in recent years. These developments illustrate the high procyclical - instead of the intended anticyclical - nature of an 'active' labour market policy financed via the anticyclically varying volume of the unemployment insurance fund.

In the United States, the Comprehensive Employment and Training Act of 1973 consolidated previous employment programmes under one statutory measure. It currently consists of eight separate titled programmes, two of which mandate adult training. Within these mandated programmes, State and local governments contract to receive federal funding for local initiatives. These local government 'prime sponsors' have a great deal of discretion in the types of services they choose to offer, and within certain national parameters, are chiefly constrained by the amount of federal funding they receive. However, certain standards of non-discrimination are laid down for these prime sponsors. If services provided for a targeted group fall short of target levels by more than 15 per cent, an inquiry and corrective action must be undertaken (43). In

218

this way if women's representation as a target group in a training programme falls far below their representation among the eligible population, there should be some legal remedy.

In Britain the position of women in training measures is in part regulated by the Sex Discrimination Act of 1975. This makes it unlawful to discriminate either directly or indirectly on the basis of sex in the provision of training, though positive discrimination in favour of a targeted group is allowed for by special application under section 47 of the Act. This section permits training bodies to "train or encourage women only to enter areas of work where they have been under-represented in the previous year. They may also train for employment those people who have a special need because they have been out of regular full-time employment for some time because of their domestic or family responsibilities" (44). The Manpower Services Commission, to whom application should be made, consists of three branches which administer placement, training and special employment programmes. Though ultimately accountable to the Department of Employment, the MSC is able to formulate policy quasi-autonomously, and within the MSC the three branches operate more-or-less independently. Many of the individual programmes and schemes are autonomously administered, and some could be said to be 'merely funded' by the MSC.

In Sweden the National Labour Market Board (AMS) has a statutory duty to "lead planning and take measures on its own account to cope with unemployment or labour shortages and thereby promote the equality of women" (45). Swedish labour market policy differs from that in the other three countries in that it is more centrally directed and administered than elsewhere. Training in Sweden occurs in the 60 special centres run by the National Board of Education on behalf of the AMS, or in specially designed courses given in the state school system. A small proportion of training also takes place in private firms, but in general training is directly provided. This allows for a high degree of control in targeting, and greater ease in monitoring the position of targeted groups.

In contrast, the Federal Employment Agency in Germany contracts out training to various, partly commercial, course-providers along the lines of a 'voucher' system: Each programme participant who is deemed eligible for training and the reimbursement of costs has more or less free choice in enrollment for training courses.Thus, most who participate in adult training under FEA programmes do so on virtually a 'self-service' basis: The FEA is not allowed to advertize training opportunities, and eligible individuals may find for themselves a training sponsor - a system which emphasizes the orientation towards individuals who have 'paid' for training through their insurance contributions. In the United States and Britain training is also subcontracted, and responsibility for schemes develops upon State and programme administrators. These forms of training provision are less amenable to direct influence, so that the promotion of a particular target group is more difficult to implement or monitor. The structure of labour market administration may therefore be an important factor in women's participation in training.

3.3   Eligibility

We have seen the way in which access to unemployment compensation is limited by eligibility requirements which, though apparently neutral, serve   to exclude many unemployed women. Access to training in all the countries is indirectly influenced by this, as the under-registration of women means that they are less likely to contact the employment services and therefore less likely than men to be advised of training or re-training opportunities.

In Germany, as we have seen, labour market policy is more strongly tied to the unemployment insurance system than elsewhere, and because programmes are largely financed through insurance contributions, the FRG sets requirements for participation in training which are extremely restrictive. This greatly limits the type of targeting which can be practiced. Applicants for training programmes must meet an exceedingly complex series of work requirements, and different requirements are set for three kinds of benefits: the general right to participate, eligibility for training allowance and for the reimbursement of course costs and other requirements. To be eligible for further training or retraining an applicant who has already had some vocational training must have completed at least three years of work experience outside of a training programme. For the unqualified or those who did not complete occupational training this requirement is six years. In both cases years spent as a housewife are counted equally towards eligibility.

To require that applicants have past work experience in employment as a precondition for training is both discriminatory and inappropriate. Groups who would be ineligible for training due to the necessity of a three to six year work history include academics who are unable to find work in their chosen field (the experience of many female social scientists), immigrants - particular women - who have no history of (insured) employment. Paradoxically the unqualified and (unqualified) housewifes have to stay in low paid employment or in their homes for a longer period until they become eligible for participation.

In the other three countries further training or retraining encompasses those who have either personally approached the employment service or training establishments, or who have been processed through the employment service as part of a benefit application. Under most schemes youth programmes are administered separately, and therefore an age requirement (usually 18) is common.

For some targeted programmes requirements for participation may be more specific. In the United States, for example, low income groups are emphasized in targeting, while some emphasis is given in Sweden to combating job segregation. All countries operate some special further training programmes to promote women, and in other cases, the young long-term unemployed or handicapped workers are targeted. More will be said about targeting later in this chapter in relation to individual schemes, but in general targeting which stresses low income or skill levels rather than employment status is more beneficial to women. Specific targeting of women, of course, is also beneficial depending upon the scale of the programme.

3.4   Allowances

Training allowances in the four countries follow four entirely different models and range from a direct incentive for the unemployed to a distinct disincentive for certain groups. Here the Swedish and American system seem to do the most to encourage the training of women. In Sweden, training allowances must not be higher than former income, and there is a maximum allowance which is equal to the maximum unemployment benefit rate and a minimum which is somewhat higher than cash labour market assistance. Until recently there was a small incentive increase (ten Sw.Kr. per day in 1980) to induce the unemployed to prefer training to unemployment, but this incentive payment was cancelled in 1981. Prior to 1976 allowances were also meanstested, which was a barrier for unemployed women whose husband's incomes would make them ineligible to receive an allowance. Now, however, the meanstest no longer applies.

In the United States CETA regulations prescribe a basic hourly allowance for individuals in training which is equivalent to the State minimum wage, or in the case of work placement, the standard rate for the job. There is also an allowance for dependents, and an additional incentive payment may be added by individual States to encourage those on public assistance to seek training. This incentive payment is disregarded when entitlement to meanstested benefits is calculated, so that even married women in welfare families would receive some extra financial assistance during CETA training.

Training allowances for adults in Britain are paid at a uniform rate which is set at a low level ($ 35 per week in 1982). The allowance is higher than unemployment benefit for a single person and roughly equivalent to unemployment benefit for married couples, so that in either case training might be attractive as an alternative to unemployment. A single person with no dependents who is in receipt of supplementary benefit would also be financially better off in training, but difficulties arise with married couples on supplementary benefit, single parents and families receiving Family Income Supplement. In these circumstances allowances are deducted from meanstested benefits, which leaves the claimant with little or nothing extra to cover the added costs associated with training. A single parent who requires childcare in order to be free for training for instance, could find this interaction of allowances and benefits prohibitive.

Finally, in the FRG subsidized allowances are only paid to those individuals who fulfill certain eligibility requirements over and above the conditions for entry into training. Since 1982 training allowances are limited mainly to the insured or those in receipt of benefits. Recent amendments of the Employment Promotion Act in 1982 have given the allowances the character of a provisional loan, so that anyone who does not fulfill certain work requirements after training must repay all allowances. Thus, a trainee has four years directly after completion of training in which to pay back allowances, but if the individual is in insured employment or available for work during at least three of the four years then the debt is cancelled. Furthermore, those whose training is not 'necessary' for the procurement of work but merely instrumental to upward mobility - usually those who are in training accompanying employment - are only given a discretionary loan during training which cannot be amortized with a period of work. Allowances themselves, like unemployment benefits, are set at 68 per cent of former net income (75 per cent for trainees with dependents), or 58 per cent for those whose training is not 'necessary', which mainly is promoting training accompanying a job.

Overall, this system of training allowances tends to further exclude those who are already at a disadvantage in the labour market. The applicant must have worked in insured employment for at least two out of the three years directly prior to training in order to be eligible for a training allowance and for the costs of the measure. This period of three years can be extended by four years per newly born child for persons re-entering the labour market; so that for persons, mainly women, with one child, the requirement is normally two years of work during a seven year period. Until recently it was possible to waive these work requirements in special cases of great need and following insured employment, but this is no longer allowed. Furthermore the applicant must guarantee to take up insured re-employment for at least three years out of the four years directly following the scheme.

Past, present and future work requirements make the German eligibility tests for training allowances the most restrictive. Under the requirement which calls for recent work experience, re-enrants to the labour market after a prolonged absence (mostly older women) would not qualify for training even if former employment had been of a long duration and fully insured. Both requirements discriminate against uninsured part-time workers and all others who are not fully covered by unemployment insurance, as even an extensive work history is insufficient if it does not consist of insured employment. Also newly entering women are excluded from training allowances.

In particular the post-training work requirements discriminate against those part-time workers who are neither fully insured nor available for full-time employment. Nor is there any exemption for women who bear a child during that period: no prolongation of this four year period is provided. Thus private decisions concerning marriage and children are strongly restricted, which may prevent some women from participation. Women who wish to develop new skills for promotion or non-traditional skills might also find that their training is considered 'unnecessary' and therefore unsubsidized; whereas for men promotion is not so dependent on further training, and is more often enabled by inplant training schemes or by other means sponsored by the employer.

Both eligibility requirements and allowance payments can serve to exclude groups who should otherwise be a priority for targeting. In Britain, men and women in welfare families (who by definition are living at a poverty level) receive no additional State support when they take up training, despite the additional expenses incurred. Ironically, the better-off receive a non-meanstested flat-rate payment. In the FRG a wide range of groups tend to fall outside the eligibility rules, including some labour market re-entrants, immigrants, structurally unemployed academics, uninsured part-time workers, and young mothers with poor work histories.

Those who manage to pass the eligibility tests may be discouraged all the same by the allowance requirements, and those who are seeking to improve their labour market status are forced to subsidize themselves. Especially in Germany eligibility and allowance rules may render those who are vulnerable in the labour market or who seek to improve their skills ineligible for training or support. Targeting for programmes in such circumstances is considerably hampered.

3.5   Women's Participation in Training Schemes

Eligibility rules for training programmes and for the receipt of training allowances have a market effect on the participation of women in training. In Sweden where regulations and entry requirements are least restrictive, and in the United States where women are indirectly preferred among potential   participants, the proportions of women in training are highest (at over half of all trainees). In Sweden the incentive to register with the employment service in order to receive KAS may be an important factor in this, while in the United States the highest proportions of women in some schemes is a direct result of targeting low income and disadvantaged groups. In the U.K. women are proportionately represented in training overall compared with their labour force participation, but in certain programmes which set special qualification conditions women are only a small minority. Finally in the FRG the restrictive entry requirements and the emphasis on insurance payments have yielded the lowest female participation rate of the four countries surveyed: Although women comprised more than half of all registered unemployed they formed only one third of all participants in training schemes sponsored by the FEA in 1980.

Table 2
Women as a percentage of all participants in training programmes
and of all the registered unemployed

	FRG		U.K.		SWE		U.S.	
	part.	unempl.	part.	unempl.	part.	unempl.	part.	unempl.
1971	17	45	4	16	46	44	-	-
1974	22	44	38	16	51	51	46[1]	44[1]
1978	27	51	42	29	51	48	51	50
1981	29	49	31	29	47	49	53[2]	44[2]

1) 1975
2) 1980

Source: Gruppe Politikinformationen, Chronik 11, January 1983.

In all countries, however, whatever the gross porportions of women in training the occupational distribution of female training continues to follow a traditional pattern. It is this aspect of women's participation in training - the type of training received and the choice of occupations - which will now be considered.

In the United States, CETA titles IIB/C form the 'counterstructural core component' of adult training. Targeting for enrollment is based on various definitions of labour market disadvantage: Overall, in 1980 92 per cent of participants are considered 'economically disadvantaged' (i.e., have a poverty level income) (46), 49 per cent are non-white, nearly one-third are high school drop-outs, and 53 per cent are women. The emphasis on 'disadvantage' as opposed to insurance status is illustrated by the fact that only five per cent of participants under Titles IIB and C were unemployment insurance claimants (47).

But despite the fact that a majority of Title II enrollees are women, there is evidence that they are less favourably treated than men. Training under Title

II can be given as either classroom training, on-the-job training in sponsored workplaces, or adult work experience through short-term placements. As described by the National Commission for Employment Policy of the Department of Labor; "on-the-job training integrates the participant into the labor force more than does classroom training. PSE (public service job creation) seems to be preferable to adult work experience since PSE jobs are intended to lead to unsubsidized employment, whereas adult work experience jobs are shorter in duration, more likely than PSE to be part-time, and lower paying than PSE jobs." (48) However, in fiscal year 1979-80, when women comprised 58 per cent of those eligible under Title II, they were 60 and 59 per cent of those participating in classroom training and adult work experience, and only 37 per cent of those receiving on-the-job training. Under Title IID public sector job creation, women were also under-represented by about 20 per cent (49).

Part of the explanation for the under-representation of women in certain types of training has to do with the approach of those responsible for programme assignment. Although CETA participants have some say in the sort of activity they undertake, one study found that; "for those who wanted job training, females were much more likely to get classroom training than OJT (on-the-job training). For those who wanted jobs, they were more likely to get adult work experience than PSE jobs" (50). Berryman and Chow conclude that CETA integrates women less into the workplace and less into 'serious' jobs which are intended to provide permanent employment opportunities. But as they point out; "at least the classroom training/OJT difference may just reflect where training for traditional female jobs usually occurs. In this case any inequities resolve into occupational, not activity, assignment issues" (51). In other words, although the priorities of placement officers may led to discriminatory patterns of assignment, traditional female job and training opportunities also have a role to play.

Unfortunately, no data exists for the occupational distribution of women in CETA training, but some indication may be obtained from the pattern of job placement. The types of employment found have tended to be low paid, sex-stereotyped and unskilled. For women, the most common placement was in clerical employment, accounting for 47.6 per cent of all women placed by CETA. For men the job of non-farm labourer was the most popular, with 26.7 per cent of all male placements. Overall about two-thirds of adults placed by CETA were in a traditional job for their sex, one-quarter were in mixed jobs and the remaining ten per cent obtained non-traditional employment (52).

In October 1982 the Job Training Partnership Act (JTPA) was introduced by the Reagan administration. Under this Act emphasis is given to job-linked training schemes rather than job creation. The targeting of groups remains the same as under CETA; persons with incomes below the poverty level, recipients of welfare benefits and the handicapped - though ten per cent of programme recipients may have incomes above the limit if they suffer from other disadvantages. But JTPA restricts the budget for indirect costs, which directly cover course fees, to 30 per cent of all expenditure: under CETA, where no limits have been set in this respect, 80 per cent of overall costs were spent for training allowances, services such as childcare and other enabling allowances (53). This newly balance in favour of employer subsidies is likely to reduce the total number of available participants, particularly among unemployed mothers.

In the United Kingdom, adult training is largely the responsibility of the Training Services Division (TSD) of the MSC. The main policy instrument   of   the

TSD, accounting for 70 per cent of expenditure in 1980/81, is the Training Opportunities Scheme (TOPS). In 1978, women were 41 per cent of all TOPS trainees, which was roughly proportionate to their representation in employment. In recent years female placements have dropped relative to men, so that in 1980/81 women formed only 38 per cent of placements (54). Moreover, "insofar as women take part in (TOPS) they do, in the main, choose training for traditional female occupations in the clerical and commercial field" (55). Three-quarters of all women participating in TOPS in 1978 were in clerical and commercial courses, compared to only four per cent of male participants. On the other hand, the most popular male course of study was in the engineering and automotive field, involving 48 per cent of all male trainees. Only two per cent of women were enrolled in that area. Moreover, only five per cent of women were enrolled in a higher level TOPS course in management, compared to ten per cent of men (56).

TOPS training takes place in either colleges of further education (CFEs) and private colleges (both providing classroom training), skill centres (which ressemble small factories), employers' establishments and residential training centres. Nearlyhalf (49 per cent) of all training occurs in CFEs, and another 35 per cent is in skillcentres. The remainder is mostly conducted on employers' establishments (15 per cent) (57). Within these categories there is a distinct sexual division in training undertaken: 42 per cent of men train in skillcentres, compared to 1.6 per cent of women. The large majority of women train in CFEs and other institutions. Of the minority who do take skillcentre courses, nearly half trained in sewing machining and men's hairdressing, although 28 per cent enrolled in such non-traditional courses as capstan setting machining and bricklaying. In gross numbers, though, only 186 women out of 40,000 female trainees studied non-traditional manual trades in skillcentres.

In a 1979 survey of TOPS trainees by OPCS, about half of all women interviewed had dependent children. Four out of five women with dependent children had children aged five years or over, which suggests that "many women with young children see TOPS courses as a means of re-entering the labour force after their children enter full-time schooling" (59). The success rate of obtaining employment after a TOPS course would indicate that TOPS might indeed provide good re-entry training: only six per cent of trainees interviewed 15-17 months after completion of training had had no work experience during that interval (60). However, 'housewives' comprised 58 per cent of this group, though just 28 per cent of the total trainee population (61).

Even then a 94 per cent achievement rate in job placement belies the actual impact of TOPS training. Eighteen per cent of trainees interviewed by OPCS were not in work at the time of the interview, and a further 22 per cent were in employment which was unrelated to the skills they had learned. Labour turnover was relatively high - 52 per cent of all trainees who had found work had held two or more jobs during the 15-17 month interval. Over half of these had left their first jobs because of low pay and bad working conditions, and over a quarter were made redundant. Altogether at least 46 per cent of TOPS trainees found either no work or work which was unstable or unsatisfactory, and a quarter of all TOPS trainees were unable to make use of their new skills. However, there are no major differences between the sexes in these features.

In the FRG, the large majority of participants in adult training administered by the Federal Employment Agency are men: in 1980, an average of 71.6 per cent. Training offered consists of further training, re-training and on-the-job training. The most popular of these schemes is further training, accounting for 70.8 per cent of all enrolled trainees in September 1980. Second to this is re-training (at 21.6 per cent of trainees) and a small majority take part in on-the-job training (7.6 per cent) (62). As in the other countries, the representation of women in training programmes varies according to the type of training offered. In 1981, 25.1 per cent of those enrolled in further training - the largest programme - were women. The proportions taking part in re-training and on-the-job training were somewhat higher, at 40.0 and 34.9 per cent respectively (63).

Three types of training course are offered within the category of further training; adaptive training to overcome a lack of skill, training which promotes career advancement and refresher courses in skills previously learned. Here again there is an apparent sexual division in training programmes. In 1980 half of all men newly entering further training were in career advancement courses, compared to just one quarter of female participants. In contrast 56 per cent women and only 35 per cent of men undertook refresher training (1980) (64). This is partly due to the fact that women are more likely to be re-entrants into the labour market, and are twice as likely as men to have had not previous occupational training; which explains their under-representation in further training courses which build upon current skills (65). Moreover, traditional occupational patterns still obtain: Overall 80.1 per cent of women newly entering all three kinds of training schemes trained in service sector skills in 1980 (66).

The greatest representation of women in training is under retraining schemes, although it must be noted that here also they are under-represented in relation to the female share of unemployment. Retraining involves learning a new, and hopefully, more marketable skill. It could therefore provide a means of reducing job segregation by training men and women in new, non-traditional skills. In fact the pattern of this type of training has been a reflection of typical work patterns too: In 1980, more then two-thirds of men were retrained in manufacturing skills, while over 80 per cent of women received training for service sector employment (44 per cent of which was in clerical skills) (67).

Lastly, on-the-job training is provided through a subsidy to participating employers of up to 80 per cent of wage costs, lasting from a minimum of four weeks to one year. Only applicants who are unemployed or threatened with unemployment may take part, and enrollment in the scheme has shown an equal split between the two groups. As a means of reducing unemployment, on-the-job training is the most sucessful of all programmes, with only one per cent of participants being made redundant unemployed upon termination of training. However, of participants in on-the-job training in 1980, 54 per cent of female trained in service occupations, compared to only 24 per cent of men (68). It is also notable that the majority of women in on-the-job training were under 25, which indicates that labour market re-entrants are less likely to participate (69). This is certainly true where participation rates in training schemes overall are considered: Despite the stated aim of the EPA to promote the 'occupational integration of women', in 1980 female labour market entrants and re-entrants who had been without employment of six years or more made up only 3.8 per cent of all female trainees; these 3,000 participating newly entering and re-entering women (1980) comprise a neglectable minority compared to around 300,000 women who re-enter the labour market per year (70).

226

In Sweden, as we have seen, the participation of women in training schemes is relatively high. But in spite of the fact that the County Labour Boards have been directed to give priority to the under-represented sex in applications for training, the pattern of training in Sweden also follows traditional lines. During 1979 the most popular course of vocational training for men was in manufacturing skills (62 per cent of all male trainees), whereas only nine per cent of female participants trained in that area. For women, training in health and social services predominated, encompassing 46 per cent of all female trainees, while a further 34 per cent of women trained in clerical and office work. Only 16 per cent of males received vocational training in these areas (71). There also appears to be some sex bias in the type of training undertaken: In 1980/81, only 33.4 per cent of participants in on-the-job training were women (72).

The programmes which have been described so far are the major providers of labour market training in the countries surveyed. However, there exist other substantial adult training initiatives which are different in approach. One in particular deserves mention here; the Work Incentive Program in the United States. This programme combines training with placement which, unlike work experience, is intended to lead to permanent employment.

The Work Incentive Program (WIN) in the United States, operating since 1967 is seen as a means of securing employment and self-sufficiency for people dependent on welfare benefits, Aid to Families with Dependent Children (AFDC). All those who claim AFDC must register with the WIN programme unless they are legally exempt from doing so, though exempt claimants may also volunteer to join. Exemptions include people looking after young children or ill or disabled relatives, and women married to or living with men who are already registered with WIN. To encourage this first group to volunteer, child care costs and other expenses can be paid by the WIN administrators if necessary (73).

The primary aim of WIN is job placement; this has been emphasized by the amendment in 1971. Some classroom and workplace training is conducted, and depending upon the registrant remedial education, childcare and other forms of support may be provided. But placement which removes a claimant from the welfare rolls or at least partly relieves the burden of payment is considered to be the measure of WIN success. In 1979, over 80 per cent of those enrolled under WIN did so as a precondition for receipt of meanstested benefits. The majority were women, which fits the pattern of family poverty which occurs in the United States (74).

But various rules of WIN administration actually disadvantage women compared to male participants. For example, the disbursement formula for federal funding of State programmes award a higher subsidy for the number of sucessful job placements and the average wage and duration of employment of those placed. WIN administrators prefer to concentrate effort on placing male registrants, as men have higher average wages and exhibit less labour turnover than women (75). 'Unemployed fathers' are also given priority in placement, which is reinforced by the fact that any male AFDC recipient who is employed for more than 100 hours a month loses benefit entitlement - a rule which does not apply to women. In practice this has been the effect of forcing WIN administrators to seek better quality and higher paid employment for male registrants, who lose their entitlement once they are placed.

Perhaps for these reasons, though women comprise over three-quarters of   all

WIN registrants, they are only two-thirds of job entrants. Because of the emphasis on quick placement rather than quality of placement, the types of jobs they go into tend to be low paid, traditionally female employment. In 1979 66.1 per cent of female placements went into clerical and service work. In contrast, only 17.8 per cent of unemployed fathers did so, while 45.7 per cent were placed in manufacturing and construction employment (76). Nearly half (47.6 per cent) of all women placed in jobs through WIN had earnings in 1979 which were less than $ 3,00 per hour. Only 14.3 per cent of unemployed fathers had such low earnings (77). Thus, while selectivity for WIN participation tends to favour women (because of their relative poverty), priority is given to men in placement. Where the placement of women does occur under WIN the emphasis is on reducing the welfare rolls rather than providing women with career opportunities. As the WIN experience illustrates, the quality of women's participation in training measures is as important a consideration as their representation in training overall.

3.6   Special Training Programmes for Women

We have seen that in all the 'core' training programmes for adults described, women's participation has been largely confined to traditional clerical and social service skills. In this section we shall examine programmes which are more specific in targeting women for training, and which in some cases concentrate on non-traditional skills. The first of these, the Equality Grant in Sweden, is intended as a means of obtaining permanent positions for trainees while providing government subsidies during training - an aim also common to WIN in the U.S.. But the similarity between the two programmes stops there.

The Equality Grant in Sweden is only available to employers who hire and train men and women for non-traditional occupations; defined as an occupation in which there is at least 40/60 bias in favour of one sex. An employer receives 20 Sw.Kr. per hour for training a person in such non-traditional fields. Until 1979, a precondition for receipt of the grants was that the job be hard-to-fill. Since this requirement was lifted, take-up of the grant has more than doubled. However, in 1980 only 693 trainees (78) were placed by aid of the grant, or just 1.5 per cent of all persons in training.

By definition, the Equality Grant does not suffer the same stereotypical placement pattern as WIN training. However, there is some reason to believe that employers only find the grant attractive when there are shortages in traditionally male skills. Admittedly this was more likely to occur when the regulation concerning hard-to-fill places was in force, but even in 1980 subsidies for male employees in female jobs were only four per cent of the total (79). There is thus a danger that women will train in non-traditional jobs merely to fill fluctuations in demand. Worse still, they may replace male labour in a skill which is in the process of being degraded, or which offer poor prospects of future employment.

Another type of scheme in operation in all the countries surveyed is that of 'work orientation' for men and/or women. These schemes are usually short in duration and offer a curriculum of preparation for unskilled or semi-skilled work through improving self-presentation, practicing rusty skills, and consulting with vocational counsellors. Some courses involve job sampling and short periods of specific training. They may also be used, as with the WIN programme in the U.S., to gauge job prospects, arrange placements, or motivate applicants to take on further training. In general their intention is to facilitate enry or re-entry into the labour market. Though open to both men and women (with the exception of the Wider Opportunities for Women courses in Britain), separate all-women classes which give prominence to women's re-entry problems are a feature of this type of scheme. However, "short and fairly modest non-skilled training and assessment courses may not improve the employment prospects of participants, particularly at a time of rising unemployment" (80).

The German experience underlines this general result: Orientation courses for which participants may receive training allowances were introduced under the fifth amendment of the Employment Promotion Act in August 1979 (section 41a). The courses have a duration of four to six weeks and mainly take place as full-time training. Some of these orientation courses are provided on a women-only basis. Until August 1980 around 7,100 unemployed people of whom 37 per cent were female had taken part in this scheme (81). By the end of August 1980 41 per cent were still unemployed, and only 28 per cent had found employment. Another 15 per cent were enrolled in further training and five per cent were in job creation measures. A final eleven per cent were no longer seeking work, though information about their new status was not available (82).

Because no indepth training occurs, work orientation cannot be a means of placing women in non-traditional jobs unless further training follows, nor does it greatly improve their employment prospects. On the other hand participants may be helped in knowledge and technical know-how concerning job application, and in the process their self-confidence may be strengthened.

Finally, all the countries surveyed arrange non-traditional initial training schemes for women on a small scale (training schemes for employed, re-entering or unemployed women are rare). Examples of this type of scheme can be seen in recent initiatives of the Industrial Training Boards (ITBs) in the U.K.. In 1981, for example, the Engineering ITB awarded 26 bursaries to young women to train for degrees in engineering. The fact that there were 112 applicants for these 26 places shows that a demand exists for training of this sort (83). The EITB also offers special grants for enginneering employers who recruit and train female technicians. In 1981 about 150 girls were recruited under this programme, bringing the total number of women engineering trainees in skilled grades to 200 out of 14,500. A comment by the EITB head of research adds perspective to these 'experimental' forays into traditionally male sectors: "there has been no serious backlash as everybody in the industry knows that the female intake is very small in relation to the total" (84). Such programmes are of importance as models which could be used to combat traditional notions of the capabilities of women and the sexual division of labour. However, they can equally be used by governments as a means of evading the accusation that labour market policy does not help women. It is therefore important that such schemes do not remain marginal, but are taken up on a much larger scale.

Of the countries examined, only Sweden offered a variety of activities in a range of occupational areas, promoting non-traditional placement for both women and men (85). However, a general problem arising with an expansion of policies in this direction is that they become too expensive if they rely upon financial incentives for their take-up among employers. Hence, broader implementation necessitates a quota regulation or some other means of ensuring the adequate representation of men and women on programmes.

3.7   Conclusions

In our examination of training measures we began by looking at the impact of different approaches to training administration on the participation of women in training schemes. Of all the countries, Swedish labour market administration is the most highly centralized, and as such could have a greater potential for directing training initiatives than in the other three countries. But so far as the participation of women in training schemes is concerned, an equally crucial factor appears to be the extent to which eligibility is linked to either unemployment insurance or meanstested benefits. In Sweden, where women who are not eligible for unemployment benefit have an incentive to register in order to receive KAS, women have a closer contact with the employment service than elsewhere. They are thus more likely to be included in training schemes, and their participation in training overall is relatively high for the countries surveyed. In the United States, where women are under-represented among the insured unemployed, women form a majority of social security benefit recipients of Aid to Families with Dependent Children. As it is mandatory for many of these welfare claimants to register for training, and as they are a target group for labour market programmes, women are also relatively well represented among trainees in the United States. In contrast to both Sweden and U.S., women's participation is very low in the FRG where lack of insurance coverage and extremely restrictive, insurance-based entry requirements effectively rule out training for many women.

But within these variations in the proportions of women who receive training, in all the countries women continue to pursue traditionally female skills in the fields of office work and social services. Moreover, there appears to be a sex bias in the type of training undertaken by women, so that women tend to be better represented in classroom than on-the-job training. From the German experience there is some indication that of those women who do take part in on-the-job training, younger women are strongly favoured compared to older women: Female re-entrants to the labour market are thus less likely to receive on-the-job training. By definition on-the-job training provides a more direct entry into work than classroom training, as contact with employers may be maintained after training is completed. But at least part of the female bias towards classroom training may be explained by their predominance in traditional female skills which are more likely to be tought in a classroom setting, and their relative lack of intitial training. Not surprisingly, where placement occurs after training it also tends to follow traditional patterns.

Finally, in each country there are a number of much-publicized special training schemes for women. Under the terms of the Euqality Grant in Sweden, where non-traditional recruitment is stressed, the take-up is low and probably limited to sectors where there are shortages of male labour. Those which involve work orientation are ineffective - and indeed, not intended - as a means of obtaining skilled jobs, though they could be of potential value in encouraging individuals to train in non-traditional skills. Other schemes which place women in skilled, traditionally male employment are at present so marginal that their quantitative impact on women's employment is virtually negligible.

4.   JOB CREATION, PRESERVATION AND PROMOTION

4.1   Introduction

With rising unemployment labour market policies are aimed increasingly at a reduction in the number of jobless. Other aims, such as combatting job segregation, may be lost in the pursuit of this goal. We have seen that adult training in the countries examined - with some exeptions - tended to maintain or reinforce the traditional job structure. But apart from further training there are other policy instruments which more directly intervene in the labour market.

The most important of these policies, numerically, has been job creation, and is still a major arm of policy in some of the countries. Most of our attention will therefore be focused on this type of scheme, which involves the funding of new jobs on a temporary basis. But we shall also describe some measures aimed at promoting targeted groups and measures which attempt to prevent redundancies from occuring.

Our concern in this section is with the participation of women in all of these programmes. As we shall see again, where any of these types of scheme has emphasized counter-cyclical policy its effectiveness in influencing the pattern of women's employment has been poor. However, where counter-structural aims have been foremost there has been a greater, though limited, measure of success.

4.2   Job Creation

In all four countries examined, job creation came into vogue in the mid1970's and by 1980 - with the exemption of the FRG and Sweden - decreased in importance as a policy instrument. In the United States, for example, as late as 1979 public employment schemes accounted for 54 per cent of total CETA participants. In 1982 public service employment forms an insignificant part of CETA outlays, and the main programme under Title VI of CETA is close to abolition. Under the newly-introduced unlimited Job Training Partnership Act job creation is no longer provided. However, a new counter-cyclical job creation programme has been set out, which intends to provide 320,000 new jobs in bridge-building and road-construction. Obviously this will mostly favour men (86).

The reasons for this vogue and decline in job creation are complex, but among other factors it was found to be both expensive and insufficient to stem the rising tide of unemployment. Where such policies have been maintained they have tended to target participating groups more stringently.

Job creation schemes in the four countries have certain common features: First, their intention is to create employment and not displace it, so that the jobs involved tend to be only marginal. Second, the overwhelming majority of jobs created are in public sector employment or non-profit agencies. Third, it is specified that the work done should be of some social value, a criterion which also applies in some schemes that allow job creation in profit-making enterprises. Finally, in each of the countries we examined women have been under-represented among participants in job creation.

231

In the United States job creation schemes are mandated under Titles IID and VI of CETA, described as Public Service Employment (PSE). Although originally a countercyclical measure, since 1976 eligibility requirements have limited entry to the long-term unemployed or underemployed, welfare recipients and others on low incomes. PSE is operated through prime sponsors who receive a grant-in-aid for each job created, so long as the job does not (in theory) displace regular employment. One means of insuring against displacement has been to prescribe a salary limit for PSE jobs (in 1978, $ 7,200 p.a.for most jobs). There is some flexibility in that this limit can be supplemented by local funds or a higher hourly rate can be obtained by a reduction in working time (87). PSE employment has a maximum duration of 18 months for each participant. The jobs themselves have occured predominantly in the public sector, totalling 75 per cent of all positions, the remaining 25 per cent being in private non-profit organizations.

In the United Kingdom, the first programme of this type was the Job Creation Programme; its target group was mainly the younger unemployed between 16 and 24 years, and duration of unemployment was not specified. The two subsequent schemes, the Special Temporary Employment Programme (STEP), the Community Enterprise Programme (CEP) and the Community Programme, have concentrated more on the long-term unemployed; which indirectly excludes women since - among other reasons - their propensity to register is low and decreases with the duration of unemployment. Job creation until 1982 was embodied in STEP: in order to participate applicants had to be over 19, out of work for a minimum of 6 months (for those aged 19-24) to one year (for those 25 and over), and resident or registered for employment in a designated priority region. STEP jobs were offered in sponsored, temporary employment. Most positions therefore occured in public sector employment or voluntary organizations. But unlike PSE, participants were paid the standard rate for the job (up to a maximum of Ł 89 per week in 1980/81).

Since October 1982 CEP is being replaced by the new Community Programme, in which around 130,000 work places are planned to be promoted. Participants will be paid according to agreements, but maximum payments are limited to a much lower level. By this it is intended to stimulate a greater number of part-time jobs. One effect is, that the unemployed with families will have a much lower incentive to take part in the scheme since wages are too low. In relation to the target group and rising unemployment the measure provides jobs for less than ten per cent of potential participants (88).

In the FRG job creation occurs through the Employment Creation Measures (ECM) of the Employment Promotion Act. These provide for temporary employment in work which is "in the public interest". The aim of these measures has also been primarily countercyclical, though the long-term unemployed, older workers and the hard-to-place are priority groups for selection. The maximum duration of employment is one year, although it may be extended to two (89) years in individual cases. During this time the project sponsors receives a wage subsidy of 60-100 per cent of wage costs, which should conform to union or recognized rates for the job. In addition there has been the 'Special Programme' of 1979 for regions with unemployment rates above the federal average. Under this programme subsidies are generally 100 per cent of wage costs, and part-time employment for women in social services (90) is specially encouraged. In both these measures employment is again almost entirely within the public sector, although the Special Programme places more emphasis on social services and environmental work.

Job creation in <u>Sweden</u> consists of a number of different measures, including sheltered work places for the handicapped and some wage subsidies. But in its narrowest sense job creation occurs mainly as relief work (beredskapsarbeten). Relief work is aimed primarily at the unemployed who are either unable to find suitable work or are waiting for a training course to begin. Under the scheme, participants are temporarily placed in jobs of social benefit - work which without sponsorship would not be done. Most relief work occurs in public sector service employment or in voluntary agencies, though private firms are allowed to take part. Employment is limited to six months, during which time a subsidy of 75 per cent of wage costs is paid. In 1972 an additional special programme was established which temporarily substituted relief workers for regular employees engaged in training courses. The subsidy was paid only for the relief worker, and the employer continued to pay the wages of the regular staff member. But due to its administrative difficulty, its low employment effects and problems for the relief worker arising from the return of the regular staff member, the scheme was abandoned in 1981. Relief work in itself continues to be a major policy instrument, however, though declining in importance since 1975 (when in terms of public expenditure, it was the main active labour market programme in Sweden) (91).

Table 3

Women as percentage of all job creation participants and of all the unemployed

	Percentage of women in job creation		Percentage of women of all unemployed	
	1975	1980	1975	1980
FRG (ECM)	28[1]	39	51	52
U.K. (JCP, STEP)	24[2]	17[3]	20	31
SWE (beredskaps-arbete)	16	37	53	53
U.S.A. (CETA IID and IV)	32	48	44	44

1) 1978; before 1978 not available.
2) Job Creation Programme 1975 - including February 1977.
3) STEP; financial year 1980/81.

Source: Gruppe Politikinformationen, Chronik 11, January 1983.

233

Women have been under-represented in all of these job creation schemes. In the United States in 1979-80, when women comprised at least 63 per cent of those potential participants for public service employment, they were only 48 per cent of those enrolled (92). In Sweden in 1981 only 35 per cent of relief work participants were women (a decrease from 40 per cent in 1979). In Britain under the STEP programme the proportion of female participants was as low as 17 per cent in 1981/82 (93). In Germany the record was better than elsewhere (and has been improving), but even then in 1981 women were under-represented in relation to their share of unemployment by about three per cent (94).

These figures tend to suggest that, with the possible exeption of Germany, women are not a priority target group in job creation. Indeed, in the United Kingdom where the proportion of women participating was lowest of all, the high proportion of male participants has been interpreted as a sign of sucessful targeting: "A recent (MSC) study confirmed that the longterm unemployed tend to be male manual workers with no formal qualifications...". "A follow-up survey of STEP participants who entered the programme in January 1979 shows that STEP, even at an early stage in the year, was concentrating increasingly on those who form the majority of the long-term unemployed. 81 per cent of respondents were male and just over half were aged 24 or less" (95). In this case at least, the under-registration of unemployed women (who cannot therefore be defined as 'long-term' unemployed) may lead to their under-proportionate targeting in labour market programmes.

But what is perhaps more important than the gross proportions of women involved in job creation is the type of employment they obtain within such schemes. In the United Kingdom, under an earlier job creation programme in 1975-6, half of the jobs created were in the field of construction and environmental improvement. Of these jobs, "virtually none (went) to women" (96). Where women were employed it was among the remaining activities, which occured predominantly in social service and cultural employment (35 per cent of all jobs) and administration and research (nine per cent). Production work was only one per cent of all jobs created. In the FRG this pattern also holds true, where in 1980 90 per cent of women in employment creation were employed in either office work or the social services (97).

In the United States, women's participation in CETA overall has been in traditional fields of employment, with 47.6 per cent of all female jobs falling under the heading of clerical work (98). Within CETA, data for public service employment titles show that 63 per cent of jobs created are either clerical, service work or general labouring - a pattern characteristic of CETA as whole - but the distribution of women in these jobs is unspecified. However, women are a majority of those assigned to PSE jobs in non-profit organizations, which are "largely confined to social service and cultural activities" (99).

Sweden is no exception to this general pattern: In 1979/80 about half (49 per cent) of all jobs created were in the service and nursing sector; while women formed 82 per cent of relief workers in nursing and 57 per cent of those in other service sector jobs (100).

Where targeting is concerned, then, two issues are important; the representation of women in job creation overall and their occupational distribution within the schemes. In relation to the first issue the experience of targeting in the United States is pertinent. As we have seen, eligibility for CETA   programmes

234

is not dependent upon qualification for unemployment insurance, and in fact only just over 10 per cent (1979) of CETA participants in Titles II/II-D and VI are in receipt of unemployment compensation (101). CETA targeting for job creation has instead concentrated on those who fall below set standards of poverty and low income. These standards have been restricted further over the years so that only those who fall under the very lowest income levels are counted among targeted groups. Because of women's lower earnings this has tended to both increase the proportion of women among the target population and increase their participation in job creation schemes: In 1977, when women formed about 60 per cent of those eligible, they were only 29 per cent of PSE participants; by 1980 these proportions were 63 and 48 per cent, respectively (102).

However, although this type of targeting may have a quantitative effect on women's participation, the issue of the quality of their participation still remains. Where job creation re-creates traditional employment patterns it is unlikely to be a long-term solution to women's low pay and restricted employment prospects.

Finally, some points should be made about the nature of job creation in itself. It is significant that in each of the four countries job creation is a temporary solution and not a means of providing permanent employment. The jobs created must also not displace regular jobs, and excepting relief work, must be primarily of social benefit. The project-based or short-term nature of job creation, coupled with criteria of non-displacement and social value, greatly limits the types of employment which can be created and the transferability of skills used by participants. For example, non-profit organizations: "by their very nature...may engage in activities that neither the government nor the private sector will undertake. If participants gain skills and experience that are specific to their jobs in non-profit agencies, they might not be able to use those skills elsewhere. Innovative use of (job creation) in non-profit organizations may therefore ultimately work to the disadvantage of the participants themselves" (103).

Public sector employment in general may involve skills which are more readily transferable to outside agencies than those used in nonprofit organizations. But here again, in order to prevent displacement of the regular workforce jobs created should be marginal and inessential to the normal provision of services. More attention should therefore be given to the types of jobs created.

4.3   Job Preservation

A second type of policy instrument particularly favoured in recent years is job preservation. Job preservation, like job creation, is essentially a counter-cyclical measure, but leaves less scope for targeting special groups. Job preservation schemes normally involve a wage-cost subsidy in return for a reduction in working time, which enables an employer to continue operating during a temporary slump in demand. With a subsidy to wages, it is intended that jobs should be saved from redundancy and employees with needed skills might remain on hand until the product market recovers.

Examples of job preservation schemes exist in all four countries. In the U.K. there is the Temporary Short-Time Working Compensation Scheme   (TSTWCS), administered by the Department of Employment. Under this scheme, any employer who notifies the Department of an impending redundancy affecting a minimum of ten workers may be eligible for a wage subsidy if the job is preserved. Available work is then divided among employees, who must be paid at least 75 per cent of their normal wages (plus insurance contributions) while working on short time. The employer is then reimbursed for 50 per cent of normal wage costs, and this may be paid for up to nine months.

In Sweden there has been a more ambitious programme which combines training with a job preservation subsidy. The Employment Maintenance Training Subsidy (EMTS) provides a flat-rate payment to the employer for every hour that employees on short-time spend in training. In this way: "Instead of subsidizing the productive employment of workers threatened with redundancy, the programme combines short-time working, which cuts down production, with the subsidization of in-firm training, which should both serve to improve the future job prospects of the subsidized workers, and to contribute to that adjustment in workers' qualification necessary for structural change" (104). Since 1978 the subsidy has been set at 25 Sw.Kr. per hour for the first 480 hours of training provided for each employer. All employees in the firm are eligible, not just those facing redundancy, but before any subsidy can be paid the employer must produce a comprehensive training plan approved by the relevant trade unions.

In Germany, characteristically, job preservation is closely tied to unemployment insurance: The onus is on the employer to claim compensation for hours lost through short-time working, and only insured individuals are eligible to claim. The German scheme requires a minimum three per cent reduction in working time for both the individual claimant and the firm as a whole, and pays compensation at 68 per cent of hourly earnings for a maximum of six months (extended to 24 months in special cases).

A similar arrangement exists in the United States which is in fact a form of unemployment insurance and, at a national level, is not really a separate job preservation scheme as such. As described in Chapter II, those eligible for unemployment compensation who choose to work part-time as an alternative to unemployment may claim an allowance equal to (or even greater than) the difference between their level of entitlement to unemployment compensation and their part-time wages. Individuals threatened with redundancy are equally eligible, so that in practice the scheme may function in the way of job preservation. But individual States have elaborated upon this facility: In California the Work Sharing Unemployment Compensation Scheme is only payable to individuals in firms or work groups who have suffered a ten per cent reduction in work time. The maximum length of payment is 20 weks, and as payment is a form of unemployment compensation any unemployment benefit paid thereafter is accordingly reduced in duration.

These schemes have the virtue of reaching potentially large numbers of people. In the United Kingdom, in 1980/81 the number of individuals subsidized through the TSTWCS amounted to nearly 80 per cent of all participants in special government measures to combat unemployment (105). In the FRG participants in short-time work measures numbered around 830,000, compared to 1,920,000 registered unemployed in October 1982 (106). In Sweden in its peak year (1977) the EMTS subsidized around 41,300 workers (107), which comprised around one per cent of all employed. No figures are available for the numbers of workers in the U.S. on short-time and in receipt of unemployment compensation, but in California the take-up does not appear as great as elsewhere - with only 84C

236

firms out of 500,000 claiming the subsidy in 1980 (108). But when redundancies are at a high level, the tendency in most cases has been to stem the tide   of unemployment by subsidizing shorter working hours.

In each country, however, the take-up of the scheme has been limited to certain sectors of industry. In Britain, for example, more than half the jobs subsidized under the TSTWC scheme were in engineering, and virtually all jobs were in manufacturing employment. In Sweden over two-thirds of all EMTS subsidies went to manufacturing work, as did over three-quarters of those paid out under the California WSUC. This pattern is not unexpected, given the high incidence of redundancies in those sectors. But the sectoral distribution of short-time working suggests that women are under-represented in the over-all take-up of the subsidy. In those countries for which statistics broken down by sex are available, women are indeed in the minority among recipients of short-time work subsidies: Men make up two-thirds of WSUC participants in California and over 70 per cent (1980) of participants in the German short-time work scheme (109).

By its nature job preservation seeks to maintain the status quo, so that job segregation and other aspects of inequality are not at issue. The Swedish approach, which combined a work subsidy with training, is the only one which has any potential for structural change, though even there employers have tended to exploit the scheme without offering training of a good quality (110). But unless job preservation is linked to other measures which strike more directly a labour market inequality, the tendency is for it to be used to delay unemployment in predominantly male manufacturing industries which are suffering a long-term decline.

4.4   Job Promotion

A final type of policy instrument affecting patterns of employment is job promotion. In some cases job promotion for a target group may take the form of a direct wage subsidy, such as the Young Workers' Scheme in Great Britain, or an indirect subsidy to employers, as in the American Targeted Job Tax Credit. Under such schemes employers are only eligible to receive the subsidy for new recrutis who are members of a targeted group. In none of the four countries examined, however, were there any notable examples of these types of employment subsidies aimed at the promotion of women. But apart from wage subsidies or tax credits, other forms of job promotion exist which provide inducements or sanctions to encourage the recruitment of women. Chiefly, in the United States and Sweden public sector employers and firms receiving or seeking state finance may be required, as a condition of funding, to submit detailed plans for the recruitment and promotion of women. These programmes - Affirmative Action in the United States and Regional Grants for Swedish industry - will now be described.

Affirmative action for women in the United States came into existence in the 1960's along with regulations prohibiting discrimination among government contractors on the basis of race, religion or ethnic origin. Executive Orders 11246 and 11375 established the principle that government and those under federal contract should be model employers, or should at least be able to demonstrate their progress towards eliminating discrimination. The Office of Federal Compliance Programs, which is responsible for checking compliance with the Orders, has the power to prevent would be contractors from receiving   federal funds and may even cancel existing contracts if necessary. But compliance with affirmative action is not merely a matter of enforcement following an inspection: All employers who wish to remain eligible for federal contracts must provide documentary evidence of non-discrimination in their firms, and time-tables for future improvements. This continual examination of the position of women employees, however unpopular among employers, may potentially influence employment practice over a wide range of industries which service the federal government. As put by O'Neill and Braun: "The paperwork involved in the (detailed affirmative action plans) has been a constant source of complaint by firms. But the threat of loss of federal contracts is believed to be a potent tool" (111).In Sweden since 1974 firms applying for regional development grants have been required to employ a minimum of 40 per cent of each sex, or to develop recruitment plans which redress any imbalances in the firms employment. When applying for a grant the firm is aided by the County Labour Board to formulate appropriate recruitment plans, and is helped by the employment services to fill whatever jobs are offered. In turn, if male or female candidates for the job offered not readily available, an opportunity must be given for the employment services to train individuals for the positions. Although it is possible to apply for an exemption from these rules most employers have in fact followed the advice of the County Labour Boards.

Like U.S. federal contracts under the affirmative action programme, the use of development grants as a lever for changes in employment practice is potentially a powerful tool. Though the impact it has had on women's employment is perhaps not so great as could be desired, there is evidence that some improvement has occured. During the first two years of the scheme's operation, the proportion of female employment in the firms concerned increased from 19 to 21 per cent; a somewhat greater increase than for corresponding company branches elsewhere. Furthermore, women formed 35 per cent of all new recruits to those firms. Jonung and Thordarsson suggest that the policy may have other effects in those regions where the grants are in operation: the share of women in education and training for non-traditional skills is higher in those areas than elsewhere in the country (112).

These two schemes are different from other labour market policy instruments in that they give specific attention to the recruitment of women and/or men in non-traditional jobs, and place the onus on employers to show that they have made progress to that effect. In making positive discrimination a precondition for the assignment of government contracts or development grants, these schemes recognized and reward good employment practice - unlike other policies which rely on employers taking up inducements in respect to individual employees.

A further favourable aspect of job promotion through development grants is that whatever female employment is generated takes place within industries which are targeted for growth and fit into the local economy and local development plans. Similarly, affirmative action requires some long-term planning by employers, so that the issue of equal opportunities is kept alive. However, it is possible that unless properly vetted, both schemes could become window-dressing exercises for the firms involved. To be effective, these types of scheme must be actively pursued.

4.5   A Special Case: The British Job-Splitting Scheme

In January 1983 a new government scheme for the unemployed came into operation in the U.K.. This scheme, the Job-Splitting scheme, combines elements of job creation, preservation and promotion in that it aims to create employment for unemployment benefit claimants, prevent redundancies and "generate additional part-time work opportunities" (113). The scheme gives a flat-rate grant of £ 750 to employers who split a full-time job into two part-time jobs, so long as it results in the recruitment of at least one unemployment benefit claimant or prevents the redundancy of someone who would otherwise claim benefit. Each part-time job must average out to at least 15 hours weekly. A job split in this way could be shared by two unemployment benefit claimants; one benefit claimant and one existing full-time employee; two existing full-time employees (where one or both would otherwise be made redundant); or two full-time employees who change to part-time work while an unemployment benefit claimant is recruited to do the rest of their work. In reducing the number of unemployment benefit claimants by these means, the government has estimated that "the large savings in benefit payments should mean a net saving in public expenditure" (114).

In requiring that the scheme involve only unemployment benefit claimants the take-up among women is likely to be less than the demand for part-time work. Ironically, the 51,800 people who were registered as unemployed in 1982 but ineligible for benefit because they were actively seeking part-time work would not have been allowed to participate in a job split. But despite this it is probable that the job-splitting scheme will have its greatest take-up among women, purely because of the types of job which tend to be offered on a part-time basis: low paid, female dominated types of work (115).

The subsidy for each job-split is not very substantial in relation to wages in the professions or higher paid occupations. However well- or ill-founded, employers in Britain maintain that "the standard costs of employing a part-timer is pro rata, generally higher than a full-timer" (116). For this reason the subsidy should prove less of an inducement when it comes to highly paid jobs. In the case of low paid jobs, however, the subsidy is likely to add to the attractiveness of part-timers who earn less than the national insurance contribution limit.

Moreover a memorandum sent by the Confederation of British Industry to all its members illustrates that employers regard the scheme as a means of avoiding responsibilities associated with full-time labour. In Britain basic employment protection such as the right to claim compensation if unfairly dismissed, maternity rights, the right to a written statement of terms and conditions of employment, and a number of other employment rights are subject to a one-year qualification period for all employers working over 16 hours weekly. For part-timers working between 8-16 hours weekly, however, the qualification period is five years, and those working less than eight hours are excluded altogether. A job-splitting specifies a minimum week of 15 hours it leaves the door open to the avoidance of employment protection legislation. This feature of the scheme was noted by the CBI, who have advised their members to use part-timers working less than sixteen hours weekly or to arrange job-splits on an alternative day basis (so that every second week the employee works less than 16 hours) (117).

Though superficially a programme which encourages the creation of   part-time job opportunities might sound particularly beneficial to women, it is probable that the British Job-Splitting scheme will have the opposite effect. Moreover, while each unemployment benefit claimant (or would-be claimant) who takes part in the scheme saves the government money which would have gone to the payment of benefits, the fact that many participants earning less than the contribution limit will be rendered ineligible for future benefits should augment government savings.

5.   Conclusions

For reasons that we have already mentioned, women should claim a high priority as a target for labour market policies. However, despite the facts that the rate of female unemployment has accelerated rapidly in recent years, and that in all the countries surveyed - with the exeption of the United Kingdom - the female unemployed comprise the majority of all unemployed, women still predominate among the unregistered unemployed. Among other effects, this under-registration of women makes them less accessible as a target for employment policies, and could serve to perpetuate the view that male unemployment is somehow a more serious problem.

As we have shown, the nature of unemployment insurance systems operating in the countries surveyed is an important factor in the propensity of women to register. Systems based on the contributory principle which tend to exclude low earners, part-time workers, seasonal and casual labour thereby exclude substantial numbers of women from liability and benefit. If they are unlikely to be eligible for benefit there is less incentive for the unemployed, particularly discouraged workers, to register.

However, under the non-contributory system examined in our paper, the KAS system in Sweden, the propensity of women to register is much greater than elsewhere. Eligibility for benefit under KAS is not dependent upon contributory tests but on registration for work, including part-time work. This model of unemployment compensation not only improves the rate of female registration and thus the visibility of female unemployment: It also ensures that some extra financial support, often vital in enabling childcare arrangements to be made, is received during a period of job search.

In the same way that unemployment insurance system based on contributory tests tend to exclude women and marginal workers, labour market policies which concentrate on the insured unemployed fail to meet the needs of these groups. This was particularly apparent when the West German provisions for adult training and retraining were considered. There, qualification for fully subsidized adult training is strongly dependent upon a claimant's past and future work histories and insurance record. Those groups - and this holds partly true for men as well - who are most prone to unemployment (for reasons which may include a lack of skill, domestic constraints and simple discrimination), and who therefore have inadequate work and contribution records, are less well-serviced by government adult training and retraining provisions than the core groups in the labour market.

Furthermore, countercyclical policies which have as their objective a reduction in the numbers of registered unemployed can lose sight of those who fail to register or whose employment is tenuous. This is illustrated by the   experience of public sector job creation in the United States: The greater was the emphasis on rapid placement of the unemployed, the fewer women were serviced by the scheme. However, when counterstructural criteria were stressed the proportions of women included grew. But perhaps the worst example of countercyclical policies, as far as women are concerned, is job preservation. In all countries these schemes are overwhelmingly dominated by primary workers in traditional male manufacturing industries. By definition such schemes are ill-equipped to tackle the problem of job segregation unless, as in the Swedish relief work, some element of training has been incorporated within them.

Finally, we have noted throughout that where women are defined as a priority group and policies are designed with sex inequalities in mind, the result is more favourable than with apparently 'sex-neutral' policy measures. Of the four countries examined in Sweden has been the most successful in this repsect. However, as with the Swedish Equality Grant, there is still a danger that schemes which promote non-traditional employment are limited to areas in which there is a shortage of male labour due to declining wages. But Swedish labour market policies at least have the virtue of making non-traditional employment a consideration if not a general requirement. Other measures elsewhere which are often held up as evidence of government action against women's labour market ineqality all too often involve only a handful of women. The importance of such schemes is limited to their pubilcity-value and the example which they set. As a means of eradicating women's labour market disadvantage the targeting of women must take place on a larger scale, and not merely as an 'experimental' or 'model' programme.

NOTES AND REFERENCES

(1) OECD, Equal Opportunities for Women, Paris 1979.

(2) Arbetsmarknadsstyrelsen (AMS), Cash Unemployment Assistance, Solna, Sweden, January 1982, p. 8.

(3) Gruppe Politikinformationen am Internationalen Institut für Management und Verwaltung, Internationale Chronik zur Arbeitsmarktpolitik, Berlin, Oktober 1981, p. 10.

(4) Arbetsmarknadsstyrelsen (AMS), op.cit., p. 1.

(5) Lillemor Gladh and Siv Gustafsson, Labour Market Policy Related to Women and Employment in Sweden, Manuscript, Berlin: International Institute of Management, December 1981, p. 104, own calculations.

(6) Current Labor Statistics, Monthly Labor Review, Vol. 105, Washington D.C.: U.S. Dep. of Labor, February 1982, p. 74.

(7) Alison Donaldson, The Measurement of Unemployment in Britain, Berlin: International Institute of Management, No. 1a - 1979, p. 6.

(8) Simon Crine, The Hidden Army: Homeworkers, Low Pay Pamphlet no. 11, London: Low Pay Unit, November 1979.

(9) U.S. Department of Labor, Employment and Training Report of the President, Washington D.C.: U.S. Government Printing Office, 1980, p. 244.

(10) Christian Brinkmann and Hans Kohler, "Am Rande der Erwerbsbeteiligung - Frauen mit geringfügiger, gelegentlicher oder befristeter Arbeit", Beiträge aus der Arbeitsmarkt und Berufsforschung, No. 56, (1981), p. 120-146.

(11) Statistisches Bundesamt, Wirtschaft und Statistik, No. 3 (1981), p. 181.

(12) Jim Lester, M.P., House of Commons Hansard, London: H.M.S.O., May 21, 1980, col. 203.

(13) Current Labor Statistics, Monthly Labor Review, Vol. 105, no. 2, (February 1982), p. 73.

(14) Arbetsmarknadsstyrelsen (AMS), op.cit., p. 3.

(15) Arbetsmarknadsstyrelsen (AMS), De erkanda arbetsloshetskassornas verksamket och Det kontanta arbetsmarknadsstodet ar 1980, Solna; AMS, 1980, p. 17.

(16) Chris Pond and Emma MacLennan, Insuring Poverty at Work, London: Low Pay Unit, April 1981, p. 5.

(17) Gladh and Gustafsson, op.cit., p. 104.

(18) Quarterly Statistical Series, Department of Employment Gazette, November 1982, p. 538.

(19) Herta Däubler-Gmelin, Frauenarbeitslosigkeit oder Reserve zurück an den Herd!, Reinbek bei Hamburg: 1977.

(20) Renate Weitzel, Labour Market Policy Related to Women and Employment in the Federal Republic of Germany, Manuscript, Berlin: International Institute of Management, May 1982, p. 59.

(21) Equal Opportunities Commission, I Want to Work but What About the Kids?, Manchester: September 1978, p. 7.

(22) Dahlberg, Anita, Arbetslöshetsersättningar, andra upplagan, första upplagan 1974 Arbetslöshetsstöd, AWE/Gebers, Stockholm: 1979, quoted in Gladh and Gustafsson, op.cit., pp. 31-32.

(23) We do not have comparable data for this from all the four countries surveyed: Although regulation of penalties potentially is likely to hit more women than men, for the FRG it surprisingly turned out that women are underrepresented among temporary suspensions from eligibility for unemployment benefit and unemployment aid. This could be due to the fact that there are fewer suitable job offers for women (arising from the sex-specific segmented labour market) thus making the female unemployed less likely to refuse job or training offers. One study of the regional variation in suspensions supports this hypothesis, as suspensions occured more often in regional labour markets with good employment prospects and less often in areas where prospects were poor. Werner Karr and Rudolf Leupoldt, "Unterschiede im Leistungsbezug zwischen den Arbeitsamtsbezirken der Bundesrepublik Deutschland", Mitteilungen aus der Arbeitsmarkt- und Berufsforschung, No. 1 (1979), pp. 16-23.

(24) U.S. Department of Labor, The Unemployment Insurance Program, Background paper for the Conference with the Ministry of Labor and Social Affairs of the State of Israel, August 24-31, 1979, p. 10.

(25) ibid.

(26) U.S. Department of Health and Human Services, Social Security Programs Throughout the World, Research Report No. 54, Washington D.C., 1980, p. 252.

(27) Diana Runner, "Unemployment Insurance Laws: changes enacted during 1981, Monthly Labor Review, Vol. 105, No. 3, (February 1982), p. 17.

(28) U.S. Department of Labor, op.cit., p. 368.

(29) Gladh and Gustafsson, op.cit., p. 104.

(30) Robert Elliott, Pauline Glucklich, Emma MacLennan and Chris Pond, Women in the Labour Market. A Study of the Impact of Legislation and Policy Toward Women in the U.K. Labour Market During the Nineteen Seventies, Manuscript, Berlin: International Institute of Management, September 1981, p. 178, own calculations.

(31) Bundesanstalt für Arbeit, Amtliche Nachrichten der Bundesanstalt für Arbeit, Nürnberg: September 1981, p. 1111; own calculations.

(32) Special Unemployment Assistance (SUA) was a temporary programme running from 1974-78 in the U.S., which provided a special benefit for those who were unemployed but ineligible for regular unemployment compensation.

(33) OECD, Unemployment Compensation and Related Employment Policy Measures, U.S.A., Paris: OECD, 1979, pp. 278-279.

(34) Elliott et.al., op.cit., pp. 131-132.

(35) Weitzel, op.cit., p. 80.

(36) Anders Björklund, The Measurement of Unemployment in Sweden, Berlin: International Institute of Management, No. 1d, 1979, p. 16.

(37) June O'Neill and Rachel Braun, Women and the Labour Market: A Survey of Issues and Policies in the United States, Manuscript, Berlin: International Institute of Management, November 1981, p. 50.

(38) Arthur Padilla, "The Unemployment Insurance System; Its Financial Structure", Monthly Labor Review, (December 1981), p. 32.

(39) Gruppe Politikinformationen, op.cit., April 1982, p. 9.

(40) OECD, Unemployment Compensation and Related Employment Policy Measures, U.S.A. Country Study, Paris: OECD, 1979, p. 280.

(41) National Commission for Employment Policy, Increasing the Earnings of Disadvantaged Women, Washington D.C., 1981: p. 70.

(42) Weitzel, op.cit., p. 96.

(43) National Commission for Employment Policy, op.cit., p. 90.

(44) Department of Employment Gazette, April 1982, p. 179.

(45) Arbetsmarknadsstyrelsen (AMS), Annual Report 1979/80, Solna, 1980, p. 4.

(46) Gruppe Politikinformationen, op.cit., January 1982, p. 9.

(47) U.S. Department of Labor and the U.S. Department of Health and Human Services, Employment and Training Report of the President, Washington D.C., 1980, p. 27.

(48) National Commission for Employment Policy, op.cit., p. 94.

(49) National Commission for Employment Policy, op.cit., p. 91.

(50) Sue Berryman and Winston Chow, "CETA: Is it Equitable for Women? in: National Commission for Employment Policy, op.cit., p. 155.

(51) Berryman and Chow, op.cit., p. 155.

(52) National Commission for Employment Policy, op.cit., pp. 97-99.

244

(53) Gruppe Politikinformationen, op.cit., October 1982, p. 6.

(54) Department of Employment Gazette, July 1982, p. 312.

(55) CEDEFOP, Equal Opportunities and Vocational Training; Training and Labour Market Policy Measures for the Vocational Promotion of Women in the United Kingdom, December 1979, p. 9.

(56) P. McGill, "Post-training experience of TOPS trainees", Be Gazette, July 1981, p. 325.

(57) Manpower Services Commissions, Annual Report 1980/81, London 1981, p. 12.

(58) CEDEFOP, ibid.

(59) McGill, op.cit.

(60) ibid.

(61) ibid.

(62) Weitzel, op.cit., p. 122.

(63) Weitzel, op.cit., Appendix 49.

(64) Bundesanstalt für Arbeit, Förderung der beruflichen Bildung, Ergebnisse der Teilnehmerstatistik über berufliche Fortbildung, Umschulung und Einarbeitung von 1980, Nürnberg, December 1981, p. 12.

(65) Eberhard Sommer, Benachteiligung von Frauen in der beruflichen Weiterbildung und beim beruflichen Aufstieg, in: D. Posser, R. Wassermann (ed.), Von der bürgerlichen zur sozialen Rechtsordnung, Heidelberg, Karlsruhe, 1981, p. 62.

(66) Bundesanstalt für Arbeit, op.cit., p. 29.

(67) Bundesanstalt für Arbeit, op.cit., p. 24 and 28.

(68) Bundesanstalt für Arbeit, op.cit., pp. 22 and 27.

(69) Bundesanstalt für Arbeit, op.cit., p. 27.

(70) Renate Weitzel, Berufliche Weiterbildung nach dem Arbeitsförderungsgesetz. Rechtliche und institutionelle Bedingungen der Teilnahme von Frauen im Vergleich zu Männern. IIM/LMP 83-12, Wissenschaftszentrum Berlin 1983.

(71) Gladh and Gustafsson, op.cit., p. 102.

(72) Arbetsmarknadsstyrelsen, Arbetsmarknadsstatistik, Arbetsmarknadsutbildning under budgetåret 1980/81, p.3.

(73) No special provisions are made for the second group, and there seems little reason for their exemption.

(74) U.S. Department of Labor and the U.S. Department of Health and Human Services, op.cit., p. 52.

(75) National Commission for Employment Policy, op.cit., p. 129.

(76) U.S. Department of Labor and the U.S. Department of Health and Human Services, op.cit., p. 53.

(77) U.S. Department of Labor and the U.S. Department of Health and Human Services, op.cit., p. 54.

(78) Arbetsmarknadsstyrelsen, Statistics on Training in Enterprises, Table FÖ.A.3.5.

(79) ibid.

(80) Manpower Services Commission, Review of Services for the Unemployed, London, March 1981, p. 31.

(81) Bundesanstalt für Arbeit, arbeit und beruf, April 1981, Nürnberg, pp. 97 and 98.

(82) ibid.

(83) Department of Employment Gazette, November 1981, p. 462.

(84) Financial Times, April 5, 1982, p. 12.

(85) For detailed further information see: Nordic Council of Ministers' Secretariat, Measures for Equality between Men and Women in the Labour Market in the Nordic Countries, Stockholm, 1979, pp. 76-117.

(86) Thus, one study found that PSE workers in administrative, technical craft and professional positions had higher earnings than clerical staff, service workers, para-professionals and labourers. Richard Nathan, Robert Cook, V. Lane Rawlins et al., Public Service Employment, The Brookings Institution, Washington D.C., 1981, p. 73.

(87) Gruppe Politikinformationen, op.cit., January 1983, p. 8.

(88) Gruppe Politikinformationen, op.cit., October 1982, p. 7.

(89) It may be prolonged up to three years if after the third year of ECM the promoted employee is guaranteed lasting employment in the establishment.

(90) Fritz Scharpf, Dietrich Garlichs, Friederike Maier, Hans Maier, Implementationsprobleme offensiver Arbeitsmarktpolitik, Frankfurt/Main: 1982.

(91) Peter Auer, Internationaler Vergleich von Arbeitsbeschaffungsmaßnahmen, Berlin: International Institute of Management, forthcoming 1983.

(92) National Commission for Employment Policy, op.cit., p. 93.

(93) Manpower Services Commission, Annual Report 1980/81, London, 1981, p. 3.

(94) Weitzel, op.cit., Appendix 16.

(95) Manpower Services commission, Review of the second year of Special Programmes, London: MSC, 1980, pp. 15-16.

(96) M.J. Faulkner, Schemes of Direct Job Creation in Member States of the European Community, first draft, Brussels: Commission of the European Commuity, May 1978, p. 69.

(97) Weitzel, op.cit., Appendix 47.

(98) National Commission for Employment Policy, op.cit., pp. 97-99.

(99) Nathan et al., op.cit., pp. 113-115.

(100) Arbetsmarknadsstyrelsen (AMS), Tekniska enheten planeringssektionen.

(101) National Commission for Employment Policy, Sixth Annual Report to the President and the Congress, Washington, D.C., December 1980, p. 112-113.

(102) National Commission for Employment Policy, op.cit., p. 91; Nathan et al., op.cit., p. 40.

(103) Nathan et al., op.cit., p. 115.

(104) André Calame, Impact and Costs of Wage Subsidy Programmes, Berlin: International Institute of Management, No. 1a, 1980, p. 10.

(105) Manpower Services Commission, Annual Report 1980/81, London 1981, p. 11.

(106) Bundesanstalt für Arbeit, Amtliche Nachrichten der Bundesanstalt für Arbeit, Nürnberg, November 1982, p. 1461.

(107) Calame, op.cit., p. 12.

(108) Fred Best, Short-Time Compensation in California, Statement before the Subcommitte on Public Assistance and Unemployment Compensation, U.S. House of Representatives, Sacramento, U.S.A., June 1980, p. 4.

(109) Weitzel, op.cit., Appendix 44.

(110) Calame, op.cit., p. 32.

(111) O'Neill and Braun, op.cit., p. 115.

(112) Christina Jonung and Bodil Thordarsson, "Sweden", in: Yohalem, Alice (ed.), Women Returning to Work, Landmark studies, Montclair, 1980, p. 151.

(113) Department of Employment Gazette, December 1982, p. 519.

(114) Department of Employment Gazette, August 1982, p. 323.

(115) Renate Weitzel and Andreas Hoff, Öffentliche Förderung der Teilzeit-arbeit?, in: F.W. Scharpf et al. (ed.), Aktive Arbeitsmarktpolitik. Er-fahrungen und neue Wege, Frankfurt/Main, New York, 1982, pp. 181-206.

(116) Confederation of British Industry, Evidence to European Communities Committee Report no. 19, Voluntary Part-Time Work, House of Lords, July 27, 1982, p. 137.

(117) The Guardian, October 6, 1982.

11 ESTIMATING THE IMPACT OF LABOR MARKET POLICIES ON WOMEN: A DISCUSSION OF THE FOUR-COUNTRY STUDIES ON THE EMPLOYMENT OF WOMEN

GLEN CAIN

1. INTRODUCTION

The four studies on women in the labor force in England, the Federal Republic of Germany, Sweden, and the United States, which were presented at this conference (1) deal with three main themes: (a) the large increase in market employment by women, especially during the last 20 or 30 years; (b) the persistent gap between the wage rates earned by men and women; (c) the increase in government programs during the past 20 years that affect the work and earnings of women. The themes pervade all four countries and, indeed, industrialized nations generally.

Social scientists, economists in particular, may usefully analyze these themes with three objectives in mind: to describe (measure), forecast, and explain the labor supply and earnings patterns. Explaining these events means estimating their causal determinants. Ideally, the explanatory models would permit an evaluation of government programs.

Evaluation involves estimating the quantitative effect of a policy and, ultimately, measuring its efficiency or benefit/cost ratio. At some point value and political judgments enter, about which social scientists may have little to contribute. Nevertheless, these judgments are usually implicit in social science research. Behind the objectives listed above lie the deeper and more exclusive goals of measuring the economic well-being of men and women and how their well-being is affected by the operation of the economy and government policies.

This comment will develop the following propositions about the three objectives listed above.

(1) Economists have been moderately successful in measuring work and earnings, less successful in predicting and explaining trends in work and earnings, and least successful in evaluating the impact of government programs.

(2) There is room for improving our measures of work and earnings, and additional measures are suggested below.

(3) Labor supply has been measured and explained more successfully than wages. In particular, labor market discrimination, which accounts for some unknown portion of the wage gap between men and women, is crudely measured.

(4) Measuring the impact of government programs depends on our ability to predict and explain labor market behavior in more general situations - for example, long-term trends. In the absence of controlled experiments, the evaluation of government programs must be embedded in such general models.

2.   MEASURING LABOR SUPPLY AND EARNINGS AND THEIR INTER-
      PRETATION FOR MEASURING THE ECONOMIC STATUS OF
      WOMEN

2.1   Labor Supply

The conference papers for the four countries mainly use labor force participation rates (LFPRs) to measure the increase in market work by women. Trends in LFPRs are closely related to trends in hours worked, and a more comprehensive measure is "hours worked per lifetime" for each cohort of women. However, at best this measure can only be approximated by observing LFPRs and hours worked (for those working) for different age groups and different years. Sometimes these two statistics are available only for the week of the survey. In the U.S., for example, the LFPRs and hours worked for women who were 15 years old in 1920 may be partially traced until the women reach retirement age in 1970 or 1980, using data from the six (or seven) census years and interpolating values for the between-census years.

My calculations with this type of measure of lifetime labor supply for the United States show the increase in women's market work to be less dramatic than that illustrated by LFPRs, but it is still substantial. With the data for the LFPRs and weekly hours worked from the decennial censuses from 1890 to 1970, I first estimate the lifetime hours of work for each cohort, assuming that the span of working life begins at age 14 and ends at age 70. I wish to express the measured total hours of work as a fraction of the total hours "available" during this age span. Although there are 24 hours per day, I assume that 8 of these are required for sleep and personal maintenance. This leaves 16 hours per day of discretionary time that are potentially available for market work for each person. The ratio of total hours worked to total hours available for the 56-year span (age 14 to 70) represents the fraction of the average man's or woman's adult lifetime spent in market work.

I find that around 1900, the average woman could expect to spend about 8 percent of her adult life (age 14 to 70) in market work. By 1970 this fraction had increased to 13 percent. The increase is mainly attributable to the increase in LFPRs of married women, which has offset the decrease in: (a) LFPRs of young women (especially those age 14 to 18); (b) the LFPRs of categories of single women (such as widows); and (c) the hours of work of women who worked full-time. The typical working day was much longer in 1900 than in 1970.

The average man in 1900 could expect to spend about 43 percent of his adult life in market work, and by 1970 this percent had decreased to 25. There are two main sources of this decline. First, the decline in hours worked by men who worked. From 1880 or so to 1940 the typical working day decreased from 12 hours (or more) to 8, and the number of days per week declined from 6 (or 7) to 5. Second, from 1940 on the decline in the fraction of time that men spend at work is due more to decreased LFPRs of younger and, especially, older men. The typical work week has remained around 40 hours.

A rough translation of the above statistics on hours worked into terms that apply to a typical work year for a man in 1900 and 1970 will illustrate the nature of the decline. In both periods the number of hours per year available for work are, of course, the same: 16 x 365 = 5,840. Consider 1900: 43 percent of 5,840 is 2,511, which translates to slightly over 48 hours per week. Both the probability of working - that is, the LFPR - and the number of hours worked by prime-age men (ages 18 to 65) was, of course, higher, and the 2,511 (or 48) hours represents an average over all ages. Now consider 1970: 25 percent of 5,840 is 1,460, which represents an average of say, 2000 hours per year for men age 22 to 62 and many fewer hours for younger and older men, among whom both LFPRs and hours worked are lower. The 1900 to 1970 decline in the average of hours worked per year, 2,511 - 1,460 = 1,051, is impressive, indeed. It reveals that the man's average work year over a 56-year span (age 14 to 70) decreased by about 1000 hours for each of those 56 years. Meanwhile, the average amount of hours of market work for women increased from around 470 hours per year in 1900 (8 percent of 5,840) to 760 (13 percent of 5,840) (2).

Consider our contrasting judgements of these statistics. For men the decline in market work is judged to reflect an important component and source of the rise in their standard of living and economic well-being. For women the increase in market work is judged to reflect increased opportunities and a rise in their economic well-being. The following points shed light on these seemingly contrasting views.

(1) For some periods we observe a slower increase or even a decrease in work rates by young women, older women, and single women with dependent children. These changes are all consistent with an improved labor market for women, given that the well known alternatives to market work for these groups have improved: respectively, increased school attendance, increased voluntary retirement because of improved retirement benefits, and less market work because of improved government income-transfer programs.

(2) The large increase in LFPRs for married women in all the countries - even during the periods when their fertility and their husbands' incomes increased - is strong evidence for the pull of demand forces. But how has time spent in home work changed? The long-run rise in leisure attributed to men will also be true for women only if the decrease in women's home work has been greater than the increase in their market work. I know of no persuasive study of this issue.

251

(3) The quality of jobs held by women has surely improved, on average, in terms of both real wages and nonpecuniary aspects, such as fringe benefits, working conditions, and so on. Quantifying these improvements, especially in comparison with men's jobs, is difficult, however. This issue will be discussed below.

Comparisons across countries have all of the foregoing issues to contend with, plus others. Labor force definitions are not exactly comparable. For example, there are differences in defining unemployment status (including eligibility for unemployment insurance), part-time work, and the labor force status of women who are on maternity leave or in various training programs.

Sweden has the highest LFPR of women among the four countries, and Germany (FRG) has the lowest. In both countries the increase in female employment is largely or totally due to the increase in female employment in the public sector. In Germany the public sector accounts for 63 percent of the growth in female employment from 1963 to 1980 (Weitzel, Table on p. 24 of Appendix). In Sweden this sector alone accounts for 102 percent (!) of the growth for roughly the same period, 1965 to 1980 (Gladh and Gustafsson, p. 117 and correspondence with Christina Jonung). Thus, female employment in Sweden declined by 2 percent in the private sector. (The decline in private sector employment includes the category, "self-employed and members of their family," where a decline of 22,000 women workers more than offset the increase of 13,000 women in the category, "private" employment.)

The opportunities for and conditions of work by women probably were more favorable in the public sector, but I expect this sector to grow much more slowly in the next 20 years than it has in the past 20 years. As a result, the LFPRs of women in Sweden, in particular, may become closer to those in England and the United States. Despite the expected declining trend of employment in the public sector, the market work rates of the two sexes should continue to move closer together.

2.2   Earnings

If the quantity of market work is moving toward equality between the sexes, what about the quality of market work? We would like to measure the total remuneration, nonpecuniary as well as pecuniary and for the lifetime as well as the current status, of women's and men's jobs. This ideal is unobtainable, and the practical alternatives are to use wages (or salaries) and occupational indicators at different points in time. I will discuss wage rates, which are easier to measure and facilitate measuring changes over time within a country or for making comparisons across countries.

Both wages and occupational measures show considerable inequality between the sexes. Women's wages and salaries are about 60 to 80 percent of men's and the upward trend in this percent in many countries, especially the U.S., is very slight. There are two predominant interpretations about both the levels and the trend. One view of the level is that labor market discrimination is largely responsible for the lower relative wages of women. An opposing view is that the gap represents a voluntary division of labor between home and market sectors and that men's specialization in the market rationalizes their larger investments in market-earnings capacities and resulting higher wages (3).   The critics of the discrimination hypothesis contend that labor market experience, which is assumed to reflect unobserved on-the-job training, should be "held constant" when comparing men's and women's wages.

Regarding trends, one view is that labor market discrimination has not much lessened over time. Another view is that: (a) the voluntary division of work between home and market sectors has changed only slightly, and (b) although women have become more committed to market work, the increase in women's LFPRs has "diluted" the measured productivity of women workers, because the recent entrants have less work experience. The hypothesis is that the "dilution" by recent entrants has offset the "enrichment" by those women workers who are increasing their work experience. Let us analyze this hypothesis.

A Potential Bias in Measuring Trends. The changing composition of the work force does complicate the measurement of relative wage trends between men and women. This is one of the reasons wage comparisons are more difficult to interpret than labor supply comparisons. Wages are measured for a truncated population of only those in market employment. LFPRs are based on the entire population.

When the fraction of women who work is increasing, it is easy to show that the average wage of working women can decrease even though the market wage of every woman may have increased. Assume that women who did not work in the initial period had a lower market-wage capacity than those who did work. Assume further that an overall increase in women's wages entices the former group into the labor market in a subsequent period. Clearly, if the average wage of the new entrants is less than the average wage of the existing women workers, the overall average wage may decrease. (Let us here assume that the average experience of women workers decreases because the inexperience of the new workers dominates the increased experience stemming from a simultaneous reduction in the exit rate of women workers.)

During the period when women's LFPRs increased, the LFPRs of men decreased. The men who left the labor force, particularly the elderly or those with disabilities, are likely to be the low-wage workers. Thus, the stock of working men and women is changing to decrease the ratio of average women's wages to average men's wages, even though there may have been a rise in the market wage offered to the population of women relative to the population of men. Correcting for these selection (or compositional) biases is difficult.

One useful measure of the change in relative wages for men and women could be obtained by longitudinal data for those who worked continuously during the period. However, if women tend to exit from the labor force more than men, then restricting the comparison to continuous workers would create a probable selection bias that would overstate the change in the female/male wage ratio. This is because the change in wages, or "wage offers", would tend to be smaller for those who drop out of the labor force.

There is a similar selection bias in measuring the change in the average occupational status of men and women. By restricting the occupational measures to workers only, the common change for women from housewife to a market occupation is ignored, and the new entrant probably has a lower-than-average occupation. I doubt if a satisfactory ranking for the occupation of housewife can be devised to permit us to measure the changing occupational status of all adult women. If we had such a measure we could avoid the selection bias.

A Conceptual Problem in Measuring Discrimination. The main controversy about the wage gap between men and women concerns the measurement of sex discrimination, which we may define as a higher wage paid to men than to women who are equal in productivity. Although sex discrimination in the labor market is defined as wage discrimination, wages will usually reflect discrimination in a variety of labor market events. For example, the hiring, placement, and promotion processes may restrict women to (or "crowd" women into) lower paying jobs. Thus, discrimination may serve to increase the supply of women into certain occupations and thereby lower the wage in those occupations. Using wages as a measure of market discrimination will not, however, capture all of the nonpecuniary aspects of employment. Holding wages constant these aspects are sometimes favourable to women, who for example, tend to be in cleaner working environments, but are in other aspects, such as the "authority" inherent in the job, unfavourable to women.

Note that above I used the phrase, "equal in productivity", when defining sex discrimination in wage differentials. I believe that the term, "productivity", should refer to the ability of the worker to perform a task, given an equal opportunity and willingness to do so. At any moment in time the occupational distribution will show men with more training and higher skills on average. A central question is: To what extent does this occupational or skill distribution reflect the voluntary choices of men and women regarding the division of labor between market and home sectors? Conversely, to what extent does this reflect market discrimination that is imposed on women? For some policy purposes this latter question is focused on whether the employer, other male workers, or customers are the specific sources of market discrimination.

I doubt whether the usual econometric procedures for measuring labor market discrimination can answer these questions. The usual measure is the residual in average wages between working men and women after accounting for their "endowments" (or productivity characteristics). The residual is usually obtained from multiple regression models of the following kind:

Let y = wage; x_j = the jth productivity trait and let the collection of productivity traits be abbreviated as x; B_j = the "effect" of x_j, interpreted as the market return (or "payoff") to x_j; e = a random error; and i = f, m for f = female and m = male.

(1) $\quad y^i = \sum B^i x^i + e$, with $\hat{y}^i = \sum \hat{B}^i x^i$ as the regression-predicted value of y, given x.

(2) $\quad \bar{y}^m - \bar{y}^f = \sum \hat{B}^m (\bar{x}^m - \bar{x}^f) + \sum \bar{x}^f (\hat{B}^m - \hat{B}^f)$.

Equation (2) is a standard decomposition of the male-female wage difference. The first term on the right-hand side shows the product of the male coefficients, B^m, and the difference between the mean values of the "endowments". Usually $\bar{x}^m > \bar{x}^f$, on average, where the x's are positively related to y (i.e., B > 0), so the first term is presumed to express the component of the predicted difference that is attributable to unequal endowments. As a corollary, if the endowments could be equalized, $\bar{x}^m = \bar{x}^f$ (for each x or "on average"), this source of a wage gap would be eliminated. (4).

The second term on the right-hand side is conventionally attributed to market discrimination. The endowments are held constant (here, at the mean values for females), and the (on average) excess of B^m over B^f is said to reflect   the market's favored treatment of males. In other words, the same good (x) is valued at different prices, which defines discrimination.

Equation (2) is useful for its descriptive content and, I believe, for clarifying some inherent weaknesses in the econometric attempt to measure market discrimination. The major problem is the ambiguity of the x's as representations of "endowments". Frequently the x's reflect market discrimination directly, and such x's should not be held constant. A glaring example occurs when the x's measure occupations, perhaps as a collection of dummy variables (1 if in the occupation; 0 otherwise). Occupational segregation may well be the most serious form of market discrimination.

A more subtle example is the use of an x that measures labor market experience, defined as some measure of the quantity of labor supplied. Experience does have a theoretical basis in the human capital model for affecting wages, as we have noted. The positive relation may reflect explicit training or perhaps "learning by doing". However, in our previous discussion of female labor supply we also noted the positive effect of market wage rates on labor supply. Clearly, in the market as a whole and over time, wage rates and labor supply are mutually causal. The interpretation of the statistical relationship is generally ambiguous, although there are circumstances when one or the other variable may be realistically considered exogenous, permitting a one-way causal interpretation.

The study of women in the U.S. labor market (O'Neill and Braun) is the most explicit in emphasizing the causal role of experience in determining wages. As a result, it is the most "conservative" in its discussion of market discrimination against women. The study of England (Elliott, et al.) did not "hold experience constant" in its comparisons, and this is an important reason why it attributed more of the wage gap to discrimination. Consider the following deterministic path diagram, with arrows designating causal paths, to illustrate the two interpretations, which I will label (in an oversimplification) as the U.S. and English models:

PATH DIAGRAM FOR ALTERNATIVE MODELS OF WAGE
DISCRIMINATION AGAINST WOMEN

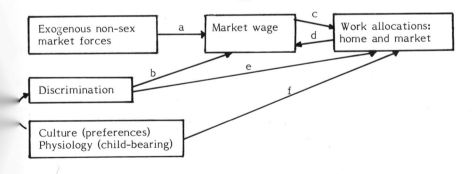

The U.S. model may be expressed (with some injustice to the authors perhaps) as asserting that f is large, which makes d important, and that b = e = 0. The English model (in extreme form) asserts that b and e are large and that f = 0.

A focus on g is not likely to reconcile the two views. One could postulate that noneconomic forces are the source of discrimination and preferences, and that discrimination is predetermined (exogenous) to the labor market agents. In this instance discrimination becomes part of the culture. This would merely shift the debate to the question of whether the labor market agents - employers and unions, say - affect g in the long-run and whether, in the short-run, policies can be implemented on the assumption that b and e are nonzero.

My methodological point is, in any case, that the existence of causal paths c and d do not address the question of how much discrimination exists. The point holds for any x variable that is endogenous - that is, affected by the operation of the labor market. Economists view education, for example, as an investment that is to some extent responsive to rewards in the labor market. The number of children women desire may plausibly be influenced by the labor market opportunities for women, and so on. Indeed, I can think of few variables besides age and ethnicity that are exogenous among the variables conventionally used in earnings functions. This is not to say that the labor market is the only or even the major determinant of education, training, the number of children, and so on. Rather, it is that the conventional practice of "holding constant" such variables in equations (1) and (2) tends to understate discrimination against women in the labor market as a whole.

It may be illuminating to mention the use of multiple regression models like (1) and (2) in the analyses of discrimination in individual firms. In the U.S. the regression analyses are sometimes offered as evidence in court cases or other litigation proceedings stemming from antidiscrimination laws. These analyses have three advantages over nationwide studies. First, the objectives are explicit - a guilty or innocent verdict! Second, a variety of characteristics - x variables - may well be exogenous to a given employer, even though they are not exogenous to the labor market as a whole. Third, explicit information about the employer's criteria for hiring, retention, promotion, or pay may be used to determine the x-variables. Regression analyses with nationwide samples usually suffer from ambiguities and vagueness about all these points.

Unfortunately, the analyses of data from a single firm have two serious faults that (I believe) invalidate their use for assessing market discrimination. First, the selection rules for becoming part of the data base are seldom known; second, the sampling variability is unknown but probably very large. If the company under study was randomly selected, or believed to be "representative", and was known to select their male and female employees randomly, then only the problem of a small sample size would detract from the inferences and estimates obtained. However, the companies studied in court cases are not a random sample of all companies, and their recruitment policies are certainly not random.

In some cases the company records apply only to a narrowly defined skill group - insurance salespersons or college teachers or entry-level unskilled laborers - so the measure of discrimination would at best apply to this occupational group. The role of market discrimination in determining the sex distribution in those occupations would not be examined. In other cases, even this narrowly defined analysis of discrimination would be rendered invalid because of the lack of information about the company's recruitment (selection) procedures. Perhaps the company has a reputation for discrimination against women that restricts the pool of female applicants. (Maybe only a small number of new-comers to the community constitute the pool of female applicants.) The statistical analyst usually deals with the employees on board or, at best, with persons who have applied to the company. Under these circumstances, generalizations about discrimination to the market as a whole cannot be validly based on studies of one or several companies.

I have said little about the second term on the right-hand side of equation (2). Consider Solomon Polachek's argument that larger values of B^m do not re-present discrimination because the same x-values will typically represent more market productivity when embodied in males. In his words:

> ... structural differences (B's) (may) be attributed in part to the division of labor within the household which could come about either be-cause of direct market discrimination, societal discrimination, or the optimal mating process.... It is because of such a division of labor ... that familiy characteristics have differing effects (B's) for males and females. For this reason... namely, the assumption that family characteristics have the same effect on both male and female wages - many of the current estimates of the male-female discrimination coefficients are seriously biased. (5)

Thus, Polachek argues that equation (2) is biased toward overstating market discrimination against women. His conclusion may be correct, but I find his line of reasoning unnecessarily awkward. Polachek in effect simply defines the interaction term, "maleness" times x, to have a positive effect on the basis of a priori arguments. His conclusion may be reached more conventionally by specifying omitted variables in equation (2) that are positively (negatively) cor-related with maleness and positively (negatively) correlated with productivity (and therefore, with y).

An Alternative Measure: "Societal" Discrimination. The core of the controversy about labor market discrimination against women concerns the division of labor between home and market. The view that women specialize in home production has led some to accept the higher market wages of men as an efficient out-come of market forces. The fact that econometric estimation of market wage functions does not predict equal wages among men and women of equal measured productivity is dismissed as the fault of errors in the specification of the model and/or errors in the data. Needless to say, both our models and our data are inadequate to estimate the "home wages" of women or men.

If we assume that the specialization in work is voluntary, then, even though the choices are made by persons of equal average innate abilities, it becomes a seemingly small step to conclude that the allocation of work and wage pay-ments are equitable as well as efficient. A measure that, under certain as-sumptions, tests this "benign" theory is presented next.

My point of departure is to shift from the previous focus on market wage rates to income received during one's adult life, and, as a corollary, to shift from the individual market worker as a separate unit of analysis to the indi-vidual as a member of a household that shares the household's income receipts. Income received is intended to represent earnings for services rendered. Ideal-ly I want to measure:

$$W^{*f} = \frac{w^f M^f + p^f H^f}{M^f + H^f} \qquad \text{and} \qquad W^{*m} = \frac{w^m M^m + p^m H^m}{M^m + H^m}$$

where: w = market hourly wage; p = home hourly wage; M = hours of market work; H = hours of home work; f = female; m = male.

The question I want to ask is: Does $W^{*f} = W^{*m}$? (6). Because neither p or nor H is observed, I will use income receipts to attempt to answer this question.

The home work of a wife, in particular, is assumed to be paid for by her share of household income. For illustrative purposes I will assume, for each period, that the husband and wife share equally in consumption of market purchased goods and in leisure, defined as: total time - (H + M). In my illustration I assume that all men and women become married.

Definition of terms:

(1) Six life-cycle periods of adult life are indicated by subscripts: 1 ... 6. The superscripts remain f and m. The fact that women live longer than men is reflected in a zero value for income of men in the final period.

(2) Earnings in the market equal E, where E is a discounted average. Although E equals wages times hours worked, the decomposition may be ignored because leisure is assumed to be equal for men and women in each period.

(3) A equals retirement income and returns on savings from earnings. Wealth at the beginning of adulthood is assumed to be equal among men and women.

(4) C equals payments made to a divorced, separated, or widowed woman. These payments are mainly for the support of dependent children. The fraction of C paid by the husband who separates from his wife is k, and (1 - k) C is the government's contribution. The tax revenues for these payments are not accounted for below, but they may be considered proportional to market earnings.

(5) P equals the probability that the woman and man are divorced, and P' = 1 - P.

These definitions are contained in the terms of Table 1, which illustrates the measure of "lifetime income", which in turn is intended to measure lifetime earnings for the average man and woman. The comparison between men's and women's economic well-being, and, provisionally, the issue of equitable treatment is examined by summing the income amounts in each of the last two columns. Empirical approximations for entries in these columns may be obtained from longitudinal data or from cross-section surveys from different years. What would the comparison show?

The qualitative point that the present value of the sum for men exceeds that for women seems clear. The sum of the male excess in periods 1, 4, and 5

258

Table 1

Income Received Over the Adult Lifetimes of Women and Men

Period	Approximate Age	Woman's Income	Man's Income
1	18-22	E_1^f	E_1^m
2	23-25	$1/2(E_2^f + E_2^m)$	same (as women's)
3	26-33	$1/2(E_3^m + E_3^f)^*$	same
4	34-64	$1/2(P')(E_4^f + E_4^m) + P(E_4^f + C)^{**}$	same first term + $P(E_4^m - kC)$
5	65-71	$1/2(P')(A_5^f + A_5^m) + P(A_5^f)$	same first term + $P(A_5^m)$
6	72 +	A_6^f	0 (or negative!)***

* E_3^f is presumed to be much less than E_3^m or even than E_2^f, because this age period is assumed to be when 1, 2 or 3 children are born and when the maximum amount of child-care is provided by the mother.

** E_4^f, E_4^m, A_5^f, and A_5^m may differ depending on whether the separation occurs. The same symbol is used to avoid clutter.

*** When the man is assumed dead his earnings are, of course, zero. In all other periods, well-being (or "utility") was assumed equivalent to leisure - plus - income. Perhaps a negative value is required to express the worse - than - zero utility associated with dead.

surely exceeds the female advantage in period 6. (Recall that the E's are discounted by a factor $(1 + r)^{-n}$, where r is the annual discount rate and n is the number of years in the future when income is received.) On the other hand, the assummed sharing of E's when the couple is married probably makes the ratio of the two totals more equal than the ratio of the typical w^f and w^m, which, for example, tends to be around 0.6 in the U.S.

Several questions and qualifications about Table 1 and my use of it may be mentioned. Is leisure consumption the same for men and women, on average? Do women feel a stigma if their market wages are lower or if they receive transfer payments (C), even though their incomes may equal men's? Is the longer life span of women attributable to the division of work? Biologists tell us that women are probably endowed with more longevity, but whether the sex difference in market work adds to this endowment is unknown.

Although the ratio, E^f/E^m, has increased, so has P - the probability of divorce and separation. The variance in expected income has increased, particularly among women, as a consequence of rising P values. Accounting for the risk aversion suggests that the simple sums of the expected values overstate the value of women's total income relative to men's. More importantly, the excess of $P(E^m - kC)$ over $P(E^f + C)$, along with the rising P, has lowered the lifetime income (as defined above) for women relative to men in recent years. Moreover, my impression is that leisure is sharply reduced for women who are left with the responsibility of raising children, unless the women are on the welfare (public-assistance) rolls, in which case their total income is very low. It may seem counter-intuitive that women's lifetime income (as defined above) would be declining relative to men's in recent years, because we know that E^f has risen relative to E^m. One must ask whether the rise in P is a consequence of the relative rise in E^f and whether all of this reflects an overall improvement in women's well-being. This is not a question that economists are well equipped to answer.

The above measure of equitable treatment has not been empirically implemented, so my comments about it are speculative. Note that it avoids the question of why market wage rates are lower for women and does not attempt to measure discrimination in the labor market. Under the assumptions described above, the procedure attempts to measure economic discrimination in the combined market and nonmarket (home) sectors. The procedure deals with the following question: Regardless of why men are paid higher wages, are women compensated in whole or part by alternative income receipts? Even if this question can be answered, I doubt that economists can answer the following questions: If there is equalizing compensation, does this imply that there is no market discrimination? If there is market discrimination in wages, does equal income or, perhaps, equal compensation (in the form of leisure-plus-income) remedy that inequity? I believe it is better to ask the right questions even if we cannot (yet) answer them.

3.   MODELS FOR POLICY ANALYSIS

Economists have developed general models for predicting and explaining labor supply behavior and the determination of wage rates. The term, "general", implies that the model is intended to apply to a wide variety of conditions, and that it has not been developed for any particular situation. Ideally, the general model is tested with a variety of data sets. In the labor supply model, for example, income and wage parameters have been estimated in many different contexts.

One approach to predicting the effects of various policy changes, such as tax changes, wage subsidies, and training programs is to translate the policy change into equivalent changes in the variables in the general model and then use the parameter estimates previously obtained from the general model. Another approach, which may be useful when a policy has been implemented, is to use the general model to predict the counterfactual outcome if the particular policy had not been implemented. The measure of the policy's effect is, then, estimated as the actual value minus the (counterfactual) predicted value.

Unfortunately, there are serious obstacles to using these approaches with confidence. In the first approach, the general models have too often produced a wide range of parameter estimates, and the policy changes often do not correspond closely to the types of variation in variables found in the general model. In the second approach there are usually a variety of unmeasured events that occur during the time when the program has been in operation. Thus, causal inferences about a program's effect are problematic.

Path diagrams may illustrate some of the problems. Let y = outcome, measured for a person; $\underline{x}$ = vector of general explanatory variables (measuring market and personal characteristics); T = the policy "treatment;" and e = an error term. The function to be estimated and its path diagram are shown below:

$$y = f(\underline{x}, T) + e_y$$

Single arrows represent causal paths, and double arrows represent correlations that may or may not be causal. We seek to obtain an unbiased estimate of the change in y with respect to the change in T. We assume that T is measured accurately.

A necessary and sufficient condition for an unbiased estimate is that the e_y source of variation in y is independent of T, or, as a weaker condition, uncorrelated with T if the relation we want to estimate is linear. This condition is met if $\underline{x}$ exhausts all the systematic factors except T that affect y, or if, given that there are omitted x-variables, these omitted variables are, on average, not related (uncorrelated) with T. A general expression for a source of bias in measuring the effect of T occurs when the unmeasured e_x and T are correlated, as shown below:

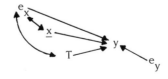

261

I see no methodological substitute for the requirement that we must have sufficient knowledge about the process by which people are selected into the T status to be able to determine when the correlation between e_x and T is zero. Obviously, a random assignment of T values among the sample observations is a special case in which we know both the process and that a zero correlation may be assumed, so the effect of T will be unbiased. However, random assignments are seldom practical, and, in any case, do not apply when T is educational attainment, unemployment status, or any event that is only partially determined by policy manipulation.

In summary, social scientists have two major tasks in developing methods for program evaluation. One is to improve our general models of the form $x \rightarrow y$. The other is to model the determination of T.

4.   CONCLUSIONS

The four-country studies have provided us with excellent descriptive material about work and wages of women and about government policies affecting women in the labor market. I have suggested additional measures, but I recognize that these are difficult to obtain.

On the basis of the implicit theoretical framework of the authors and our shared value judgements, we may view the increased work rates of women as progress toward a more efficient and equitable economy. Interpreting the trends in the wages of women, particularly their relation to the wages of men, was found to be less clear. The government policies that were described were not analyzed to determine their effectiveness, but this reflects the limits of our science, not of the authors.

The conference has taken place during a time when economic growth has slowed and unemployment has risen in all four countries. It is a time when scepticism surrounds governmental attempts to reverse these trends. Thus, there is great value in theoretical guidance about policies and in empirical techniques for evaluating the policies. At the same time, the more modest goal of improving our measurements of the changes in the economic status of women is also worthy of attention.

NOTES

(1) The four background papers listed below were prepared for the conference on "Regulation Theory of the Labour Market. International Comparison of Labour Market Policy Related to Women" at the International Institute of Management, Berlin, December 8-9, 1981.

Elliott, R., Glucklich, P., MacLennan, E., and Pond, C., "Women in the Labor Market: A Study of the Impact of Legislation and Policy Toward Women in the UK Labor Market During the Nineteen Seventies;"

Gladh, L., and Gustafsson, S., "Labor Market Policy Related to Women and Employment in Sweden;"

O'Neill, J., and Braun, R., "Women and the Labor Market: A Survey of Issues and Policies in the United States;"

Weitzel, R., "Labour Market Policies Related to Women and Employment in the Federal Republic of Germany."

(2) These statistics are derived from the author's unpublished tabulations.

(3) The two views of the wage difference between men and women reflect views that differ in the emphasis they give to the role of "voluntary choice" versus "market-imposition." The following studies appear to emphasize the role of voluntary choice because they take as given (that is, hold constant) time spent at home (or, conversely, time spent in the labor market): O'Neill and Braun (cited in footnote 1), p. 67 in particular; and Polachek, S., "Potential Biases in Measuring Male-Female Discrimination," Journal of Human Resources, X, Spring 1975. Examples of studies that appear to emphasize market imposed discrimination and which do not "hold constant" labor market experience are: Blinder, Alan, "Wage Discrimination: Reduced Form and Structural Estimates," Journal of Human Resources, VIII, Fall, 1973; and see also Chapter 3 in Elliot, et al., especially pp. 81-92, where employer-imposed constraints on women's career choices are emphasized.

(4) Note that an alternative "price" for these endowments is the vector, B^f. The use of B^f in the first term and x^m in the second term provides an alternative decomposition. These and other scaling devices reflect the inherent "index number" problem in aggregating heterogeneous goods (x's) with different weight (B's). I will ignore this problem.

(5) Polachek, cited above, p. 227.

(6) Economists often postulate that in equilibrium $w = p_*$ "at the margin" for any given worker. This equality is not required for W^*, however, because w and p (and W^*) are averages, not marginals.

12 THE POLITICAL ECONOMY OF LABOR MARKET DISCRIMINATION: A THEORETICAL AND COMPARATIVE ANALYSIS OF SEX DISCRIMINATION

GÜNTHER SCHMID

1. INTRODUCTION[*)]

Labor market discrimination has a long history. However, discrimination has seldom been a focus of debate in economic theory. One reason for this is the predominance of neoclassical theory, for which discrimination is a paradox or a deviation from the rule: In a market economy which fulfils the conditions of perfect competition, wages are equal to the value of the marginal product of labor, and two equally productive persons receive - at least in the long run - the same wages, independent of sex, age, or race. Another reason for the neglect of the issue of discrimination is that the development of theory is dependent on economic and social movements. To put it simply: Where there is no anti-discrimination movement, or where other socio-economic problems - such as mass unemployment or inflation - are overriding concerns, economic or political theory will not bother much about the issue of discrimination. The Civil Rights Movement and the Women's Liberation Movement of the 1960's and 1970's succeeded for a time in placing discrimination problems in the fore-front; however, it might well be that rising and continuing mass unemployment will now displace that issue.

The last development is in fact paradoxical, since discrimination increases as economic conditions deteriorate for a longer period (Jain/Sloane 1983). It can be shown that labor market discrimination is itself a means to solve employment problems. Discrimination is a common mechanism of "labor rationing", and women are - among other groups - the "victims" of this process. If this observation is correct, a first (and much neglected) conclusion can be drawn: discrimination is a relative term, comparable to the notion of "relative deprivation". Discrimination may be perceived as being more serious in   a   society closer to equality than in a society far away from that goal, and even increasing discrimination may be perceived as being less serious when people are concerned with other problems.

Labor market discrimination, therefore, cannot be reduced to the pure economic question of whether and why wages are different among people with the same productivity. Apart from the fact that an empirical test of this relationship is almost impossibly, the perception of discrimination is also a matter of tastes, value judgements, conflicting interests, and - therefore - a relative concept. How the issue is brought into the political arena, and how it is solved, depends on political institutions and the organization of interest groups. The theory of labor market discrimination has to be based, not on economics but on political economy.

This is all the more necessary when, as in this article, we are primarily interested in the real or potential effects of anti-discrimination policies. Discrimination is not only a relative concept but also a complex issue. Policies which focus on a single cause might be self-defeating: A regulation equalizing wages might end up fostering discrimination by causing employers to be less willing to retain or hire the protected group, resulting in even greater unemployment or underemployment differentials; pure quota rules might result in increased prejudice, with stigmatizing effects, and with artificial work reorganization that reestablishes the old differentials. Policies will have to be directed to the specific causes and to the different dimensions of discrimination, and they will have to take into account the institutional context in which they are working; indirect strategies might in the long run be more effective than the direct approaches to the problem.

The purpose of this essay is to present and to evaluate theories of discrimination, to develop policy options for reducing labor market discrimination, and to assess their prospective impact on equal opportunity in the labor market. While the article focuses primarily on problems of discrimination against women, it also claims to be of some value with respect to anti-discrimination policies for other groups. I start with definitions of discrimination and distinguish the most important dimensions of discrimination (section 2). This is followed by a sketch of theories of discrimination, most of which provide complementary rather than competing views of the issue (section 3). Section 4 deals with the functioning and the effects of different equal opportunity policies, and section 5 summarizes the main results.

2. DEFINITIONS AND TYPES OF DISCRIMINATION

2.1 Definitions

Discrimination can be defined as a mechanism of excluding individuals from a group by assigning them pejorative characteristics or by the unjustified assumption of the lack of characteristics which are deemed to be necessary for group membership (1). Discrimination, therefore, affects individuals, but it can only be identified at the level of the group. As a result, it is not possible for a society to determine whether it is or is not an equal opportunity society without collecting and analyzing economic data on groups (Thurow 1980:180).

It is quite obvious from this definition that to be efficient, the discriminating characteristic must be outstanding and clearly observable. In other words, other things being equal, discrimination is an increasing function of outstanding characteristics: Having black hairs among blondes or being a "black sheep" among whites makes an excellent candidate for discrimination. An outstanding characteristic is a necessary, but not a sufficient condition for discrimination. That women can be easily distinguished by readily observable external differences, is one condition - although surely not the cause - for the enduring and efficient discrimination by sex. Not too long ago, female sex connoted inferior intelligence or political capabilities, and such prejudices might still be deeply rooted in many minds. Easy external distinctions reinforce prejudices. Where an outstanding characteristic is lacking, it may be created by assigning one (e.g. the "Jewish star") or by confining people in ghettos.

Apart from this structural condition of discrimination, the concept of labor market discrimination has been defined in three different ways since the first days of explicit anti-discrimination policies; this change has been well summarized in an article by Jain and Ledvinka (1975) on "Economic Inequality and the Concept of Employment Discrimination": Initially, discrimination was defined as "prejudiced treatment", i.e. as harmful acts motivated by personal antipathy toward the group of which the target person was a member. However, since it is difficult to prove intent to harm, that first definition was ineffective as a means of solving the problem of labor market inequality.

Consequently, discrimination later came to be defined in the courts as "unequal treatment". Under this second definition, the law was said to mean that the same standards be applied to all employees and applicants. In other words, the employer was allowed to impose any requirements, as long as they were imposed on all groups alike. Yet many of the most common requirements, such as education and testing, had unequal effects on various groups, even though they were imposed on all groups equally. In other words: this second definition was not suitable for dealing with indirect discrimination. Employers were still allowed to ignore the inequities built into the society, especially into the processes by which people acquired credentials that were used as discriminatory mechanisms.

In recognition of such concerns, the U.S. Supreme Court articulated the third definition of employment discrimination in Griggs v. Duke Power Co. (2). There the Court struck down employment tests and educational requirements that screened out a greater percentage of blacks than whites. Those practices were prohibited simply because they had the result of excluding blacks disproportionately, and because they bore no relationship to the jobs in question. Thus, the concept of labor market discrimination shifted from a concept of intent to a concept of "adverse impact"; and consequently, the focus shifted from individuals to groups. According to this approach, the problem of labor market inequality is to be solved by eliminating those employment practices that had unequal impact on the groups covered by equal employment law, independent of whether there was conscious discrimination or not. What matters are consequences and not intentions.

But what consequences are to be judged as labor market inequalities, and what factors or practices lead to such inequalities? We obviously need a causal theory of labor market discrimination. Distinguishing different types of discrimination is a first step in this direction.

2.2   Types of Labor Market Discrimination

Earnings of women may differ from average earnings or from those of men for several reasons:

- Women have less access than do men to productivity augmenting opportunities such as schooling, accumulation of experience through continuous work or training, and regional mobility. This can be called "pre-market discrimination" because the lower education, less work experiences and training, and restricted regional mobility of women is not a consequence of labor market discrimination but a consequence of discrimination that ocurred before entering the labor market. Of course, there can also be anticipated labor market discrimination, which deters individuals from investing, for example, in education. Sex role stereotypes restricting tastes for jobs also belong to this category of pre-market discrimination.

- Women occupy less favourable jobs than do men or they receive no job at all, for a given set of qualifications such as education, experience. In this case, if tastes for jobs do not differ, and differences in qualifications have been properly allowed for, employment discrimination can be observed. One can distinguish three main forms of employment discrimination: Hiring discrimination occurs when groups other than, for example, women are preferred in the recruitment process; the preference can be expressed in direct or indirect forms, e.g. sex specific advertisements or screening tests which sort out women from the "waiting queue". Promotion discrimination happens when men in the same job are preferred over women in promotion decisions for further training, jobs with higher status, better working conditions etc.. Firing discrimination occurs when women systematically are sorted out at dismissals or lay-offs, either directly because of respective tastes of the employers or indirectly by applying criteria such as seniority that are disadvantageous to women. Hiring and firing discrimination lead to unemployment differentials between women and men.

- Women receive lower pay than men for the same job. This reflects wage discrimination if similar jobs are in fact being compared. Wage discrimination can take different forms: Collective agreements can explicitly discriminate against women by creating sex specific wage groups with lower pay for women (e.g., so-called light pay groups); this practice has been only recently forbidden by law in most countries. Another mechanism of wage discrimination is just to pay women less hourly wages than men even when the same or similar work is being done. A third, and probably nowadays more important, mechanism is the unequal treatment of women in terms of fringe benefits.

Leaving aside the possibility of "post-market discrimination", i.e. the unequal treatment of women's earnings by tax or social security regulations, we can summarize the reasons for earning differentials in a kind of decision tree or in a decision matrix as follows:

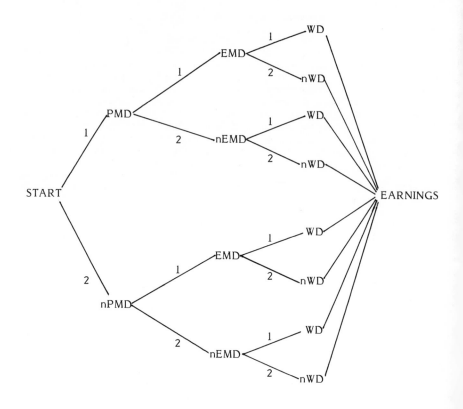

Where: (n)PMD = (no) pre-market discrimination
         (n)EMD = (no) employment discrimination
         (n)WD = (no) wage discrimination

$$
\text{START} \quad \left\{
\begin{array}{ccc}
1 & 1 & 1 \\
1 & 1 & 2 \\
1 & 2 & 1 \\
1 & 2 & 2 \\
2 & 1 & 1 \\
2 & 1 & 2 \\
2 & 2 & 1 \\
2 & 2 & 2
\end{array}
\right\} \quad \text{EARNINGS}
$$

Figure 1: Types and Combinations of Labor Market Discrimination

The worst case is obviously the "decision sequence" (1, 1, 1), whereas (2, 2, 2) results in no earnings differentials between women and men. The figure makes also obvious that wage discrimination is only in one case the single reason for earning differentials; in all other cases the impact of equal pay policy will be of limited effect because of preceding pre-market or employment discrimination, or because employers have the alternative of changing from wage discrimination to employment discrimination.

Pre-market discrimination, on the other hand, is a much more complex phenomenon than employment discrimination, depending on deep cultural traditions, tastes and individual attitudes. It is very difficult to influence traditions, tastes, and attitudes, and the means used affect other goals such as liberty and self-determination. This is not to suggest that nothing be done in this sphere, but anti-discrimination policy might be well advised to concentrate on employment discrimination, and to rely on indirect means of countering pre-market discrimination which would affect tastes and attitudes in the long run.

3.   THEORIES OF LABOR MARKET DISCRIMINATION

3.1   An Analytical Framework for the Identification of Theories

There are several possible ways to describe and characterize theories, but the criteria for classification are seldom explicitly stated. Such criteria are, however, important for assessing the purpose, the comprehensiveness, and the relevance of the theories considered. The following figure provides an analytical framework for the proper identification of labor market discrimination theories.

First of all, one has to distinguish between different actors on both sides, on the discriminating and on the discriminated side. Discrimination can be caused by employers, by employees, and by consumers, and all three categories can be the victims of discrimination. Theories of labor market discrimination tend to emphasize employer discrimination and to neglect employee or consumer discrimination. In special circumstances, employee or consumer discrimination can be of great importance: We know of coalitions between employers and part of the employees to discriminate against other employees; consumer discrimination might be important especially in personal services where clients reject the contact, e.g., with members of an ethnic minority or with elderly women.

We can then distinguish two different motivating forces of the actors, endogenous as well as exogenous causal factors. Theories of discrimination usually identify three main sources of motivation on the discriminating side: tastes, social customs or rules, and income maintenance or maximization. I will use this distinction as the basis for a classification of theories of discrimination (see parts 3.2 to 3.4).

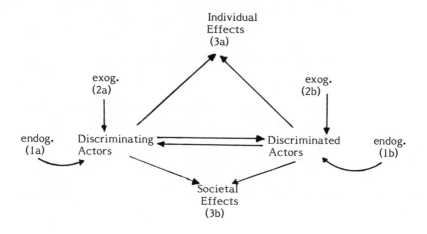

(1) Basic Utility Considerations, Creating Motivation
    (Endogenous Causal Factors)

    (1a)   - tastes
                - social customs
                - income maintenance or maximization

    (1b)   - social role orientation
                - labor market commitment

(2) Context Conditions for Actors, or "field determinants"
    (Exogenous Causal Factors)

    (2a)   - intensity of social contacts
                - informational constraints or imperfections
                - monopsony or monopoly
                - high bargaining power

    (2b)   - low labor supply elasticity for a given firm
                - low bargaining power

(3) Effects of Discrimination for Individuals and for Society

    (3a)   - pay differentials
                - employment or unemployment differentials
                - position differentials

    (3b)   - lower or higher productivity
                - inequity, and social conflicts

Figure 2: Analytical Framework for the Identification of Theories of Discrimination

On the discriminated side, inflexible or restricted role orientations and low labor market commitment are often mentioned as motivational sources for labor market discrimination.

Each individual acts within an environment or "action field" which exercises pressure or attraction on the individual in terms of exogenous constraints or options (push or pull factors). Tastes can be reinforced by close social contacts with the rejected group; profit maximization under uncertainty might lead to discriminatory behaviour without any intent to discriminate against anybody (known as "statistical discrimination"); a monopsony position in the market can tempt employers as well as employees to discriminate; high bargaining power can be the reason for discrimination, or the maintenance of high bargaining power can even become the objective of, e.g., occupational discrimination. A combination of monopsony and low labor supply elasticity for a given firm provides ideal conditions for discrimination - relevant especially to women whose spatial mobility is limited to a narrow local labor market; this can be further reinforced by the low bargaining power of the discriminated group. Thus, we have to keep in mind that endogenous and exogenous factors are interrelated, sometimes producing chains or spirals of cumulative and self-reinforcing discrimination. Most theories of discrimination, however, tend to concentrate on one or two of the above mentioned factors (Myrdal 1968; Lundahl/Wadensjö 1982).

Finally, different effects of discrimination can be identified, and theories can be classified by what kind of effects they emphasize and how they relate these effects to discrimination. Neoclassical theories, for example, concentrate on individual pay differentials, and on societal allocational inefficiences. Institutional approaches, on the other hand, pay much more attention to employment or positional discrimination, e.g. the dual labor market theory, or on problems of inequity and social conflicts as societal consequences of long-lasting discrimination.

Figure 3 summarizes the topics I dealt so far, and provides a structure for the following discussion of approaches to labor market discrimination. It is neces-

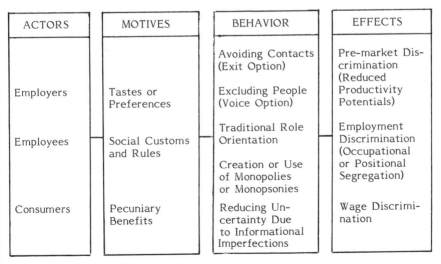

ACTORS	MOTIVES	BEHAVIOR	EFFECTS
		Avoiding Contacts (Exit Option)	Pre-market Discrimination (Reduced Productivity Potentials)
Employers	Tastes or Preferences	Excluding People (Voice Option)	
		Traditional Role Orientation	Employment Discrimination (Occupational or Positional Segregation)
Employees	Social Customs and Rules	Creation or Use of Monopolies or Monopsonies	
Consumers	Pecuniary Benefits	Reducing Uncertainty Due to Informational Imperfections	Wage Discrimination

Figure 3: Dimensions of Labor Market Discrimination

sary to distinguish between actors, their motives, their actual behavior, and the outcomes or effects. Theories of discrimination can be classified by the most important categories within these dimensions, and different combinations of theories are possible. I have chosen the dimension motives and behavior for the following classification of existing theories.

3.2 Gary Becker's Theory of "Taste for Discrimination"

The publication of Gary Becker's The Economics of Discrimination in 1957 was the initial effort in neoclassical economics to deal seriously with discrimination as a deviation from market equilibrium. In good neoclassical tradition, Becker identified a "non-pecuniary motivation" as the source of disturbance in market equilibrium, i.e. the "taste for discrimination", and in his view the major contribution of the book was to develop a theory of non-pecuniary motivation and to apply it quantitatively to discrimination in the market place (Becker 1957:3).

"If an individual has a 'taste for discrimination', he must act as if he were willing to pay something, either directly or in the form of a reduced income, to be associated with some persons instead of others." (Becker 1957:6). The taste for discrimination is due to the fact that individuals have preferences for making transactions with certain persons instead of others, and this taste can - according to Becker - vary in strength from person to person. Becker does not provide a full-fledged causal theory of taste, however, he refers at several points in his study to the socio-psychological theory of prejudice. According to this theory, prejudice is related to the degree of personal contacts: If contact with members of a certain group is completely lacking, there is no taste for discrimination. The taste will also be weak or non-existent if contacts are very common and intensive. Thus, by definition, there are no pecuniary motives for discrimination, which Becker excludes from his study.

Employers, therefore, who discriminate against one group (e.g. negroes or women) pay a premium on the wages of the preferred group which they would not pay if they had been guided by the criterion of marginal productivity; Becker calls this premium "discrimination coefficient" (3). This mechanism leads to wage differences and to segregation between discriminated and preferred groups, and - almost by definition - to pecuniary loss by the discriminating employer as well as to imperfections in factor allocation, and - as a consequence - to welfare losses from a societal point of view.

It follows also from this approach that the resulting disequilibrium is unstable and tending toward equilibrium, i.e. to the disappearance of wage differences whereas segregation may be stable. Assuming taste differences among employers, firms with low or no discrimination coefficients will employ the discriminated group and, due to lower labor costs, receive higher profits than firms with high coefficients. This leads to a further expansion of firms with low coefficients, and to a gradual elimination of the firms with a strong taste for discrimination. By definition firms that have a monopoly in a commodity market run no competitive risk if they discriminate. However, if there is competition in the capital market and if the monopoly is transferable (which is not the case with state monopolies), entrepreneurs without a taste for discrimination will buy up monopoly companies. Competition in the capital market, therefore, will have the same effect as competition in the commodity market in the previous case. Increased competition works against employer discrimination. Thus, if the aim is to decrease discrimination, the endeavor should be to increase competition in different markets (Lundahl/Wadensjö 1982).

The effects of employee discrimination depend on the extent to which the discriminating and discriminated groups can be substituted for each other in production. If they are perfect substitutes, the result will be segregation. Every firm that chooses to have a work force consisting of people from both groups will have higher costs than the firm whose employees come from only one of the groups. With non-discriminatory employers the wage rate will be the same for both groups. The market discrimination coefficient (see footnote 3) will thus be zero. If the groups are not perfect substitutes, the results will be different. Assume that we have three groups, for example male foremen, male workers and female workers; that the foremen and the workers are perfect complements in the production process; and that male foremen discriminate against female workers. In this case, the market discrimination coefficient will not be zero. Women will get lower wages than men. In the case where the groups are neither perfect substitutes nor perfect complements, the market discrimination coefficient falls somewhere between these cases (Lundahl/Wadensjö 1982).

Even in the case of perfect substitutes we may get - according to Becker - a market discrimination coefficient which is greater than zero when trade unions discriminate, for example, by not allowing members of a certain group to join and by controlling the employment policy of the firm (e.g. via closed shop clauses).

Labor market discrimination can indirectly arise when consumer discrimination exists. Because of "tastes for discrimination", consumers may avoid buying goods or services from employers not discriminating against a group. Thus, even if an employer has no taste for discrimination, it might be rational for him for economic reasons to discriminate, because the economic advantage from non-discriminating in employment might be outbalanced by consumer discrimination. Again, however, Becker assumes that market forces will negatively sanction consumer discrimination in the long run - discriminating consumers will have to pay higher prices than less or non-discriminating consumers - so that there is a tendency toward downward adjustment in "tastes for discrimination."

An important conclusion from Becker's analysis is, however, that discrimination by employers, employees, trade unions, consumers, and even governmental discrimination (5) may cumulate and reinforce each other, a process which might retard the anti-discrimination tendencies of market forces. Thus, according to Becker, discrimination is very much related to market failures.

Becker's microeconomic analysis of labor market discrimination can now be summarized: Discrimination does not lead only to wage differences but also to segregation; different types of discrimination can have additive effects; discrimination is regarded as in essence an example of market failure because it leads to inefficient factor allocation from a societal point of view; however, there are forces in the economic system which tend to reduce wage differences among employers, if preferences vary between different employers and commodity markets are competitive or monopolies transferable.

Meanwhile, various modifications and criticisms have been developed. This is not the place to deal with them at length (see especially Lundahl/Wadensjö 1982). The central problem with Becker's theory of discrimination, however, should be mentioned briefly: It cannot explain why wage differences between the discriminating and the discriminated groups, e.g. between men and women, remain in the long run. It also fails to explain the empirically more relevant cases in which employers discriminate, sometimes in coalition with employees, for pecuniary motives. The question of where "tastes for discrimination" originate remains underdeveloped in Becker's analysis. Becker's basic explanation - avoiding contacts with other groups - can hardly be relevant for discrimination against women, with whom men seek contact for other than economic reasons. Indeed, concern about emotional and social contacts interfering with work might just be the reason for employer's discrimination against women in some cases. In the following section I briefly describe the most important alternative theories.

3.3   Theories of Social Customs and Rules

One of the most frequently cited reasons for lower wages for women in the same jobs or for the exclusion of women from certain occupations has always been been traditions or customs. In principle, however, the criticism of Becker's theory, that it fails to explain the stability of discrimination in the long run in a competitive economy, is relevant here as well. Firms that do not follow tradition but instead hire (lower-paid) women in male occupations or only employ the lower-paid female labor force in mixed occupations ought to make greater profits than other firms. These firms could then expand until the differences in wages and employment possibilities between men and women disappear. Certainly, this is precisely what happened in some branches of the economy, but the empirical evidence still shows long-lasting discrimination in other parts of the economy.

There are several approaches which explain this outcome by the stability of social customs (traditions) and rules. One explanation for the stability of traditions refers to the theory of games (e.g. Akerlof (1)); another approach - especially related to the Women's Liberation Movement - is based on, what can be called, the theory of social reproduction (e.g. Beck-Gernsheim/Ostner (2)), and a third approach explains the stability of social customs by reinforcing factors of work organisation, e.g. the dual labor market theory of which Michael Piore is the outstanding representative (3).

(1) Akerlof (1976, 1980) assumes that individual utility depends not only on consumption but also on prestige in society. This prestige, in turn, is assumed to depend in part on whether the person follows social codes or not, in part on the percentage of the population which support them. If someone in a caste system, for example, hires untouchable for a job reserved for a certain caste, the employer himself becomes untouchable. Thus, Akerlof's model does not require per se that people have tastes for discrimination. It suffices that everyone believes or fears that the others do. This situation is comparable with the "prisoner's dilemma" in game theory: Thinking that others are racists or patriarchal chauvinists can make it economically rational to take actions which seem to be those of an irrational racist or patriarchal chauvinist. What matters are the players' perceptions of the payoffs and choices, not the real facts.

Lundahl/Wadensjö summarize Akerlof's approach in the following way: Opposing a norm can be economically advantageous but at the same time may lead to diminished prestige. The percentage supporting a norm is assumed to be endogenously determined in the model. The change in this percentage depends on the difference between the percentage that follows and that which does not support the norm. If this difference is positive, the percentage supporting the norm increases; if negative, it decreases. Akerlof indicates that with a given norm, the economy can end up in one of two equilibria. In the first one almost everybody believes in and follows the norm; in the other, almost nobody does. In a system having many different norms, there can be many different equilibria.

From this it would follow that once a minimum coalition for breaking a rule is reached, the system might quickly change to another equilibrium. In other words, for example, once a substantial minority of employers are willing to change their discriminatory behavior toward women, labor market discrimination against women might quickly disappear. Policy strategies should aim to bring about such minimum coalitions. Akerlof, however, does not provide a theory of the origins of social customs and rules, nor does he suggest policy proposals as to how such minimum coalitions can be achieved to end labor market discrimination.

(2) A theory of social customs - their origins and their stability - is provided by sociological role theory. An example, among many others, is the approach of Beck-Gernsheim and Ostner (1978) (6). The key explanatory variable of discrimination in the labor market is the basic division of labor between housework and market work and the ascription of the roles to women and men respectively. Discrimination in the labor market occurs not because of "tastes for discrimination" but because of role traditions which are created and supported by several mechanisms: early childhood socialization, sex specific schooling, and, last but not least, biological or anthropological differences between men and women.

Modern anthropology and ethnology, for example, have provided persuasive material against the myth of the matriarchy in the sense of female rule in ancient societies, an idea put forward by Morgan (1877), Bachofen (1861/1948), and Engels (1884). They show that even in matrilineal or matrifocal societies there was never a dominance of women; in a few examples, e.g. the Hopi-Indians or the Iroquois, women enjoyed at best equity of status (Reiter 1975, Wesel 1980). The present fundamental division of labor between men and women goes back to the "primitive" hunting societies, or more precisely to the origin of the family (50.000 to 500.000 B.C.): Through a combination of biological changes (neoteny) (7) and changes in the mode of production (hunting, food gatheering and conservation), women became more and more absorbed by "homework" or, what is called in modern language, by "social reproduction." The competitive advantage of men over stay-at-home-women arose especially in connection with tool production and trade: The multiple functions of women in their breeder-and-feeder roles did not allow them to spezialize as much as men in production roles; and women were not able to work the trading networks to the extent the men were, because they were too busy with production for family consumption (Boulding 1976:99). This deepening of the division of labor between production (hunting, land cultivation, tool production, and later trade, war, and market work) and social reproduction, during a long historical process, had repercussions on social attitudes and norms.

According to this approach, labor market discrimination is essentially a matter of premarket and employment discrimination. Women are trained in non-market roles, and they are acknowledged in the labor market only as "reserve army"; therefore they are allocated only to low-grade and low-paid positions. This approach suggests three policy conclusions as anti-discrimination strategies: Abolition of the sex-specific allocations of housework and market work (i.e. equal division of tasks in housework between men and women), change in the role attitudes of both women and men, and a fundamental change of market work organization which allows a synchronization of family and market roles.

Beck-Gernsheim and Ostner emphasize especially the latter point. They argue that the need for a changed work organization is not only a matter of intro-ducing flexible working time arrangements - especially not a matter of in-troducing more part-time jobs for women - but also a matter of changing working conditions in favour of female specific abilities, attitudes and behavior. This means, e.g., a reduction of competitive performance behavior, a reduction of the separation between hand and head work, and a reduction of hierarchical structures. In other words, they argue that there are not so much "tastes" or preferences but rather anti-feminine work organization which is responsible for discrimination. Thus, given this anti-feminine work organization, it is even rational when women have a very restrictive orient-ation towards specific jobs which seem to correspond to their female specific abilities. A break up of occupational segregation per se, therefore, will not be an adequate antidiscrimination strategy, and labor market policies training women in non-traditional jobs might even be counterproductive if the job characteristics do not correspond to the alleged "female specific abilities."

Whereas the strength of this approach lies in the explanation of the origins and stability of social customs, its weakness results from the lack of economic and political-institutional considerations. As we will see below, there are strong economic forces which induce discriminatory strategies independent of the sex-specific allocation of homework and market-work. The policy conclusions, although normatively acceptable, have an idealistic bias because they do not take into account political-institutional arrangements which foster sex-specific division of labor, such as tax and social security regulations, and the low re-presentation of women in interest groups (see section 4).

(3) The dual labor market theory can be understood as an approach which tries to combine sociological role theory with economic theory. The well known dis-tinction between a primary and a secondary labor market is clearly related to the distinction between primary and secondary roles (Doeringer/Piore 1971, Berger/Piore 1980). Discrimination arises because of the job security and advancement opportunities which exist for the internal work force (in the primary sector) and because of the economics of developing and retaining a trained work force which the internal market provides to employers. Employers very often face the problem of uncertainties due to market fluctuations and technological "shocks." This problem can be solved by dividing jobs and work organization into two segments: jobs with permanent tasks, and incidental jobs. To this basic "job division" there corresponds a division of employees: an internal work force with secure and permanent jobs, connected with current training and retraining, good wages and internal promotion ladders; an external work force with insecure or time-limited work contracts, no current invest-ment in human capital, low wages, and restricted promotional opportunities. Discrimination in this sense has a clear economic and social rationale for both

employers and employees and need not have racial or sexual implications as such (Doeringer/Piore 1971:133) (8).

In practice, however, it has precisely such implications because the fundamental division of homework and market work by sexes provides an easy and economically efficient criterion for selecting persons for primary or secondary segments of the labor market. "The capitalist system finds these classes and does not create them. ... The migrants (foreign and domestic), the rural workers, and the women are attractive precisely because they belong to another socio-economic structure and view industrial employment as a temporary adjunct to their primary roles. They are willing to take temporary jobs because they see their commitment to these jobs as temporary, and they are able to bear the flux and uncertainty of the industrial economy because they have traditional activities upon which to fall back." (Berger/Piore 1980:50). Contrary to Becker's approach, discrimination is not an end but a means, and elimination of discrimination is likely to reduce the efficiency of the labor force adjustment process, at least in the short run, thereby imposing costs upon both the employer and the society (Doeringer/Piore 1971:136).

Why such costs arise in eliminating discrimination has much to do with the uncertainty in evaluating prospective job performance in the recruitment and internal promotion process. I will return later to this point when I discuss the income or profit maximization theories of discrimination, especially the concept of statistical discrimination. An important policy conclusion is that any anti-discrimination policy that does not take this costs aspect into account will necessarily fail.

3.4   Theories of Income or Profit Maximization

With the theory of segmented labor markets we already have build a bridge to theories which explain discrimination by economic motives. Three basic approaches can be distinguished which I will briefly consider: Monopsony theories (1), monopoly theories or theories of bargaining (2), and informational theories (3).

(1) A profit-maximizing monopsonistic firm will offer a higher wage to men than to women because the supply of women is likely to be more inelastic for a given firm than that of males. The principal reason for this is that women tend to search for jobs in closer proximity to the home than males because of housework responsibilities. This line of argument implies a further distinction between married and single women, since the supply of the latter is likely to be more elastic (Gordon/Morton 1974). The simple monopsony model, however, explains - if at all - only a small part of labor market discrimination against women; for a criticism of this point see Blau/Jusenius 1976. The explanatory power of this approach depends obviously on the empirical relevance of monopsonies in the labor market. In rural areas monopsonies are probably more frequent than in agglomerated areas, and if monopsonies in the labor market are combined with monopolistic or oligopolistic elements in the commodity market, the discriminatory potentialities of employers might become important.

(2) Combined with employee discrimination monopsony possibly can explain even more of labor market discrimination against women. The dual and the

racial labor market theories (Gordon 1972, Reich 1981) assume a high significance of monopsonistic and monopolistic elements despite the presence of other types of firms due to specific employment strategies. An internal labor market is characterized by the fact that an individual can only be hired for certain positions or ports of entry in the firm, from which he commences a career in a (hierarchical) promotional system. Women are less likely to be hired at such ports of entry due to employers assumption that they have no long-term labor market commitment. The firms then have only a monopsonistic position with respect to such ports of entry and to external slots providing no promotional opportunities.

On the other hand, the employees within the "internal segment" have a monopolistic position vis-a-vis the employers because of skills specific to the firm. In this way, the wage level of this segment is not regulated by market forces. The monopsonistic power that firms may possess with respect to ports of entry can be counteracted, for example, by the formation of trade unions. This is especially relevant when trade unions are organized by occupations and when they maintain a "closed shop" by agreement with employers. One should expect, therefore, that discrimination is greater in labor markets with trade unions organized by occupations than in labor markets with trade unions organized by industries; however, I do not know of any research which confirms this hypothesis (9).

(3) Finally, informational theories explain discrimination by employers even in cases in which the firms are profit-maximizing, non-monopsonistic or non-monopolistic, and without "tastes" for one group over another. Informational theories are based either on the idea of incomplete or incorrecte information (prejudice) with respect to the prospective productivity of groups (a), or on the idea of uncertainty concerning the expected productivity of each separate individual within one group, known as statistical discrimination (b).

(a) The only true test of a person's ability or productivity for most jobs is performance on the job. The criteria in terms of which hiring or allocation decisions are based are surrogates for such performance, and the correlation between the two varies according to the completeness or correctness of information on which the criteria are based. The main reason for incomplete information is the cost of acquiring information, which might vary among different groups, and the main reasons for incorrect information are prejudice and obsolete information. A group's productivity can be influenced by the degree of pre-market discrimination, for example, in the school system. If the extent of such discrimination changes, a previously accurate assessment of the productivity differences can become erroneous. In this situation, if the wage is set for a certain position without taking group affiliation into account and the firms have prejudices about the productivity of different groups, those who belong to the group that the firms believe has the lowest productivity will be hired last (Lundahl/Wadensjö 1982:2:48).

Prejudice can vary with the labor market situation: the discriminated group will be hired to a greater extent during periods of low unemployment, which enables firms to acquaint themselves faster with the actual productivity of the group; this would be an argument for job acquaintance subsidies for disadvantaged workers during periods of high unemployment. Correspondingly, prejudices ought to disappear faster during periods of prosperity. Prejudices of employers can also have repercussions for the behavior of the discriminated group by inducing lower investments in qualifications or in searches for jobs for which discrimination is expected (Arrow 1973, Spence 1974).

These explanations of economic discrimination suffer - at least in principle - from the same weakness as Becker's theory: It is difficult to explain enduring discrimination. The firms who do not discriminate make larger profits and will expand at the expense of discriminating firms. In this case, there should be an effect via dissemination of information among the firms about the actual productivity of different groups (Lundahl/Wadensjö 1982:2:48). Stiglitz, however, developed an argument that one can construct perfectly competitive models in which there are no competitive pressures for the elimination of discrimination. This is the case where the productivity of a worker is an increasing function of his wage. "This increased productivity may, as perhaps in some less developed countries, be due to nutrition, but in the more developed countries it is likely to be associated with psychological factors of the kind that Henry Ford recognized: 'Pay a worker more and he feels he ought to work harder.' There is, then, a wage w , which minimizes labor costs. Firms then hire laborers up to the point where the marginal productivity of labor equals the wage. The cost-minimizing wage may be at a level above that which assures full employment; although all those working have a positive marginal product, there is no competitive pressure to lower the wage. In this world, firms exercise their prejudices in selecting among applicants with impunity. The model may be more appropriate to discrimination in earlier stages of development, but it may have some applicability to individuals who are very unskilled. Their 'norms' concerning a reasonable wage are defined largely by the norms for the population as a whole and may not be very dependent on the distribution of wages for individuals performing comparable work requiring comparable skills to their own." (Stiglitz 1973:290).

(b) The statistical theory of discrimination assumes that employers have an idea about the productivity of different groups which is on the average correct, but that they do not know the productivity of each individual. Group affiliation, e.g. on sex grounds, serves then as an inexpensive aid when making employment decisions. Such selection criteria based on group affiliation lead to discrimination under the condition that the variation in productivity and the variation in the random term differ between groups. Groups with higher variation will be discriminated against as the following figure shows:

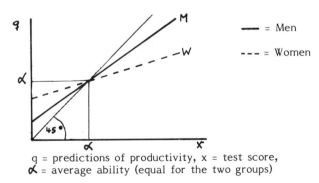

q = predictions of productivity, x = test score,
α = average ability (equal for the two groups)

Source: Aigner/Cain 1977:180.

Figure 4: Predictions of Productivity by Sex and Test Scores

Assuming that the tests are less reliable for women than for men (10), but average test values and productivity are equal for both groups, a steeper regression slope is obtained for the relation between test results and productivity for men than for women. Men with high test values should receive higher wages than women with the same values, while the opposite should be valid for low test scores. The average wage will be equal for both groups. In both groups, however, those with high productivity lose if the precision of the test is low, but this must be weighted against what those with low productivity in the group gain. Aigner and Cain, therefore, doubt whether it is appropriate to talk in this case about economic discrimination, as Phelps (1972) has done in introducing this concept. However, it might well be the case that firms set a minimum level of test values for hiring people, i.e. a level that women - due to pre-market discrimination - cannot meet as often as men; in this case, indirect discrimination of women would be the result.

Aigner and Cain suggest that it only makes sense to talk of economic discrimination if the information concerning the variance in the employee's expected productivity is not cost-free, and if the employers include these costs in their profit function. An individual woman might then be discriminated because of the higher uncertainty of the expected productivity, and because of employer's risk aversion: given an equal test value, the risk conscious employer will discount the expected return for female labor more than for male labor; the consequence of this will be unequal pay or employment discrimination.

Aigner and Cain argue, however, that wage differences which can be explained in this way should not be overestimated. If the wage differences are great, the economic incentives will be great to develop better test instruments and to organize the production in such a way that variation in the difference between actual and expected productivity becomes less important for the production result (Aigner/Cain 1977:182 f). If the labor market is characterized by wage competition, there is a further argument that limits the explanatory power of statistical discrimination for wage differentials: individuals affected by discrimination because they belong to a group with greater productivity uncertainties could undercut the ongoing wage rate; when they have got the job, they can demonstrate their skills and their productivity potentials and ask for wages which correspond to their marginal productivity.

However, statistical discrimination will be of much greater importance where wages are determined by institutional forces, and where individuals are not able or even not allowed to bid wages lower than regulated by laws or by bargaining processes between employers and trade unions. In addition, statistical discrimination will endure where labor markets are characterized by job competition instead of by wage competition (Thurow 1975:75 ff). In a job competition model, wage bidding is counterproductive because skills are acquired on the job and transferred from employee to employee. Employees will be reluctant to transfer their knowledge to potential wage competitors. Thus, it is in the interest of the employer to pay uniform wages for a job, to provide employment security for the qualified employees, and to reward seniority in order to insure the necessary knowledge transfer between newcomers and more senior employees in the firm.

At this point theories of statistical discrimination merge with segmentation theories of the labor market mentioned above. If skills are not sold on the market but produced on the job, capability of learning and long-term as well as permanent employment prospects become a decisive criterion   for   hiring people. Statistical discrimination, then, occurs when one group shows on the average lower capabilities of learning and lower degrees of life-time labor force participation or lower daily or weekly availability in the labor market (not that this assumption differs from that in figure 4). In such a situation, it is efficient for an employer to establish rigid "either/or" hiring rules and to exclude systematically individuals from that group which - on the average - has less of the desired characteristic than another group. An individual who belongs to such a group is not paid less. Rather, he or she is completely excluded from the job in question, and being excluded, there is no way that he or she can demonstrate the desired characteristic even if he or she as an individual fulfils completely the requirements.

This mechanism is especially relevant to sex discrimination. Consider the phenomenon of lifetime labor force participation or part-time supply of labor. For a wide variety of historical and cultural reasons, women have had, and continue to have, lower participation rates in the paid labor force than do men. Further, many more women then men have held, and are still holding, part-time jobs voluntarily (see the contribution by Brinkmann in this volume). An employer - and also many employees - faced with these differences in work probabilities will practice statistical discrimination even though a significant proportion of women will be in the fulltime paid labor force for their entire lifetimes. Ex ante, the employer cannot tell which women will be lifetime year-round full-time employees and which women will leave the labor force or become part-time employees. Indeed, many young women starting their job career cannot tell this either. To the extent that the employer and the employees provide on-the-job training, they will want to invest in those who are more likely to stay in the full-time labor force. If they provide training to women, they are less likely to be able to recoup their investment (Thurow 1975:170 ff) (11).

4.   EQUAL OPPORTUNITY POLICIES FOR WOMEN

The preceeding sections have made it clear that labor market discrimination is a complex phenomenon. Assuming that there is substantial amount of sex discrimination (12), and holding the normative view that discrimination should be reduced as much as possible, no single policy will serve as a catch-all remedy. Policy effects will vary depending on what kind of motives, behavior or attitudes are prevalent, depending on who is discriminating and who is discriminated (employers, employees, consumers), and depending on what kind of discrimination (pre-market, employment or wage discrimination) the policy is concerned with. There obviously is a need for a "policy mix", i.e. a set of complementary policy interventions weighted according to the dominance of discriminatory causes.

However, this is more easily said than done. As we have seen, there are mainly complementary but also competing theories of discrimination, and most theories have not been satisfactorily tested. We have also observed that "intention to discriminate" is in principle difficult to prove. There is, finally, much evidence that labor market discrimination is to a significant extent a consequence of pre-market discrimination. Policies concentrating narrowly on employment and especially on wage discrimination will be ineffective. It seems to be appropriate, therefore, to concentrate the policy debate more on the outcome and not so much on the motivational input of labor market processes.

I have, thus, consciously chosen the title "equal opportunity policies" for this section, i.e., I will not restrict the following discussion to anti-discrimination policies in a narrow sense, and I will concentrate more on effects than on intentions.

The objective of the following section is twofold: First to identify the principle policy options in order to broaden the usual narrow perspective which considers only one or just a few policies; second to consider their potential (or intended) effect on the different modes of discriminatory behavior or attitudes (see figure 4, p. 29).

In some cases I will also illustrate policy options with examples in selected countries in order to present some evidence of their effectiveness. The state of theory and empirical analysis, however, is not developed enough to undertake any serious evaluative analysis of these policy options. The following analysis, therefore, is intended to be an exploration of plausible relationships between policy strategies and causal patterns of the problems that policies are intended to solve. A further aim is to detect functional equivalents for individual strategies and promising combinations ("policy mixes") of different strategies.

4.1   Compensatory Public Finance or Public Employment as a Strategy for Equal Opportunity Policy

How can discrimination be eliminated - be it direct or indirect, intentional or unintentional? One strategy is not to attempt to change behavior or attitudes of individuals, but to compensate for discrimination (e.g. for pre-market discrimination) or to prevent discrimination (especially statistical discrimination) by generating equal chances via public finance or public employment.

The state (or another collective group) can finance <u>and</u> produce goods and services which the market does not provide. If the market provides jobs for some groups and not for others, the state can compensate by extending its services and creating additional jobs for the discriminated. The state can also provide training for women who have underinvested in human capital because of a false discounting of future returns, possibly due to low labor market commitment as a result of traditional role orientations. Another form of public provision of goods and services would be public or publically financed day care facilities. The public can also produce or distribute information by councelling and placement services, which are classical functions of public employment agencies.

The state can also compensate for discrimination by redistributing income in favor of the discriminated groups (idemnity payments, reparations) or by arranging the tax system in such a way that systematically disadvantaged groups are compensated, for example, by a negative income tax. Transfers in kind are another possible way to compensate for unequal chances, for example, the provision of in home services for young mothers (provision of household help, nurses, baby-sitters).

One should, however, bear in mind, that public finance and production (or respective employment) can also be a source of discrimination (see the contribution by MacLennan and Weitzel in this volume for a discussion of discrimination in unemployment insurance, public training schemes, and public job creation).

In as far as the state itself is a consumer and a buyer on the market, it can compensate for discrimination by favoring the products and services of discriminated groups. In combination with a ban on discrimination, the state can also make conditioned purchases, i.e. make public contracts dependent on non-discriminatory behavior or even on affirmative action by the firms receiving them. As experience in the United States shows, this strategy seems to be especially promising (see the contribution by Braun in this volume).

Based on the assumption that informational deficits and social customs play an important role in sex discrimination in the labor market, strategies for reducing uncertainties with respect to long-term female labor supply, and strategies for compensating the lower average productivity of women seem promising. Both "deficiencies" have much to do with the sexual division of homework and market work and womens basic attachment to homework. Within this context, a key issue is who is responsible for child rearing and how it is financed. Thus, I shall briefly discuss different forms of child care provisions and their potential impact on labor market discrimination.

(1) Two quite different questions are involved with respect to child care. One is whether child care in any form should be subsidized by taxpayers. According to one view, parents choose to have children and derive pleasure and benefits from them. Therefore, they should make their decision to have a child based on their own evaluation of the costs and benefits. Other taxpayers who do not benefit should not be required to assist them. The opposing view stresses that child care largely falls on women and remains an obstacle to their ability to pursue work opportunities outside the home. As long as society values children, a subsidy is appropriate to help overcome this financial obstacle to women's employment. A third view is that many working women with small children are overloaded, and that the double role of labor market work (mostly for financial reasons) and child care is detrimental to the children; thus, child care should be subsidized to some extent by child care allowances (in Germany: "Erziehungsgeld") which allow working women to withdraw from the labor market.

It is evident that the first view is not concerned about labor market discrimination. The third view's underlying philosophy is also not motivated by any desire to improve the labor market chances of women; its implementation would rather stabilize sex role stereotypes and reduce the labor market participation of women (13).

(2) With respect to the second viewpoint, the goal of improving the labor market chances of women and at the same time respecting the needs of small or ill children for intensive care, the next question is what form a government subsidy for child care should take. A government might provide low or no-cost day care centers; in this case the good or service "child care" would be publicly produced as well as publicly financed. Proponents of this option argue that such centers are needed - apart for opening employment opportunities - to ensure quality child care and to support redistributional objectives by giving low income families preference in access to public day care facilities. This form of public day care provision is also favored for developmental reasons, i.e. to compensate for the negative consequences of single child families on the socio-psychological development of children.

283

Alternatively, a voucher or tax credit can be provided to parents who then choose their own form of care. Proponents of vouchers argue that parents know what is best for their children and should be able to choose the form of day care they prefer (O'Neill/Braun 1982:134). Moreover, vouchers can readily be provided in varying amounts, whereas day care centers usually imply a large average expenditure per child.

A third alternative is to compensate only to some extent for the loss of income during parental leaves for the sake of child care, and guarantee a right to return to the former work place. Different models for the implementation of this alternative can be conceived. With respect to the potential anti-discriminatory impact, two criteria are important: Whether the child care sabbatical can voluntarily be chosen by either parents (as for example in Sweden) or only by the mother (as it is the case in the Federal Republic of Germany), and the extent to which the costs are "socialized" or to be borne by the employer. It is evident that statistical discrimination will be reinforced to the extent that individual employers have to bear the costs, and when child care sabbaticals are subsidized only for women. Some empirical illustrations are given in the following paragraph.

(3) The provision of public day care is not well documented. However, Table 1 shows some interesting patterns:

Table 1

Percentage of children in public day care centers according to age groups

	0 - 2		3 - 6		7 - 12	
	1965	1979	1965	1979	1965	1979
FRG	0.6	1.6	33.2[*]	77.8[*]	1.2	2.1
SWE	n.a.	n.a.	9.6[**]	27.2[a]	n.a.	13.0
UK	n.a.	n.a.	n.a.	4.0[b]	n.a.	n.a.
USA	n.a.	5.0	n.a.	20.0[c]	n.a.	4.0[d]

a) age group 0-6; including 10.9 % places with publicly subsidized day-care mothers (i.e., parents pay the same fee as at the day-care center); 1981 the figure was 33.9.

b) age-group 0-5.

c) age group 2-5.

d) age group 6-11.

[*] including part-time places!
[**] 1971

n.a. = not available.

FRG: Weitzel 1982, pp. 59-61; data refer only to Kindergarten or Hort-Places (table 38, Appendix); Statistisches Jahrbuch - own calculations.

SWE: Gustafsson/Jacobsson 1983, table 11, Appendix.

UK : Elliott et al. 1982: 145 (2 % were in workplace nurseries, 18 % in private day nurseries, 23 % in local authority day nurseries, 57 % with childminders). Figures refer to full-time day care places.

USA: O'Neill/Braun 1982 : 133.   284

First, as far as data are available, there seems to be an increasing tendency to provide child care in public day care centers. The fiscal crisis of the state, however, will probably slow down this process: In 1976, for example, the Swedish parliament adopted a program to increase the number of places by 100,000; since the budget deficit soared, it has not been possible to implement this goal, and the increase in the number of day-care places has slowed considerably.

Germany provides the most public day care for the age group 3-6. Almost 80 per cent of children in this age group have places in a Kindergarten (1979), whereas in the United Kingdom there are only few public day care places available; Sweden and the United States lie in the middle. Although the German figures seem to be somewhat inflated (no distinction between part-time and full-time places), the difference remains remarkable. This pattern should mean - all other things being equal - that German mothers receive more support from child care "service" than do mothers in other countries included in this study. Is this reflected in differences in employment participation?

We must answer such questions in order to evaluate the impact of policy strategies. One possibility would be a systematic comparison across countries. Unfortunately, the available data do not allow this. The following tables present some evidence by comparing the labor force participation rates of mothers with children in different countries over time.

Table 2
Mothers of children under 16 in the labor force
(independent of family status)

| | 1960 - 65 | | | | 1974-80 | | | |
	< 3	3-6	< 6	7-16	< 3	3-6	< 6	7-16
FRG	29.7^a	n.a.	31.3^a	n.a.	31.5^b	n.a.	34.0^b 36.4^g	n.a.
SWE	n.a.	n.a.	38.0^c	57.7^h	n.a.	n.a.	75.4^d	85.2^d
UK	n.a.	n.a.	n.a.	n.a.	21.5^e	45.9^e	n.a.	n.a.
USA	n.a.	n.a.	n.a.	n.a.	54.2^f	57.5^f	55.5^f	n.a.

a) 1961   b) 1976   c) 1963, under 7   d) 1980, under 7   e) 1974
f) 1978   g) 1981   h) 1965   n.a. = not available

FRG: Deutscher Bundestag, 8. Wahlperiode: Drucksache 8/3121, Tab. 4, p. 25; Statistisches Jahrbuch 1982.

SWE: Jonung 1982: Tab. 2, p. 304; AKU årsmedeltal 1980.

UK : Elliott et al. 1982, Tab. 1.6, p. 27.

USA: O'Neill/Braun 1982, Tab. 10, p. 29.

It is interesting to note that in Sweden mothers of children below 7 have nowadays a labor force participation rate which is double that in Germany (table 2) although the availability of public day care centers is much less than in Germany (table 1). In addition, the labor force participation of German mothers increased only slightly despite the rapid increase in the number of Kindergarten-places after the Kindergarten-Law of 1970, whereas the labor force participation rate of Swedish women has doubled since the early sixties. How can this be explained?

One explanation is that the figures for the provision of child care in table 1 do not accurately reflect actual relief for parents with small children. As noted above, the German figures are exaggerated in the sense that a large (but un-known) part of German kindergardens are providing only part-time places. The Swedish data, on the other hand, refer only to full-time places. In addition, Sweden provides pre-school for all six-year-olds and for about 50 per cent of five-year-olds. This, however, can probably explain only part of the difference. Another explanation can be found in the different methods of financing pro-tective provisions for mothers and parental leaves for child rearing or the care of sick children as described in the following section.

(4) The Swedish model relies much more on a strategy of the collective organization of the finance of child care while the German model relies more on the compensatory public provision of child care (this holds true for children below 6). In other words: More child care is provided privately in Sweden than in Germany, but it is to a large extent publicly financed. In addition, the Swedish model is combined with strong employment protection during child care (see also section 4.2). What does the model look like?

In Sweden, every parent who is member of the health insurance system (which means all parents) has the right to child care benefits. The concept of parents is quite widely defined (Gladh/Gustafsson 1982:72). There are three different kinds of child care benefits:

     - child care benefits in connection with the birth of a child,

     - special child care benefits, and

     - child care benefits for casual care of a child.

The Childcare benefit at birth resembles motherhood benefits in other countries with one important exception (at least with respect to Germany): The benefit is the same as sick pay benefits (with a minimum of 32 Swedish Kronors (SKr) per day), which means almost full wage compensation. In Germany, the health insurance contribution is a flat rate contribution of 750,-- DM per month, whereas the employer has to pay the difference between this amount and the wage rate the women received before motherhood. This works as a disincentive to hire young women or as an incentive to dismiss young women first. This may have strong repercussions for the long-term employment prospects of those women, and it has been, therefore, recommended that maternity benefits be financed out of a collective fund into which all employ-ers would have to pay contributions (Pfarr 1981:86).

There is one interesting indication which might reflect this important differ-ence. Table 3 shows unemployment rates for women in the four countries. Apart from Britain which is a special case (see the contribution by Björklund

Table 3
Unemployment rates of women according to age groups

	Total*		20 - 24		25 - 34		35 - 44	
	1975	1980	1975	1980	1975	1980	1975	1980
FRG	4.8	3.7	6.6	6.1	6.9	6.4	4.9	3.7
SWE	1.6	2.3	3.5	3.9	1.8	2.2	1.1	1.4
UK	4.5	7.7	5.2*	9.4*	1.7	5.1	2.7	2.4
USA	8.5	7.1	n.a.	n.a.	9.1	7.2	6.9	5.3

*) Men and women together; n.a. = not available

FRG: Schmid 1982:43

SWE: Schmid 1982:43; AKU årsmedeltal 1980.

UK : Department of Employment Gazette

USA: Employment and Training Report, 1981:166.

and MacLennan/Weitzel in this volume), the pattern of female unemployment by age compared to total unemployment is almost the same, with one important exception: The German unemployment rate for women in the age group of 25 to 34 is double the average unemployment rate, whereas for Sweden and the United States the unemployment rate for this age group equals the average unemployment rate. Motherhood is most frequent to this age group, and the difference between Sweden and Germany might be explained by the different regulations for the financing of maternity benefits mentioned above. In the USA, there is also no such similar disincentive to hire women of this age group.

Sweden is also unique with respect to two other forms of child care benefits: the special child care benefit which pays either the father or the mother wage compensation during six additional months of leave time that can be taken at any time up until the child is 8 years old. Employment is protected during that time, and there are flexible leave options (full-time, part-time, quarter-time). During the first three months this benefit is the same as the sick pay benefit, and during the last three months the benefit is a flat rate of 37 SKr per day.

The child care benefit for occasional care can be received during a maximum of 60 days per year and child until the child is 12 years old in the following special cases: (a) the child is ill or has contagious disease, (b) the ordinary caretaker of the child is ill or has a contagious disease, (c) for visiting health institutions, and (d) 10 days for the father at the birth of a child (Gladh/Gustafsson 1982:72 ff).

All three forms of child care benefits together reduce substantially for both, employers and employees, the risks and uncertainties connected with mother-hood that we found to be one of the most important reason for statistical or indirect discrimination against women. In addition, because some forms of parental leave in Sweden require a minimum record of employment before parenthood, there is even an incentive for young women first to start an employment career and then to plan for a family.

If the financial and social costs of parenthood are borne more by society rather than by individuals, and if the entitlement to those parental rights is closely linked with a former employment career, a change in family planning is to be expected: Couples will postpone their wish to have children until they are settled in the labor market. An indicator for such a change would be an average increase in the age of mothers at the birth of their first child, and according to the comparison of parental provisions above, this change would be expected to be most pronounced in Sweden.

The figures in table 5 confirm this expectation: Since 1965 the birth rate decreased in all countries considered in this study, most drastically in Germany and in the United States. What is interesting within the context of our argument, however, is the change in birth rates by age groups in relation to the total birth rate which is shown in the second part of the table. Whereas the relative birth rate in the youngest age group did not change much in Germany, United Kingdom, and even increased in the United States, it decreased drastically in Sweden relatively to the total birth rate. Correspondingly, the highest increase in the relative birth rate of the age group 30-34 can be found in Sweden, and Sweden also shows the lowest decrease in the relative birth rates for the 35-39 age group (see next page).

(5) A final option is to compensate for employment discrimination in the private sector by enlarging the employment possibilities for women in the public sector. Whether this option has been taken consciously or not, table 4 clearly shows that women have substantially increased their share of public employment in all four countries considered during the last 15 years, and Sweden shows the highest proportion.

Table 4
Female share of Public Sector Employment in Selected Countries
- Percentages -

	1965	1970	1975	1977	1981
FRG	24.4[a]	26.7[b]	38.9[c]	38.5	n.a.
SWE	52.0	57.9	62.1	63.9	66.6
UK	n.a.	48.8[d]	53.4	54.3	n.a.
USA	40.9	45.4	47.5	49.5	n.a.

a) 1963, b) 1969, c) 1974, d) 1971; n.a. = not available

FRG: Wirtschaft und Statistik 7/81, 5/75, my calculations
SWE: AKU årsmedeltal; Gustafsson/Jacobsson 1983, table 12, Appendix.
UK : OECD 1982, table 7, p. 30.
USA: dito

Live births per thousand women by age of the mother;
below: total birth rate = 100

		15-19	20-24	25-29	30-34	35-39	40-44	Total Birth Rate
FRG	1964	31.9	143.3	163.7	105.1	49.9	14.9	86.8
	1980	15.3	81.1	106.6	61.5	20.2	3.9	46.7
SWE	1965	48.6	140.9	154.0	89.3	39.3	9.9	80.7
	1980	15.8	95.6	124.2	70.7	24.9	4.3	56.0
UK[+]	1965	45.4	179.5	180.5	102.6	48.1	12.6	92.1
	1980	30.9	114.1	135.8	71.3	22.6	4.4	65.0
USA	1965	70.4	196.8	162.5	95.0	46.4	12.8	96.6
	1979	53.4	115.7	115.6	61.8	19.4	3.9	62.0
FRG	1964	36.8	165.1	188.6	121.1	57.5	17.2	100.0
	1980	32.8	173.7	228.3	131.7	43.3	8.4	100.0
SWE	1965	60.2	174.6	190.8	110.7	48.7	12.3	100.0
	1980	28.2	170.7	221.8	126.3	44.5	7.7	100.0
UK[+]	1965	49.3	194.9	196.0	111.4	52.2	13.7	100.0
	1980	47.5	175.5	208.9	109.7	34.8	6.8	100.0
USA	1965	72.9	203.7	168.2	98.3	48.0	13.3	100.0
	1979	86.1	186.6	186.5	99.7	31.3	6.3	100.0

+) Includes only England and Wales

FRG: Statistical Yearbook 1982, own calculation (unweighted average of yearly cohorts)

SWE: Gustafsson/Jacobsson 1983, Table 9; own calculation of total birth rate

UK : Office of Population Censuses and Surveys, Series FM1 no. 6, Parent's age, Table 3.1 (a)

USA: O'Neill/Braun 1982, Table 6, p. 17; own calculation of total birth rate; for 1965: Statistical Abstract of the U.S., Ed. 1972, Table 65, p. 51.

4.2   Regulation as a Strategy for Equal Opportunity Policy

Whereas public finance or employment normally have only an indirect impact on employment discrimination in private spheres, regulation aims at directly changing discriminatory behavior or attitudes. Regulation is probably the most common form of intervention by collective organisations, especially the state. Examples of equal opportunity regulation are anti-discrimination laws, anti-trust laws, minimum wages or wage equalization laws (14), quotas, affirmative action programs, special protective clauses such as dismissal protection for pregnant women. Such norms are often quite general so that they require specification by administrative action or by court in order to be effective.

Regulations can directly specify desired behavior through requirements, e.g. quotas or making public contracts with private firms dependent on the fulfilment of equal opportunity standards; they can prohibit certain acts, e.g. through bans on discrimination; and they can set general objectives, e.g. increase the share of women in qualified positions by a certain percentage in a certain period without, however, specifying how to reach such goals. It is evident that the potential effects of regulation depend on many factors: its content, form, and specificness; the degree of consensus; its period of validity. This makes it difficult to formulate general statements about potential effects on discriminatory behavior or attitudes. The potential effects of anti-trust regulations are briefly considered (1); the hotly discussed issue of quotas is examined more carefully (2); and finally some ideas for affirmative actions are mentioned (3).

(1) According to the theory of "taste for discrimination" (Becker), countervailing measures against discrimination should be aimed at improving the operation of markets - both product or capital and labor markets - in order to accelerate the effects of competitive forces. Thus, anti-trust regulation would be the policy conclusion of this conception of discrimination. This recommendation also applies where prejudices or incorrect information rather than preferences are the cause of discrimination. Increased competition raises the cost of being prejudiced. An equilibrium with discrimination based on social custom, however, will not disappear simply by increasing competition in the different markets; nor will statistical discrimination, except in cases where the costs of mistakes due to statistical discrimination are high; in the latter case, relative costs increase with competition (Aigner/Cain 1977; Lundahl/Wadensjö 1982).

(2) If discrimination is due to prejudice or incorrect information about a particular group, enforcing contact by quotas might improve the information of employers and thereby reduce discrimination. If, however, discrimination is due to strong preferences - i.e., employers pay higher wages to avoid contact -, open discrimination might disappear as a result of quotas but preferences will continue to exist because Becker's competitive market forces will no longer be effective, and discrimination might develop hidden and subtle forms. There is especially the danger that employee discrimination will increase because of increasing prejudice: Any female employee will be suspected of having been hired because of the quota or affirmative action clause and not for her qualifications or performance. This might produce much anguish and great bitterness both among the preferred and the disadvantaged workers and undermine good work relations in the firm ("Betriebsfrieden"); furthermore, bureaucratically enforced quotas might make established skilled workers reluctant to   transfer

their job specific knowledge to the preferred group.

If quotas are used to compensate for pre-market discrimination, they might lead to a less satisfactory resource allocation by imposing additional costs on the employer. The group formally benefiting could again end up with negative consequences as a result of stigmatizing effects (Sowell 1976; Lundahl/Wadensjö 1982). The results can even be worse when employers have the possibility of influencing the size of the discriminated group, e.g. counting more people as "handicapped" than would have been the case without quota rules. With respect to sex discrimination, employers might use the counter-strategy of increasing the female labor force in unskilled jobs, thus formally fulfilling the quota but of resulting in segregation within the firm. The response of state regulation might well be a differentiation of quotas by occupation or status, and this again might lead to another counter-strategy of increasing occupational and status differentiation. Thus, quota regulation probably will end up in a bureaucratic spiral (Sowell 1976; Schmitt Glaeser 1982).

Quota regulation is, therefore, a doubtful equal opportunity strategy for two reasons: It conflicts with other norms that have high priority (e.g. freedom of contract, idividual justice), and its efficiency is highly questionable because of negative side effects or counter-strategies. This does not mean, however, that quota regulation should in every case be avoided. There are situations where quotas can be effective:

(a) Quota rules might be more effective if discrimination is due purely to the existence of social customs which are maintained by different forms of social or economic sanctions. In this case the existence of quotas provides support for those groups who wish to break with discrimination but have not done so because of the risk of losing social reputation or having economic sanctions imposed against them (Masters 1975:158 f.).

(b) Quota rules might be necessary where the long-term damages due to dis-crimination are very high. In such cases, the infringement of individual free-dom or, in some cases, individual injustice caused by the enforcement of quotas might be justified from the point of view of social policy. Thus, one can imagine that the actual disadvantages suffered by women in the area of primary vocational training might be compensated for - at least for some time - by quota regulation in that area (Schmitt Glaeser 1982, Pfarr 1981).

(c) Quota regulation, finally, might be effective at critical decision points in organizations: The equal representation of women in important decision boards, e.g. in works councils, in top level party committees or in governmental cabinets (15) might in the long run have more impact for the realization of equal opportunity for women than any other mandatory quota regulations. However, mandatory quotas are hardly feasable in this area.

(3) The use of indicative rather than mandatory quotas in affirmative action programs seems to be more promising. Several forms can be imagined: (a) re-quiring affirmative action programs for women as a condition for government contracts with private firms; (b) setting sex specific goals in governmental training and job creation programs; (c) targeting wage cost subsidies in such a way that women will be favored, e.g. by subsidizing only low wage earners; (d) developing "gentlement's agreements" between employment agencies and firms in which firms promise to set affirmative action goals in favor of women, and

employment agencies promise to support the firm if any problems arise.

There has been considerable experience with strategies (a), (b), and (c), especially in the United States (see contribution by Braun in this volume), whereas strategy (d) - to my knowledge - has only be applied in Sweden with respect to handicapped persons.

4.3 Financial Incentives or Disincentives as Strategy for Equal Opportunity Policy

Attitudes or behavior might also be changed by financial incentives or disincentives. Possible instruments are wage cost subsidies, investment allowances, tax increases or decreases either to reward non-discrimination or affirmative action, to punish discrimination, or to stimulate change in discriminatory social customs. A subtle form of negative incentive would be the threat to take action in the future if a desired behavior is not forthcoming, e.g. a special tax on employers who are reluctant to hire young women. Such revenues, then, could be used for positive incentives for employers to hire this group of employees.

Positive incentives have the great advantage of flexibility: they can be differentiated according to regions, industries, size of firm, and income; they can be progressive or degressive, a percentage of income, of tax or a flat rate; and they can be introduced for any time period. Positive incentives, however, also have great disadvantages: they cost money, and they can easily be avoided since compliance is voluntary; they can also be abused by taking the incentive payments without any change in actual behavior. Negative incentives have the great advantage that they cannot be easily evaded, except where there are loopholes in the law or in administrative controls (Lange 1982); as a matter of fact, however, such loopholes are often more the rule than the exception, and there is no evidence that negative incentives are in principle more effective than positive incentives.

In the case of strong preferences among the majority of firms to discriminate, incentives might stimulate or support non-discriminating firms to hire even more of the discriminated group thus accelerating the diminuition of discrimination by competitive forces; corresponding disincentives may have the same effect. The same is also true where social customs are supported by economic sanctions against non-discriminating actors; these sanctions might be compensated for by incentives, whereas disincentives could - at least in principle - break discrimination based on social customs.

Incentives to increase labor mobility could lead to a reduction of discrimination if the cause of discrimination is monopsony in the labor market: The greater the opportunity for mobility, the greater the extent to which wages for the individual firm are determined by competitive market forces. Prejudices or incorrect information might be reduced by incentives to hire more of the discriminated group, thus providing an opportunity for contact which should correct existing prejudices.

Since we have found that social customs with respect to the division between homework and market work and statistical discrimination are the most important factors in sex discrimination in the labor market, I shall consider shortly two policy options related to these types of discrimination: financial incentives for employers to create more part-time jobs (1), and the tax system as an incentive or disincentive to change traditional sex roles (2).

(1) Because of child care and other homework obligations, women are frequently only available to part-time work in the labor market. As we know, potential supply is much greater than demand, which has recently led some countries to introduce financial incentives to employers to create more part-time jobs, sometimes both for men and women. I will briefly summarize the experiences of some experimental programs in Germany (for more details see Weitzel/Hoff 1982).

In some states (Länder) within the Federal Republic of Germany lump-sum payments were given to employers who created additional part-time jobs for unemployed women (in some cases also for men). Where men were included in the target group, participation by men was very low. The subsidy amounted to approximately 20 to 30 per cent of the annual average wage.

None of the experimental programs was extended because the results were not satisfactory. In one case, in which only qualified jobs were eligible for subsidies, participation was ridiculously low. In the other cases, where the only condition was to create additional part-time jobs, participation was only limited by the total amount of money available. However, there was evidence that deadweights or windfall profits were high, i.e., employers would have created these jobs anyhow, and there was no evidence that non-traditional part-time jobs had been created.

Among the reasons for the failure of these experimental programs, one deserves mention here because it reflects a general condition for the effectiveness of such programs. A short-term financial incentive is not likely to change behavior because of the costs of information and decisions involved in such changes. Short-term incentive programs assume that these costs are zero. This might be the case where incentives merely reinforce existing trends (e.g. interest subsidies for firms which see good market prospects), but this is not the case where a substantial change in traditional behavior is sought. In such cases, employers would need a long learning period in order to discover their true interests and the long-term effects which the desired changes entail. Thus, the incentives should be in effect for a long period, and they should be complemented by persuasive strategies and by administrative promotion, e.g. informational campaigns, and personal contacts with firms (Scharpf 1983). On the other hand, however, a long-term incentive could be extremely costly, especially since with time employers also learn how to misuse such a scheme. This trade-off is not easy to control.

(2) Any system of taxation is not only a means of providing government revenue, but also an instrument for shaping society through the redistribution of income. Since a tax is essentially a reduction in the wage, it is thought that changes in tax rates work as incentives or disincentives to enter the labor market, at least to the extent that gainful work is governed by income differentials. A large econometric literatur has found almost unanimously that the labor supply of married women is especially sensitive to wage changes, while men's labor supply response is less elastic (O'Neill/Braun 1982:125 f). Thus, differences in tax structure can be expected to make a difference in the labor force participation of married women and, potentially, also of men.

Tables 6 and 7 compare the labor force participation in the four selected countries for married women and the percentage of part-time work for men and women. Table 6 shows clearly that the labor force participation of married women is substantially higher in Sweden than in any of the other three countries. Even more interesting is the fact that the increase in labor force participation in Sweden from 1970 to 1980 was higher despite the fact that the participation rates in Sweden were already much higher than in the other countries.

One possible and plausible explanation for this latter difference could be the introduction of the obligatory individual income tax in Sweden in 1971 (Gladh/Gustafsson 1982), whereas in all three other countries the principle of aggregation or income splitting is still in effect. "Income splitting" means that a married couple can file a joint return with the combined income of both partners split in half and taxes paid on each half regardless of who earned what. Because the tax system is progressive - taxing larger incomes at a higher rate - income splitting represents a great tax savings for couples in which one spouse earns all or most of the taxable income. This is an incentive for wives to pursue homemaking: If she did choose to work for pay, her first income unit (dollar, mark, pound) earned would be taxed at the same marginal rate as the last income unit earned by her husband. In Britain, however, this disincentive is reduced by the Wife's Earned Income Allowance" (Elliott et al. 1982:197) which might explain the relative high proportion of female part-time workers in Britain (see table 7) the bulk of which belongs to he lowest income bracket. The likely effect of this disincentive has also been reduced recently in the United States in granting a deduction to the "second earner" of 5 per cent of the first $ 30,000 of earnings in 1982 and 10 per cent in 1983 (O'Neill/Braun 1982:126). But the disincentive still exists, especially in Germany where there is only a small tax exemption for a wife's earned income.

A tax system that makes it profitable for spouses to divide home and market work between them in an equitable way would be a preferable system from the point of view of equality between men and women. Not only would it give the women an income of her own in the present but it would also foster a buildup in her human capital endowments making her more competitive in the labor market in the future. Furthermore, it gives her a pension of her own that can support her in old age at a standard of living to which she is accustomed even in the event of divorce. The present Swedish tax system combines a high marginal tax with separate taxation of income. In general it will be more profitable for the family income if the spouse who works the smallest number of hours in the labor market increases his/her market work (Gladh/Gustafsson 1982:63) (16), and there is even an incentive for the high earning man to decrease his market work in favor of his wife. Thus, it is to be expected, that part-time work of men will increase in reaction to the introduction of individual taxation (in combination with a very progressive tax system which is the case in Sweden). Table 7 seems to confirm this expectation: Whereas part-time work of men even decreased in Germany and United Kingdom (at a very low level) from 1973 to 1979 and only increased marginally in United States, part-time work has risen strongly in Sweden. (17) The income tax structure, therefore, seems to have a considerable impact on equal employment opportunities, and it would be worthwile to concentrate policy as well as research on this point.

Table 6
Labor Force Participation Rates of Married Women by Age Groups

	25 - 34		35 - 44		45 - 54	
	1970	1980	1970	1980	1970	1980
FRG	41.7[a]	53.3[a]	41.7[a]	50.8[a]	39.6[a]	44.5[a]
SWE	55.1	78.1	64.9	84.3	62.2	83.7
UK	38.4[b]	51.5[c]	54.5[b]	67.1[c]	57.0[b]	65.6[c]
USA	39.3	59.3	47.2	62.5	49.5	55.7

a) averages of the age groups 25-29/30-34; 35-39/40-44; 45-49/50-54.
b) 1971; c) 1979.
FRG: Schmid 1982, p. 41.
SWE: AKU årsmedeltal.
USA: O'Neill/Braun 1982, p. 4.
UK : Elliott et al. 1982, p. 23.

Table 7
Part-time Employment of Men and Women in Percent
(less than 35 hours per week)

	Men		Women	
	1970	1979	1970	1979
FRG	1.0[a]	0.9	20.0	26.2
SWE	4.0	7.0[b]	39.0	46.0[b]
UK	1.8[a]	1.3	38.3	37.7
USA	10.2	11.5[b]	27.9	28.6[b]
	(7.0)	(8.3)	(25.1)	(25.4)

a) 1973
b) 1980

FRG, UK: arbeit und beruf 5/1981
USA   : O'Neill/Braun 1982, Table 14, p. 35

(The figures for United States are somehow inflated by the high rate
of part-time work of teenagers 16-18 years old; figures in brackets show
the part-time rate for persons 20 years and over; an additional "inflation
effect" results from including the group 65 and over).

SWE   : Internationale Chronik zur Arbeitsmarktpolitik, No. 6
          (IIM/LMP - Science Center Berlin), Oct. 1981, p. 7.

Institutional Regulation and Persuasion as Strategies
       for Equal Opportunity Policy

A much neglected policy option is the indirect influence on discriminatory behavior and attitudes of changes in the institutional framework for decision-making with respect to hiring, pay, promotion or job protection. This policy can take different forms; the common feature, however, is the increase in the decision-making power of disadvantaged groups or at least giving them the opportunity to articulate and to present their interest. This strategy is especially important where the discriminated group, either due to its size or its heterogenous interests, is less capable of organizing its own interest than is a small and homogenous interest group (Olson 1971). This is certainly the case for women, with the possible exception of the United States where women's liberation groups gained some strength, which may explain the relative success of equal opportunity policy in that country (Janssen-Jurreit 1979:268 ff).

Examples of "institutional regulation" are special commissions or committees for anti-discrimination policy at different decision levels (firms, traditional interest organizations, governmental agencies), or "women's commissioners" (ombuds (18), or "affirmative action groups").

The potential effect of this policy option can hardly be estimated in advance because it depends much on the real shift in power (especially the capacity of these institutions to enforce their decisions), on the personalities representing the interests of women, and on the way such institutions use or are able to use the complementary policies mentioned above. Some examples and experiences are reported in the contributions by Braun, Gustafsson, Jackson, and Pfarr in this volume.

Last but not least, cognitive or moral suasion are further policy options to influence discriminatory attitudes and behavior. It is obvious that this strategy mostly affects discrimination based on social customs and discrimination due to informational imperfections or prejudices. Examples are information campaigns for the cause of women's rights, moral rewards for non-discriminatory firms or for firms undertaking affirmative action programs, widespread publicity to either spectacular cases of discrimination or spectacular cases of non-discriminatory behavior or affirmative actions.

5.   SUMMARY AND CONCLUSIONS

On a very general level, discrimination can be defined as an unjustified mechanism of selection: individuals are identified because they belong to a group with outstanding characteristics (sex, race, religion, nationality) and are denied certain rights based on law or merits. For the discriminated individual, it does not matter whether this exclusion is intentional or not. What matters are the consequences, for example, long-lasting and group specific inequalities in the labor market.

Today, the change in meaning of discrimination from a concept of "prejudiced treatment" to a concept of "unequal treatment" or "adverse impact" (indirect discrimination) is generally recognised. However, this did not help to clarify the issue. On the contrary, this led to even greater disagreement. On the one hand, there is a tendency to see discriminatory forces at work behind each group specific difference, on the other hand there is also a tendency to deny the existence of discrimination and to justify group-specific differences by market forces or by the tastes of the disadvantaged individuals themselves. Both tendencies are especially evident with respect to the labor market disadvantages of women.

Given this situation, it is necessary to clearly define discrimination, to distinguish of different types of discrimination, and to identify the causes of discrimination. However, such a definition inevitably implies a value judgement as to which selection mechanism is justified or not. In a society in which the fundamental division of labor between homework and market work and the respective role assignments of women and men are generally accepted, preferential treatment of men in allocating market jobs cannot be called "labor market discrimination" as long as market efficiency criteria are not violated. It was only consequent, therefore, that earlier theories restricted the concept of discrimination to selection mechanisms unjustified in terms of efficient market allocation (e.g. Becker). The situation becomes different, however, when we assume a fundamental change in the value system toward the view that women and men should share responsibilities for homework and market work equally, or each individual should at least be able to freely choose between them and enjoy equal opportunity. In such a value system, preferential treatment of men in allocating market jobs is clearly discrimination against women. This value judgement is the normative foundation of this study.

Three types of labor market discrimination have been identified: Pre-market discrimination when women have less access to productivity augmenting opportunities such as schooling, accumulation of experiences through continuous work or training, and regional mobility; employment discrimination when women occupy less favourable jobs than do men or when they receive no job at all for a given set of qualifications; wage discrimination when women receive lower pay then men for the same job. Equal opportunity policy requires different strategies to deal with each type of discrimination.

Anti-discrimination policies are ultimately aimed at changing the behavior of individuals who act within the constraints of organizations. Thus a clear identification of the discriminating as well as the discriminated persons and the rationale of their behavior is essential. Theories of discrimination have been collected and evaluated, therefore, according to the type of actors, their motivation and the mode of discrimination (see the summarizing figure 3). Not all theories are equally relevant to sex discrimination in the labor market. The most influential theory of discrimination in economics, the theory of "taste for discrimination" developed by Gary Becker, has little explanatory power for sex discrimination. More important but controversial in their empirical relevance are theories of monopsony based upon the assumption of the lower supply elasticity of women relative to men. The most promising approaches to explain sex discrimination in the labor market are theories based on the motivational force of social customs and on pecuniary benefits with respect both to employers and employees, and theories based on the behavioral assumptions of traditional role orientation and on reducing uncertainties due to informational imperfections.

Whereas social customs and traditional role orientation explain in particular pre-market discrimination, pecuniary benefits or efficiency considerations and the aim of reducing uncertainties probably play a larger role in explaining employment discrimination against women; within the latter context, statistical discrimination probably is most important in explaining persisting sex discrimination in the labor market. The theory of statistical discrimination assumes that employers have an idea about the productivity potential of different groups which is on the average correct, but that they do not know the productivity potential of each individual. Group affiliation serves then as an inexpensive aid in making employment decisions. Women as a group are assumed to have lower productivity than men because of lower labor market commitment, and this implies a systematic disadvantage for each individual woman when applying for a job. Especially for higher qualified jobs, employers tend to establish rigid "either/or" hiring rules, that is to exclude women almost totally from such positions. And because these very often are jobs in which an individual's productivity can only be demonstrated on the job or in which productivity is accumulated during a long learning process, the "either/or" hiring rule tends to be self-confirming, and a vicious circle for the excluded group is created.

Despite the well known fact that women's earnings is substantially lower, only about two thirds of the average earnings of men, this differential is more a consequence of pre-market and employment discrimination than of wage discrimination. Equal employment policies, therefore, seem to be more promising than equal pay policies as strategy to tackle the problem of sex specific labor market discrimination. Even where wage discrimination occurs, equal pay policies or bans on wage discrimination can easily be evaded by employers by resorting to employment discrimination. Pre-market discrimination, on the other hand, is an extremely complex phenomenon rooted in cultural traditions and institutions with a long history. It has been argued that indirect strategies - such as changes in the tax or social security system - will be more effective in the long run than direct efforts to change tastes and attitudes.

Four principal forms of policy interventions to reduce labor market discrimination have been identified and evaluated: First, the state itself can play a compensatory role through public finance or public employment; second, the state may try to directly influence the behavior of market actors through bans on discrimination or through quota rules; third, the state can provide incentives in order to influence individual behavior or attitudes indirectly, and fourth, the state can change the institutional framework of decision-making with respect to hiring, pay, promotion or job protection:

(1) Based on the assumption that employment discrimination against women has two main causes - lower average productivity and informational uncertainties with respect to long-term female labor supply -, strategies which focus on these problems seem to be most promising. Both "deficiencies" have a common reason: the sexual division of labor between homework and market work. In this context, a key issue is who is responsible for child rearing and how is it financed. It has been found that the Swedish form of providing child care seems to be the most appropriate. It provides relatively long and especially flexible forms of parental leave, and the financial burden does not have to be borne by individual employers and not as much by individual parents as in other countries (for the latter point see Kamerman/Kahn 1982). Because the entitlement to child care provisions is related to prior market work, there is an incentive for women to start an employment career before establishing a family. Due to relatively generous social benefits single parents - most of which are women - are also better-off than in other countries, and no other country provides as many public employment opportunities for women as Sweden. Compensating the lower average productivity of women by publicly

financed training measures, especially for women reentering the labor market, is also an important element of equal opportunity policy (see MacLennan/Weitzel in this volume).

(2) Bans on discrimination and quota rules are the most common measures to directly influence discriminatory behavior. Bans on discrimination require an appropriate legal and administrative framework in order to ensure fair and effective procedures for discriminated individuals. Important features of such a framework are the establishments of institutions to support individual law suits or to initiate legal actions in their own right. Such institutions need adequate resources and effective sanctions. In this respect, most can be learned from the experiences in the United States. The conclusions with respect to quota regulation, however, are rather sceptical. The negative side effects (stigmatization, the danger of a bureaucratic spiral), the incompatibility with principles of equality and liberty, and the likely ineffectiveness due to evasive counter-strategies are all factors reducing the usefulness of quotas. Only a few cases can be imagined where quota rules might be necessary, at least for a while, especially when long-term damages for the discriminated group are considerably high, e.g. in the case of primary vocational training. Indicative rather than mandatory quotas in the context of affirmative action programs seem to be more appropriate. Here again, the United States and to some extent Sweden have developed the most promising models.

(3) Attitudes and behavior might also be changed indirectly through financial incentives or disincentives. Some possible instruments are wage cost subsidies, investment allowances, or tax provisions designed either to reward non-discrimination or affirmative action or to punish discrimination, or - most importantly - to stimulate change in discriminatory social customs. It has been found that short-term incentive programs are not likely to be effective; experiments in Germany, e.g., to induce employers to create more part-time jobs for women, confirm this view. Long-term and institutionalized incentive structures, however, are of great importance. The income tax system, in particular, seems to be an effective equal opportunity instrument in the long run. The present Swedish tax system which combines a high marginal tax with separate taxation of income clearly provides incentives for a more equal sharing of market work (and as a consequence, hopefully, also of homework) between men and women.

(4) The institutional framework for making decisions on hiring, pay, promotion, and employment protecting can also be changed in favor of women, e.g. by establishing special commissions, committees or "ombuds" for anti-discrimination policies at different levels of decision-making (firms, interest organizations, governmental agencies).

The principal options for equal opportunity policy enumerated above are often only effective in combination, but sometimes they can also be seen as functional equivalents. When the state provides training programs, e.g., for women reentering the labor market, there is less need to use positive incentives for employers to retrain or to acquaint women to jobs. When affirmative action groups or commissioners for women are institutionalised at the firm level, administrative enforcement of equal opportunity policy might be less necessary.

In practice, however, combinations of the different policy options mentioned above will be more important. What is needed is a polyformal steering instead of monoformal steering. Policy options should be combined in such a way that the individual instruments complement each other, i.e. the weakness of one instrument is compensated by another, or the potential effectiveness of one instrument is complemented or reinforced by the catalytic effect of another. To be effective, a regulatory norm must be widely known, strongly felt and symbolically manifest. This requires a combination of normative, institutional and cognitive regulation. Just as traffic symbols or signals represent traffic norms, analogous symbols or signals have to be developed to make anti-discrimination or affirmative action rules effective, and institutions are needed to control deviant behavior and to represent women's interest in the labor market.

NOTES

*) I am much indebted to Hugh Mosley for improving considerably my English in style and grammar. Thanks for critical comments go to Siv Gustafsson, Bob Hart, Christina Jonung, Fritz W. Scharpf, Klaus Semlinger, Michael Wagner, and Renate Weitzel. Ralf Schmarje helped to fill some gaps in the tables.

(1) This meaning of discrimination seems to be the essence of any definition to be found in dictionaries. It is interesting to note that the term "Discrimination" in its political sense became prominent only in the second half of the 19th century, in connection with the Liberation Movement in the United States, and in connection with liberal theories of international trade. For example, the German Dictionary "Vollständiges politisches Taschenwörterbuch. Ein Handbuch zur leichten Verständigung der Politik" (by E.F.L. Hoffmann, Leipzig 1849) does not include the term "discrimination".

(2) Griggs v. Duke Power Co., 401 U.S. (1971), 3 EPD § 8137; Alfred W. Blumrosen 1972; see also the contribution by R. Braun in this volume. An important further consequence was the increasing use of "statistical evidence" to prove unfair selection (Rosenblum 1982), and even regression analysis (Bloom/Killingsworth 1982).

(3) Assume that the wage for a group against whom an employer discriminates is w and that the employer acts as if the wage is w(1 + d), due to his bias against members of that group. The discrimination coefficient thus is d and wd are the non-monetary costs which for the employer are connected with avoiding contact. Using the discrimination coefficient as a tool, Becker analyzes the economic effects of discrimination on, among other things, wage differences. In order to measure the effect of discrimination on wages, he employs the concept of <u>market discrimination coefficient</u> (MDC), which is defined as the difference in wage rate between the discriminated (W_D) and the non-discriminated groups (W_N) divided by the wage rate for the discriminated group:

$$MDC = \frac{W_N - W_D}{W_D}$$

(4) For a very useful summary of this development, and especially for different improvements of the Beckerian approach see Lundahl/Wadensjö 1982.

(5) Governmental discrimination can also occur directly and indirectly. Direct discrimination is almost excluded in western democratic society by the development of constitutional provisions which prohibit discrimination by race, religion, and sex. However, neutrally formulated laws may have indirectly discriminatory effects by requiring characteristics which are unequally distributed in society.

(6) Within the large literature of "role theory" see e.g. Myrdal/Klein 1971; Safilos-Rothschild 1972; Beck-Gernsheim 1976.

(7) The origin of the family is older than assumed by Bachofen, Morgan, and Engels. It probably goes back to the beginning of upright movement of men, which had two anatomical consequences: In the course of milleniums human heads became larger and the pelvis smaller. Children had to be born earlier. They were less developed at birth and increasingly dependent on the care and nutrition by the mothers. This is called "neoteny".

(8) Although Doeringer and Piore discuss discrimination only in the context of "racial discrimination", their analysis can be extended to women as well.

(9) The basis of the radical labor market theory (sometimes called neo-marxist) is profit-maximizing firms with a monopsonistic position in the labor market. By dividing, i.e. by pitting different ethnic groups against each other, the employer conquers, i.e. he can lower wages (Lundahl/Wadensjö 1982, 2:58). For overviews of the radical theory see Gordon 1972 and Reich 1981. The radical theory of discrimination is not relevant to sex discrimination.

(10) A specific explanation for the differences in the variance of the random term is that the efficiency of the test instrument depends on the group tested. If it is devised and tried out on one group, it measures the performance of other groups less accurately. Aigner and Cain give a concrete example of this: "The Scholastic Aptitude Test has been found, for example, to be a less reliable indicator of college grades for blacks than for whites." (Aigner/Cain 1977:180).

(11) "As far as the employer is concerned, the higher probability of women leaving the full-time labor force is not counter-balanced by the higher probability of job switching among males. Even though the average period of employment by any employer is not much different between males and females, employers are still interested in lifetime labor force participation. If a skilled male employee threatens to leave one employer for a better job opportunity elsewhere, the employer at least has the option of bribing the employee to stay. Such countervailing bribes will be much less effective in stopping women from having children, for here the trade-off is not between two basically similar economic opportunities where economic rewards can make a big difference. Nonmarginal and non-economic decisions are being made." (Thurow 1975:178 f.).

(12) It cannot, however, be said that well founded theoretical and empirical literature in this area abounds. For Germany see Langkau 1979; Pfarr/Bertelsmann 1981; Beck-Gernsheim 1976; Addison 1975; for Sweden see Jonung 1982; for United Kingdom see Siebert/Sloane 1981; Chiplin/Sloane 1976; for United States see Long 1976; Lloyd 1975; Jain/Pettman 1976; Welch 1981; Blaxall/Reagan 1976.

(13) The third view is the favored model of the Christian Democrats in West-Germany. There was an experimental program in Lower Saxony from 1978 to 1980 which ran out because of budgetary shortages; Berlin introduced child care allowances in 1983.

(14) For the likely effects of wage equalization on different causes of discrimination see Lundahl/Wadensjö 1982:9:12 ff.

(15) The Social Democratic Party in Schleswig-Holstein, under the leader Engholm, recently formed a "Shadow Cabinett" composed by 50 % men and 50 % women.

(16) Gustafsson and Jacobsson (1983) present a numerical example to measure the net effect of tax changes between 1967 and 1973, based on a married couple with no children under 16, with no capital income, where the husband earns 30 000 SKr, and the wife's wage is 10 SKr per hour (in SKr of 1967). The wife's increasing work hours from 0 to 2 000 (full-time) would increase household disposable income by 45 per cent under the old tax system, while the corresponding increase would be more than 65 per cent in 1973.

(17) It is not clear to me why the level of part-time work for men is relatively high in the United States. In comparison with Sweden and other countries, the figures are partly "inflated" by the high rate of part-time work among male teenagers and elderly men; however, this explains only part of the difference. The Swedish figures for male part-time work also seem to be influenced by increasing part-time work by the elderly (due to the recently introduced part-time pension scheme), and by young people who work part-time while attending school; thus it is not clear how far male part-time work in Sweden is influenced by the tax system.

REFERENCES

Addison, John T., "Gleichberechtigung - The German Experience", in: Pettman, B.O. (ed.), Equal Pay for Women, Bradford 1975, pp. 99-128.

Aigner, Dennis J., and Glen C. Cain, "Statistical Theories of Discrimination in Labor Markets", in: Industrial and Labor Relations Review, Vol. 30, No. 2, 1977, pp. 175-187.

Akerlof, George A., "The Economics of Caste and the Rat-Race and Other Woeful Tales", in: Quarterly Journal of Economics, Vol. XC, Nov. 1976, pp. 599-618.

Akerlof, George A., "A Theory of Social Custom, Of Which Unemployment May Be One Consequence", in: Quarterly Journal of Economics, Vol. XCIV, June 1980, pp. 749-775.

Arrow, Kenneth J., "The Theory of Discrimination", in: Ashenfelter, O., and A. Rees (eds.), Discrimination in Labor Markets, Princeton 1973, pp. 3-33.

Ashenfelter, Orley, and Albert Rees (eds.), Discrimination in Labor Markets, Princeton 1973: Princeton University Press.

Bachofen, Johann Jakob, Das Mutterrecht, 1861 (quoted according to the ed. by Karl Meuli, 2 Vol. 1948).

Beck-Gernsheim, Elisabeth, and Illona Ostner, "Frauen verändern - Berufe nicht?", in: Soziale Welt, No. 3, 1978, pp. 257-286.

Beck-Gernsheim, Elisabeth, Der geschlechtsspezifische Arbeitsmarkt. Zur Ideologie und Realität von Frauenberufen, Frankfurt 1976: Aspekte Verlag.

Becker, Gary S., The Economics of Discrimination, Chicago 1957: The University of Chicago Press (sec. ed. 1971).

Berger, Suzanne, and Michael J. Piore, Dualism and Discontinuity in Industrial Societies, Cambridge et al. 1980: Cambridge University Press.

Blau, Francine, and Carol Jusenius, "Economists Approaches to Sex Segregation in the Labor Market: An Appraisal", in: Blaxall, M., and B. Reagan (eds.), Women and the Workplace, Chicago 1976, pp. 181-199.

Blaxall, Martha, and Barbara Reagan (eds.), Women and the Workplace. The Implications of Occupational Segregation, Chicago and London 1976: The University of Chicago Press.

Boulding, Elise, "Familial Constraints on Women's Work Roles", in: Blaxall, M., and B. Reagan (eds.), Women and the Workplace, Chicago 1976, pp. 95-117.

Bloom, David E., and Mark R. Killingsworth, "Pay Discrimination Research and Litigation: The Use of Regression", in: Industrial Relations, Vol. 21, No. 3, Fall 1982, pp. 318-339.

Blumrosen, Alfred W., "Strangers in Paradise: Griggs v. Duke Power Co., and the Concept of Employment Discrimination", in: Michigan Law Review, Vol. 71, November 1972, pp. 59-110.

Chiplin, B., and Peter J. Sloane, Sex Discrimination in the Labor Market, London 1976: Macmillan.

Doeringer, Peter B., and Michael Piore, Internal Labor Markets and Manpower Analysis, Lexington, Mass. 1971: D.C. Heath and Company.

Elliott, Robert, and Pauline Glucklich, Emma MacLennan, Chris Pond, Women in the Labor Market. A Study of the Impact of Legislation and Policy Toward Women in the UK Labour Market During the Ninetine Seventies, Aberdeen and London 1982: Mimeo.

Engels, Friedrich, Der Ursprung der Familie, des Privateigentums und des Staates, 1884, in: Marx/Engels, Werke (MEW), Vol. 21 (1972), pp. 25-173.

Gladh, Lillemor, and Siv Gustafsson, Labor Market Policy Related to Women and Employment in Sweden, Stockholm 1982: Arbetslivscentrum, Mimeo.

Gordon, Nancy, M., and Thomas E. Morton. "A Law Mobility Model of Wage Discrimination - With Special Reference to Sex Differentials", in: Journal of Economic Theory, Vol. 7, March 1974, pp. 241-253.

Gordon, David M., Theories of Poverty and Unemployment, Lexington, Mass. 1972: D.C. Heath and Company.

Gruppe Politikinformationen, Maßnahmen zugunsten einer besseren Vereinbarkeit von Familie und Beruf. Erfahrungen aus der DDR, Frankreich, Großbritannien und Schweden sowie Empfehlungen für die Bundesrepublik Deutschland, Discussion Paper IIM/LMP 82-27, Wissenschaftszentrum Berlin 1982.

Gustafsson, Siv, and Roger Jacobsson, "Trends in Women's Work, Family Formation, Education and Earnings", Mimeo, Stockholm/Umea 1983.

Jain, Harish C., and James Ledvinka, "Economic Inequality and the Concept of Employment Discrimination", in: Labor Law Journal, Sept. 1975, pp. 579-584.

Jain, Harish C., "The American Anti-Discrimination Legislation and its Impact on the Utilisation of Blacks and Women", in: International Journal of Social Economics, Vol. 3, No. 2, 1976, pp. 109-134.

Jain, Harish C., and Peter J. Sloane, "The Impact of Recession on Equal Opportunities for Minorities & Women in the United States, Canada and Britain", Research and Working Paper Series No. 205, McMaster University, Faculty of Business, Hamilton, Canada 1983.

Janssen-Jurreit, Marielouise (ed.), Frauenprogramm. Gegen Diskriminierung. Gesetzgebung - Aktionspläne - Selbsthilfe. Ein Handbuch, Reinbek bei Hamburg 1979: Rowohlt.

Jonung, Christina, "Kvinnorna I Svensk Ekonomi", in: Bo Södersten (ed.), Svensk Ekonomi, Stockholm 1982.

Kamerman, Sheila B., and Alfred J. Kahn, "Income Transfers, Work and the Economic Well-being of Families with Children: A Comparative Study", in: International Social Security Review, No. 3, 1982, pp. 345-382.

Kolstad, Eva, "Three Years with an Act on Equality", in: Equal Opportunities International, Vol. 1, No. 4, 1982, pp. 1-6.

Lange, Klaus, "Kriterien für die Wirksamkeit von Instrumenten und Programmen des Verwalungshandelns", in: Die Öffentliche Verwaltung, Vol. 34, No. 1, 1981, pp. 73-83.

Langkau, Jochem, Lohn- und Gehaltsdiskriminierung von Arbeitnehmerinnen in der Bundesrepublik Deutschland, Bestimmung und Analyse des geschlechtsspezifischen Einkommensabstandes 1960-1976, Bonn 1979.

Lloyd, Cynthia B. (ed.), Sex, Discrimination, and the Division of Labor, New York 1975, Columbia University Press.

Long, James E., "Employment Discrimination in the Federal Sector", in: The Journal of Human Resources, Vol. XI, No. 1, 1976, pp. 86-97.

Lundahl, Mats, and Eskil Wadensjö, Unequal Treatment. A Study in the Neoclassical Theory of Discrimination (Preliminary Version), Stockholm (Swedish Institute for Social Research) 1982.

Masters, Stanley H., Black-White Income Differentials, New York 1975: Academic Press.

Morgan, Lewis H., Ancient Society, 1877 (quoted according to the German translation by W. Eichhoff and K. Kautsky: Die Urgesellschaft, 1908, Repr. 1976).

Myrdal, Alva, and K. Klein, Die Doppelrolle der Frau in Familie und Beruf. Dritte und überarbeitete Auflage, Köln und Berlin 1971.

Myrdal, Gunnar, Asian Drama. An Inquiry into the Poverty of Nations. New York 1968: Pantheon.

OECD (Organisation for Economic Cooperation and Development), Employment in the Public Sector, Paris 1982.

Olson, Mancur, Jr., The logic of Collective Action. Public Goods and the Theory of Groups. Cambridge, Mass. 1971: Harvard University Press.

O'Neill, June, and Rachel Braun, Women and the Labour Market: A Survey of Issues and Policies in the United States, Washington 1982: Urban Institute, Mimeo.

Pettman, Barrie O. (ed.), Equal Pay for Women. Progress and Problems in Seven Countries, Bradford 1975: MCB Books.

Pfarr, Heide M., and Klaus Bertelsmann, Lohngleichheit. Zur Rechtssprechung bei geschlechtsspezifischer Entgeltdiskriminierung (Vol. 100, Schriftenreihe des Bundesministers für Jugend, Familie und Gesundheit), Stuttgart et al. 1981: Kohlhammer.

Pfarr, Heide M., "Gleichstellung der Frau im Arbeitsleben - Vorschläge zur Rechtsreform", in: Posser/Wassermann (eds.), Von der bürgerlichen zur sozialen Rechtsordnung, Heidelberg and Karlsruhe 1981, pp. 75-90.

Phelps, Edmund S., "The Statistical Theory of Racism and Sexism", in: American Economic Review, Vol. 62, No. 4, September 1972, pp. 659-61.

Reich, Michael, Racial Inequality. A Political-Economic Analysis, Princeton 1981: Princeton University Press.

Reiter, Rayna R. (ed.), Toward an Anthropology of Women, 1975.

Rosenblum, Marc, "Evolving EEO Decision Law and Applied IR Research", in: Industrial Relations, Vol. 21, No. 3, Fall 1982, pp. 340-349.

Safilios-Rothschild, C. (ed.), Toward a Sociology of Women, Lexington, Mass. 1972.

Scharpf, Fritz W., "Interessenlage der Adressaten und Spielräume der Implementation bei Anreizprogrammen", in: Mayntz, R. (ed.), Implementation politischer Programme II: Ansätze zur Theoriebildung, Opladen 1983: Westdeutscher Verlag, pp. 99-116.

Schmid, Günther, "Arbeitsmarktpolitik in Schweden und in der Bundesrepublik", in: Scharpf, F.W. et al. (eds.), Aktive Arbeitsmarktpolitik. Erfahrungen und neue Wege, Frankfurt 1982, pp. 29-62.

Schmitt Glaeser, Walter, Abbau des tatsächlichen Gleichberechtigungsdefizits der Frauen durch gesetzliche Quotenregelungen, Stuttgart et al. 1982 (Schriftenreihe des Bundesministeriums des Innern, Bd. 16): Verlag Kohlhammer.

Siebert, Wolfgang S., and Peter J. Sloane, "The Measurement of Sex and Marital Status Discrimination at the Workplace", in: Economica, Vol. 48, May 1981, pp. 125-141.

Sowell, Thomas, "Affirmative Action Reconsidered", in: The Public Interest, No. 42, Winter 1976, pp. 47-65.

Spence, Michael A., "Job Market Signaling", in: Quarterly Journal of Economics, Vol. 87, No. 3, August 1973, pp. 355-74.

Spence, Michael A., Market Signaling, Cambridge, Mass. 1974: Harvard University Press.

Stiglitz, Joseph E., "Approaches to the Economics of Discrimination", in: American Economic Review, Papers and Proceedings, Vol. 63, No. 2, May 1973, pp. 287-295.

Thurow, Lester C., The Zero Sum Society. Distribution and the Possibilities for Economic Change, New York 1980: Basic Book/Penguin Books.

Thurow, Lester C., Generating Inequality, Mechanisms of Distribution in the U.S. Economy, New York 1975: Basic Books.

Weitzel, Renate, Labour Market Policy Related to Women and Employment in the Federal Republic of Germany, Berlin 1982: IIM-Labor Market Policy, Wissenschaftszentrum Berlin, Mimeo.

Weitzel, Renate, and Andreas Hoff, "Öffentliche Förderung von Teilzeitarbeit?", in: Scharpf, F.W. et al. (eds.) Aktive Arbeitsmarktpolitik. Erfahrungen und neue Wege, Frankfurt am Main 1982:181-206.

Welch, Finis, "Affirmative Action and Its Enforcement", in: The American Economic Review. Papers and Proceedings, Vol. 71, No. 2, May 1981, pp. 127-133.

Wesel, Uwe, Der Mythos vom Matriarchat. Über Bachofens Mutterrecht und die Stellung von Frauen in frühen Gesellschaften, Frankfurt am Main 1980: Suhrkamp.